The Vulnerable

JOHN L. PALMER
TIMOTHY SMEEDING
BARBARA BOYLE TORREY

Editors

The Vulnerable

The Changing Domestic Priorities Series

John L. Palmer and Isabel V. Sawhill, Editors

THE URBAN INSTITUTE PRESS
Washington, D.C. 1988

THE URBAN INSTITUTE PRESS
2100 M Street, N.W.
Washington, D.C. 20037

Library of Congress Cataloging in Publication Data
The Vulnerable

(The Changing Domestic Priorities series)

Bibliography: p. 449   Includes index.
1. Children—United States—Social conditions. 2. Children—United States—Economic conditions. 3. Aged—United States—Social conditions. 4. Aged—United States—Economic conditions. 5. United States—Social policy. I. Palmer, John Logan. II. Smeeding, Timothy M. III. Torrey, Barbara Boyle. IV. Series.
HQ792.U5V85 1988 305.2'3'0973 88–17397
ISBN 087766-420-X
ISBN 087766-419-6 (pbk.)

Printed in the United States of America

9 8 7 6 5 4 3 2

Distributed in the United States and Canada by
University Press of America 4720 Boston Way Lanham, MD 20706

iv

THE URBAN INSTITUTE is a nonprofit policy research and educational organization established in Washington, D.C. in 1968. Its staff investigates the social and economic problems confronting the nation and government policies and programs designed to alleviate such problems. The Institute disseminates significant findings of its research through the publications program of its Press. The Institute has two goals for work in each of its research areas: to help shape thinking about societal problems and efforts to solve them, and to improve government decisions and performance by providing better information and analytic tools.

Through work that ranges from broad conceptual studies to administrative and technical assistance, Institute researchers contribute to the stock of knowledge available to public officials and private individuals and groups concerned with formulating and implementing more efficient and effective government policy.

Conclusions or opinions expressed in Institute publications are those of the authors and do not necessarily reflect the views of other staff members, officers or trustees of the Institute, advisory groups, or any organizations that provide financial support to the Institute.

Titles available in the Changing Domestic Priorities Series

Books

THE REAGAN EXPERIMENT
An Examination of Economic and Social Policies under the Reagan Administration (1982), John L. Palmer and Isabel V. Sawhill, editors

HOUSING ASSISTANCE FOR OLDER AMERICANS
The Reagan Prescription (1982), James P. Zais, Raymond J. Struyk, and Thomas Thibodeau

MEDICAID IN THE REAGAN ERA
Federal Policy and State Choice (1982), Randall R. Bovbjerg and John Holahan

WAGE INFLATION
Prospects for Deceleration (1983), Wayne Vroman

OLDER AMERICANS IN THE REAGAN ERA
Impacts of Federal Policy Changes (1983), James R. Storey

FEDERAL HOUSING POLICY AT PRESIDENT REAGAN'S MIDTERM
(1983), Raymond Struyk, Neil Mayer, and John A. Tuccillo

STATE AND LOCAL FISCAL RELATIONS IN THE EARLY 1980s
(1983), Steven D. Gold

THE DEFICIT DILEMMA
Budget Policy in the Reagan Era (1983), Gregory B. Mills and John L. Palmer

HOUSING FINANCE
A Changing System in the Reagan Era (1983), John A. Tuccillo with John L. Goodman, Jr.

PUBLIC OPINION DURING THE REAGAN ADMINISTRATION
National Issues, Private Concerns (1983), John L. Goodman, Jr.

RELIEF OR REFORM?
Reagan's Regulatory Dilemma (1984), George C. Eads and Michael Fix

THE REAGAN RECORD
An Assessment of America's Changing Domestic Priorities (1984), John L. Palmer and Isabel V. Sawhill, editors (Ballinger Publishing Co.)

ECONOMIC POLICY IN THE REAGAN YEARS
(1984), Charles F. Stone and Isabel V. Sawhill

URBAN HOUSING IN THE 1980s
Markets and Policies (1984), Margery Austin Turner and Raymond J. Struyk

MAKING TAX CHOICES
(1985), Joseph J. Minarik

AMERICA'S CHILDREN: WHO CARES?
Growing Needs and Declining Assistance in the Reagan Era (1985), Madeleine H. Kimmich

TESTING THE SOCIAL SAFETY NET
The Impact of Changes in Support Programs during the Reagan
Administration (1985), Martha R. Burt and Karen J. Pittman

REAGAN AND THE CITIES
(1986), edited by George E. Peterson and Carol W. Lewis

PERSPECTIVES ON THE REAGAN YEARS
(1986), Edited by John L. Palmer

SINGLE MOTHERS AND THEIR CHILDREN
A New American Dilemma (1986), Irwin Garfinkel and Sara S.
McLanahan

THE REAGAN BLOCK GRANTS
What Have We Learned? (1986), George E. Peterson, Randall R.
Bovbjerg, Barbara A. Davis, Walter G. Davis, Eugene C. Durman, and
Theresa A. Gullo

MEDICAID
The Trade-off between Cost Containment and Access to Care (1986),
John F. Holahan and Joel W. Cohen

CHALLENGE TO LEADERSHIP
Economic and Social Issues for the Next Decade (1988), Isabel V.
Sawhill, Editor

Conference Volumes

THE SOCIAL CONTRACT REVISITED
Aims and Outcomes of President Reagan's Social Welfare Policy
(1984), edited by D. Lee Bawden

NATURAL RESOURCES AND THE ENVIRONMENT
The Reagan Approach (1984), Edited by Paul R. Portney

FEDERAL BUDGET POLICY IN THE 1980s
(1984), edited by Gregory B. Mills and John L. Palmer

THE REAGAN REGULATORY STRATEGY
An Assessment (1984), edited by George C. Eads and Michael Fix

THE LEGACY OF REAGANOMICS
Prospects for Long-term Growth (1984), edited by Charles R. Hulten
and Isabel V. Sawhill

THE REAGAN PRESIDENCY AND THE GOVERNING OF AMERICA
(1984), edited by Lester M. Salamon and Michael S. Lund

CONTENTS

Text Tables

Text Figures

This book is part of The Urban Institute's Changing Domestic Priorities series, a collection of volumes that assess the impact and significance of shifts in domestic policy under the Reagan administration and analyze the critical economic and social issues that will face the nation in the 1990s and beyond.

One of the most important of these issues is the changing needs of children and the elderly in our society. Recent trends of rapid population aging, rising poverty rates of children, escalating health care costs, slower economic growth, and enduring federal deficits have led to growing public debate over our nation's fiscal priorities and social policies as they affect our two largest dependent groups. The purpose of the book is to lay a solid conceptual and analytic foundation for this debate, which promises to become even more heated in the years ahead.

Its origins lie in an August 1985 workshop sponsored by the National Academy of Sciences on "Demographic Change and the Well-Being of Children and the Elderly," which was stimulated by Samuel Preston's presidential address to the Population Association of America on the same topic. That workshop brought together interested social scientists with three objectives in mind: to develop a multifaceted picture of levels and trends in well-being among children and the elderly in the United States; to explore the relative importance of demographic change, the performance of the economy, and public policies for the well-being of these two groups over time; and to grapple with the policy implications of what was known about the first and second topics. The main outcome of the workshop was to clarify how little, rather than how much, was known about these three concerns. As a consequence, several of the participants decided to invite other colleagues to join them in analyzing and discussing these topics more systematically. The subsequent activity over two years included two more workshops in the United States followed by an international conference in Luxembourg. The resulting volume deals primarily with the United States, but it also contains extensive comparative analysis and discussion of numerous other industrial democracies.

The brief editors' introduction (chapter 1) succinctly sets out the rationale and organization for the specific topics covered, so I need not repeat them here. Suffice it to say that the volume makes an invaluable contribution to the growing debate over "intergenerational equity" and how public policies in the United States might more adequately adapt to the changing needs of children and the elderly.

William Gorham
President

Acknowledgments

The research project and series of meetings that produced this book was made possible primarily by the financial support provided specifically for this purpose by the Alfred P. Sloan Foundation, through a grant to the University of Utah. Additional support was provided by the Ford Foundation and John D. and Catherine T. MacArthur Foundation through the Changing Domestic Priorities project of The Urban Institute.

We particularly want to thank Michael S. Teitelbaum, Sloan Program Officer, who contributed considerable time and encouragement, including participating in the workshops organized around draft chapters of the volume. Thanks are due also to our colleagues Thomas Espenshade and Patricia Ruggles, who provided helpful input at several stages of the project, and to the numerous other colleagues who participated in discussions of the chapter drafts in meetings at The Urban Institute and Luxembourg.

At the University of Utah, at The Urban Institute, at the U.S. Bureau of the Census, at the Centre d'Etudes de Populations, de Pauvreté et de Politiques Socio-Economiques (CEPS) in Luxembourg, and finally at Vanderbilt University, Donna Dove, Ann Foster, Ann Guillot, Evelyn Houtmann, Rene Krier, Ralf Mehlhorn, Ann Peterson, Susan Piontek, Jolaine Randall, Ginette Schickes, Jeanne Ward, and Rosalie Webb provided expert secretarial and conference assistance. The entire project was tremendously aided by the organizational and editorial skills of Felicity Skidmore.

Finally, we would like to thank Gaston Schaber, Director of CEPS for the marvelous ambience of the conference he hosted in Luxembourg.

Chapter One

EDITORS' INTRODUCTION

The allocation of public resources for the support of dependent populations in the United States has become a matter of increasing concern in recent years. In part, the concern stems from demographic shifts: because the make-up of our population has been changing so rapidly, the level and type of need for social support has also been changing—but in ways that we do not yet well understand. Also, evidence is accumulating that the recent cutbacks in social programs have affected different population groups very differently—again with results that we do not well understand. Finally, the enduring federal deficit will continue to constrain spending for all social purposes for the foreseeable future, thus heightening competition among groups for dwindling resources. All these developments add up to a powerful argument for reexamining our public purposes in social program spending. This book was undertaken to lay some necessary groundwork for such a reexamination.

RATIONALE FOR THE VOLUME

Changes in well-being among the nation's two largest dependent groups—children and the elderly—are the focus of the book. These two groups were chosen not only because they account for the vast bulk of all public expenditures for social purposes, but also because both groups have been subject to powerful forces for economic, demographic, and social change over the last few decades. Economically, the elderly appear to have improved their position considerably relative to the rest of society, so that old persons today face a smaller probability of being poor than at any time in our nation's history. Among children, in contrast, poverty has been on the increase, rising from 14 percent of the child population in 1969 to

20 percent in 1987. Demographically, the elderly constitute an increasingly large share of our population, whereas the proportion of children has shrunk considerably. Socially, the breakdown of the traditional family unit affects both groups by curtailing private alternatives to public support; but it has particularly negative consequences for children, more and more of whom are growing up in single-parent households, with much higher risk of poverty.

These developments have major implications for public policy. Just to maintain the current levels of support for both groups will require large increases in the tax burden (on a substantially smaller workforce). But there is ample reason to expect that the level of support needed by both groups will increase in the future. For the elderly this will occur simply because of increasing longevity: given current population projections, more and more elderly will be counted among the "old-old" (those over 85), and these people will be both "needier" and more likely simply to outlive their private means. For children the rising poverty rate of today is likely to translate into a lower productivity rate tomorrow; that is, today's poor children will be less well-equipped as adults to support their own dependents and the productivity of the workforce as a whole will suffer.

Sketched in these broad terms, the future—for taxpayers and dependents alike—looks bleak indeed. Certainly, coming to terms with the issues outlined above will require more coherent and farsighted policy making than has generally characterized this country's approach to social problems. In the concluding chapter of this volume, we propose some directions for future policy; but for the most part in this book we are concerned more with description than with prescription—with drawing as clear and complete a picture of the condition of dependency for young and old in the United States as possible.

Toward that end, we address three broad categories of questions:

□ What is the current economic status of the elderly and children in this country, and their probable future status (that is, in the absence of policy changes), and how do we evaluate their status? (How reliable are indicators of economic status, how have they changed over time, and how do they vary among countries?)
□ What broader factors translate economic status into a fuller sense of well-being for individuals, and how are these factors changing over time and across countries?

□ What are the cultural, political, social, and economic forces that shape change in the well-being of dependent groups?

In formulating these questions, we have been mindful of the unwieldiness of the concept "well-being." We focus here primarily on material well-being, not because we think material factors are more important than subjective ones, but simply because they are more measurable and more susceptible to the influence of public policy. As is apparent from chapter 2, even with the narrowest possible definition of material well-being as income, measurement problems abound. How do you assess a child's income? How do you balance income with need? Does a financial asset translate into the same level of well-being for a 6-year-old as for a 60-year-old?

Consideration of all these sorts of questions leads us to conclude that comparisons of well-being between elderly and children are extremely equivocal—even analytically perilous—undertakings. But if we stopped at this point, there would be no volume: only a journal article on "methodological problems in comparing the well-being of different age-groups." We persevered with the volume because we thought enough *could* be said with confidence to be useful in shaping policy. Data on the well-being of the two groups have been used to justify policy in the past (indeed, have been credited with launching policy) and undoubtedly will be used to justify changing policy in the future. We want to ensure that the data will be as complete and timely as possible and serve to counteract the current tendency to make naive and potentially distorting comparisons. More positively, we believe that the dramatic changes now transpiring in our fiscal and demographic circumstances *do* argue for a reexamination of our social policies and that information and analyses of the sort provided here can and should inform the reexamination.

Because of the difficulties in defining well-being and comparing well-being, however defined, of different groups, the chapters that follow are as intertemporal and international in coverage as possible, given the availability of data. In the course of our analyses, all contributors to this book became more mistrustful of cross-sectional comparisons between age groups; but all recognize that the concept of well-being is, in every society, necessarily comparative. People interpret their well-being in relation to something: how they were yesterday, how they hope to be tomorrow, how their neighbor is, and so on. Comparisons along some dimensions prove much more fruitful than others. We emphasize the ones that seem most fruitful.

ORGANIZATION OF THIS VOLUME

The book is organized to correspond roughly with the three categories of questions noted earlier. The first section considers income as a measure of well-being; this measure is the one most commonly used and the one for which data are most abundant. Chapter 2 should be read both as a general caveat against too facile a use of income measures and as a context in which to weigh the income comparisons provided in the rest of part I, with the alternative indicators of well-being provided in part II. The remaining papers in part I look at income variations from three perspectives: historical, individual, and geographical. Chapter 3 examines changes in income among United States population groups over time. Chapter 4 examines changes over the life cycles of individuals. Chapter 5 examines differences in income among groups across countries.

Part II broadens the picture of dependency in the United States to encompass those factors other than income that most clearly contribute to the material well-being of the young and the elderly. What we are interested in highlighting from these broader comparisons is the extent to which other factors in American life either offset or augment the influence of income on well-being. Chapters 6 and 7 look at changes in the distribution of private resources in the United States over the past two decades, with chapter 6 focusing on those resources of particular importance to children—family assets and parental time, as well as income—and chapter 7 comparing changes in the distribution of overall wealth among elderly and child households. Chapter 8 examines the one aspect of well-being— health—for which the United States has assumed major public responsibility. The authors survey changes in both public and private resources for health care for both groups over the past twenty years. Chapter 9 then broadens the picture of the contribution of public resources to the material well-being of the two groups by comparing the patterns of United States expenditures for general social purposes with those of the major industrial countries of Western Europe. Chapter 10 concludes the section by using a variety of nonmonetary measures both to obtain a fuller picture of the changes in well-being for young and old Americans and to assess the implication of these changes for the "social health" of the United States vis-à-vis other developed societies.

Part III consists of two country studies. The intent is to bring the picture of dependency in the United States into clearer focus by sighting it against the backdrop of two very different but highly developed societies. Chapter 11 discusses Japan; chapter 12 discusses Sweden. We view these chapters, first, as benchmarks against which to assess American problems and progress, and second, as diagnostic tools, to aid us in identifying those demographic, economic, political, and cultural phenomena most critical to shaping the changes in well-being documented in the earlier chapters.

This last task—comprehending the causal factors at work—is the central concern of the final section of the book. We are concerned with causation for two reasons: first, policymakers need to have some idea of what forces have shaped present outcomes to anticipate adequately the dimensions of future dependency and the problems connected with it, absent any change in policy; and second, the design of successful public policies to deal with these problems will depend on an understanding of the dynamics of dependency. If policymakers do not pay sufficient attention to the multiple factors contributing to the well-being of dependent groups, they will be at risk of being misled by simplistic nostrums—such as those that, in the 1960s, induced uncritical reliance on the "social engineering" potential of federal policies, or those that, in the 1980s, induced uncritical reliance on the private economy to "lift all boats."

We see, and are concerned with throughout this book, three major determinants of material well-being: economic conditions, demographic change, and public policy. Ideally, we would like to identify precisely the relative contribution of each to the material well-being of different groups at different times. In practice, of course, this is impossible; such phenomena are simply too interrelated and human behavioral responses too unpredictable. But what we can do is identify those large economic, demographic, and policy changes that have had clear effects on the well-being of American children and the elderly. We can also use history and the experience of other countries to illuminate the interaction of social policy and social welfare. That is, we can take a further step back from the changes in well-being examined in this volume to look at how social policies in other countries as well as our own have in fact evolved in response to the changing needs of dependent populations. Chapter 13 does this for the elderly, chapter 14, for children.

These two chapters, in concert with chapter 15 on political

strategies, are aimed at enhancing our understanding of the social, institutional, and political constraints within which future American social policy will be made. Whereas the earlier chapters are primarily concerned with explicating some aspect of the current state of well-being among children and the elderly, chapter 15 addresses the future: to what extent will peculiarities of the American political environment—independent of demographic and economic factors—shape public policies toward these two dependent populations?

Chapter 16 concludes the book by discussing what the data, analyses, and speculation in the rest of the book add up to. In particular, the chapter provides an overview of what we have learned about the changing economic status of children and the elderly in the United States and, in comparison to other countries, discusses the major economic and political factors that have shaped these outcomes in the past and are important in thinking about the future, and indicates some of the potentially fruitful directions for public policies concerned with these dependent populations.

Part One

INCOME AS A MEASURE OF WELL-BEING

Chapter Two

THE USES AND LIMITS OF INCOME
COMPARISONS

John L. Palmer, Timothy Smeeding, and Christopher Jencks

Discussions of the economic well-being of societies or groups within societies usually involve the comparison of income statistics in one form or another: average income, income adjusted according to some standard of need, percentage of persons with income below some standard, and so on. There are many valid reasons for this reliance on income measures, but the use of income statistics also raises many thorny analytical issues, which are all too often slighted in the course of arguments over social policies. Considering other factors that contribute to economic well-being, taking account of differences in economic needs, and paying attention to the fluidity of family units can radically alter the comparisons, making now one group and then another appear advantaged or disadvantaged.

Our awareness of the limitations of income comparisons motivates this chapter. We want to ensure that the data provided in this volume, and the larger debate over policy to which this volume is addressed, reflect an understanding of just how much income data can and cannot tell us about the material well-being of children and the elderly. Accordingly, the first section of the chapter briefly surveys the availability and limitations of income data for the two groups; the second section assesses the problems involved in using these data for comparisons.

MEASURING ECONOMIC WELL-BEING

Economists generally argue that disposable personal income is the single most important indicator of economic well-being for the

We wish to thank Marilyn Moon, for comments on an earlier version of this chapter and for her suggestion of the use of table 2.2, and Stephanie G. Gould for editorial assistance.

residents of any given country at any point in time. Income is measurable, meaningful, and concrete. Moreover, money income data are regularly available to researchers. In the United States, the Census Bureau has collected household and family money income data for a representative sample of the population annually since 1947. These data can be disaggregated by source (for example, labor earnings, income from capital, and income from transfers) and by demographic characteristics of the recipient unit, such as race and age. Income can therefore be compared across groups and within groups; summary measures of income's central tendency (means and medians) and its variability (the size distribution of income and poverty rates) also can be calculated for groups at several points in time. Such data provide a rich background to gauge levels of economic well-being for individual households and demographically distinct groups of households and for changes in the economic well-being of the latter over time.

Household income microdata sets such as the Panel Study of Income Dynamics (PSID) and the Retirement History Survey (RHS) provide longitudinal household data that allow researchers to follow the same household, or persons within those households, over time.[1] Following individuals directly as their incomes and living arrangements change allows researchers to investigate the interaction between income change and other significant life events, such as the birth of a child, divorce, long-term unemployment, disability, death of a spouse, or retirement, that either react to or produce large changes in income and economic well-being.

Finally, the recently initiated Luxembourg Income Study (LIS) project allows comparisons across eight Western industrial democracies (Australia, Canada, Norway, Sweden, Switzerland, United Kingdom, United States and West Germany) at one recent point in time (1979, 1981 or 1982).[2] Just as panel data have opened new research horizons to study income change for individuals, LIS for the first time enables researchers to make meaningful comparisons of relative economic position across countries. The three subsequent papers in part 1 of this volume use these data sets to examine various aspects of money income among the elderly and children, both within the United States and across industrial countries.

Although money income is a useful measure of economic well-being, our ultimate interest is usually in consumption rather than income. To convert income estimates into consumption estimates, we need to take account of two facts. First, economic needs, including tax liabilities and work-related expenses, can vary substantially among families depending on their characteristics, particularly the number and age of family members. Second, many resources of considerable economic value, such as homeownership and medical insurance, affect consumption but not money income.[3] Thus, two families with similar money incomes could, in fact, have very different levels of economic well-being; and two families that might generally be judged as having a similar level of economic well-being might have very different levels of money income. These limitations can be overcome at least partially by trying to estimate the value of nonmoney economic resources and by adjusting measures of economic resources to reflect tax burdens and the demographic characteristics of different families.

Adjusting for Demographic Characteristics

To see why adjusting measures of economic resources available to families by their demographic characteristics may be important, let us compare a single mother and child living together and having an income of $20,000 with a neighboring couple with three children and an income of $35,000. If we consider only total money incomes, the members of the second family appear to be better off, but this larger income has to be spread over more people; on a per capita basis, this family's income is only $7,000 per person, compared with $10,000 each for the single mother and child. Are we then to conclude that the economic status of the mother and child, in fact, is superior? Not necessarily, because the per capita measure fails to take into account the economies of scale in consuming food, housing, transportation, and child care that may be available to the larger family. Furthermore, even the needs of two families of the same size presumably depend on their composition. To the extent that the needs of adults and children for food, living space, health care, child care and the like differ, a four-person family consisting of two parents and two children might require more or less income to achieve the same standard of living as a single parent with three children.

Adjusting income for demographic characteristics is just as much a problem *within* families as it is *across* families. It is particularly problematic for children, who generally have little or no command over income independent of their parents and whose material well-being depends as much on parental time, day care services, school lunch programs, and the like, as on income. It is obviously difficult to measure children's consumption separately from the consumption of the family of which they are a part. Although children as a group can be compared with adults as a group, each child's annual economic well-being is nevertheless conventionally defined by assigning the child a share of the income received by adults in the same family. This means that the economic situation of children and adults will differ only insofar as adults with children differ from those without, or the presence of children is thought to make a family worse off. Generally speaking, families with children have about the same average income as families without children. Income differences between children and adults are thus largely dependent on how we think the presence of children affects family well-being.

It is also useful to separate families with children into those with one parent (90 percent of which are headed by women) and those with two parents. Because of time constraints and the labor market disadvantages of women, single-parent families are significantly worse off than two-parent families in terms of money income. In fact, the number of one-parent versus two-parent families and the number of children in each type of family are two of the major factors that make adult and child income differ *within* the "families-with-children" group.

In making comparisons, we obviously must adjust family income statistics to account for differing family circumstances, but it is far from obvious just how to do this. Although some methods of adjustment are intuitively and empirically more appealing than others, they all entail a certain degree of arbitrariness and can yield quite different results.

The most commonly employed and generally accepted method of adjustment in the United States is to consider the relationship of a family's income to its poverty threshold as determined by official federal government standards—yielding what is called an "income-to-needs" ratio or an "adjusted" or "equivalent" income measure. These poverty thresholds vary according to the number and ages of persons in a family as shown in table 2.1, which displays the levels for 1985. In that year, for example, a two-parent, four-person family with an income of $21,798 would have had an income-to-needs ratio of 2.0, whereas an elderly person living alone would have achieved the same ratio with an income of only $10,312. The various chapters in this volume use this or related methods of adjustment to the extent possible.

Broader Measures of Well-Being

As noted earlier, families often have resources of economic value other than money income available to them. They may also be

Table 2.1 POVERTY THRESHOLDS IN 1985 (dollars)

Number of family members	Head under 65 years		Head over 65 years	
	Income	Marginal cost of next member[a]	Income	Marginal cost of next member
1	5,593	1,638	5,156	1,347
2	7,231	1,342	6,503	—
3	8,573	2,416	—	—
4	10,989	2,018	—	—
5	13,007	1,689	—	—

For a family of four

4 adults	11,085
3 adults, 1 child	11,268
2 adults, 2 children	10,899
1 adult, 3 children	10,937

Source: U.S. Bureau of the Census (1983). Data are updated to 1985 using the Consumer Price Index.
a. For a family of one, for example, the cost of the next member is $7,231 − $5,593 = $1,638.

required or choose to give up some of their income to others (through taxes or repayment of debt, for example) or they may choose to give some of it away, reducing the amount that is indeed available to them. Ideally, all the resources and transactions listed in table 2.2 should be considered in any assessment of economic well-being. In practice, of course, data and measurement constraints limit what it is possible to do.

The first group of resources in table 2.2 constitute the traditional definition of money income, which is generally confined to payments made in cash to the family regularly or at least periodically. Thus, the contribution of financial wealth to economic well-being above and beyond the income it produces is excluded, as are resources tendered in kind and one-time resource flows, such as gifts and inheritances. Moreover, contributions that one family regularly makes to other families, such as alimony payments or taxes that support public transfer payments, are not subtracted from this total. The various categories of adjustments are listed further down in the table.

Knowledge of a family's financial wealth adds an important dimension to our sense of its economic well-being. For instance,

Table 2.2   RESOURCE FLOWS TO AND FROM INDIVIDUALS AND FAMILIES

Traditional or regular income
  1. Salaries, wages, interest, rent, dividends
  2. Public cash transfers
  3. Private cash transfers, such as pensions and alimony
Additions
  4. Wealth contribution (cash or in kind) above dividends, interest, rent (counted in 1 above), and loans
In-kind transfers received
  5. Public in-kind transfers
  6. Business (employment related) or charity in-kind transfers from a regular source
  7. Continuing transfers of time from relatives, such as child care
Intermittent transfers received
  8. Gifts from relatives including inheritances and bequests
  9. Cash settlements, such as insurance
  10. One-time transfers of time from relatives
Subtractions
  11. Cash or goods given to others
  12. Debt repayment
  13. Time given to others
  14. Mandatory contributions through taxes
  15. Resources set aside for own future needs

Source: Authors and Marilyn Moon.

although income measures are intended to capture the stream of returns to most wealth, these returns may be variable or unrealized and are thus not reflected well in annual or panel income measures. And one major return to a common form of wealth—the rent or mortgage interest not paid because of equity in a home—is not captured at all. Even when returns to wealth such as interest, rents, and dividends are included in income, they are greatly underreported; and there are systematic biases related to age and income. Finally, even a good estimate of the income flow from wealth is liable to underestimate the economic benefits (or costs) from the presence (or absence) of wealth holdings, because they provide a form of insurance that can be drawn on in times of need. (See chapters 6 and 7 for further discussion of wealth.) But even among families without wealth, access to credit is a valuable resource that allows them to maintain their consumption when their income flow is interrupted.

Of the various types of public and private in-kind transfers received from nonrelatives, the most important to children and the elderly are education and health care. The educational attainment of children is an important part of their human capital, or nonfinancial wealth, and a major determinant of their future earnings capacity. Health status and health insurance against financial risk independently affect the well-being of children and the elderly. Although functional health limitations may impose substantial costs in well-being, particularly for the very old, the less than ideal health status of poor children (due to nutritional inadequacy, for example) may have significant long-term physical and mental health care costs. Moreover, families with inadequate health insurance may forgo necessary medical treatments or face financial catastrophe when illness occurs. Particularly among the very old, a lengthy stay in a nursing home can be a catastrophe. (See chapter 8 for a treatment of health care and chapter 9 for a broad view of public in-kind transfers.)

Relatives not in the nuclear family unit often care for children or elderly family members; this care can be a partial substitute for the education and health care discussed earlier or can complement it. But usually the most important in-kind transfer children and the elderly receive is care from parents or a spouse within the nuclear family. This help needs to be considered in addition to those resources noted in table 2.2. (See chapter 7 for treatment of parental time.)

Occasional transfers of resources either in cash or in kind add yet another dimension to the measurement issue. Income surveys generally instruct respondents not to report sporadic inflows on the grounds that a one-time infusion of cash or goods does not produce the same benefit as the same amount received in regular payments. Nonetheless, a particularly large one-time payment can help a family over many years. For instance, when housing and education costs are high, many parents may contribute to the down payment on a home for their adult children, and grandparents may help pay college tuition for their grandchildren. Such a transfer means a permanent increase in the well-being of the family member who receives it. Similarly, much of the growing wealth of the elderly will at some point trickle down to their offspring and other relatives.

For these reasons, such resources ought to be included in the total available to the family unit, although they should be valued differently from periodic flows. Intermittent resource flows are also particularly likely to complicate any attempt to sort out the difference between "normal" access to resources and the potential for greater resources through informal family "insurance" mechanisms. As a practical matter, however, there are no good data that allow researchers to gauge at all accurately even the aggregate flows of intermittent resources, let alone their distribution among families, with or without children.[4]

Subtractions from this list of resources are also needed to reflect how well families are faring. Just as borrowing can augment the resources of a family without current income, so, too, repayment of debt can deplete the resources of a family with substantial income. Similarly, if alimony and child support to custodial spouses and other cash and in-kind transfers are included on the positive side of the ledger, they should also be debited from the resources of the families who directly provide or otherwise finance them. A critical question is whether to include all tax liabilities or only those liabilities necessary to support the transfers that are added to families' resources. The simplest approach is to subtract all tax payments, even those that are not directly contributory; this practice stresses the role of taxes in limiting discretionary resources.

COMPARING ECONOMIC WELL-BEING

The meaning one imputes to various measures of economic well-being derives primarily from making comparisons within and across groups, across countries, and over time. We make all these comparisons to some extent in this volume, because the authors are interested in painting as complete a picture as possible of changing patterns of well-being for children and the aged in the United States. But certain comparisons are more useful than others, depending on the issue being examined and the limitations of the available data.

Point-in-Time Comparisons between Different Age Groups

The simplest and most frequently cited comparison is between levels of adjusted income (or some other index of economic well-being) for different subgroups of the United States population at a single point in time. Unfortunately, this comparison is both conceptually and analytically troublesome when the subgroups are at substantially different stages of their life cycles. There are two main reasons for this. First, the economic position of individuals varies systematically with age. Consider figure 2.1, which shows the normal bow-shaped age-income distribution in the United States associated with the typical age distribution of parents and children taken together, labor force participation, career advancement, and retirement. Because of

Figure 2.1   PHASES IN THE SIMPLE INCOME LIFE-CYCLE

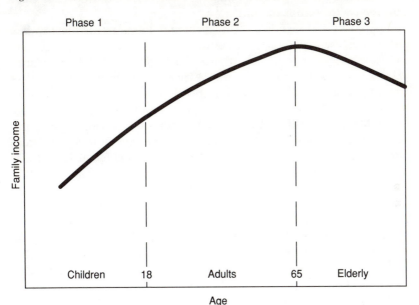

this variation, two different age groups might appear to have substantially different levels of income at any point in time; and yet they might experience essentially the same pattern of income over their lifetimes.

Second, the needs of people differ with their ages. This problem is even more intractable. It is troubling enough when the issue requires adjusting for the numbers or ages of children, but how does one construct an index that appropriately adjusts for different needs among three groups so fundamentally different as, say, teenagers needing a college education, young adults who are potential first-time homeowners, and chronically ill octogenarians? We noted earlier that any such index entails some degree of arbitrariness, but to illustrate more fully what is at issue let us examine in some detail the problems associated with the official poverty thresholds used so extensively in this volume and elsewhere.

The official poverty thresholds derive from the work that Mollie Orshansky (1965) did during the first year of the War on Poverty. The work was done somewhat hastily, and Orshansky never expected her methods to be viewed as definitive. When the federal government began publishing "official" poverty statistics in 1968, however, it adopted Orshansky's poverty thresholds intact (adjusting them only for annual changes in the Consumer Price Index); and they have survived with minor modifications ever since.

Orshansky's thresholds were designed to measure the level of income below which families could not eat adequately. To construct her estimates, she used the United States Department of Agriculture's (USDA) "economy" food plan as the measure of the amount families of varying composition needed to spend on groceries. Then, because a 1955 USDA survey had shown that families of two or more typically spent a third of their income on food, she set the poverty level income thresholds for families of three or more at 3.0 times the cost of the USDA food plan. She used higher and essentially arbitrary multipliers for families of one and two, on the basis that nonfood expenditures depended less on family size than food expenditures.

Orshansky was probably right that there are fewer economies of scale in purchasing food than in purchasing housing, medical care, transportation, and the like. But this assumption also implies that if the "food multiplier" is more than 3.0 for families of one and two and is exactly 3.0 for families of three, it should be less than 3.0 for larger families. Orshansky's decision to use one set of rules for families of less than three and another set of rules for larger families led to rather bizarre results, as shown in table 2.1. Note that the fourth and fifth family members allegedly cost substantially more than the second and third. This is decidedly counterintuitive.

If we assume that the overall economies of scale in purchasing housing, transportation, medical care, and the like are about the same as for food, the official poverty thresholds for small families are too high relative to those for families of three or more. In that case, official statistics overestimate poverty among small families, and hence among the elderly. If we assume, like Orshansky, that there are greater economies of scale in those things than in food consumption, the thresholds for large families are too high relative to those for families of three. In that case, official statistics overestimate poverty in large families, and hence among children.

In order to settle the question of how much the poverty line should vary with family size, we would need indicators of material well-being that have roughly the same meaning for families of all sizes. If adults in families of all sizes assigned the same priority to eating steak rather than hamburger, for example, we could ask how much income it took to keep the consumption of steak relative to hamburger the same for families of varying size. No one has actually tried to estimate family equivalence scales using intuitively understandable criteria of this sort. Several econometricians have tried to do something akin to this by looking at the way family size changes the overall pattern of expenditures, but this approach also has its conceptual and methodological problems.[5]

The fundamental difficulty with using expenditure patterns to estimate the amount of income that families of different sizes need to be equally well off is that family composition may alter a family's tastes as well as its overall need for money. Suppose, for example, that the steak-to-hamburger ratio is lower for a couple with two children and $25,000 a year than for a couple with no children and $15,000 a year. It is tempting to conclude that the larger family is worse off. But one might alternatively conclude that children prefer hamburger to steak, and that parents prefer cooking the same thing for everyone. In other words, tastes, custom, and a host of other factors are relevant and ideally should be considered.

Another problem is that, from the viewpoint of the parents, children are themselves akin to consumer goods. Most parents have children because they want them, and they want children even though they know that children are expensive and present problems in other ways. If adults choose to spend their money on children rather than on steak, this may be because they find eating hamburger with their children more satisfying than eating steak alone. It is not obvious, therefore, that having children makes adults worse off in any meaningful sense, even if it reduces their consumption of "luxury" goods, reduces a previously two-earner family to a one-earner one with less income, and increases the fraction of their income that they allocate to "necessities."[6]

Table 2.1 also shows that the poverty threshold falls by 8 percent when people living alone reach age 65, and by 10 percent when the head of a two-person family reaches age 65. These reductions reflect the fact that the USDA "economy" food budget is lower for persons over 65. Orshansky simply assumed that if food costs fell after people reached 65, all their other expenses would fall by the same percentage. Everyday experience suggests that the elderly do, in fact, have smaller appetites than younger adults. But it hardly follows that they also need 8 to 10 percent less money for housing, medical care, telephone service, and transportation. Some additional examples help further clarify these differences:

■ *SHELTER*

The elderly are much more likely than the young to own their own homes, and elderly homeowners are much more likely to have paid off their mortgages than younger homeowners. Even when the elderly do not own their homes, they have usually accumulated a stock of furniture and other durables, so they do not have to spend as much on these items as younger adults.

But elderly homeowners are also less able to maintain their own homes than younger adults. As a result, the elderly must either pay more for maintenance and utilities, adapt to a lower standard of repair, or both. Whether the net result is that the elderly pay 8 to 10 percent less than younger adults for similar housing is anybody's guess. (In fact, some data sources indicate that they pay less, and others that they pay more.)

■ MOBILITY

The elderly are less likely to own cars than younger adults, partly because they are less likely to be able to drive. To be as mobile as younger adults, the frail elderly would need a chauffeur as well as a car. When mobility becomes this expensive, people usually reallocate their limited resources to other things and live with less mobility.

■ HEALTH

Despite eligibility for Medicare, the elderly spend a slightly larger fraction of their money income on medical care than do younger adults. The elderly also spend more on what we might think of as "health-related" goods and services, such as keeping their homes warmer in the winter.

These examples all suggest that if the poverty line (or any given multiple of it) is supposed to represent the same level of material well-being for different groups, it may vary quite significantly with age. But deductive reasoning cannot even tell us whether the thresholds should be higher or lower for the elderly, much less tell us *how much* higher or lower.

One way to assess the adequacy of the official poverty thresholds for comparing the elderly with younger families is to look at families with the same income-to-needs ratio and then ask how often families of different ages report various problems. In 1984, for example, the Gallup Organization asked respondents whether there had been a time during the previous year when they did not have enough money to pay for food, clothing, or medical care that they or their family needed. Table 2.3 shows how respondents with family incomes that were varying multiples of the poverty line answered

Table 2.3 RESPONDENTS REPORTING LACK OF SUFFICIENT INCOME DURING THE PREVIOUS YEAR FOR BASIC NEEDS, BY AGE AND POVERTY STATUS, 1984 (percentage)

	All respondents	<50 percent of poverty line	50–149 percent of poverty line	Income 150–249 percent of poverty line	250–349 percent of poverty line	>349 percent of poverty line
Food						
Under 65	21.8	51.9	46.0	19.4	12.6	6.0
Over 65	13.1	39.0	24.0	2.8	2.4	0
Clothing						
Under 65	28.0	64.5	49.3	28.0	18.7	12.0
Over 65	17.9	39.0	30.0	5.5	9.4	4.7
Medical care						
Under 65	25.8	51.8	52.4	26.3	13.8	9.2
Over 65	21.9	49.4	34.1	8.7	11.7	8.4
Number of cases						
Under 65	1,242	65	285	252	287	352
Over 65	226	13	95	46	24	49

Source: Computations by authors from unpublished Gallup Survey data for January 1984.
< less than > greater than.

these questions. At any given income level, respondents over age 65 were less likely than younger respondents to report not having had enough money. Indeed, elderly respondents with incomes near the poverty line were only marginally more likely to report these problems than were younger adults with incomes twice the poverty line.

Table 2.3 suggests that the poverty line represents a significantly higher level of material well-being for the elderly than for younger adults. But this conclusion only holds if getting food, clothing, and medical care has the same priority (relative to other possible uses of money) for persons of all ages. We are not certain that this condition holds. The elderly may, for example, worry more than younger adults about having enough money for food or chronic health care. If that is so, the elderly may forgo other pleasures in order to be sure that they will not run out of money for groceries or medical emergencies before their next check arrives. Prudence of this kind could produce the results in table 2.3 without necessarily meaning that the elderly were better off in other respects than younger adults with the same income. The young might be having more fun, even though they run out of money more often. And the young people may also have more alternatives for supplementing their income in emergencies than do the old.

These considerations suggest that no single measure can tell us how well one age group is doing relative to others. Such comparisons require a full description of how different age groups live. And such descriptions must tell us not only what each age group gets, but also what it wants and needs. Income statistics alone, however adjusted, cannot definitively address such issues, although they can be a useful beginning point.

Ideally, then, cross-sectional comparisons between two age groups whose needs are as different as those of children and the elderly would be based on a wide range of social indicators, including physical and mental health, access to medical care, nutritional status, housing conditions, physical mobility, social connectedness, the quality of family life, access to education and entertainment, intellectual stimulation, and the like. Taken together, these indicators might tell us something about different age groups' need for money income, and might allow us to say something about whether those needs are being met relatively better for one group than the other by the economic resources available to each at any given time.

We do not attempt the task in this volume. One reason is that we do not know how to combine various indicators into a single meaningful measure. What are we to make of the fact that children are as likely as the elderly to see a doctor if they are sick enough to restrict their activities in some way? The two groups suffer from different medical problems and diseases, which require different amounts of medical attention. We have no good way of knowing whether they get comparable care relative to their needs. Nor do we know whether they "should" get comparable care. If inadequate care will shorten a child's life by 70 years but will shorten an octogenarian's life by only a few, it may not make sense to assume that the two have equal claims on our collective medical resources. But the main reason we cannot make an overall comparison between the young and the elderly is that we have found it impossible to identify social indicators that mean the same thing for children and the elderly in the first place. Even when superficially comparable data are available—on health status, for example—they do not really mean the same thing for different age groups.

Similar problems arise in every area. Does failure to eat what the National Academy of Sciences regards as an acceptable diet mean the same thing for an 8-year-old and an 80-year-old? Or can we conclude that housing conditions for children are worse than those for the elderly because children are more likely to live in households with more than one person per room? Does privacy really have the same value for a grandchild as for a grandparent? Similarly, does the fact that children and the elderly are equally likely to live in air-conditioned households mean that they are equally well off, or does one group "need" air-conditioning more than the other?

These are all extremely difficult questions. All we can do is point out the folly of imputing too much meaning to any single point-in-time measure, however adjusted, of the relative well-being of two widely different age groups. Also, we can reiterate the value of constructing a picture of relative needs and resources that is as multidimensional as possible. To this end, various chapters in this volume go beyond income measures and deal, at least to some extent, with such things as wealth, spending on health care and education, and other broader indicators of well-being.

Other Types of Comparisons

So far we have been concerned with point-in-time comparisons between different age groups. But, as we noted earlier, two other approaches illuminating the changing well-being of the aged and children in the United States also are employed in this volume wherever data permit: comparisons within similar age groups at a given time and of similar age groups over time. Both these types of comparisons also pose difficult conceptual and analytical problems. We will not burden the reader further by going into them in any detail here, but these limitations are generally less severe than those inherent in points-in-time comparisons between different age groups. For example, as should be clear from the earlier discussion, needs vary along dimensions other than just the various stages of the life cycle. Nevertheless, we think it fair to conclude that if, on average, elderly men have an income-to-needs ratio twice that of both elderly women and children, that fact says far more about the reality of the economic status of elderly men compared with elderly women than it does about that of elderly men compared with children.

In a similar vein, comparisons of any given measure of economic resources for similar age groups are conceptually more meaningful across time than across age groups. If the average income-to-needs ratio of the aged today is twice as high as that of the elderly 20 years ago, one can fairly confidently conclude that, other things being equal, the typical elderly person today is substantially better off than the typical elderly person of 20 years ago. Of course, we cannot conclude from such data that the same elderly people who are still alive today (those over 85) are substantially better off than they were 20 years ago. Not only have their needs changed in ways that complicate direct comparisons with their younger selves, but the data cited seldom distinguish between an increase in the average adjusted income of the elderly that is due to widespread improvements (for example, as a result of general increases in Social Security benefits) and an increase that is due simply to the fact that successive generations (cohorts) of the new elderly have higher incomes than the already elderly who have a work history of lower earnings (and therefore receive lower Social Security benefits). Fortunately, some sorting out of these various kinds of factors is possible—and done in the two subsequent chapters of this volume—with panel data or several waves of cross-sectional data that enable researchers to track the members of a given age group over time.

Because cohort analysis is able to abstract from life-cycle differences, such analysis carried out over a long enough time period will yield quite meaningful comparisons of economic status across generations. Although generations can be broken down in several ways, figure 2.2 presents the income life cycle for three separate groups as of 1988: group 1, today's children (born 1971–88); group 2, today's nonaged adults (born 1924–70); and group 3, today's

Figure 2.2   GENERATIONAL PHASES IN THE INCOME LIFE-CYCLE

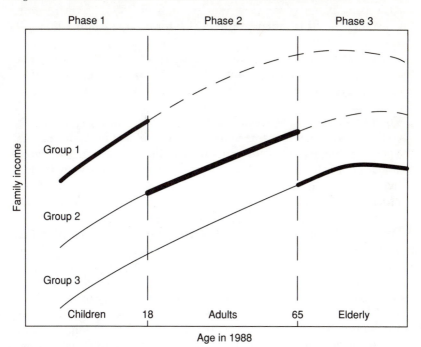

elderly (born 1923 or before). The boldly lined segment of each group's income life cycle in figure 2.2 represents that group's life-cycle position from figure 2.1. The lightly lined segment of each group's life cycle represents its socioeconomic "life history" before 1988. The broken-lined sections indicate each group's expected future economic course. A perspective such as this permits consideration of trends in well-being for successive generations. Assume for a moment that data restrictions are nonexistent, that is, that we have income data back to 1900. Such data would allow us to compare the income of today's children to today's elderly when they were children, or, in general, to compare incomes (or ideally consumption) over the life cycle for successive generations.

It is clearly more speculative to compare the well-being of today's elderly to tomorrow's elderly (today's adults), and even more speculative to ask what will happen to today's children when they become elderly in the twenty-first century. Nonetheless, such comparisons are often inferred by social commentators and analysts interested in the question of "intergenerational equity." Those who fear that the Social Security system will fail to provide adequately for the baby boom generation and for their children in retirement, for instance, envisage income life cycles for groups 1 and 2 that fall below that of group 3. They assume that successive generations may not always be better off than the preceding generation and that today's children and young adults (part of group 2), in particular, may find themselves less well off in old age, if not before, than today's elderly.

Today's children are certainly better off as children than their parents or their grandparents were. But some recent evidence makes the generational equity argument worth serious attention. If we were to make finer differentiations or to consider particular demographic subgroups within any of the large groups in figure 2.2, these comparisons might not always indicate that successive generations are better off than preceding ones as drawn in figure 2.2.

For example, as is documented in subsequent chapters, over the past 15 years the average income in the United States of families with children has declined slightly, and child poverty rates have risen substantially. On the basis of these data, one could argue that, on average, children born since the early 1970s are worse off than those born in the previous 15 years when incomes were rising and poverty rates falling sharply, violating the common assumption that succeeding generations are better off than previous generations. Similarly, if today's adults are separated into the baby boom generation (ages 24 to 42, born from 1946 to 1964) versus those born earlier, there is evidence that the younger generation may not be faring as well in adulthood as did their recent predecessors.

CONCLUSION

As we noted at the beginning of this chapter, conventional measures of money income have serious limitations as indicators of the material well-being of different age groups in poverty. These limitations differ in kind and degree; hence the value of the measures varies with the purposes for which they are being used—whether researchers are considering well-being within age groups or across age groups and at a point in time or over time. We have attempted to illuminate these concerns so that the reader will have a better understanding of the appropriate role of income comparisons in the large policy debate to which this volume is addressed. The overriding message is that such comparisons should be handled with care.

Notes

1. For a description of these data sets, see chapter 4.

2. For a description of the Luxembourg Income Study, see chapter 5.

3. Comparisons over time entail additional complications because adjusting the purchasing power of income received in different years depends on comparing the value of goods and services that are often not comparable. Because the Consumer Price Index (CPI) generally ignores technical improvements in consumer goods and services, for example, inflation-adjusted income statistics generally understate improvements in living standards.

4. The Federal Reserve Board's 1986 Survey of Consumer Finances does contain some data on intermittent resource flows, but they were not available for public use when the chapters in this volume were written.

5. See Watts (1977).

6. Matters look quite different, of course, from the child's viewpoint. Parents may have a lot of children because children make their lives more enjoyable, but children do not generally have a voice in how many brothers and sisters they will have. Research suggests that children who grow up in large families, other things being equal, labor under a significant handicap in terms of cognitive development, educational attainment, economic success, and most other indicators of well-being. But no one has tried to construct an "equivalence scale" that tells how much additional income a child's parents must have to offset the negative effect of an additional sibling. Certainly the poverty thresholds were not constructed with this goal in mind.

References

Orshansky, Mollie. 1965. "Counting the Poor: Another Look at the Poverty Profile." *Social Security Bulletin* 28, no. 1 (January):3–29.

Roper Center for Public Opinion Research. 1984. *Gallup Survey Data, January 1984.* Storrs, Conn.: Roper Center for Public Opinion Research.

U.S. Bureau of the Census. 1986. *Census of Population and Housing: 1980.* PK-35. Washington, D.C.

Harold Watts. 1977. "The Iso-Prop Index: An Approach to the Determination of Differential Poverty Income Thresholds." In *Improving Measures of Economic Well-being,* edited by Marilyn Moon and Eugene Smolensky. New York: Academic Press.

Chapter Three

THE DECLINING SIGNIFICANCE OF AGE IN THE UNITED STATES: TRENDS IN THE WELL-BEING OF CHILDREN AND THE ELDERLY SINCE 1939

Eugene Smolensky, Sheldon Danziger, and Peter Gottschalk

In the past several years, academics, policymakers, and the media have widely discussed the declining impoverishment of the elderly and the growing poverty among children. Here are the facts concerning poverty as officially measured:

□ The poverty rate for all elderly persons has fallen substantially since 1939, but particularly since 1969.
□ The poverty rate for all children fell substantially between 1939 and 1969, but has risen since 1969.
□ Beginning in 1974, the poverty rate among children exceeded that among the elderly.

This chapter places these facts in historical perspective by extending the official series on poverty rates back to 1939. We find the decades of the 1940s and 1970s to be decisive. The elderly have indeed improved their position faster than have children since 1969. However, children made more rapid progress than did the elderly between 1939 and 1949 and between 1959 and 1969. Between 1949 and 1959, the rate of poverty decline was similar for the two groups.

A popular interpretation of the period since 1969 is that government policy has benefited the elderly relative to the young. The longer historical perspective poses a challenge to this interpretation. Although government policy is primarily responsible for the recent

The data creation and analysis reported here were sponsored in part by a grant from the U.S. Department of Health and Human Services, Office of the Assistant Secretary for Planning and Evaluation, to the Institute for Research on Poverty and by the Center for Demography and Ecology, which receives core support from the National Institute of Child Health and Human Development (HD-5876). The views expressed are those of the authors and not necessarily those of any sponsoring organization or agency. Luise Cunliffe and George Slotsve provided valuable research assistance. We wish to thank Ross Finnie, Robert Haveman, John Palmer, Christine Ross, and Timothy Smeeding for comments on a prior draft. Many of those comments have influenced what appears here.

decline in poverty among the elderly, the disappointing trend in the earnings of the parents of children—not reductions in government benefits—is primarily responsible for rising poverty among children. Poverty among children also rose because of the increase in the percentage of all children living in single-parent families and the very high poverty rate of these families.

MEASURES OF POVERTY

An important measure of economic well-being is the incidence of poverty. For all years since 1959, we have a detailed record of the proportion of the total population in poverty according to the official measure, which is fixed in real terms. We also have a description through time of changes in the relative importance of the major socioeconomic correlates of poverty—age, race or ethnicity, family size, and sex and educational achievement of the household head.

The recent release of public use sample tapes for the 1940 and 1950 censuses permits us to extend the historical record on the incidence of poverty and the changing role of various socioeconomic correlates. It is in the latter area that the largest gain can be made, because the previously published Current Population Survey (CPS) data have made possible some rough estimates of the aggregate incidence of poverty over the 1947 to 1959 period (see, for example, Fisher 1985).

Our measure of poverty is the set of official poverty lines. They vary by age and sex of the household head, by residence (farm or nonfarm), and by family size. We extended the 1959 census lines back to 1939 and 1949 via the Consumer Price Index (CPI).[1] A poverty line that reflects only price changes and not changes in real incomes yields what strikes many as an implausibly high incidence of poverty in 1939 (Smith 1988). This poverty line for a family of four is about 9 percent higher than mean household income in 1939, whereas it is only 41 percent of the 1979 mean. In fact we have simply extended the poverty line via the CPI back from 1959 by 20 years, in the same way that the Office of Management and Budget has extended the official line forward since 1959 by more than 20 years. The years 1939 to the present seem to us an era with enough commonality so that poverty lines fixed in real terms have some intuitive meaning. If our 1939 and 1949 lines are considered too high, then, by analogy, the current official poverty lines must be too low.[2] Yet this case is rarely made.

It is important to note that the data presented here for 1939 are not directly comparable with the data for later years because in the 1940 census only earned income (wages and salaries) is reported.[3] It is also important to note that what we are interested in—the poverty rate for children *relative* to the rate for the elderly in each year—is, as shown below, less influenced by different income concepts than is the trend in the absolute value of the poverty rates.

Beginning in 1950 and continuing through the 1980 census, households were asked about all sources of cash income.[4] Total cash income, commonly referred to as census money income or posttransfer income, provides the income measure for the official poverty series.[5] We measure poverty by comparing the total resources of all persons in a household unit with the appropriate poverty line. Our definition of household includes the Census Bureau's concepts of families and unrelated individuals. Only those household members related to the head are included as members of an income-sharing unit.[6] Related persons living in the same dwelling are thus assumed to pool their income.

The income of elderly persons and their probability of living alone are positively correlated. If, over time, the elderly increasingly live apart from their adult children because the incomes of the elderly are rising, then, paradoxically, the data will show increasing poverty rates for the elderly if the poverty line is above the income level at which a substantial number of elderly choose to live alone rather than share living quarters and pool incomes with their children.

How important this shift in living arrangements has been historically is not known.[7] To the extent that it matters, it probably leads to an underestimate of the improvement of the well-being of the elderly relative to the well-being of children over the past two decades.

We measure poverty for all persons classified by their own age, race, and sex in 1939, 1959, 1969, and 1979. In 1949 we have to classify persons by the characteristics of their household head. This is because in 1950 the Census Bureau collected income information from a sample of persons rather than households. Unfortunately, the respondents in this 20 percent subsample were not asked about the incomes of other members of the household unless the respondent was the household head. For example, if the wife was the person sampled, we know only her own income; if the husband was sampled, we know both his own and the household's total income. Because poverty is defined by household income, we can include only household heads and unrelated individuals in our analysis.

Consider, for example, a 70-year-old woman married to a 75-year-old man in a family for which the husband was the respondent. In 1949 the woman will be counted in the tables that follow as a person living in a household headed by an elderly man. In the other census years, she will be counted as an elderly woman. Thus, for 1949, only persons living in households headed by an elderly woman without a husband present are counted in the tables that follow as elderly women. Children are classified consistently in each of the censuses.

In sum, we provide measures of poverty that correspond as closely as possible to the officially published poverty statistics. However, there are differences over time in the measures presented here, as well as differences between these measures and those based on the CPS.

TRENDS IN POVERTY

The well-being of children and of the elderly depend on different sources of income. Historically, the well-being of children has depended overwhelmingly on access to the current earnings of prime-age workers, whereas the well-being of the elderly has depended primarily on the level of Social Security benefits and hence the long-term trend in earnings. There is no necessary connection between the rate of growth of wages and Social Security benefits in the short run; hence the well-being of the elderly and the young can diverge.

This divergence is illustrated in table 3.1, which presents poverty rates for children and the elderly by decade since 1939 in the first five columns, and the poverty rate of each group relative to that of men ages 65 to 69 in the second five. Even though, as mentioned above, the 1939 rates shown here are biased upward because they are based only on earned income, it is clear that poverty rates for children declined relative to rates for either elderly men or women between 1939 and 1969 and that the incidence of poverty among children actually rose after 1969. As we shall see, this pattern reflects primarily the path of mean earnings of prime-age men over time. Periods of rapidly rising real Social Security benefits are what cause

Table 3.1 POVERTY RATES FOR CHILDREN AND THE ELDERLY, SELECTED YEARS, 1939–79

Age group	Percentage of persons who are poor					Poverty rate relative to rate for men age 65–69				
	1939[a]	1949[b]	1959	1969	1979	1939[a]	1949[b]	1959	1969	1979
Children										
Under 4	79.4	45.0	26.2	15.9	18.2	1.08	1.00	1.04	0.91	2.33
5–9	80.5	48.2	26.4	16.1	16.6	1.09	1.08	1.05	0.93	2.13
10–14	78.6	50.7	25.5	14.9	16.5	1.07	1.13	1.02	0.86	2.12
All	79.5	47.6	26.1	15.6	17.1	1.08	1.06	1.04	0.89	2.19
Elderly men										
65–69	73.6	44.8	25.1	17.4	7.8	1.00	1.00	1.00	1.00	1.00
70–74	78.2	58.1	33.8	20.4	10.8	1.06	1.30	1.35	1.17	1.38
75–79	85.4	62.7	42.1	23.5	14.5	1.16	1.40	1.68	1.35	1.86
80–84	83.6	67.4	44.7	30.9	12.5	1.14	1.50	1.78	1.78	1.60
85+	83.2	68.7	47.1	36.7	14.5	1.13	1.53	1.88	2.11	1.86
All	78.0	55.3	33.2	22.2	10.6	1.06	1.23	1.32	1.28	1.53
Elderly women										
65–69	75.5	65.5	32.6	26.4	15.7	1.03	1.46	1.30	1.52	1.88
70–74	79.3	69.5	40.4	31.1	17.6	1.08	1.55	1.61	1.79	2.26
75–79	78.6	71.4	44.1	35.2	19.9	1.07	1.59	1.76	2.02	2.55
80–84	78.3	71.2	46.6	37.8	19.1	1.06	1.59	1.86	2.17	2.45
85+	80.4	74.7	39.3	35.4	27.0	1.09	1.67	1.57	2.03	3.46
All	77.5	69.4	38.6	32.1	18.0	1.05	1.55	1.53	1.84	2.44
All persons	68.1	39.8	22.1	14.4	13.1	0.93	0.89	0.88	0.83	1.68

Source: Computations by authors from decennial census computer tapes.

a. For 1939, based on household earnings; for other years, based on household cash income from all sources. The 1939 rates are biased upward because self-employment income was not counted as earnings.

b. Because the 1950 census sample frame differs from that of the other censuses, the poverty rates for 1949 are for persons classified by the age of the household head, and not for persons classified by their own ages. The treatment of children, however, is consistent across all censuses. See text and note 7.

Figure 3.1   POOR PERSONS: CHILDREN AND ELDERLY, 1939–85

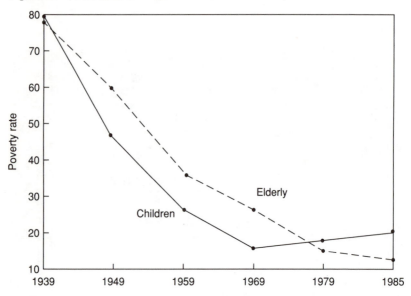

the periodic steep declines in the incidence of poverty among the elderly.

The relationship between the economic well-being of the elderly and that of the young is extremely sensitive to the choice of the date at which the initial comparison is made, as table 3.1 and figures 3.1 and 3.2 together illustrate. Beginning such comparisons with 1966, when the CPS continuous series begins (as in figure 3.2), highlights the relatively rapid progress of the elderly, who eventually overcome the substantial advantage originally held by the young (Radner 1986). Tracing the record from 1939 (as in figure 3.1 and table 3.1) emphasizes in contrast that, although the time path of progress of the two groups was quite different, they both have experienced substantial and similar gains over the past four decades. Only by concentrating on the recent past does the story become one of great gains by the elderly as compared with the growing impoverishment of children (Preston 1984). In fact, the greatest divergence occurs after 1979 (see figure 3.2). From a longer historical perspective this divergence is a brief anomaly. However, it has occurred, and because the anomaly lies in the most recent period, it—rather than the history of the entire postwar period—may better foreshadow the future. We return to this point later in the chapter.

Figure 3.2   POOR PERSONS: CHILDREN AND ELDERLY, 1966–86

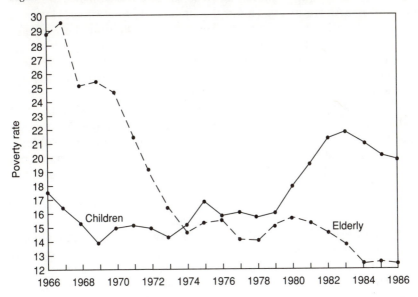

Further detail for age and sex subgroups, reported in table 3.1, indicates differences both over time and among groups. The declines in poverty between 1939 and 1969 were smaller for the elderly than for children. For example, children were slightly more likely to be poor than were men between the ages of 65 and 69 in 1939, 1949, and 1959, but slightly less likely in 1969.

But over the entire 40-year period, the differences in poverty rates among the elderly groups widened. As table 3.1 shows, both children and elderly men ages 65 to 69 gained relative to elderly men and women (over 70 years of age). The ratios for men over age 70 ranged only from 1.06 to 1.16 in 1939, but ranged from 1.38 to 1.86 in 1979. The ratios for all elderly women rose from 1.05 in 1939 to 2.44 in 1979.

The gains between 1969 and 1979 of all elderly men and women of all ages relative to children are also apparent in table 3.1. Poverty rose somewhat for children but dramatically declined for the elderly. Whereas children were less likely than men ages 65 to 69 to be poor in 1969, they were more than twice as likely to be poor by 1979. And whereas children were less likely to be poor than men over age 70 in every year prior to 1979, they were more likely than these men to be poor in 1979. Even in 1979, however, poverty rates for children were quite similar to those for elderly women below the age of 85. As we discuss later, the time path of earnings relative to Social Security benefits plays a key role in explaining these trends.

But why did the position of elderly women relative to elderly men deteriorate so much over the period? In 1939 there was little divergence by sex; by 1979 the rates for elderly women in any age group were 1.5 to 2.0 times those of men of the same age. Higher incidences of poverty for elderly women are not surprising, but that the trend is so adverse needs to be explained. Part of the explanation is due to the increased longevity of elderly women relative to elderly men. As a result, a much greater percentage of elderly women were widows in 1979 than in 1939. And widows have always had higher poverty rates than have elderly wives.

The other part of the explanation is policy-related but quite mechanical. Social Security benefits for a widow fall by one-third when a husband dies, whereas the poverty line for a single elderly person is 20 percent below that for an elderly couple. As a result of the differences in these two implicit equivalence scales, a husband's death can trigger an increase in measured poverty. We refer to this effect as mechanical because it results from two explicit, but inconsistent, policy decisions. Measured poverty would not increase if Social Security benefits used the poverty-line equivalence scale— that is, fell by only 20 percent at the death of a spouse—or if the poverty line for a single person were one-third below that for a couple. We could not find in the literature a discussion of whether these equivalence scales should be the same or whether each one is appropriate for the purpose it serves. That two different equivalence scales are in use side by side by policymakers, however, suggests that the economic problem faced by widows is not simply a mechanical failure.

We recomputed poverty rates by adjusting the poverty-line differ- ence so that it was as large as the Social Security benefit difference in 1985. For white elderly widows, poverty rates fell to 14.1 percent from 21.4 percent; for black elderly widows, the rates fell to 35.7 percent from 45.4 percent. Scaling the incidence of poverty by these amounts for elderly women as reported for 1979 (table 3.1) would eliminate much of the difference in poverty rates among elderly men and women at ages below 85.

Changes in poverty, especially among children, reflect changes in demographic characteristics as well as changes in the economic circumstances of each demographic group. The data in table 3.2 on the composition of the population and the composition of the poor

Table 3.2 COMPOSITION OF THE POPULATION AND OF THE POOR, SELECTED YEARS 1939–79 (percentage)

Age group	1939[a]		1949[b]		1959		1969		1979	
	All persons	Poor persons	All persons	Poor persons	All persons	Poor persons	All persons	Poor persons	All persons	Poor persons
Children under 15	25.1	29.3	28.3	33.8	31.6	36.8	28.8	31.4	23.2	30.4
Living with two parents	22.6	26.0	25.9	29.2	29.2	29.6	25.3	18.9	18.9	14.8
Living with single parent	2.5	3.3	2.4	4.6	2.5	7.2	3.6	12.5	4.3	15.6
Adults, 15–64	68.1	63.0	63.0	53.2	59.7	50.1	62.3	51.3	66.1	57.3
Elderly, 65 and over	6.7	7.7	8.8	13.0	8.7	14.1	8.9	17.3	10.7	12.3
Men	3.3	3.8	6.5	9.1	3.9	5.8	3.8	5.8	4.3	3.5
Women	3.5	3.9	2.3	3.9	4.8	8.3	5.2	11.5	6.4	8.8
Total	100.00	100.00	100.00	100.00	100.00	100.00	100.00	100.00	100.00	100.00

Source: Computations by authors from decennial census computer tapes.

Note: totals may not add to 100.00 because of rounding.

a. For 1939, earnings poverty; for other years, income poverty. See note a, table 3.1.
b. The 1949 classification is not consistent with those of the other census years. The largest difference is in the classification of elderly wives. See note b, table 3.1.

detail the rapid demographic as well as economic changes over this period. Between 1939 and 1959 the share of children in the population increased from 25.1 percent to 31.6 percent, while their share among the poor increased from 29.3 percent to 36.8 percent. During this period the much higher-than-average poverty rates of children living in single-parent (mostly female-headed) families began to emerge as a major issue. In 1959 children in two-parent families constituted about 29 percent of all persons and all poor persons, whereas children in single-parent families were about three times their share of the poor relative to their share of all persons (7.2 percent versus 2.5 percent). By 1969 children in two-parent families for the first time had a poverty rate that was below average—10.7 percent versus 14.4 percent for all persons (data not shown). Children in two-parent families made up a smaller part of the population (25.3 percent) than in any earlier year, but an even smaller percentage of the poor (18.9 percent). Even today, as discussed later, children in two-parent families have a poverty rate lower than that for all persons.

The declining relative well-being of children, then, is exacerbated by the post-1959 increase in the share of children living in single-parent families and the very high poverty rates of those families. For example, in 1939 the poverty rate of children in single-parent families (90.0 percent) was about one-third higher than the 68.1 percent rate for all persons. In 1949 these children were almost twice as likely to be poor as the average person; and in 1959, almost three times as likely. By 1979 their rate of 47.4 percent was more than three-and-one-half times the aggregate rate of 13.1 percent. In 1979 as table 3.2 shows, despite their small numbers in the population (4.3 percent), poor children in single-parent families composed a larger share of all poor persons (15.6 percent) than either poor children in two-parent families (14.8 percent) or poor elderly persons (12.3 percent).

Disaggregation by race and ethnic group also shows divergent patterns of change. Table 3.3 compares the experiences of children and the elderly classified by race or ethnicity and sex. The average experience, dominated by data for whites, is not representative of the minority experience. Between 1939 and 1969 white children gained relative to elderly white men as well as relative to black and Hispanic children, elderly black men, and all elderly women. And black and Hispanic children, black elderly men, and black and white elderly women had smaller declines in poverty than elderly white men during virtually each subperiod. Thus, the post-1969 trend of

Table 3.3   POVERTY RATES FOR CHILDREN AND THE ELDERLY, BY RACE OR ETHNICITY, AND SEX, SELECTED YEARS, 1939–79

Age group	Percentage of persons who are poor					Poverty rate relative to rate of white men age 65 and over				
	1939[a]	1949[b]	1959	1969	1979	1939[a]	1949[b]	1959	1969	1979
Children under 15										
White	76.6	41.2	18.8	10.4	11.7	1.00	0.78	0.62	0.52	1.36
Black	97.5	87.0	63.3	41.1	36.1	1.27	1.65	2.10	2.04	4.20
Hispanic	96.2	73.0	53.3	33.3	28.3	1.26	1.38	1.77	1.66	3.29
All	79.5	47.6	26.1	15.6	17.1	1.04	0.90	0.87	0.78	1.99
Elderly men, 65 and over										
White	76.6	52.8	30.1	20.1	8.6	1.00	1.00	1.00	1.00	1.00
Black	95.3	86.4	65.2	43.7	26.5	1.24	1.64	2.17	2.17	3.08
Hispanic	c	c	c	c	c	c	c	c	c	c
All	78.0	55.3	33.2	22.2	10.6	1.02	1.05	1.10	1.10	1.23
Elderly women, 65 and over										
White	76.2	67.3	36.4	30.4	15.8	0.99	1.27	1.21	1.51	1.84
Black	94.6	92.3	64.9	50.0	35.3	1.23	1.75	2.16	2.49	4.10
Hispanic	c	c	c	c	c	c	c	c	c	c
All	77.5	69.4	38.6	32.1	18.0	1.01	1.31	1.28	1.60	2.09
All elderly persons	77.8	59.0	36.2	27.9	15.0	1.01	1.12	1.20	1.39	1.74

Source: Computations by authors from decennial census computer tapes.
a. See note a, table 3.1.
b. See note b, table 3.1.
c. Less than 200 observations in sample; figures are included in the total.

Table 3.4   POVERTY RATES FOR CHILDREN AND THE ELDERLY, BY RACE OR
ETHNICITY, AND SEX OF HOUSEHOLD HEAD, 1985

| | Percentage of persons who are poor | | |
| | Whites (non-Hispanic) | Blacks and Hispanics | All |
Age group			
Children under 18[a]			
Living with two parents	8.3	21.8	11.4
Living with single parent	35.7	64.3	49.9
Persons living in households where heads are:[b]			
Men, 18–64	6.2	15.2	7.9
Women, 18–64	20.2	40.2	26.8
Men, 65 and over	5.6	19.6	7.4
Women, 65 and over	20.3	39.2	23.1
All persons	9.9	28.2	14.0[c]

Source: Computations by authors from the Current Population Survey of March 1986.
a. Census data in previous tables are for children younger than 15 years of age.
b. These data, like those from the 1950 census, are for persons classified by the age of the household head and not for persons classified by their own ages.
c. In 1985, there were 236.59 million persons in the United States; 33.06 million were poor according to the official definition of poverty.

rising poverty among children largely reflects the fact that poverty declined more among elderly white men than it did for any other group, whereas among white children it rose for the first time.

How have these patterns changed since 1979? We will not have data from the 1990 decennial census for several years, but we have similar data for the year 1985 from the March 1986 CPS. These data are not directly comparable to the decennial census data, but they are sufficiently similar to indicate that the pattern of poverty rates across subgroups of the population has not changed much since the last census. Between 1979 and 1985, the difference between the poverty rates for children and the elderly, as reported in the CPS, increased from less than one to more than seven percentage points. In 1985 these rates were 20.1 percent and 12.6 percent, respectively.

There continues to be great diversity across groups defined by the age, race or ethnicity, and sex of the household head (see table 3.4).[8] For example, in 1985, children living in two-parent families were less likely to be poor (11.4 percent) than persons living in households headed by elderly women (23.1 percent) or nonelderly women (26.8 percent), or persons living in households headed by black or Hispanic elderly men (19.6 percent).

The poverty rate for all children is high in large part because the rate for children living in single-parent families is extraordinarily high, 49.9 percent. The poverty rate for all elderly persons is low primarily because the rate for persons living in households headed by elderly white men is low, 5.6 percent.

Female headship has obviously become an important contributor to child poverty, especially since 1969. However, the rise in child poverty during the 1970s and 1980s was due primarily to the impact of poor economic performance on parents' incomes. A demographic standardization shows that if children's living arrangements had remained the same between 1969 and 1985—that is, if 12 percent instead of 24 percent of all children lived in single-parent families— but if the poverty rates for children in single- and two-parent families were at the 1985 levels shown in table 3.4, then the child poverty rate in 1985 would have been 16.1 percent instead of 20.1 percent. A similar standardization, also based on 1969 living arrangements, shows that if the poverty rate for all children had declined between 1969 and 1985 at the same rate as it did between 1959 and 1969, then the 1985 rate would have been 6.3 percent.

The actual child poverty rate in 1985, 20.1 percent, was 13.8 percentage points higher than this standardized rate. About one-third of the difference was due to the increase in children living in single-parent families; about two-thirds was due to the failure of poverty rates to decline as fast as they had in the period before 1969.

Race and ethnicity contribute significantly to the poverty of children, but they also contribute to the poverty of the elderly. The combination of female headship with race and ethnicity is extremely potent—almost two-thirds of children living in households headed by black and Hispanic women are poor. In 1985 these children were about five times as likely to be poor as the average person. For all black and Hispanic subgroups of the population, except persons living in households headed by men between the ages of 18 and 64, the incidence of poverty equals or exceeds the national poverty rate of 20 percent that led President Johnson to declare war on poverty more than 20 years ago.

Before closing this section, we should repeat a caveat. Poverty rates have been defined on the basis of cash income (for 1939 our measure includes only earnings). Income in kind is omitted in every year, although it is obviously of some significance throughout the period. In the early years it is an important omitted component of the income of particular low-income groups—farm proprietors, farm laborers, domestics, and some service workers. Whether children or the elderly are more likely to be affected by this lack of data is problematic.

In recent years in-kind income has been an important component of transfer benefits, especially in the form of medical benefits to the elderly. Such benefits have come to rival in scope the large in-kind transfers to children through public education. The significance of these trends will become clear in other chapters in this volume. The issue that in-kind income raises for this chapter is its effect on relative trends in the poverty rates for the young and the elderly.

The U.S. Census Bureau (1986) has evaluated the effects of the food, housing, and medical programs on the incidence of poverty, under a variety of assumptions, for each year since 1979. These in-kind programs benefit both children and the elderly, but their antipoverty effect is greater for the elderly. The appropriateness of including medical benefits in measures of poverty is hotly contested. Even when they are excluded, however, the elderly benefit more than children from in-kind transfers. When medical care is excluded, in-kind benefits for food and housing in 1985 removed about 12 percent of poor children from poverty and about 15 percent of poor elderly persons. Because these benefits were virtually nonexistent in 1939, their omission from decennial census data implies that we have somewhat understated the recent relative gains of the elderly.

TRENDS IN AVERAGE EARNINGS AND TRANSFERS

Trends in mean earnings affect the incidence of poverty among children and the elderly in two quite different ways. First, changes in the mean income of a group are often associated with much larger percentage changes in the same direction in the incidence of poverty. That is, cyclical decreases in average income are usually associated with increases in inequality that further raise poverty rates. Second, changes in earnings affect poverty differently for children and the elderly. For example, if nominal earnings are rising but real earnings are falling, as occurred during much of the 1970s, the incidence of poverty rises because the poverty lines are indexed to prices.

Poor children are more dependent on real earnings, especially if they are in intact families, than are the elderly. Hence large swings in the rate of growth of earnings such as those the United States has experienced, especially recently, have a greater impact on the incidence of poverty and well-being among children. The elderly are less affected because benefit levels under Old Age and Survivors Insurance (OASI) and wage income in the short term are not necessarily connected. Thus the well-being of children relative to that of the elderly depends not only on rates of growth of earnings, but also on rates of growth of earnings relative to rates of growth of OASI benefits.

We now turn to the role of the relationship of trends in earnings relative to transfers, and of transfers to elderly persons relative to transfers to children, as the proximate causes of these observed trends. Table 3.5 shows in the first three columns real median wages and salaries for all men (assumed to be representative of the income of parents and hence of children in two-parent households), the percentage of elderly men who have retired, and real average annual Social Security benefits for a retired worker and his wife. The last three columns show the ratio of Social Security benefits to median male earnings, to the poverty line for an elderly couple, and to mean welfare benefits for a three-person family.

Social Security benefits and the percentage of elderly men retired changed very little between 1940 and 1950. However, real median earnings increased by more than 50 percent. As a result, benefits increased from 50 percent to 57 percent of the poverty line for two elderly adults, but declined from 45 percent to 33 percent of median male earnings.[9] Between 1950 and 1960 real Social Security benefits increased by about 40 percent and real earnings by about 25 percent. Social Security benefits increased to 37 percent of earnings and 81 percent of the poverty line, which is constant in real terms for the entire period. Between 1960 and 1970 benefits and earnings each increased by about 20 percent. Benefits grew rapidly again between 1970 and 1980—by about 35 percent—while real earnings declined by 7 percent. As a result, in 1980 the average benefit for a worker and his wife was 1.3 times the poverty line and 55 percent of median earnings.

Thus from 1940 to 1970 earnings growth was more rapid than Social Security growth, and children benefited more than the elderly. In the 1970s, growth in Social Security benefits quickened while earnings fell. As a result, poverty among the elderly fell, and poverty among children increased. The beginning and ending decades are the ones that diverge the most for the two groups. Forecasts depend on the weight given to one or the other of these decades.

If it can be assumed that the poverty line specifies a minimum annual retirement income for the elderly, mean Social Security benefits can be viewed as having changed from a retirement supple-

Table 3.5 EARNINGS AND SOCIAL SECURITY BENEFITS, SELECTED YEARS, 1940–80 (1980 dollars)

Year	Median wage and salary earnings of male workers[a] (1)	Percentage among retired men age 65 and over[b] (2)	Mean annual Social Security benefit, worker and wife[c] (3)	Ratio of mean Social Security benefit to		
				Male median earnings[d] (4)	Poverty line[e] (5)	Mean AFDC benefits for 3-person family[f] (6)
1940	5,494	58.2	2,492	0.45	0.50	1.40
1950	8,667	58.6	2,845	0.33	0.57	1.47
1960	10,782	69.5	4,026	0.37	0.81	1.62
1970	13,100	75.2	4,882	0.37	0.99	1.43
1980	12,128	80.1	6,632	0.55	1.34	1.90

a. U.S. Department of Health and Human Services, Social Security Administration (1983), Table 22, 80. Computed for wage and salary workers only. Includes workers of all ages and those working parttime or part-year.

b. U.S. Bureau of the Census (1976), 26–41.

c. U.S. Department of Health and Human Services, Social Security Administration (1983). Table 78, 153. Mean computed for Social Security recipients only.

d. Computed as column 3 divided by column 1.

e. The poverty line for an elderly couple is about $4,950 in 1980 dollars for each year.

f. U.S. Department of Health and Human Services, Social Security Administration, (1983). Mean monthly amount per recipient multiplied by 3.

ment paying half the minimum in 1940 to a minimum guaranteed income by 1970 and something well beyond the minimum by 1980. If the cash value of the benefits the elderly have received from Medicare since 1965 were to be added in as well, the gains of the elderly relative to both the poverty line and median male earnings would be even greater. Similarly, the elderly's relative well-being would further increase if we valued the increased leisure associated with increased retirement.

The Social Security system is on a pay-as-you-go basis. As a result, the trend in real earnings in column 1 of table 3.5 is overstated because we have not subtracted the growing payroll tax required to finance the increased real Social Security benefits.[10] And, because tax rates were so much lower in the earlier than the later years, the unprecedented rise in Social Security benefits relative to earnings since 1970 can be viewed as a direct transfer from workers and their children to the retired. For example, Burkhauser and Warlick (1981) show that, on average, less than 30 percent of Social Security benefits in 1972 could be viewed as a return to the individual's total (employer plus employee) Social Security tax payments.

Column 6 of table 3.5 shows that Social Security benefits rose relative to cash benefits for children in recent years. Benefits from the transfer program most important to children—Aid to Families with Dependent Children (AFDC)—were always lower than Social Security benefits, but they grew at a similar rate up to 1970. Benefits for a retired couple were typically about 40 percent greater than AFDC benefits for a three-person family over the 30-year period. However, since 1970 Social Security benefits have increased in real terms, whereas AFDC benefits have remained stagnant. By 1980 the typical retired couple received almost twice the benefits of a three-person family with a prime-age head.

Because the census has only limited information on cash income maintenance transfers, we used the March CPS data to provide more detailed evidence of these transfer differences. The first two rows of table 3.6 show that pretransfer poor families with children (those who would have been poor had their only incomes been from market sources) receive a disproportionately small and declining share of all transfers. They were about 26 percent of all pretransfer poor families in both 1967 and 1984, but their share of cash transfers declined from 19.8 percent to 16.8 percent.

The bottom rows of table 3.6 show that pretransfer poor families with children received much smaller transfers than households headed by a person over 65 years of age. The average transfer to the

Table 3.6   POVERTY AND TRANSFER RECEIPT, SELECTED YEARS, 1967–84

	1967	1973	1979	1984
Pretransfer poor families with children, as a percentage of all pretransfer poor households	26.2	25.3	24.5	26.8
Percentage of all cash transfers to pretransfer poor households received by pretransfer poor families with children	19.8	22.5	17.9	16.8
Average cash transfer received by the pretransfer poor (1984 dollars)				
Two-parent families with children	1,832	4,024	3,776	2,946
Female-headed families with children	3,908	5,217	4,056	3,276
Households headed by elderly persons	4,756	6,484	6,926	7,322

Source: Computations by the authors from the March Current Population Surveys of 1968, 1974, 1980, and 1985.
Note: Pretransfer poor households are those whose cash incomes, excluding government transfers, fall below the poverty line.

elderly poor increased over the entire period. Transfers to families with children increased substantially between 1967 and 1973, but then declined. Thus, in 1984, when the poverty line for a family of four was $10,609, the typical pretransfer poor family with children received only about $3,000. This contrasts with the situation of the elderly, for whom the poverty line for a couple was $6,282 and the average transfer was $7,322. In the recent period, declining real transfers and declining real earnings along with an increase in families headed by women combined to produce the unprecedented rise in child poverty beginning in 1969 and accelerating after 1979. (See figure 3.2 presented earlier.)

IMPLICATIONS OF RECENT POLICIES

For most of our history, there has been a dependent population of young and old whose standard of living was virtually determined by the income of the working population with whom they resided.

That remains true today only for children in intact families. It is no longer true for the many children in single-parent families dependent on child support and AFDC, and it is certainly past history for the elderly.

The Social Security Act ruptured the connection between current living standards and the income of the family in which the elderly resided as a subfamily. A political link remained and benefits were frequently raised by legislative mandates that tapped trust fund surpluses in prosperous times. Finally, however, indexing, as it was intended to do, ended the connection altogether.

The well-being of children in two-parent families depends largely on rates of income growth of the heads of the household in which they reside, but this would no longer be true for the elderly even if they still lived with their children. This situation leads to an observation and a question. First, the observation: To describe the past and to forecast future living standards for children and for the elderly involve different independent variables. The children's equation needs real income and living arrangements. To forecast the distribution of economic well-being for children a variable such as cohort size is also needed to predict the income distribution of the working population (Easterlin 1986). Since 1972 real benefits for the elderly have remained constant. In contrast to the situation of children, we need to estimate a relationship for the elderly only if we intend to forecast politically motivated changes in benefit levels.

The question is, how does one evaluate the political decision to separate the well-being of the elderly from the current earnings of their children, while leaving the well-being of their grandchildren dependent on those same income earners and their current earnings? To answer this question requires a look back at the policy changes that shaped the transfer system over the past two decades.

The floor for minimum consumption of the elderly is now set by the Supplemental Security Income program (SSI) plus food stamps. Children are eligible only for food stamps, so that the fundamental difference, at least in the basic safety net, is SSI. Enactment of SSI in October 1972 resulted from the long and futile effort by the Nixon administration to pass the Family Assistance Plan (FAP). Introduced in Congress in 1969, FAP was initially a negative income tax with a low guarantee and a low tax rate but with universal coverage of families with children. The legislation was later expanded to include elderly, blind, and disabled persons as well. Although FAP passed the House twice, it never succeeded in the Senate. Only the part of the legislation that aided elderly, blind, and disabled persons—

SSI—was enacted. If FAP had been enacted, children would now have the same income floor as the elderly.

As things stand, however, the income floor for children in one-parent families is AFDC. For two-parent families, in the 26 states (and the District of Columbia) that have it, the floor is the Unemployed Parent part of AFDC. Otherwise the floor is composed of food stamps and General Assistance, a county-administered program that varies widely within states and even more widely across states.

That the income floors of the elderly and of children differ, then, and differ substantially, is a deliberate policy choice. According to the major study of the effort to enact FAP (Burke and Burke 1974), the Senate's objection was that it extended welfare to able-bodied men expected to work. That is, parents of children in poverty were presumed to reduce their work effort if the income of their children were to rise. However, adult children of elderly poor parents were not expected to reduce their work effort if the income of their parents were to rise. The rationale for these different expectations, we suppose, is that working-age parents have access to the transfers to their dependent children but would not have access to transfers to their dependent parents. On economic grounds, the distinction makes sense only if children are dependents and dependents can be exploited, whereas parents are not dependents and hence cannot be exploited. It is an ugly view of twentieth-century family life, but it could be right. We need to know more than we do about intergenerational transfers to know whether there is substance to this view. What little we know casts considerable doubt on it, however.

Marilyn Moon examined intrafamily transfers between young and old as they could be inferred from the patterns of living arrangements in extended families. She concluded that "aged couples or individuals who reside in larger extended family groups fall at the extremes of the income distribution. The income levels of their younger relatives tend to fall at the opposite extremes. Consequently, . . . [intrafamily transfers] exhibit a strong equalizing effect" (1977, 111). In other words, extended families of adult children and parents continue to exist, and they live together in order to help each other. That is, they share resources. Sharing must mean that the labor market decisions of prime-age men are affected by transfers to parents. Yet, at least for the foreseeable future, policy will be made on the presumption that labor supply is seriously affected by cash transfers to children, which may be inadequate, whereas benefits to the elderly, fixed in real terms, are adequate and do not affect labor supply.

It is possible to get a rough estimate of the cost to poor children of rejecting FAP but accepting SSI. In 1986 the SSI benefit level for a couple without other income was $504 per month (or, including food stamps, somewhat more than 80 percent of the poverty line). For that same year, the Congressional Budget Office (CBO) (U.S. Congress 1985) estimated the effects— on the incidence of poverty, on the poverty gap, and on the federal budget—of establishing a national minimum for AFDC plus food stamps at 65 percent the poverty line. Under this simulated plan, the guarantee would be raised for 2.2 million families (60 percent of existing AFDC families) an average of $73 per month, and 190,000 families would be added to the rolls. The cost to the federal government of the plan would have been about $3.5 billion, or 40 percent of federal AFDC benefit payments but less than 2 percent of Social Security benefits.

These data suggest how small the nation's largest cash welfare program for children really is. Nevertheless, raising benefit levels to 65 percent of the poverty line from the current level of around 40 percent would significantly affect the incidence of poverty and the poverty gap. "About 80 percent of new and increased benefits would go to families below the poverty level, which would cause the poverty gap—as measured by official poverty statistics—to decline by about $2.7 billion. Roughly 0.1 million families would be moved above the poverty level, about 5 percent of the poor families affected" (U.S. Congress 1985, 37). Moving the guarantee up to the SSI level would not be as target efficient as going from 40 percent to 65 percent of the poverty level, but another 7 percent of poor people would undoubtedly be taken out of poverty.

In addition to higher benefits, had FAP passed, coverage would have been extended to intact families with children. No estimate has been made of the effect of such a change. It would be considerably more expensive than the current program, but with the guarantee level set at 80 percent of the poverty line, it would have a substantial impact both on the incidence of poverty and the poverty gap, particularly for poor children in male-headed households.

The CBO estimates were conducted for viable bills introduced into the Congress. These bills have not attracted sufficient support, however, to move them out of committee, and they are unlikely to become law. Amid the current passion for workfare, their labor supply disincentive effects would be sufficient to kill them, even in a time of budgetary surplus.

In 1988, with unemployment rates expected to remain over 5 percent for the rest of the decade, poverty among children will remain high even if the economy—already into the second longest expansion since World War II—continues to grow without recession and even if the percentage of children living in single-parent families could be reduced. One must also recognize that because Social Security benefits will no longer grow faster than inflation, the best forecast for poverty rates among the elderly is that they will decline slowly. Newer retirees will have higher lifetime earnings and hence higher Social Security benefits. Newer retirees are also more likely to have private pensions than existing retirees; only about one-third of retirees currently have them, but about one-half of current workers are covered by them. Most of the benefits of tax-deferred Individual Retirement Accounts (IRAs) and private pensions will accrue to the well-off. But some people who might have been strapped in retirement—for example, lower-middle-income workers, the group that Smeeding (1986) calls "tweeners"—will also be helped. They are now too wealthy to qualify for Medicaid, but not wealthy enough to buy Medigap insurance, that is, insurance designed to fill the gaps in Medicare coverage. They are economically insecure and vulnerable to unexpected health problems. They are not, however, poor.

IMPLICATIONS FOR FUTURE POLICIES

Our recommendations for aiding the poor, in an era in which the significance of age has declined, would avoid expansion of welfare programs but involve increased income testing through the income tax. That is, funds can be raised through higher taxes on the nonpoor elderly and nonelderly and spent on higher tax credits for poor children.

Such changes can aid poor children and avoid hurting the poor elderly. In contrast, a policy of across-the-board cuts in Social Security would hurt the poor elderly; and a policy of across-the-board benefits to children, such as children's allowances, would help those who are not needy.

We would also strengthen policies targeted on the poor elderly by, for example, attempting to raise the SSI participation rate or changing the program so that it serves a greater percentage of the elderly poor.

Public policy has recently shifted in the direction of taking back some of the special tax provisions that disproportionately aid the nonpoor elderly. These changes include repeal of the double personal exemption and taxation of one-half of the Social Security benefits of those filing joint returns with incomes above $30,000 or single returns with incomes above $25,000. A further move would be to tax the implicit subsidy in Medicare in the same way that we are taxing Social Security, as well as to repeal the tax-free status of employer-provided health insurance.

The Tax Reform Act of 1986 has made an important step in the direction of aiding poor children by removing most of their families from the rolls through expansion and indexation to the cost of living of the earned income tax credit, the standard deduction, and the personal exemption. We could move further in the direction of using the income tax to aid poor children by making the child care tax credit refundable or by turning the $2,000 personal exemption into a refundable credit of $560 (its value to taxpayers in the 28 percent bracket). It is now worth only $300 to taxpayers in the 15 percent bracket; it is worth nothing to some poor families whose tax liabilities have been eliminated but who still have unused personal exemptions.

Both these changes can help restore the relative position of the children of the working poor and near poor, who have been hurt the most by the recent retrenchment in government benefits and the erosion of real family incomes in the period since 1973. The Tax Reform Act of 1986 corrects the harm done them by tax changes over the last decade, but not the harm done by market and transfer system changes.

We conclude that poverty remains high by historical standards for many subgroups—elderly white widows, all minority elderly people and children, and white children living in single-parent families. These subgroups in 1985 constituted about 16 percent of all persons but about 37 percent of all poor persons. Taken as a group, their poverty rate was almost 33 percent. Given current public social insurance and welfare policies and private pension policies, poverty among these groups will fall very little over the next decade, even if the economy continues to grow without recession.

To reduce further the incidence of poverty requires a redirected antipoverty effort, in which age has little significance. If the resources devoted to such an effort are effectively targeted to people in need, children will gain disproportionately. But if the policy merely shifts from a bias in favor of the elderly to a bias toward children, the poor—both children and the elderly—will gain disproportionately little. Targeting benefits to the elderly may have proceeded for too long, but such targeting has been more successful than any other policy in reducing poverty. An alternative group as target-efficient as the elderly and a policy as politically acceptable as raising Social Security benefits will be hard to find.

Notes

1. For example, in 1939, the poverty lines for an elderly couple and a family of four were $841 and $1,408, respectively; in 1979, they were $4,392 and $7,355. A detailed description of the process by which the poverty lines were extended back in time is available from the authors. Also, see Ross, Danziger, and Smolensky (1987).

2. We also analyzed a relative poverty threshold set at 44 percent of the median income for every year. (This measure was first used by Plotnick and Skidmore, 1975.) The relative poverty rate is much more stable over the 40-year period. These results are available from the authors. Smith (1988) adopts a definition that is a hybrid of the official measure and a relative measure. His poverty threshold increases by 0.5 percent for every 1 percent growth in real median income. He finds that poverty declined from 34 percent of persons in 1940 to 11 percent in 1980.

3. The census does contain an indicator denoting whether the household received $50 or more in other income. We found that adding $50 to total income for households with this indicator did not significantly change the 1939 poverty rate, so we do not use it. To obtain a consistent series for the 40-year period, we have computed an earnings poverty series based only on wages and salaries, but those data are not reported in this paper. See Ross, Danziger, and Smolensky (1987).

4. The decennial census has never collected information on in-kind transfers received and taxes paid, although both affect a household's command of resources. Inclusion of in-kind transfers would lower poverty rates in each year; inclusion of taxes would raise them. These biases increase over time. If their effects were to be included, they would be small until 1969. For a discussion of their effects in a recent year, see Smeeding (1986).

5. The difference between earnings poverty and posttransfer poverty in any year is accounted for by income from self-employment, interest, dividends, rent, government income-transfer programs, private pensions, and other miscellaneous sources. Because of data limitations, income from government programs cannot be distinguished from other sources of income until the 1960 census. For this reason, we do not focus on the antipoverty effects of government programs in this paper.

6. Unrelated persons age 15 and over and secondary families are counted as separate units. For example, two unrelated persons living in a single dwelling unit are assumed not to share income, and each is counted as a separate one-person household. They would also be counted as separate one-person households if they shared a dwelling unit with another family. Subfamilies, by definition, are related to the household head and thus are included as part of the primary family's income-sharing unit.

7. Danziger, van der Gaag, Smolensky, and Taussig (1984) found that in 1973, classifying all persons by their own age instead of the age of their household head slightly increased the relative economic status of the elderly. In that year, 13.1 percent of all elderly persons lived in households headed by nonelderly persons; 2.7 percent of nonelderly persons lived in households headed by the elderly. Holden (1988)

found that in 1950 about 24 percent of women over age 60 lived in a household where the head was a relative other than a husband, whereas only 10 percent were in this category in 1980.

In this chapter, the data we used from the 1950 census and the March 1986 Current Population Survey classify persons by the age of their household head. All other census data classify by the age of persons. Computational costs prevented us from testing the sensitivity of the poverty rates shown in these years to this classification. However, this evidence suggests that classification by age of household head probably leads to a slight understatement of elderly poverty rates in 1949, when a greater percentage of the elderly lived with the nonelderly, and a slight overstatement in 1985, when a smaller percentage lived with the nonelderly. If anything, adjusting for these differences would only reinforce our major theme.

8. Like the 1949 census data, the CPS data reported in table 3.4 classify persons by the age of their household head. In addition, children are defined as persons under 18, not under 15.

9. Note that earnings are for all male wage and salary workers, including those of all ages working parttime and part-year.

10. Employees and employers each pay half the payroll tax. The employee shares were 1.0, 1.5, 3.0, 4.8, and 6.13 percent of annual earned income (up to a maximum taxable wage base) in 1940, 1950, 1960, 1970, and 1980, respectively.

References

Burke, Vincent J., and Vee Burke. 1974. *Nixon's Good Deed*. New York: Columbia University Press.

Burkhauser, Richard, and Jennifer Warlick. 1981. "Disentangling the Annuity from the Redistributive Aspects of Social Security." *Review of Income and Wealth* 27:401–21.

Danziger, Sheldon, Jacques van der Gaag, Eugene Smolensky, and Michael Taussig. 1984. "Implications of the Relative Economic Status of the Elderly for Transfer Policy." In *Retirement and Economic Behavior*, edited by H.J. Aaron and G. Burtless. Washington, D.C.: Brookings Institution.

Easterlin, Richard A. 1986. "The New Age Structure of Poverty: Permanent or Transient?" University of Southern California. Photocopy.

Fisher, Gordon. 1985. "Tabulations of Poverty Rates from Current Population Survey." U.S. Department of Health and Human Services, Washington, D.C. Photocopy.

Holden, Karen. 1987. "Poverty and Living Arrangements among Older Women." *Journal of Gerontology* 43(1):522–27.

Moon, Marilyn. 1977. *The Measurement of Economic Welfare: Its Application to the Aged Poor*. New York: Academic Press.

Plotnick, Robert, and Felicity Skidmore. 1975. *Progress against Poverty*. New York: Academic Press.

Preston, Samuel H. 1984. "Children and the Elderly: Divergent Paths for America's Dependents." *Demography* 21:435–57.

Radner, Daniel B. 1986. "Changes in the Money Income of the Aged and Nonaged, 1967–1983." *Studies in Income Distribution,* no. 14. U.S. Department of Health and Human Services, Washington, D.C.

Ross, Christine, Sheldon Danziger, and Eugene Smolensky. 1987. "The Level and Trend of Poverty, 1939–1979." *Demography* 24 (November):587–600.

Smeeding, Timothy. 1986. "Nonmoney Income and the Elderly: The Case of the 'Tweeners." *Journal of Policy Analysis and Management* (Summer).

Smith, James P. 1988. "Poverty and the Family." In *Divided Opportunities: Minorities, Poverty, and Social Policy,* ed. Gary D. Sandefur and Marta Tienda. New York: Plenum Press.

U.S. Bureau of the Census. 1976. *Historical Statistics, Colonial Times to the Present,* Series D. Washington, D.C.

U.S. Bureau of the Census. 1986. *Estimates of Poverty Including the Value of Noncash Benefits: 1985.* Technical paper 56. Washington, D.C.

U.S. Congress. Congressional Budget Office (CBO). 1985. *Reducing Poverty among Children.* Washington, D.C.: CBO.

U.S. Department of Health and Human Services, Social Security Administration. 1983. *Social Security Bulletin, Annual Statistical Supplement, 1983.*

Chapter Four

LIFE EVENTS, PUBLIC POLICY, AND THE ECONOMIC VULNERABILITY OF CHILDREN AND THE ELDERLY

Richard V. Burkhauser and Greg J. Duncan

The degree of hardship caused by an economic setback is determined not only by its magnitude, but also by the ability of the persons affected to cope with it. The ability to cope varies over life; but two groups, the young and the elderly, are especially vulnerable to such setbacks. Children are completely dependent on others for their economic security, and a growing body of evidence links outcomes such as years of completed schooling to the economic resources available during childhood (Sewell and Hauser 1975, White 1982, and Hill and Duncan 1987). The elderly, for their part, are less able than younger adults to turn to the labor market for help in coping with economic adversity or to remarriage after the death of a spouse. The opposite ends of the life course have traditionally been associated with lower levels of well-being and greater risks of poverty and have increasingly been the target of social transfer policy over the past half-century.

THE DYNAMIC NATURE OF FAMILY WELL-BEING

Much of our knowledge of the economic position of children and the elderly is based on cross-sectional data on family income. Such data provide snapshots of the relative percentages of population subgroups in poverty when the picture is taken, but they offer no direct information on the volatility of income or the duration or risk of poverty as people age. More sophisticated studies compare snapshots at several points and chart changes in the risk of poverty as groups of people age. Such studies, although useful, are still unable to identify the life events most associated with poverty and economic adversity.

This chapter focuses directly on the dynamic nature of family well-being through the use of two longitudinal data bases that enable us to trace experiences of the same persons over a decade or more. In contrast to the image of fairly stable incomes during most life-cycle stages that is often inferred from cross-sectional data, we find substantial variation and volatility in economic well-being both within and across age groups.

We investigate patterns of life events—dissolutions of families, retirement, unemployment, illness—that threaten individuals with substantial decreases in economic well-being. For children, divorce is found to be the most important family composition event and the unemployment of the household head the most important labor force event associated with such decreases. For the elderly, retirement and the death of a spouse are the life events most associated with dramatically reduced income.

Once the life events that most seriously threaten the well-being of children and the elderly are identified, the unique strength of the longitudinal data can be fully used. For children, we focus on the effect of unemployment and, especially, divorce on the level and composition of family income. Although unemployment is found to be implicated more frequently than divorce in major income losses, the duration of most unemployment episodes appears to be short. Long-term unemployment is shouldered by a rather small fraction of those who ever experience unemployment.

In contrast, the economic effects of divorce or separation on the women and children involved often last for many years. Living standards fall substantially for divorced women and their children, despite our system of private (for example, alimony and child support) and public (for example, Aid to Families with Dependent Children—AFDC) transfers. In contrast, the living standard of divorced husbands rises following divorce. As time passes, the living standards of women and children involved in a remarriage are restored to predivorce levels; when no remarriage occurs, the standards remain at essentially the same low level because falling child support payments offset increases in the earnings of the mothers.

For the elderly, we focus on the transition from market work to retirement and on the transition of elderly women from wives to widows. Couples who receive both Social Security and private pension benefits face a small chance of falling into poverty as long as both spouses are alive. For couples without private pension benefits, the likelihood of a fall into poverty in retirement is greater. However, the risk of falling into poverty is largest in the initial period of retirement. It diminishes greatly as long as both marriage partners survive. The greatest threat of poverty for elderly women in retirement, however, occurs with the onset of widowhood. Private pensions by no means eliminate the risk of poverty for widows.

DATA AND METHODS

Data

The findings that follow are based on data from two longitudinal surveys, the Panel Study of Income Dynamics (PSID) and the Retirement History Study (RHS). Since 1968 the PSID has interviewed annually a representative sample of some 5,000 families. At least one member of each family was part of the original families interviewed in 1968 or born to a member of one of these families. (For a fuller discussion of PSID data, see Survey Research Center 1984.) The RHS, conducted by the Social Security Administration, interviewed households headed by a person who was between the ages of 58 and 63 in 1969 and repeated the interviews at two-year intervals over the following ten-year period. In 1969, single men and women and husbands of couples were interviewed as primary respondents. When a spouse died, the survivor became the primary respondent and was followed during the remainder of the survey period. (For a fuller discussion of the RHS data, see Ireland 1976.)

Measures of Economic Status

It is natural to use the family as the unit for measuring economic status. Families pool their resources, transferring income to members too young, too elderly, or too involved with nonmarket activities such as childrearing to secure an adequate income for themselves. Total family money income is the most common yardstick of economic status, and it is also one of the measures we use.

However, there are many reasons why total family cash income is less than ideal (Moon and Smolensky 1977). Among the most important are the dramatic differences among families in the number and ages of family members who share a given income. Adjustments for family size can be made by dividing family income by the federal government's annually calculated poverty thresholds for families with different compositions based on the number, sex, and age of family members, producing what we term an income-to-needs ratio.[1] The poverty threshold for a family of four in 1985 dollars was approximately $11,000. A family of four with a family income of $33,000 would have an income-to-needs ratio of 3.0. A family of four with an income of $5,500 would have an income-to-needs ratio of 0.5 and be deemed poor.

The Unit of Analysis

Official poverty thresholds take the family to be the appropriate unit for the measurement of economic status. We share this assumption in the sense that we assume that all members of a family move into and out of poverty together when family income climbs above or falls below the poverty threshold. But our unit of analysis is the individual. Family composition changes dramatically over time; and the identity of families, given changes such as divorce, is virtually impossible to define. Only individuals retain their own identity. Changes in family composition are critical life events associated with changes in the well-being of individuals. These could not be taken into account by a study that, in order to maintain uniformity, ignored families undergoing radical change.

PATTERNS OF WELL-BEING ACROSS LIFE

We first examine trends and stability of family income over the 11-year period between 1969 and 1979, using the PSID. All income figures have been inflated to 1985 levels, using the Consumer Price Index (CPI). We describe the separate experiences of children, prime-age adults, and the elderly, categorizing individuals according to their age and sex in 1969, the first year of the period. The youngest group consists of children who were under the age of 5 in 1969 and therefore spent the entire 11-year period as dependent children. Given policymakers' concern for the experiences of minority children, we present separate figures for white and black children.[2] The group ages 25 to 45 consists of persons who spent the entire 11 years in their "prime" labor market and parenthood years. Most of the group ages 56 to 65 will have retired during the 11-year period. Most of the group ages 66 to 75 were retired when the period began.

Patterns by Age Group

A cross-sectional snapshot of the average 1969 family income and income-to-needs ratio shows that children and the elderly were

Table 4.1 PATTERNS OF INCOME LEVEL AND CHANGE, VARIOUS AGE
GROUPS BETWEEN 1969 AND 1979

Demographic status in 1969	Family income (thousand dollars)		Income-to-needs ratio		Average real annual growth (percentage)
	1969	1979	1969	1979	
Less than 5 years old					
White	31.1	42.7	3.0	3.6	1.2
Black	19.5	23.5	1.6	1.8	0.4
All	29.6	40.3	2.8	3.4	1.1
25–45 years old					
Men	37.8	48.0	3.7	4.9	2.9
Women	36.5	42.6	3.5	4.5	2.2
56–65 years old					
Men	35.7	23.2	5.0	3.5	− 3.4
Women	26.6	20.2	4.0	3.0	− 3.1
66–75 years old					
Men	22.3	24.7	3.2	3.0	− 1.3
Women	16.9	14.4	2.6	2.4	− 1.1

Source: Computations by authors from the Panel Study of Income Dynamics.
Note: All dollar figures have been inflated to 1985 levels with the Consumer Price
Index.

worse off than the two middle-aged groups (see table 4.1). The
average family incomes of the elderly were lower than those of
children, but adjustments for family size incorporated into the
income-to-needs measure roughly equate the average economic well-
being of the two groups. Black children had a living standard (as
measured by the income-to-needs ratio) only half that of their white
counterparts. A second snapshot, taken a decade later in 1979, shows
that the average economic status of children and prime-age adults
increased substantially as the advancing careers and higher "asset
incomes"—rent, dividends and interest—of many swelled the pool
of family income. Retirement is the most obvious explanation for
the sharply reduced average incomes of many of those ages 56 to
65. The average status of the postretirement group changed little.
Real annual growth in the income-to-needs ratio over the period
confirms that the living standard fell most sharply for the retirement
group and rose most for the prime-age group, especially the men.[3]

Taken together, the two snapshots show that men close to or beyond retirement have a living standard that usually averages at least as high as that of children, whereas the economic well-being of elderly women is generally less than that of children. Indeed, other than the vast racial differences, what is striking about table 4.1 is the increasing gap between the economic status of men and women as they age. During the prime earning years, when most men and women are married, the family well-being of men is 5 percent to 9 percent higher than that of women; in the two elderly groups, the difference is 17 percent to 25 percent.

These patterns of average family incomes across time and over the life cycle are usually taken to describe the likely path of persons as they age. Indeed, it is tempting to infer that income fluctuations are relatively infrequent and occur at discrete points in the life cycle, such as labor force entry and retirement.

But a look at the diversity of economic experiences reveals that substantial change and volatility are the rule rather than the exception. The extent of rapid increases or decreases in the family income-to-needs ratio is shown in the first two columns of table 4.2. Shown there are the proportions of persons within each group who lived in families with either large positive growth (rising more than 5 percent per year) or decline (falling more than 5 percent per year) in their income-to-needs ratio over the same 1969–79 period. Over an 11-year period, an annual real growth rate of 5 percent will raise a family's living standard by more than 70 percent; a negative 5 percent rate will cut it almost in half.

A substantial minority within every age group experienced either rapid rises or rapid falls in living standards over the period. About one child in five lived in families with rapidly rising living standards; for prime-age adults the corresponding fraction was one in three. Not surprisingly, much smaller fractions of the two elderly groups enjoyed such improvements.

Unfortunately, nearly every black child who experienced rapid growth was matched by a black child whose living standard rapidly declined. Rapid decreases were most prevalent among the group undergoing retirement and least prevalent among prime-age men. Between one-tenth and one-fifth of all other groups experienced a rapidly falling living standard.

Another measure of income volatility, analyzed in greater detail later, consists of instances in which the income-to-needs ratio fell by more than 50 percent in consecutive years. This measure of economic volatility is similar to that employed by Elder and Liker

Table 4.2 FAMILIES IN VARIOUS AGE GROUPS EXPERIENCING GROWTH OR
DECLINE IN INCOME-TO-NEEDS RATIO BETWEEN 1969 AND 1979
(percentage)

Demographic status in 1969	Income-to-needs ratio		
	Growing more than 5 percent per year	Declining more than 5 percent per year	Falling more than 50 percent at least once
Less than 5-years old			
White	24	11	26
Black	17	16	35
All	23	11	27
25–45			
Men	35	6	18
Women	32	10	24
56–65			
Men	7	38	38
Women	6	35	39
66–75			
Men	6	17	27
Women	11	16	27

Source: Same as table 4.1.

in their important studies of the effects of economic losses experienced during the Great Depression.[4] The third column of table 4.2 shows that the risk of this occurrence is substantial: more than one-quarter of all but the prime-age adults experienced such a drop at least once during the 11-year period, with the incidence for black children and the retirement group exceeding one-third. Virtually all these decreases left the persons involved with, at best, modest incomes. Some 87 percent of the persons experiencing the decreases saw their family incomes fall to less than $25,000 (data not shown in table 4.2), and more than one-third fell into poverty. A closer look at these dramatic drops in living standards, taken in Duncan (forthcoming), shows that although the spells of ensuing adversity were somewhat longer for the elderly than for children, the elderly were much more likely to have predicted the economic decline in advance and to have savings available to cushion its impact than were the families of the children.

These fluctuating living standards place substantial fractions of

Table 4.3   FAMILIES IN VARIOUS AGE GROUPS WITH INCOMES FALLING
BELOW POVERTY LINE BETWEEN 1969 AND 1979 (percentage)

Demographic status in 1969	At least once	Six years or longer
Less than 5 years old		
White	23	3
Black	73	31
All	29	7
25–45 years old		
Men	13	2
Women	20	5
56–65 years old		
Men	17	4
Women	27	9
66–75 years old		
Men	20	9
Women	35	11

Source: Same as table 4.1.

the population at risk of poverty. Table 4.3 shows what fractions of persons in the various age-sex groups spent at least 1 of the 11 years below the poverty line and more than half of the time (at least 6 of the 11 years) in poverty.[5] It is clear that children and the elderly share a higher incidence of poverty than the age cohorts they bracket. The incidence is especially high for two important subgroups of the young and the elderly. Nearly 3 out of 4 black children were poor at least once over the period and nearly 1 out of 3 was poor for 6 years or more. No other group comes close to these rates of poverty. Over 1 in 3 elderly women, the next most poverty-prone group, was poor at least once over the period and about 1 in 10 was poor 6 or more years.[6]

The strikingly high rate of persistent poverty for black children is consistent with findings from other studies of childhood poverty. For example, Duncan and Rodgers (1985) estimate poverty rates for black and white children during childhood, defined as the first 15 years of life, and find that black children are poor, on average, for more than 5 of the 15 years, compared with an average of less than 1 year for white children. More than 90 percent of the children found to be poor for at least 10 of their first 15 years were black.

Worse yet, the figures in table 4.3 doubtless understate the extent of black childhood poverty in the mid-1980s. During the 1969–79 period covered in the table, single-year poverty rates for black children in the PSID averaged 33.1 percent. Data for the 1980–83 period show an average annual poverty rate of 37.5 percent. Calculations of multiyear poverty measures for the 1980s would undoubtedly show correspondingly higher rates.[7]

The figures on black childhood poverty appear to confirm the specter of a large "underclass" of black children. One important aspect of that vision is particularly worth noting. Most discussions of the underclass cast it as an urban phenomenon. But although poverty has become more concentrated in urban poverty areas in the past decade (Danziger and Gottschalk 1987), census and PSID data show that most poor black children live outside high-poverty urban areas and that rural poverty is more persistent than urban poverty for black children (Duncan and Rodgers 1985).

Taken as a whole, the figures in tables 4.2 and 4.3 reinforce those of table 4.1 in showing the more precarious position of children and elderly persons relative to the middle-aged and of adult women relative to adult men. Black children are clearly worse off by nearly all dimensions of economic status—income level, trend, instability, and risk of long-term poverty. The group passing through retirement is the most likely to experience decreases in income during the period; for one-third of them the decreases come very suddenly. Women in their prime years are more likely to experience sharp income losses than men of comparable age, which results in an increasingly unfavorable economic position and a higher risk of poverty for them relative to men.

Incidence of Events and Their Link to Income Volatility

A substantial drop in well-being is possible at any age, as tables 4.2 and 4.3 demonstrate, but certain life events hold more danger than others. PSID data provide information on the incidence of a wide variety of economic and demographic events. We concentrate on four major demographic events (divorce or separation, widowhood, the birth of a child, and the transition to becoming a household head or spouse); two normally involuntary labor market events experienced by the household head (unemployment and major work loss due to illness), three often voluntary labor market events (major work reduction due to retirement,[8] decreases in the work hours of wives, and decreases in the work hours of other family members), and substantial drops in asset income.

As expected, retirement is the dominant life event for persons ages 55 to 65 (table 4.4). For women in this age cohort, the death of a spouse is next most frequent, with about one in five women becoming widowed over the period. For children the pattern is very different, with unemployment and illness of the household head being the dominant labor market events, and divorce or separation of parents and the birth of siblings being the dominant family composition change.

To investigate further the link between the events and the incidence of major income losses, we switch our analysis to instances where the income-to-needs ratio fell by more than 50 percent in consecutive years during the 11-year period. We investigated each such fall to determine whether it was linked to any of the seven events.[9]

The life events we measured were often associated with a loss of more than 50 percent in the income-to-needs ratio, and the links to life events varied across age groups (see table 4.5). For children, divorce or separation is the most important family composition event associated with a drop in the income-to-needs ratio. A major spell of unemployment is the most frequent labor market change, followed by reductions in labor supply because of illness of the family head. For those ages 56 to 66, retirement is most important.

For both men and women who were 66 years of age or older when the period began, the event most closely linked to a fall in living standard was a major reduction in asset income. Such a reduction appeared to be caused by a variety of factors, including depletion of savings accounts and other income-producing assets; variability in the returns to income-producing assets such as farm land or common stocks; and, in some cases, apparent misreporting of the amount of asset income. A crucial but as yet unanswered policy question is the relative frequency of these various factors, especially the loss of assets attributable to large uninsured medical expenditures. Also important in the income losses for both men and women were the death of a spouse and the drop in work hours of family members other than the household head or wife, usually grown children who leave the household.[10]

For elderly women, the transition to household head was surprisingly important as well. Inspection of some of these cases revealed situations in which elderly women were living in the households of grown children or other relatives and left those situations for reasons of health, desires for independence, or when their children married.

Identifying the link between life events and changes in well-being

Table 4.4   PERSONS IN VARIOUS AGE GROUPS EXPERIENCING VARIOUS LIFE EVENTS AT LEAST ONCE BETWEEN 1969 AND 1979 (percentage)

Demographic status in 1969	Family composition events				Labor market/health events						
	Divorce/ separation of spouse[a]	Death of spouse[a]	Birth of a child	Person became head of household or wife	Major reduction in work hours of head due to retirement	Major unemployment of household head	Major work loss due to illness of household head	Decrease in work hours of wife	Decrease in work hours of other family members	Large decrease in asset income	Any of the 10 events
Under 5 years old											
White	13	2	36	0	2	25	22	12	24	8	82
Black	20	10	36	0	8	41	33	11	33	0	90
All	14	3	36	0	3	27	24	12	25	7	83
25–45 years old											
Men	9	2	24	2	4	22	25	16	31	12	80
Women	9	4	16	2	5	21	25	14	37	11	80
56—65 years old											
Men	3	6	1	0	51	7	12	21	20	21	82
Women	2	19	1	3	31	8	10	10	16	20	76
66–75 years old											
Men	4	21	1	1	9	3	4	4	9	20	57
Women	1	28	0	4	5	3	7	3	12	20	62

Source: Same as table 4.1.

a. For persons under 5 years old, these events refer to parent rather than spouse.

Table 4.5   PERSONS IN AGE GROUP WITH A 50 PERCENT DECREASE IN THE INCOME-TO-NEEDS RATIO ASSOCIATED WITH VARIOUS LIFE EVENTS, 1969–79 (percentage)

Demographic status in 1969	Family composition events				Major reduction in work hours of head due to retirement	Labor market/health events				Large decrease in asset income	Any of the 10 events
	Divorce/ separation of spouse[a]	Death of spouse[a]	Birth of a child	Person became household head or wife		Major unemployment of household head	Major work loss due to illness of household head	Decrease in work hours of wife	Decrease in work hours of other family members		
Under 5 years old											
White	10	1	9	0	1	16	5	3	6	2	50
Black	11	8	6	0	6	13	7	2	11	0	37
All	10	3	8	0	2	16	6	3	7	2	48
25–45 years old											
Men	5	0	9	2	3	19	9	4	10	8	58
Women	9	3	3	1	4	10	5	3	17	5	52
56–65 years old											
Men	1	0	2	0	23	0	2	15	13	9	58
Women	1	5	0	6	19	1	2	8	10	11	60
66–75 years old											
Men	0	8	0	0	5	0	0	0	7	23	49
Women	0	12	0	14	0	0	0	0	11	22	48

Source: Same as table 4.1.

a. For persons under 5 years old, these events refer to parent rather than spouse.

found in table 4.5 is an important first step in uncovering the full life course consequences of such events. But a longer period is clearly needed to understand fully how an event like divorce or retirement affects the persons involved. For instance, the death of a spouse may have much more complex ramifications than can be observed in the simple one-year transitions considered here. Heavy medical bills may eat into family resources prior to a husband's death, thus dramatically reducing the well-being of the widow over several years in a more devastating way than measured here. Such a multiperiod outcome is missed by table 4.5.

Even those events captured in table 4.5 can be more fully disaggregated by multiyear analysis. For instance, certain life events produce more permanent changes than others. Unemployment or divorce followed by remarriage may cause serious but short-lived drops in well-being, whereas persons who retire into poverty may experience much more permanent drops in well-being. A multiyear analysis of the changes in well-being associated with major life events is needed to understand their effect more fully. It is to this task that we now turn, focusing on the effects of unemployment and divorce on children and the effects of retirement and widowhood on the elderly.

CHILDREN, UNEMPLOYMENT, AND DIVORCE

Parental unemployment and divorce are the two most prominent events that threaten children with a substantial decrease in living standards and even poverty. Taken together, they account for more than one-quarter of the sharp decreases in the living standard of children observed during the 1970s and a comparable fraction of the transitions into poverty observed during that same period. Unemployment appears to figure more prominently in these transitions than divorce, as shown in table 4.5, but what little comparable analysis has been done on the economic importance of these two events suggests that the economic consequences of divorce on children over the long term are more severe than those of unemployment. Duncan and Rodgers (1985) found that although a divorce or separation was associated with less than half as many transitions into temporary poverty as unemployment, the marital changes were more than twice as likely as unemployment to be associated with spells of poverty that lasted five years or more. The reason for these differences is that spells of unemployment tend to be much shorter than spells of divorce prior to remarriage.

Unemployment

The publicity accorded monthly unemployment statistics make them one of the most visible indicators of the state of the economy; what is not so obvious is that most of the burden falls on a small fraction of the unemployed. Some unemployed workers find other jobs quickly, some receive generous unemployment benefits while out of work, and some families of unemployed workers are able to cushion the losses with increases in the work of other family members. Most spells of unemployment are surprisingly short. The length of a typical unemployment spell ranges from about two to three months, depending on whether it was begun during a period of macroeconomic growth or recession (Sider 1985).

Consistent with this pattern, the effects of unemployment spells on family incomes also appear modest on average. Gramlich and Laren (1984) estimate that each percentage-point increase in the aggregate unemployment rate reduces the incomes of households headed by white and black men by between 1 percent and 2 percent; only about one-third of this decrease is offset by unemployment compensation, other transfers, or increases in other household income. Families below or near the poverty line, however, have a much higher chance of substantial income loss from recession-induced increases in unemployment than other families do.

Consistent also is the finding that, although many male heads of household experience at least some unemployment, a small fraction bear the brunt of the total unemployment costs incurred by male heads of household in the PSID. Of those unemployed at some time between 1967 and 1976, some 5 percent accounted for half of the total unemployment and lost more than $50,000 (in 1985 dollars) to unemployment during the decade (Corcoran and Hill 1979). It is likely that this extreme concentration of unemployment among a small group accounts for its predominance among transitions by children into frequent but often short spells of poverty.

Divorce

Longitudinal data provide a unique look at the effect of divorce and separation on the economic status of children by making possible comparisons of the economic status of persons in the years before and after a change in marital status.[11] The economic impact of divorce—as measured by the average amount of income, income-to-needs ratio, and proportion of persons who were poor in the year before, year after, and five years after divorce or separation—is shown in table 4.6 for the children, women, and men undergoing those events. Family incomes of the children and women include whatever alimony, child support, and welfare income was received by their families; family incomes of the men have had alimony and child support subtracted from them.

Income levels drop precipitously (by about 40 percent) between the years just before and just after divorce for children and women, and more modestly (by 15 percent) for men. Because divorce or separation initially reduces the family size of both of the resulting households, it is not surprising that income-to-needs ratio shows less severe decreases. In the year following the divorce, however, the living standards for children and women fall to about two-thirds of their former levels, whereas the average divorced man actually becomes slightly better off.[12] For women and children not involved in remarriage, average living standards change little in the five years following the divorce.

Including women and children involved in remarriage in the calculation of the economic consequences of divorce improves the average income-to-needs ratios substantially. About half of the women will have remarried by the fifth year following the divorce or separation, and their new economic status will usually exceed their predivorce status. When the remarried and still-divorced groups are combined, the "average" divorcing woman and her children are about as well off after five years as in the year before divorce. But that average, of course, is formed by two very disparate groups. Thus divorce generates much inequality in the postdivorce distribution of income among women and children.

The dramatic impact of divorce is clear when the income-to-needs figures are used to compute poverty rates. In the year before divorce or separation, about 12 percent of the children and 7 percent of the women lived in families classified as poor. In the year following a divorce or separation these figures double, to about 27 percent for children and 13 percent for women. After five years, poverty rates decline only slightly for women who are still unmarried. Poverty rates for men actually fall from 6 percent to 4 percent in the year after divorce and remain at very low levels.

The relative stability of the family incomes of women who remain unmarried masks various changes in the composition of their postdivorce income packages. The women's own labor force income was clearly the dominant component of postdivorce family income.

Table 4.6   FAMILY INCOME, INCOME-TO-NEEDS RATIOS, AND POVERTY RATES BEFORE AND AFTER DIVORCE—CHILDREN, WOMEN, AND MEN, 1969–79 (dollars)

	Children			Women			Men		
	Family income	Family income-to-needs ratio	Percentage poor	Family income	Family income-to-needs ratio	Percentage poor	Family income	Family income-to-needs ratio	Percentage poor
Level									
1 year before divorce	23,213	2.7	12	26,168	3.6	7	25,403	3.6	6
1 year after divorce	13,822	1.8	27	14,781	2.6	13	21,488	3.7	4
5 years after divorce	22,380	2.6	17	22,781	3.4	10	25,874	4.2	3
5 years after divorce for women not remarried	14,511	1.9	20	15,178	2.8	11	—	—	—
Level relative to prior status									
1 year after/1 year before	0.60	0.67	—	0.56	0.72	—	0.85	1.03	—
5 years after/1 year before	0.96	0.96	—	0.87	0.94	—	1.02	1.17	—
5 years after for women not remarried/1 year before	0.63	0.70	—	0.58	0.78	—	—	—	—

Source: Calculated from Duncan and Hoffman (1985), based on data from the Panel Study of Income Dynamics.

Labor force participation rates jumped from predivorce levels by 15 percent points—from 67 percent to 82 percent. (Interestingly, labor force participation rates for women who remarry fall to a point below the predivorce rate.) The women's labor income accounted for only 22 percent of family income before the divorce, 60 percent of total family income in the year just after the divorce, and nearly 70 percent in the fifth year after the divorce if there was no remarriage by that time.

Noncoverage and noncompliance with court awards of child support and alimony is widespread. The U.S. Census Bureau (1986b) estimates that only about half of the female-headed households containing minor children had child support awards or agreements in 1984, and only half of those due payments received the full amount; one-quarter received no payments at all. The majority of PSID women reported receiving no alimony or child support, and both the incidence and amount of such transfers decline as time passes following the divorce. Even in the year just after the divorce, when alimony and child support payments are highest, they account for only about one-tenth of the total average family income, and their average amount falls by nearly two-thirds by the fifth year following the divorce. The decline in support from the ex-husbands over time is much steeper for women coming from previously high-income marriages. Detailed in Duncan and Hoffman (1985) are patterns showing amounts of annual support from high-income ex-husbands that are nearly twice as large as from low-income husbands in the year following divorce ($2,425 versus $940) but fall below the amounts paid by low-income husbands ($746 versus $764) by the fifth year. Welfare is less important than alimony or child support as a source of postdivorce income shortly after divorce and maintains its 5 percent average share in the fifth year following divorce.

There are substantial racial differences in these income packages. But even though between one-half and four-fifths of black women report receiving welfare in the five years following a divorce or separation, in no year is the average amount received from welfare even half as large as the average amount received from black women's labor earnings (Duncan and Hoffman 1985).

THE ELDERLY, RETIREMENT, AND WIDOWHOOD

A major accomplishment of federal policy over the last two decades has been the increased well-being of the elderly. Today the incidence of poverty is no greater among the elderly than it is among the population as a whole (Danziger et al. 1984; Hurd and Shoven 1985). Despite the general increase in well-being, however, some subgroups of the elderly continue to run high risks of poverty (Quinn 1987, Smeeding 1986).

The two life events most closely associated with losses of well-being at older ages are retirement and the death of a spouse. In most cases neither event is completely unexpected and, especially in the case of retirement, substantial planning may have preceded it.[13] Hence the great majority of older workers who leave their jobs and retire do not fall immediately into poverty. But some do, and more do so over time. In addition, as time passes after retirement, most women face the transition from wife to widow. The loss of a spouse poses a new threat to their well-being and increases the risk of poverty.[14]

In this section we trace the economic well-being of a group of workers on the verge of retirement at the end of the 1960s, and the well-being of their survivors over the following decade. Our data source is the Retirement History Study (RHS). As with the divorce analysis, the emphasis is on determining the changes in well-being just before and in the years following retirement rather than simply on following this cohort through time. The measure of time used here will therefore be anchored at the point of retirement rather than at some calendar date.

Because one of our interests is in the onset of poverty after retirement, we have chosen to follow married couples who were not poor during the last year of the husband's employment. The resources at the disposal of the couples during retirement varied considerably. Social Security benefits were almost universally available for those who retired during the 1970s, but only about 60 percent of workers in our sample received pension income. When pensions were received, some plans—single-life pensions—stopped payments with the death of the worker, while others—joint-and-survivor pensions—continued to pay benefits to the survivor. We have grouped retirees according to pension eligibility and the type of survivor option chosen by the husband.[15]

Well-Being after Retirement

Despite the fact that some workers who declare themselves retired eventually return to work full-time, for the vast majority retirement is a time of substantially reduced work. Hence it is not surprising

Table 4.7   INCOME-TO-NEEDS RATIOS OF INITIALLY NONPOOR COUPLES, BY
MARITAL STATUS AND PENSION CHARACTERISTICS, 1969–79

	Intact couples			Eventually widowed couples			
	Total	No pension	Pension	Total	No pension	Single-life pension	Joint-and-survivor pension
Level							
1 year before retirement	4.7	3.9	5.2	4.3	3.6	4.4	5.6
1 to 2 years after retirement	3.6	2.9	4.1	3.5	2.9	3.6	4.8
7 to 8 years after retirement	2.3	1.9	2.6	1.9	1.5	1.8	3.1
Level relative to prior status							
1 to 2 years after/1 year before	0.77	0.74	0.79	0.81	0.79	0.81	0.85
7 to 8 years after/1 year before	0.50	0.48	0.50	0.45	0.42	0.40	0.55

Source: Calculated from Burkhauser, Holden, and Feister, (1986), table 2, based on
data from the Retirement History Survey.

that the transition to retirement is associated with a reduction in income. Table 4.7 shows the average income-to-needs ratio over two key transitions—retirement and the death of a husband.

In their last year of work, the average income-to-needs ratio of this sample of nonpoor, intact couples (4.7) is well above the poverty line. Couples who are ineligible to receive an employer pension are, on average, less well off than those who will receive a pension, but they still have income amounting to nearly four times the poverty line. The pattern is similar for the sample of eventual widows. It is important to note, however, that even before the death of the husbands the family income of soon-to-be widows was lower than that of intact couples for whom a death was not imminent.

The next two rows report average income-to-needs ratios one to two years and seven to eight years after retirement. There is a decline in the income-to-needs ratio in both periods, with the greatest drop, not surprisingly, occurring in the first year of retirement.[16] The fourth row measures the initial impact of the transition from work to retirement. It is similar to a replacement rate often used to measure the adequacy of retirement income. This replacement rate was relatively high and uniform across all groups; the income-to-needs ratio fell between 15 percent and 25 percent, on average, upon retirement.

A measure of retirement income deterioration over time is provided in the last row of table 4.7. Intact couples and widows whose husbands chose a joint-and-survivor pension plan have income-to-needs ratios that are, on average, half of what they were before retirement and two-thirds of their initial retirement levels. However, for widows whose husbands were never eligible for a pension or who were enrolled in a plan in which benefits ended with his death, there is a drop to around 40 percent of preretirement income levels.

The picture of well-being for the elderly painted in table 4.7 is a dynamic one. Average income-to-needs are high to begin with, but fall substantially for all subgroups analyzed. Not surprisingly, the steepest fall in income-to-needs occurs in the first year of retirement because increases in retirement-related income do not fully replace the husband's wage income. What follows is a much more gradual decline in average economic well-being. Those who will eventually draw pensions are considerably better off while working than are those without pension plans. This initially higher income position appears to be the reason they are better off in retirement. Although they have slightly higher income replacement rates, however, depreciation thereafter appears to occur at the same pace for both groups of intact couples. For widows the drop in status is faster, except for those whose husbands chose a joint-and-survivor pension option.

Poverty Risks

The longitudinal nature of the RHS is exploited in table 4.8 to create another dynamic measure of well-being. Here the same time periods and subgroups are used, but the measure of interest is the risk of falling into poverty at a given point after retirement.[17]

For intact couples, the risk of falling into poverty is greatest in the first period of retirement and declines thereafter. Those with a pension face a much smaller risk, 2 percent, than do those without a pension, 11 percent. But for both groups the risk of poverty falls over time. In contrast, for those who will become widows the risk of poverty is approximately the same as that for married couples in the first period, but it increases over time. This pattern of a rising risk of poverty is found across *all* subsets of widows. Somewhat surprisingly, given the average income-to-needs results reported in table 4.7, there is little difference between the risk of falling into

Table 4.8   PERCENTAGE FALLING INTO POVERTY DURING RETIREMENT, BY MARITAL STATUS AND PENSION CATEGORY, 1969–79

	Intact couples			Eventually widowed couples			
Period of retirement	Total	No pension	Pension	Total	No pension	Single-life pension	Joint-and-survivor pension
1 to 2 years after retirement	6	11	2	5	9	2	3
7 to 8 years after retirement	1	2	1	8	10	7	7
Ever poor over 8 years	9	16	5	21	28	16	15

Source: Calculated from Burkhauser, Holden, and Feister (1986), table 3, based on data from the Retirement History Survey.

poverty faced by couples with single-life pensions and those with a survivor pension.

The cumulative effect of the yearly risks of poverty appears in the final row of table 4.8. Widows are more than twice as likely as intact couples to experience poverty at least once over the first eight years of retirement. Pensions offer considerable protection from poverty in retirement. But the type of pension does not seem to affect the cumulative poverty rates of widows. The vast majority of those on the verge of retirement are neither poor nor likely to become poor, at least in their first decade of retirement. But even for those with little or no personal history of poverty while working, the transition into retirement is not without risk and is influenced crucially by pension coverage and the death of a spouse.

Exits from Poverty

As was the case for younger groups, it is important to recognize that poverty once is often not a permanent condition for the elderly. Table 4.9 shows the income-to-needs ratio of the RHS households that fell into poverty over the sample years of the 1970s.

Note the strikingly similar volatility across all rows. The income-to-needs ratio in the survey year preceding events is at least twice the poverty level. In the year of poverty, the income-to-needs ratio is about two-thirds the poverty line. In the survey year following the initial period of poverty, the income-to-needs ratio rises to about 130 percent of the poverty line. (This volatility is obscured in the average income-to-needs trends for the overall sample shown in table 4.7.) Additional evidence of fluctuations in poverty status for

Table 4.9 INCOME-TO-NEEDS RATIOS OF HOUSEHOLDS THAT FELL INTO
POVERTY IN THE TWO YEARS BEFORE, PERIOD OF, AND TWO
YEARS AFTER POVERTY, 1969–79

| Year fell into poverty | Income-to-needs ratio | | |
	2 years before poverty	Year of poverty	2 years following poverty
1970	2.67	0.66	1.33
1972	2.39	0.64	1.30
1974	2.15	0.64	1.22
1976	2.12	0.66	1.29

Source: Computations by authors from the Retirement History Survey.

the elderly is found among elderly widows. More than one-third of the widows who fall into poverty in the first year after their husbands' death are out of poverty two years later (Burkhauser, Holden, and Myers 1986).[18]

Thus, the incidence and timing of poverty for the elderly vary greatly, with retirement the key life event. Our results suggest that for the average couple with pension income, the 1970s were indeed a good decade in which to retire. The social insurance system, together with an employer pension, appears to have ensured that nonpoor workers rarely slipped into poverty after retirement. The holes in the retirement safety net were considerably larger for those without pensions. Furthermore, the combination of retirement and the subsequent death of the husband resulted in additional risks to well-being for widows. For women who became widowed during the decade, the gaps in the safety net were even larger, especially if their husbands had no pension.[19] However, just as is the case for younger cohorts, poverty is unlikely to be a persistent state even for elderly widows. At least among the "young elderly" of the 1970s, movement out of poverty was possible.

CONCLUSION

Substantial income volatility characterizes all points in the life span, placing large numbers of the population at risk of suffering significant losses and, in the extreme, falling into poverty. These risks were exceedingly high over the 1969 to 1979 decade (and are likely to have grown even more serious since then) for black children; they remain quite high for elderly women. The risks are, not unexpectedly, lowest for men in their prime earnings years.

The Economically Vulnerable Population

Divorce and unemployment were the most significant events associated with this income volatility for children; retirement and widowhood were most important for the elderly. In contrast to the effects of divorce and widowhood, the adverse economic consequences of unemployment appeared to be short-lived in most cases.

The failure of absent fathers to support their children left the mothers and their children much worse off and the fathers better off following divorce. Remarriage ended the spell of hardship for some of the women and children; without remarriage, the rising labor income of the mothers was completely offset, on average, by falling alimony and child support payments, producing no net improvement over time in the economic status of women who did not remarry.

In parallel fashion, the failure of men nearing retirement to choose a pension that provided benefits to their spouses after their deaths produced much greater economic hardship for those elderly women than they had experienced when their husbands were alive. In contrast, elderly widows with survivor benefits from a private pension fared reasonably well after retirement, although their risk of falling into poverty was still higher than it had been when their husbands were alive.

What emerges from our analysis is that the economically vulnerable population is distinguished not so much by age as by sex. The average living standard of an adult woman is lower than that of a comparably elderly man, and the sex-based gap grows over the life span. The fact that the vast majority of children live with their mothers rather than their fathers after divorce produces patterns of well-being for them that mirror the patterns for their mothers.

Policy Implications

The dynamics for family well-being at very young and old ages shed new light on old policy issues. Some of the economic fluctuations we examined began or perpetuated spells of poverty, producing situations with clear policy implications. Poverty thresholds have been formulated to reflect a minimum income level below which basic needs cannot be met. Income maintenance programs now existing in the United States (such as, Aid for Families with Dependent Children—AFDC—for families with children, and Supplemental Security Income—SSI—for the elderly and disabled) are usually designed and defended as a means of preventing recipients from enduring the hardship of an unacceptably low living standard. These programs have clearly provided needed benefits to recipients; but the continued incidence of poverty among children and the elderly, especially black children and elderly women, suggests that the coverage and benefits of these programs still leave much to be desired.

These income maintenance programs have come under attack because of the possibility that they induce dependence in recipients by reducing work incentives and promoting female-headed households (see, for example, Murray 1984). A full discussion of the debate over these issues would lead us far afield; however, it is useful to mention some of the dynamic aspects of income that bear on the debate.

Although the panel data indicate that sharp declines in income are widespread, they also show that periods of need are often relatively short and that spells of actual receipt of welfare program transfers are equally short. Only about one-sixth of all AFDC spells last more than eight years, and fewer than one-third of first-time recipients will have total welfare "careers" lasting that long (Ellwood 1986). Current programs appear to function as benign income-loss insurance programs for the majority of recipients. Whether or not they induce dependence in the minority of long-term recipients and their children is an unresolved but crucial question in designing policies to lessen the adverse effects of income variability.

Novel to our inquiry is an examination of large income losses that occur at other points of the income distribution. The vast majority of such losses left the families involved with modest incomes, although two-thirds of the affected families had incomes still above poverty and thus were generally ineligible for means-tested programs. Further research is needed to determine whether it is the losses themselves or the new, lower living standards produced by the losses that result in adverse effects. Evidence gathered to date would appear to implicate income losses in producing a variety of mental and physical health problems.

A different set of policy issues arises if the goal is to minimize the incidence or effect of preventable losses that reduce income to points above the poverty line. Here the focus is on policies tied to the events producing the losses. With divorce, the failure of fathers to support dependent children is crucial. We are not, of course, the first to reach such a conclusion. What we have done, however, is to show how the problem worsens with the passage of time after divorce, especially for women and children with above-average family incomes prior to divorce. The low earnings most divorced women can command in the labor market make remarriage rather than career advancement the more reliable route to restored economic status; this raises questions about the degree to which public policy should reduce the dependence of women's economic status upon men.

The 1970s will be remembered as a period of enormous growth in income support for the elderly. Between 1968 and 1973 Social Security benefits rose faster than at any other time in the history of the program. A worker who reached age 65 in 1973, and who made the median of Social Security covered earnings in each year of his work life, would have been eligible for benefits over 46 percent higher, even after adjusting for inflation, than a similar median worker who reached age 65 in 1968 (Anderson, Burkhauser, and Quinn 1986).

The major reason was a series of ad hoc increases in the Social Security benefit schedule by Congress over this period. The rest was due to a gradual increase in the earnings on which Social Security benefits are based. Beginning in 1974 Social Security benefits were automatically increased to offset inflation. But an error in the method used to adjust for inflation overcompensated recipients for the rest of the decade. This further increased benefits so that by 1979 a worker who reached age 65 with a median earnings history received benefits more than 51 percent greater than the benefits received by such a worker in 1968.

In addition to the overall gains in Social Security, the SSI program provided the first guaranteed income benefits to poor elderly. This system, begun in 1974, guaranteed a federal minimum to any person age 65 or over. The minimum was set substantially below the poverty line, however, and even in states that supplemented federal benefits, it does not guarantee full protection against poverty.

These two major changes in government programs targeted toward the elderly, along with an increasing percentage of elderly workers who collected private pensions, explain in large part the substantial improvement in the well-being of the elderly found by Danziger et al. (1984) and Smeeding (1986). It cannot be overemphasized that this gain in relative income vis-à-vis younger age groups happened despite a dramatic reduction in the labor supply of elderly workers. Hence, government policy in the 1970s effectively broke the previously strong link between old age and poverty.

In the 1980s Social Security benefits continued to increase just slightly ahead of inflation because of real increases in the earnings of recipients, thus making each successive generation of retired workers slightly better off than the last. But any substantial gains in the relative income of the elderly are more likely to come from greater coverage and generosity of the pension plans of the newly elderly. Ippolito (1986) estimates that, in 1980, 87 percent of private employers made payments to pension plans for their workers and that these contributions will ultimately support pension income for two-thirds of the current full-time nongovernment work force when they retire.

These unprecedented gains for the elderly as a whole are reflected in our tables. But as the tables also show, despite these gains, even in the 1970s poverty was not a rare event for certain groups of elderly, especially widows.

Women obviously gain from general increases in Social Security benefits and the growth of private pensions. But the demographic reality that most women will outlive their husbands has not been fully acknowledged by either public or private pension systems. Hence, on average, the economic well-being of women continues to fall after the death of their husbands.

Two changes in the 1970s encouraged a more equal sharing of income in households before and after the death of the husband. The 1972 Amendment to the Social Security Act increased the survivor's benefit from 82.5 percent to 100 percent of the worker's benefit. For a married woman who was eligible for only a spouse's benefit (one-half of her husband's benefit), this change effectively increased her survivor's benefit to two-thirds the level of the total household benefit when her husband was alive. This is still below the equivalence scale level of 80 percent used in official poverty statistics to make one-person households the equivalent of two-person households. It would, for example, place a woman who was just above the poverty line when her husband was alive below it after his death.

The second change had to do with a spouse's right to a worker's pension. In 1974 the Employee Retirement Income Security Act required all pension plans to offer a pension option that provided a survivor's benefit to a spouse upon the death of the worker. Although it did not require the worker to take this option, it did encourage this choice by making it the default choice for workers who made no explicit choice of payment. Despite this option, Kotlikoff and Smith (1983) estimate that only about 30 percent of male private pension holders chose a joint-and-survivor pension annuity in the 1970s. The vast majority of workers instead chose plans in which all benefits ended after their death.

The Retirement Equity Act of 1984 is the latest attempt by the federal government to encourage married workers to choose a joint-and-survivor pension. This act requires the spouse of a worker to consent in writing when the joint-and-survivor option is declined. Myers, Burkhauser, and Holden (1987) suggest that this change in the law is not likely to have a major effect on the poverty rates of widows, however, because poor widows are more likely to have come from households where the husband did not have a pension plan in the first place.

This is not to say that the economic well-being of widows as a whole will not improve over the next decade. The steady increase in the labor force participation rate of married women suggests that they will be eligible for higher Social Security benefits. In addition, women now are also more likely to be eligible for private pensions based on their own work. This is especially the case since, as part of the 1986 tax reform package, the typical length of tenure required for vesting was reduced from 10 to 5 years. Because women tend to have much shorter tenure on jobs than men, this shortening will substantially increase the likelihood of a woman's being vested.

Two major policy changes would substantially improve the lot of widows. The first, which pertains to Social Security policy, would be a move toward earnings sharing. Currently, households in which both husband and wife have substantial work histories are treated less generously than households in which a similar amount of income is earned by a single worker. (See Burkhauser and Holden 1984 for a fuller discussion of this point.) In addition, such two-earner households may suffer substantially greater drops in Social Security benefits than the two-thirds drop discussed earlier for a single-earner household. In the most extreme case—where a husband and wife earned exactly the same amount of income during their work lives—their benefits would be cut exactly in half upon the death of either spouse. Burkhauser (1984) shows that earnings sharing would prevent this dramatic drop in benefits by combining earnings records of couples and explicitly requiring a joint-and-two-thirds payment of total household benefits after the death of a spouse.

The second proposal, which involves the method by which private pensions determine pension benefits, would be to index benefits. Although it is true that the relaxing of the time until vesting will make women more likely to be eligible for benefits, in many cases these benefits will be trivial. Most private pensions are defined-benefit plans, which base benefits on the final years of earnings with the firm. In periods of high inflation, a vested pension based on wages earned years before will result in trivial benefits in the inflated currency units at retirement. Rules that require defined-benefit pension plans to index earnings in a manner similar to current Social Security rules would be a start toward overcoming this problem.

Notes

1. Other possible adjustments include the valuation of in-kind benefits (including work-related in-kind fringe benefits), taxes paid, ownership of durables (ownership of a home, for example) resource allocation within families, amount of leisure time available, and work-related expenses. Danziger, van der Gaag, Smolensky, and Taussig (1984) estimate the importance of adjustments to cash income for taxes paid, durables, family size and composition, and use of the individual rather than the household as the unit of analysis. They find that the family size and composition adjustments are by far the most important.

2. The "white" category includes all children whose race was not black.

3. The details of how this measure is constructed are available from the authors.

4. Elder and Liker and their colleagues used longitudinal data collected over several decades from a sample of Berkeley-area married couples with children as part of the Berkeley Guidance Study to perform a series of sophisticated studies of the long-term consequences of income loss (Elder 1974; Elder and Liker 1982; Elder, Liker, and Cross, 1984; Elder, Liker, and Jaworski 1984; Liker and Elder 1983). Couples experiencing a drop of one-third or more in family income between 1929 and the early 1930s were compared on a range of subsequent outcomes—marital and parent-child relationships and mental and physical health—with couples whose Depression incomes did not fall so much; some of the outcomes were measured several decades later. They found that the income losses produced uniformly harmful effects on the marital and parental behavior of men, apparently not so much from the loss of income per se as from the stress caused by the loss of status as breadwinner. Women coming from less advantaged families also experienced harmful effects on their marital and parental behavior and subsequent health. For these working-class women, the income

loss itself appeared to be the culprit, leaving them with too few resources to perform their functions as homemakers properly. Interestingly, women coming from middle-class backgrounds who experienced the income losses were better able to handle subsequent problems than were otherwise similar women who escaped such adversity. Longitudinal evidence linking income change to mental health is also presented in Pearlin, Liberman, Menaghan, and Mullan (1981).

5. The poverty rates obtained with PSID data are substantially lower than those obtained from the *Current Population Surveys* because considerably more income is reported by PSID than CPS respondents. In 1975, for example, the CPS estimate of poverty was 12.3 percent, whereas the comparable estimate from the PSID was 8.9 percent. These income differences cannot be attributed to demographic differences in the samples (Becketti, Gould, Lillard, and Welch 1983; Duncan, Hill, and Ponza 1984). A comparison with welfare program aggregates showed that the PSID accounted for more than 90 percent of total noncontributory cash transfers, while comparable rates for CPS are between 70 percent and 80 percent (Duncan, et al. 1984).

6. It is tempting to consider all persons who were poor in only 1 or 2 of the 11 years as having short spells of poverty. But this would not be entirely accurate because some who were poor only in 1979 may have been at the beginning of a long spell of poverty that extended beyond 1979; and some who were poor only in 1969 may have been at the end of a long spell that began prior to 1969. Indeed, it is possible to cast an analysis of short- and long-term poverty in terms of *spells* of poverty rather than the incidence of poverty over a specified length of time. Bane and Ellwood (1986) performed such an analysis with data from the PSID and found that 60 percent of all poverty spells lasted less than 3 years and only about one-eighth of all spells lasted more than 8 years. These spell distributions are very similar to those of welfare use (Bane and Ellwood 1983) and indicate the short-term nature of most periods of need.

7. Poverty rates for black children obtained in the *Current Population Reports* (U.S. Bureau of the Census 1986a, 1987) show similar trends. During the 1969–79 period, annual CPS poverty rates for black children averaged 40.9 percent. During the 1980–83 period, the annual rate averaged 45.1 percent; and the rate in 1984 was above the 1969–79 average.

8. Unfortunately, the data could not easily distinguish between work losses due to retirement and those due to permanent disability in some of the years studied. We are forced to assume that retirement dominates among the older groups and permanent disability among the younger ones.

9. For technical reasons relating to the difficulties in sorting out income flows during the years in which family composition changes occurred, all the income changes and events were defined between the first and third year of a three-year interval. To avoid the inclusion of drops in the income-to-needs ratio caused by measurement error, we further restricted our analysis to instances where the income-to-needs ratio in the first year of the three-year interval was not preceded in the prior year by an income-to-needs amount that was 50 percent lower or where the income-to-needs ratio in the third year was not followed in the next year by an income-to-needs ratio that was more than twice as high.

10. Burkhauser, Holden, and Feister (1986) use data from the RHS to trace the well-being of married men ages 58 to 63 and their spouses who retired during the 1970s. These couples were not poor in the year prior to retirement. This study attempted to link poverty to other events. Although the methodology is not comparable to that underlying table 4.5, one event is the same—widowhood. They find that 31 percent of their sample of poor widows fell into poverty in the first income period following the death of their husband. Hence, although widowhood is relatively unlikely for the women in table 4.5, the likelihood of a drop into poverty is quite high for those who do become widows.

11. The analysis presented here draws heavily on Duncan and Hoffman (1985), and is based on divorces or separations that occurred in the PSID between 1969 and 1975. The calendar year of divorce is treated as t, and information on income and employment is compiled in years $t-1$ through $t+5$ for the men, women, and children involved in a divorce. For both men and women, the sample was restricted to persons who were between the ages of 25 and 54 in the year prior to the divorce. Because their interest was in economic consequences, Duncan and Hoffman use a functional rather than a legal definition of marriage and do not distinguish between divorces and separations. A divorce or separation is defined as the transition from living with a spouse or long-term partner to living without that person for reasons other than death. Remarriages are defined analogously.

12. These changes differ substantially from the well-publicized results of Weitzman (1985), who found with California data that income-to-needs ratios for divorced women fell by 73 percent, whereas the ratios for divorced men rose by 42 percent. Her figures, based on a needs standard similar to that used in this chapter, are grossly inconsistent with other figures she presents based on the same data and appear to be in error.

13. Burkhauser and Wilkinson (1983) and Burkhauser, Butler, and Wilkinson (1985) look at the importance of initial wealth and other characteristics at retirement and the likelihood of falling into poverty thereafter. They find that, for couples who remained married over the period of their analysis, few fell into poverty because of unexpected events.

14. In 1984 more than one-quarter of widows age 65 and over had incomes below the official poverty line. Such women make up one-half of the elderly poor (U.S. Bureau of the Census 1985). Holden, Burkhauser, and Myers (1986) find that a large percentage of poor elderly widows were not poor while married. Boskin and Shoven (1986) find the onset of widowhood to be the most important single event associated with a drop in well-being in old age.

15. Information on the type of pension option chosen is not directly available from the RHS. This information is approximated by tracing the pension income received by women before and after widowhood. For a more complete discussion of this approximation, see Myers, Burkhauser, and Holden (1987).

16. For a more detailed discussion of the pattern of income-to-needs at older ages see Burkhauser, Holden, and Feister (1986).

17. This table is based on the life-table procedures often used to analyze the risk of death as cohorts age (Allison 1984). Note that neither measured characteristics nor heterogeneity within subcategories is controlled.

18. All income reports in a survey must be retrospective to some degree. Most survey designs include only the retrospective income of current family members in the measure of total current family members, so there are measurement problems when household composition changes during or after the retrospective incidence period. The Retirement History Survey and most data sets other than the PSID do not count as part of total family income the prior calendar year income of persons not in the household at the time of the interview. The values reported here are from widows who were in fact widowed over the entire survey year. Hence the values are not affected by this household composition problem. After adjustments are made correcting for this problem, similar results are found for all widows in the RHS sample. See Burkhauser, Holden, and Myers (1986).

19. It must be kept in mind that the sample of widows followed here includes only the widows of men who retired between 1969 and 1977 and were not poor before they died. It is clearly not representative of all widows.

References

Allison, P.D. 1984. *Event History Analysis: Regression for Longitudinal Event History*. Beverly Hills, Calif.: Sage Publications.

Anderson, K.H., R.V. Burkhauser, and J.F. Quinn. 1986. "Do Retirement Dreams Come True? The Effect of Unanticipated Events on Retirement Plans." *Industrial and Labor Relations Review* 39(4): 518–26.

Bane, M.J., and D. Ellwood. 1983. *The Dynamics of Dependence and the Routes to Self-Sufficiency*. Final Report to the U.S. Department of Health and Human Services. Cambridge, Mass.: Harvard University, Kennedy School of Government.

———. 1986. "Slipping Into and Out of Poverty: The Dynamics of Spells." *Journal of Human Resources* 21:1–23.

Becketti, S., W. Gould, L. Lillard, and F. Welch. 1983. *Attrition from the PSID*. Los Angeles, Calif.: Unicon Research Corporation.

Boskin, M.J. and J.B. Shoven. 1986. "Poverty among the Elderly: Where Are the Holes in the Safety Net?" National Bureau of Economic Research (NBER) Working Paper No. 1923. Cambridge, Mass.: NBER, May.

Burkhauser, R.V. 1984. "Earnings Sharing: Incremental and Fundamental Reform." In *A Challenge to Social Security: The Changing Roles of Women and Men in American Society*, edited by R.V. Burkhauser and K.C. Holden. New York: Academic Press.

Burkhauser, R.V., J.S. Butler, and J.T. Wilkinson. 1985. "Estimating Changes in Well-Being Across Life: A Realized vs. Comprehensive Approach." In *Horizontal Equity, Uncertainty and Well-Being*, edited by M. David and T. Smeeding. NBER Income and Wealth Conference. Chicago: University of Chicago Press.

Burkhauser, R.V., and K.C. Holden, eds. 1984. *A Challenge to Social Security: The Changing Roles of Women and Men in American Society*. New York: Academic Press.

Burkhauser, R.V., K.C. Holden, and D. Feister. 1988. "Incidence, Timing and Events Associated with Poverty: A Dynamic View of Poverty in Retirement." *Journal of Gerontology* 43(2):S46–52.

Burkhauser, R.V., K.C. Holden, and D.A. Myers. 1986. "Marital Disruption and Poverty: The Role of Survey Procedures in Artificially Creating Poverty." *Demography* 23:621–31.

Burkhauser, R.V., and J.T. Wilkinson. 1983. "The Effect of Retirement on Income Distribution: A Comprehensive Income Approach." *Review of Economics and Statistics* 65(4):653–58.

Corcoran, M.E., and M.S. Hill. 1979. "The Incidence and Consequences of Short- and Long-run Unemployment." In *Five thousand American Families: Patterns in Economic Progress*, edited by G.J. Duncan and J.N. Morgan. Vol. 7. Ann Arbor, Mich.: Institute for Social Research.

Danziger, S., and Gottschalk, P. 1987. "Earnings Inequality, the Spatial Concentration of Poverty, and the Underclass." *American Economic Review* 77:211–15.

Danziger, S., J. van der Gaag, E. Smolensky, and M.K. Taussig. 1984. "Implications of the Relative Economic Status of the Elderly for Transfer Policy." In *Retirement and Economic Behavior*, edited by H.J. Aaron and G. Burtless. Washington, D.C.: Brookings Institution.

Duncan, G.J. Forthcoming. "The Volatility of Family Income over the Life Course." In *Life-Span Development and Behavior*, edited by P. Baltes, D. Featherman and R.M. Lerner. Vol. 9, 3rd edition. Hillsdale, N.J.: Lawrence Erlbaum Associates, Inc.

Duncan, G.J., D. Hill, and M. Ponza. 1984. *How Representative is the PSID?: A Response to Some Questions Raised in the Unicon Report.* Ann Arbor, Mich.: Survey Research Center.

Duncan, G.J., and S.D. Hoffman. 1985. "Economic Consequences of Marital Instability." In *Horizontal Equity, Uncertainty and Well-Being*, edited by M. David and T. Smeeding. NBER Income and Wealth Conference. Chicago: University of Chicago Press.

Duncan, G.J., and W. Rodgers. 1985. "The Prevalence of Childhood Poverty." Unpublished manuscript. Ann Arbor, Mich.: Survey Research Center.

Elder, G.H. 1974. *Children of the Great Depression.* Chicago: University of Chicago Press.

Elder, G.H., and J.K. Liker. 1982. "Hard Times in Women's Lives: Historical Influences Across Fifty Years." *American Journal of Sociology* 88:241–69.

Elder, G.H., J.K. Liker, and C.E. Cross. 1984. "Parent-Child Behavior in the Great Depression: Life Course and Intergenerational Influences." In *Life-Span Development and Behavior*, edited by P.B. Baltes and O.G. Brim. Vol. 6. New York: Academic Press.

Elder, G.H., J.K. Liker, and B.J. Jaworski. 1984. "Hardship in Lives: Depression Influences in the 1930s to Old Age in Postwar America." In *Life-Span Development Psychology: Historical and Generational Effects*, edited by K.A. McCluskey and H.W. Reese. New York: Academic Press.

Ellwood, D.T. 1986. "Targeting Would-be Long Term Recipients of AFDC." Princeton, N.J.: Mathematica Policy Research.

Gramlich, E.M., and D.S. Laren. 1984. "How Widespread Are Income Losses in a Recession?" In *The Social Contract Revisited*, edited by D.L. Bawden. Washington, D.C.: The Urban Institute Press.

Hill, M.S., and G.J. Duncan. 1987. "Parental Family Income and the Socioeconomic Attainment of Children." *Social Science Research* 16:39–73.

Holden, K.C., R.V. Burkhauser, and D.A. Myers. 1986. "The Dynamics of Poverty among the Elderly: Income Transitions at Older Stages of Life." *The Gerontologist* 26:292–97.

Hurd, M.D., and J.B. Shoven. 1985. "Inflation, Vulnerability, Income, and Wealth of the Elderly, 1969–1979." In *Horizontal Equity, Uncertainty, and Economic Well-Being*, edited by M. David and T. Smeeding. NBER Income and Wealth Conference. Chicago: University of Chicago Press.

Ippolito, R.A. 1986. *Pensions, Economics, and Public Policy*. Homeword, Ill.: Dow Jones–Irwin.

Ireland, L.M. 1976. "Retirement History Study: Introduction." In *Almost 65: Baseline Data from the Retirement History Study*. Social Security Administration Office of Research and Statistics, Research Report no. 49. Washington, D.C.

Kotlikoff, L.J., and D.E. Smith. 1983. *Pensions in the American Economy*. Chicago: University of Chicago Press.

Liker, J.K., and G.H. Elder. 1983. "Economic Hardship and Marital Relations in the 1930's." *American Sociological Review* 48:343–59.

Moon, M. and E. Smolensky, eds. 1977. *Improving Measures of Economic Well-Being*. New York: Academic Press.

Murray, Charles. 1984. *Losing Ground: American Social Policy, 1950–1980*. New York: Basic Books.

Myers, D.A., R.V. Burkhauser, and K.C. Holden. 1987. "The Transition from Wife to Widow: The Importance of Survivor Benefits to Widows." *Journal of Risk and Insurance* 54, no.4:752–59.

Pearlin, L.I., M.A. Liberman, E.G. Menaghan and J. Mullan. 1981. "The Stress Process." *Journal of Health and Social Behavior* 22:337–56.

Quinn, J.F. 1987. "Economic Status of the Elderly: Beware of the Mean." *Review of Income and Wealth* 33:62–83.

Sewell, W.H., and R.M. Hauser. 1975. *Education, Occupation, and Earnings: Achievement in the Early Career*. New York: Academic Press.

Sider, H. 1985. "Unemployment Duration and Incidence: 1968–82." *American Economic Review* 75:461–72.

Smeeding, T.M. 1986. "Nonmoney Income and the Elderly: The Case of the 'Tweeners.' " *Journal of Policy Analysis and Management* 5, no.4: 707–24.

Survey Research Center. 1984. *User Guide to the Panel Study of Income Dynamics*. Ann Arbor, Mich.: Interuniversity Consortium for Political and Social Research.

U.S. Bureau of the Census. 1985. "Estimates of Poverty Including the Value of Non-cash Benefits: 1984." Technical Paper no. 55. Washington, D.C.

———. 1986a. "Characteristics of the Population Below the Poverty Level: 1984." *Current Population Reports*, series P-60, no. 152. Washington, D.C.

———. 1986b. "Child Support and Alimony: 1983." *Current Population Reports*, series P-23, no. 148. (Supplemental Report). Washington, D.C.

———. 1987. "Money Income and Poverty Status of Families and Persons in the United States: 1986 (Advance Data from the March 1987 Current Population Survey)." *Current Population Reports*, series P-60, no. 157. Washington, D.C.

Weiss, R.S. 1984. "The Impact of Marital Dissolution on Income and Consumption of Single-Parent Households." *Journal of Marriage and the Family* 46:115–27.

Weitzman, L.J. 1985. *The Divorce Revolution: The Unexpected Social and Economic Consequences for Women and Children in America.* New York: Free Press.

White, K.R. 1982. "The Relationship Between Socioeconomic Status and Academic Achievement." *Psychological Bulletin* 91:461–81.

Chapter Five

PATTERNS OF INCOME AND POVERTY: THE ECONOMIC STATUS OF CHILDREN AND THE ELDERLY IN EIGHT COUNTRIES

Timothy Smeeding, Barbara Boyle Torrey, and Martin Rein

The two major dependent groups in industrial countries, the young and the elderly, put the greatest demand on public resources and in turn receive most of public income transfers and services. The economic status of these two groups is therefore of particular concern for policymakers.

In the United States the economic status of the young and old changed dramatically between 1970 and 1986 (U.S. Bureau of the Census 1987). Chapters 3 and 4 of this volume have discussed in some detail how these changes occurred and what their effects were on groups within the young and the elderly. One indication of the economic change was the fall in poverty rates of the elderly as the rates for children increased. The first trend was welcomed; the second has become an increasing concern.

This reversal in the economic status of the young and the elderly in the United States occurred without an explicit policy to favor one group over the other. Rather, the reversal was the result of an accumulation of policy decisions interacting with social changes. It was not anticipated at the beginning of the 1970s and not carefully documented until the 1980s (Preston 1984).

One of the many issues raised by the changing fortunes of the young and elderly in the United States is whether this is an inevitable trend in aging societies. As the old become a larger proportion of a society, do they gain more influence and demand a disproportionate share of social resources? If this is an inevitable trend in aging

This paper was supported in part by a grant from the Alfred P. Sloan Foundation to the University of Utah, and in part by funds granted to the Luxembourg Income Study (LIS) by the National Science Foundation and the Ford Foundation. The authors are grateful to participants in the Sloan Foundation Project on the Well-Being of Children and Aged, and particularly Ross Finnie, Greg Duncan, and Michael Wolfson, for their comments, and to Brigitte Buhmann and Gunther Schmaus for their suggestions and assistance in generating the LIS data for our analysis.

democratic societies, we might expect to see similar trends in other industrial countries. If, however, the elderly in other countries do not enjoy such an obvious economic advantage relative to children, then the reversal in the fortunes of the two groups in the United States may be caused by social policies and attitudes unique to this country.

Comparable income trend data by age are difficult to find for other countries, but roughly comparable data for the 1970–84 period for Canada and the United Kingdom show trends similar to those in the United States. The incomes of the elderly increased faster than the incomes of the general population in all three countries, but especially in the United States where overall real incomes did not increase. The real incomes of single-parent families with children either increased more slowly (Canada) or fell (the United Kingdom and the United States) in real terms over the 1970–84 period.

International income comparisons in the past have been limited by the lack of comparable data for pre- and posttax/posttransfer income and for the demographic unit. Comparable income and demographic data did not exist for most countries until the Luxembourg Income Study (LIS) reported its first results at a conference in the summer of 1985. This study has created comparable cross-sectional income data files for several Western industrial countries plus the United States. As a consequence, LIS data offer the first clear economic window through which to compare industrial societies and learn the lessons such comparisons can teach.

These comparisons of the United States with seven other countries—Australia, Canada, Norway, Sweden, Switzerland, the United Kingdom and West Germany—suggest that the relative economic advantage of the elderly in the United States over the young is shared by Canada and Sweden, but in both those countries the rates of poverty for children are much lower than the rate in the United States. Four other countries (Norway, Switzerland, the United Kingdom and West Germany) have considerably higher poverty rates for the elderly than the young; in Australia the poverty rates of the two groups are similar.

These comparisons reinforce concerns about the economic status of American children. In 1979, the year of the U.S. survey examined in detail in this chapter, the poverty rate for children was only slightly higher than the rate for the elderly. The most recent official U.S. poverty rate estimates (1986) are 19.8 percent for children and 12.4 percent for the elderly (U.S. Bureau of the Census 1987), thus the child poverty rate is nearly 60 percent higher than the elderly rate. The international comparisons in this chapter suggest not only that children are at a disadvantage relative to the elderly in the United States, but also that American children have considerably higher poverty rates than the children in all the other countries examined except Australia.

After introducing the reader to LIS, this chapter examines in detail the income level and inequalities among the young and the elderly in eight countries in the 1979–81 period. It then compares the low-income and poverty levels of each group within and among countries and discusses the social, demographic, and economic factors that help to explain the differences among countries.

LUXEMBOURG INCOME STUDY DATA FILE

Between 1979 and 1982, nine countries conducted national house-hold surveys that collected detailed income data. The data from these nine surveys were adjusted for definitional differences in income and income-sharing units and have become the core of the LIS data set. The LIS data base includes nine countries, the eight included in this paper and Israel. Israel is excluded from the comparisons discussed here because its too idiosyncratic to yield much insight into comparative trends across countries. Each survey covers at least 92 percent of the noninstitutionalized population (97 percent excluding Switzerland and West Germany).[1] Although for some ethnic groups, such as Laps in Norway or Aleuts in the United States, the sample sizes are too small to be representative, the age groups that are the major concern in this chapter are well represented.

Family disposable personal income (posttax-posttransfer income) is the main measure of well-being used throughout this chapter. It includes all forms of cash income (earnings, property income, all cash transfers) net of direct taxes (that is, employer and employee payroll taxes and income taxes). In some cases we also use gross income (disposable income plus income and payroll taxes); pretax-pretransfer income (gross income minus public transfers); and posttax-pretransfer income (disposable income minus public trans-fers). Disposable income is also often adjusted for differences in family size and composition. Adjusted income is calculated by dividing disposable income by the equivalence scale appropriate to each family size and age composition. The equivalence scale is normalized to a family of three persons. A number of different equivalence scales have been used on the LIS data. For simplicity, this chapter uses the equivalence scale inherent in the U.S. poverty rate calculation. (For a more thorough discussion of the range of equivalence scales and the effect the U.S. poverty line equivalence scale has on the measurement of economic status, see Smeeding, Schmaus, and Allegreza 1985.)

The income accounting unit used in this chapter is that of the U.S. Census family (all persons living together and related by blood, marriage, or adoption). Families are also classified according to the age of the head of the family. For instance, elderly families are those headed by a person age 65 or older. Some small differences exist across LIS countries with respect to family definitions (see Smeeding, Schmaus, and Allegreza 1985, for details).

The Average Incomes of the Young and the Elderly in Eight Countries

Economic comparisons of different groups within a country require a standard measure. The national average adjusted (disposable) income for all families in each country is used as the standard for intracountry comparisons in this section. Because we are specifically interested in the economic comparisons of families with children and the elderly, we have excluded economic comparisons of nonaged families without children. In all cases the average income of the nonaged, childless family was higher than that for families with children, although for many age groups the differences were slight.

For the eight countries taken together, the overall mean income of families with children is 0.93 of the national average as compared with 0.89 for the elderly (table 5.1). In Canada and West Germany the overall adjusted incomes of elderly families and families with children are about equal. In Australia, the Scandinavian countries, and the United Kingdom, families with children have higher adjusted mean incomes than do elderly families. Only in Switzerland and the United States do we find that elderly families are better off on average than are families with children. In Switzerland adjusted incomes of elderly families are above the incomes of all families with children whose family heads are age 44 or younger. In the United States the adjusted incomes of the very old (those in families with heads age 75 and over) are only higher than those of much younger (heads age 34 or under) families with children. In Australia, Canada, and West Germany, the adjusted mean incomes of very old families are only higher than the incomes of the very youngest group of families with children (heads age 24 or under). In general, adjusted

Table 5.1 RATIO OF ADJUSTED DISPOSABLE INCOME TO NATIONAL MEAN FOR FAMILIES WITH CHILDREN AND ELDERLY FAMILIES, EIGHT COUNTRIES

Country	Families with children; age of family head						Elderly families		
	<25 years	25–34 years	35–44 years	45–54 years	55–64 years	Total	65–74 years	75 years and older	Total
Australia (1981[a])	0.68	0.80	0.89	1.07	1.05	0.90	0.88	0.80	0.85
Canada (1981)	0.65	0.84	0.93	1.02	0.96	0.91	0.94	0.81	0.90
Germany, F.R. (1981)	0.62	0.79	0.89	0.86	0.96	0.86	0.85	0.79	0.84
Norway (1979)	0.80	0.93	0.99	1.03	1.15	0.99	1.01	0.79	0.91
Sweden (1982)	0.91	0.98	1.01	0.98	1.01	1.01	0.96	0.78	0.90
Switzerland (1982)	0.60	0.77	0.89	0.98	1.16	0.91	1.11	0.91	1.02
United Kingdom (1979)	0.80	0.87	0.95	1.10	1.14	0.95	0.76	0.67	0.73
United States (1979)	0.62	0.82	0.93	1.02	0.94	0.90	0.99	0.84	0.94
Overall mean[b]	0.71	0.85	0.94	1.02	1.05	0.93	0.94	0.80	0.89

Source: Computations by authors from the Luxembourg Income Study Data File (1987).

Note: Disposable income is posttax and transfer income. Disposable income is adjusted for family size by dividing actual disposable income by the U.S. poverty line equivalence scale in table A-3. The national mean adjusted income equals 1.00. Families with children are those headed by persons ages 24–64 that include at least one child under age 18. Elderly families are those headed by a person age 65 or older. In some countries a small number of elderly families may include children under age 18.

< less than > greater than.

a. Year for which data are supplied.

b. The overall mean is the simple unweighted average of the means within each age group.

disposable income relative to the national mean of families with children is highest for those with heads ages 45 to 64. In Norway, Switzerland, the United Kingdom, and West Germany, the income of the families with heads ages 55 to 64 years with children is higher than in the 45- to 54-year-old group. Because several members of this group may already be retired, the incomes of those still working are even higher, relative to those ages 45 to 54, than these figures suggest. As people reach retirement age, their earnings begin to drop substantially, reducing their adjusted disposable income (Achdut and Tamir, forthcoming).

The older the elderly are, the lower is their income relative to the national average in every country. The average family headed by a person between the ages of 65 and 74 had an income that was 94 percent of the national average. The average income of families headed by persons age 75 and older, however, was only 80 percent of the national mean. Interestingly, the largest drops in income between families with heads ages 65 to 74 and those with heads age 75 and over are in Norway, Sweden, and Switzerland. The United States had the third highest ratio of adjusted disposable incomes for 65- to 74-year-olds and the second highest ratio for people age 75 and over (only the Swiss were higher). The average incomes of all American elderly families relative to the national mean family income is the second highest among the countries examined here (again, only the Swiss are higher). This fact is confirmed in the last column of table 5.1, where the overall mean adjusted disposable income of households with heads age 65 and over relative to the overall mean income is 0.94 in the United States and 1.02 in Switzerland, compared to an overall average of 0.89.[2]

One final comparison of interest involves single-parent families with other families. As might be expected, the adjusted disposable incomes are everywhere considerably lower for single parents with children than for all families with children. A more interesting comparison is that between the elderly families and single-parent families with children. The elderly in every country also had considerably more income than single-parent families. The adjusted income of the elderly in the United States is 88 percent higher than the income of single-parent families.

Comparisons of the incomes of various types of families to the national average in each country is a useful beginning to the study of relative economic status in the next section. However, overall averages provide no information on patterns of overall income inequality or individual poverty. These patterns, discussed later in the chapter, make a more complex picture than one taken through the simple filter of national averages.

Relative Low-Income and Absolute Poverty Rates among the Young and the Elderly

International poverty comparisons raise both conceptual and methodological issues (Rein 1970). Poverty may be defined in terms of absolute income; but deprivation is a relative concept. In this chapter, relative low income is defined as the percentage of people or families who have disposable income (adjusted by the U.S. poverty line equivalence scale) below one-half the national median adjusted income. Absolute poverty is defined as the percentage of people who have adjusted disposable income below the U.S. poverty line converted into national currencies using the purchasing power parities developed by the Organization for Economic Cooperation and Development (OECD, 1985).[3] The U.S. poverty standard is 42 percent of the adjusted median income in the United States. The effect of using the U.S. poverty standard instead of one-half the median is dramatic in the United States; it reduces the poverty rates of the elderly by a third (from 23.9 percent to 16.1 percent, see table 5.2). In four countries, the U.S. poverty line, adjusted for differences in currency using OECD purchasing power parities, is slightly above one-half the equivalence adjusted median income. In Canada, Sweden, Switzerland, and the United States, it is below half the median. Absolute poverty rates are, therefore, very sensitive to the location of the poverty line relative to the median income, as well as to a host of other factors.[4]

One fact stands out most clearly in table 5.2: The United States has a higher proportion of children in low-income families, by either the relative or the absolute measure, than any other country. In fact, with the exception of Australia and Canada, the United States has more than twice as high a proportion of children in low-income families as do the other countries.

In contrast, the poverty rate for elderly Americans using the absolute U.S. poverty definition is lower than the rate for the elderly in Australia, Norway, or the United Kingdom and not far above West Germany's rate. If we use the relative low-income line, the United States and the United Kingdom have more low-income elderly than any of the other countries. At one end of the scale, poverty among the elderly in Sweden has been virtually eliminated through the high minimum benefits in the Swedish social insurance system.

Table 5.2   RELATIVE LOW INCOME AND ABSOLUTE POVERTY AMONG
CHILDREN, ADULTS, AND THE ELDERLY, SELECTED COUNTRIES

Country and poverty measure	Percentage in poor families				Child-to-elderly poverty rate ratio
	Children	Adults	Elderly	Overall	
Australia					
Relative	15.9	9.9	15.7	12.2	1.01
Absolute	16.9	10.5	19.2	13.2	0.88
Canada					
Relative	15.5	10.7	17.2	12.6	0.90
Absolute	9.6	7.5	4.8	7.4	2.00
Germany, F.R.					
Relative	4.9	4.5	11.1	5.6	0.44
Absolute	8.2	6.5	15.4	8.3	0.53
Norway					
Relative	4.8	5.4	5.6	5.2	0.86
Absolute	7.6	7.1	18.7	8.6	0.41
Sweden					
Relative	5.0	6.7	0.8	5.3	6.25
Absolute	5.1	6.7	2.1	5.6	2.43
Switzerland					
Relative	7.8	8.1	11.4	8.5	0.68
Absolute	5.1	6.2	6.0	5.8	0.85
United Kingdom					
Relative	9.3	5.7	29.2	9.7	0.32
Absolute	10.7	6.9	37.0	11.8	0.29
United States					
Relative	22.4	13.4	23.9	17.1	0.94
Absolute	17.1	10.1	16.1	12.7	1.06

Source: Same as table 5.1.
Note: Relative low income includes all persons with adjusted incomes below half
the median adjusted national income. Absolute poverty includes all persons with
adjusted incomes below the official U.S. Government three-person poverty line
converted to other currencies using OECD purchasing power parities, where adjusted incomes are computed using the U.S. Government poverty line equivalency
scales.

At the other end, the relatively low minimum benefits in the British
public retirement system in 1979 left 37 percent of the elderly poor.[5]
    The poverty rates across the eight countries are also sensitive to
where the absolute poverty line is drawn. Table 5.3 presents the
percentage of children and elderly below not only 100 percent of
the U.S. poverty line, but also at 75 and 125 percent of that line.

Table 5.3   SENSITIVITY OF POVERTY RATES TO THE LEVEL OF THE
ABSOLUTE POVERTY LINE, CHILDREN AND ELDERLY

| | Percentage of persons falling below | | | |
Country	75 percent of poverty line[a]	Absolute poverty	125 percent of poverty line	Spread[b] (percentage points)
Poverty among children				
Australia	7.3	16.9	26.2	18.9
Canada	4.4	9.6	15.2	10.8
Germany, F.R.	2.5	8.2	21.5	19.0
Norway	2.7	7.6	17.2	14.5
Sweden	2.2	5.1	9.7	7.5
Switzerland	2.0	5.1	9.3	7.3
United Kingdom	3.8	10.7	22.7	18.9
United States	9.8	17.1	24.2	14.4
Poverty among the elderly				
Australia	2.7	19.2	38.5	35.8
Canada	1.7	4.8	16.6	14.9
Germany, F.R.	5.9	15.4	29.8	23.9
Norway	4.3	18.7	40.1	35.8
Sweden	0.1	2.1	11.2	11.1
Switzerland	2.4	6.0	13.8	11.4
United Kingdom	6.9	37.0	61.1	54.2
United States	6.8	16.1	26.6	19.8

Source: Same as table 5.1.
a. See note, table 5.2.
b. Difference between 125 percent and 75 percent of the poverty line.

Among children the U.S. poverty rates remain highest when the standard drops to 75 percent of poverty. In fact, at 75 percent of poverty, the difference between the U.S. poverty rate for children and that of the next closest country, Australia, is 2.5 percentage points (versus 0.3 percentage point at 100 percent—the absolute poverty line). When the standard is raised to 125 percent of poverty, Australia has a higher poverty rate for children than the United States. In some countries the spread in child poverty rates between 75 and 125 percent is very large—more than 15 points in Australia, the United Kingdom, and West Germany. Hence although poverty among children is sensitive to where the line is set, it appears from table 5.3 that children are deeper in poverty in the United States than in other countries wherever it is set.

Poverty among the elderly in the United States, compared with

Table 5.4   POOR PERSONS CLASSIFIED AS SEVERELY POOR (percentage)

Country	Families with children	Elderly families[a]
Australia	43.1	14.1
Canada	45.8	35.3
Germany, F.R.	30.5	38.3
Norway	35.5	23.1
Sweden	43.0	4.5
Switzerland	39.3	40.0
United Kingdom	35.5	18.5
United States	57.3	42.3

Source: Same as table 5.1.
Note: Estimates are calculated from table 5.3. "Severely poor" is defined as 75 percent of the U.S. poverty line or below.
a. See note, table 5.1.

poverty among the elderly in other countries, also depends on where the poverty line is set. At 75 percent of the poverty line, the United States has the second highest rate, nearly as high as the rate in the United Kingdom, but at 125 percent, the United States moves closer to the middle of the group of countries shown.

Obviously the extent of poverty is to some extent arbitrary—a function of definition and the social consensus of how these questions should be answered. We have chosen to stick to the poverty standards and equivalence scales developed for use in the United States because we are concerned primarily with U.S. policy.

Below a certain level of deprivation, however, things become much less ambiguous. There is broad consensus that those persons and families whose command of income is three-quarters or less of the absolute U.S. poverty line are experiencing a dire lack of resources in comparison with the consumption norms of industrial society. What proportion of the poor live at this standard of poverty? In all the countries except Switzerland and West Germany, children are more severely poor than the elderly (see table 5.4). In the United States there is more severe poverty among both groups than in any of the other countries. More than 57 percent of all the poor children in the United States are severely poor, compared with 46 percent in Canada, the next closest country. About 42 percent of all poor elderly persons are severely poor in the United States, compared to 40 percent in Switzerland, 38 percent in West Germany, and only 19 percent in the United Kingdom.

If the poverty levels of the young and the old and the relative poverty positions of the young and old in the different countries had been similar, it might have been reasonable to assume that the poverty trends were the result of fundamental, universal trends in industrial and democratic societies. The reality, however, is quite different. The rate of poverty varies considerably among groups and across countries. Three of the European countries clearly have more absolute poverty among their elderly than among their children; Sweden has more poverty among its children, but both rates are so low that the difference is very small. Poverty rates for both age groups are higher in the United States than in the other countries. In both Australia and Switzerland poverty among the elderly slightly exceeds poverty among children, even though the poverty rates of the former are more than double the rates of the latter. Most disturbing are the facts that poverty is highest among children in the United States and more severe by a large margin than in any other country in the comparison. The challenge is not only to try to understand why these differences occur, but also to assess how they might be changed in the future.

POSSIBLE EXPLANATIONS FOR DIFFERENCES IN THE POVERTY STATUS OF THE YOUNG AND OLD

Many social conditions and transfer policies may be related to the economic status of the young and the old. The ones explored in this chapter include:

1. Equivalence scales
2. Relative size of the two age groups
3. Family structure (including changing structures over the life course)
4. Heterogeneity of the population
5. Contribution of secondary earners to family income
6. Income inequality within age groups
7. Effectiveness of the tax and transfer system

Of these seven factors, the first two turn out not to be important in explaining the relative differences among the countries included here. Numbers three through six provide some insight in explaining the patterns of poverty, but none stands out as a dominant explanatory force. The last factor on the list—the tax and transfer systems of each country—plays the largest role in determining how much pretax-pretransfer poverty is reduced and hence the ultimate pattern of posttax-posttransfer poverty both within and across countries.

■ EQUIVALENCE SCALES

The proportions of children and elderly in poverty are sensitive to the equivalence scale that adjusts income for relative family size and age structure, as discussed in chapter 2 of this volume. The absolute poverty rate is much more sensitive to the choice of equivalence scale, however, than are the relative positions of different groups across countries. Particularly conspicuous is the fact that the poverty of American children is the highest of all eight countries regardless of which equivalence scale is used with one minor exception (Australia, with a subjective equivalence scale). Excluding Australia, the poverty rate for children in the United States is 58 percent, 60 percent, and 83 percent higher than the rates for the next closest country using the U.S., LIS, and subjective equivalence scale, respectively (Torrey and Smeeding 1988).

■ RELATIVE SIZE OF AGE GROUPS

There are two conflicting hypotheses about how poverty may be related to the relative size of the age group. The first hypothesis, "relative burden," is that countries with relatively large and growing dependent populations may find it difficult to allocate enough economic resources to these groups to maintain their relative economic well-being. Therefore, large numbers of elderly, children, or both in the population would increase the poverty rates for the elderly, children, or both. The second hypothesis, "political clout," is that large dependent groups will create political pressure to increase their share of the economic pie. In this case, poverty rates will be negatively correlated with group size. The evidence is not strong for either of these hypotheses. Table 5.5 presents the percentage of the total population of each country that is young (ages 0 to 17), elderly (age 65 and over), the combined total of these (sometimes referred to as the total dependency ratio), the ratio of the young population to the old population, and the ratio of child poverty to elderly poverty.

The dependency ratio varies only from 36 percent to 45 percent, and in all countries the young are a considerably larger proportion of the population than the elderly. Yet within each country, children do not have consistently more or less poverty than the elderly. In

Table 5.5   YOUNG AND ELDERLY POPULATION SHARES AND RELATIVE
POVERTY RATES

Country	Young 0–17 years	Elderly 65 + years	Young and elderly combined (dependency ratio)	Ratio of young to elderly in population	Ratio of young to elderly in poverty[a]
Australia	30	9	39	3.3	0.9
Canada	28	8	36	3.5	2.0
Germany, F.R.	24	15	39	1.6	0.5
Norway[b]	32	13	45	2.5	0.4
Sweden	23	18	41	1.3	2.4
Switzerland	26	14	40	1.9	0.8
United Kingdom	28	13	41	2.3	0.3
United States	29	11	40	2.6	1.1

Source: Same as table 5.1.
a. Taken from absolute poverty estimates in table 2, column 6.
b. The Norwegian figures for children and elderly are taken from OECD population figures. The LIS estimate of children in Norway is 36 percent and of the elderly, 12 percent. Because the Norwegian file identifies children via tax dependency, and because in Norway some tax dependents may not be children (for example, disabled adults living with other families members), we decided to use the OECD population estimates instead of the LIS estimates.

three countries children have more poverty than the elderly, whereas in five countries children have less.

The comparison of poverty rates of children in the eight countries also indicates no consistent relationship between child poverty and children as a proportion of the population in each country. Nor is there a consistent pattern of poverty and relative size of the aged population across countries. The lack of consistent relationships means that neither the relative burden nor the political clout hypothesis is supported by the cross-sectional data on the eight countries examined.

■ *FAMILY STRUCTURE*

Some family structures are less vulnerable to poverty than others. In all the countries two-adult families, both young and old, had higher average incomes than one-adult families did and were less vulnerable to poverty. Even so, vulnerability to poverty by family structure varied considerably by country. In all eight countries children in one-parent families were considerably more likely to have less than one-half the median income (table 5.6 panel A) and

Table 5.6   POVERTY AND LOW INCOME AMONG CHILDREN BY FAMILY TYPE,
SELECTED COUNTRIES

	Percentage of low-income children in each family type			
Country	One-parent families[a]	Two-parent families[b]	Other families[c]	All types of families
A. Relative low income rates of children by family type[d]				
Australia	63.5	11.4	10.2	15.9
Canada	51.0	12.0	11.1	15.5
Germany, F.R.	30.6	2.0	7.8	4.9
Norway	8.6	3.0	10.0	4.8
Sweden	8.3	4.4	0.5	5.0
Switzerland	18.4	6.4	10.0	7.8
United Kingdom	36.2	8.1	14.1	9.3
United States	59.3	13.8	22.1	22.4
B. Poverty rates[e] of children by family type				
Australia	65.0	12.4	10.6	16.9
Canada	38.7	6.8	5.5	9.6
Germany, F.R.	35.1	4.9	12.1	8.2
Norway	21.6	4.4	12.7	7.6
Sweden	8.6	4.5	0.5	5.1
Switzerland	12.9	4.1	3.8	5.1
United Kingdom	38.6	9.5	2.5	10.7
United States	51.0	9.4	16.2	17.1
C. Percentage of children by family type				
Australia	9.1	75.3	15.6	100.0
Canada	9.6	71.1	19.3	100.0
Germany, F.R.	5.5	72.2	22.3	100.0
Norway	15.7	78.1	6.2	100.0
Sweden	14.8	84.8	0.4	100.0
Switzerland	11.6	87.3	1.1	100.0
United Kingdom	8.0	76.7	15.3	100.0
United States	14.7	61.9	23.4	100.0

Source: Same as table 5.1.
a. Children in one-parent families are living with one natural parent and no other adults in the family.
b. Children in two-parent families live in units with two parents and no other adults.
c. Children in other families may live with adults other than parents: for example, living with grandparents, in extended family situations, and in foster homes.
d. Relative low income is explained in text. Children are defined as persons 17 years or under. Adjusted income was calculated using the U.S. poverty line equivalence scales.
e. Absolute poverty rates, as explained in text.

Table 5.7   THE DIFFERENCE U.S. DEMOGRAPHIC STRUCTURE MAKES TO
CHILD POVERTY IN OTHER COUNTRIES (percentage)

Country	Actual poverty rate	Poverty rate with U.S. demographic structure[a]	Increase (decrease)[b]
Australia	16.9	19.6	+16.0
Canada	9.6	11.2	+16.7
Germany, F.R.	8.2	10.5	+28.0
Norway	7.6	7.5	−1.3
Sweden	5.1	5.1	0
Switzerland	5.1	5.4	+5.9
United Kingdom	10.7	12.7	+18.7
United States	17.1	17.1	0

Source: Same as table 5.1.
a. Assumes no change in poverty rates within family types, but with 14.7 percent of children in single parent families and 85.3 percent in other types of units, the same demographic breakdown of children by family type as in the United States.
b. Poverty rate with the U.S. demographic structure minus the actual poverty rate, divided by the actual rate.

to be in absolute poverty (table 5.6, panel B) than children living in two-parent families. But, curiously, the percentage of children in one-parent families by country was unrelated to the rates of low income (table 5.6, panel C). Both Norway and Sweden have higher proportions of children in families with only one parent (15.7 percent and 14.8 percent, respectively) than the United States (14.7 percent). And Switzerland ranks next below the United States (11.6 percent of children live in single-parent units). These are the highest shares (table 5.6, panel C) among the countries studied here. Yet the low-income and poverty rates of children in the one-parent families of Norway, Sweden, and Switzerland are lower in any of the other countries studied. If anything, except for the United States, table 5.6 appears to show a slight negative correlation between the proportion of children in single-parent families and poverty rates.

So the United States is again the exception, with a high percentage of children in single-parent families *and* high single-parent poverty. The *combination* has an important influence on overall child poverty rates. If every country had the same percentage of children in single-parent families as the United States in 1980 but its own child poverty rate, the poverty rate among all children would increase everywhere but in Norway and Sweden (see table 5.7). In all other countries except Australia, however, the increase in child poverty would *still* leave those countries far below U.S. rates.

What distinguishes the situations in the United States and Australia from those in other countries is that the single-parent families are so much more vulnerable. They have lower relative incomes and their low-income rates are more than double the rates of other countries. Australia is much less rich than the United States, and it has a much lower share of children in single-parent families. The most striking element of tables 5.6 and 5.7 is the high levels of poverty in the United States compared with the levels for other high-income countries with similar demographics.

The varying family structures of the elderly also provide some insights into the pattern of poverty (table 5.8). In all the countries poverty rates are much lower among elderly couples than among elderly single persons, but poverty rates for the elderly who live alone vary widely. The percentage of elderly living alone is actually highest in Sweden (50 percent) where they have the lowest poverty rate. It is much higher than in the United Kingdom (37 percent), for example, which has by far the highest poverty rate among the aged. Few elderly live alone in Australia (about one-third), where poverty rates among the elderly living alone are very high. But not much more than one-third (36.5 percent) live alone in Canada, where poverty rates among the old are very low.[6]

Poverty varies over the life course as well as by family structure, declining as the family head enters middle age and rising again in the later years. What is less well documented is the joint role of age and family structure. Consider the U.S. experience to illustrate the point. Solo parenting in the United States is concentrated among young family heads—90 percent of these family heads are under 25 years of age. Poverty rates are especially high for this group. Solo parents account for 12 percent of all families with a head under 25; nearly two-thirds of these families are poor. In contrast, married couples account for two-thirds of all families with children in this age group; only 14 percent of children in these families are poor (still above the overall poverty rate of 2.4 percent in the United States).

Poverty again rears its head in later old age and again mainly among women. Smeeding and Torrey (1986), using the LIS data for the same eight countries, find that both low-income and poverty rates among the elderly are highest among single women living alone who are age 75 or over. In every country studied, the poverty rates for the 75-and-over group were at least 50 percent higher than among

Table 5.8   LIVING ARRANGEMENTS AND POVERTY AMONG THE ELDERLY

| | Percentage of elderly persons living | | | | |
| | Alone | | In married | Other | |
Country	Male	Female	couples	combinations[a]	Total
A. *Living arrangements*					
Australia	8.4	25.1	59.4	7.1	100.0
Canada	9.3	27.2	47.2	16.3	100.0
Germany, F.R.	6.3	36.7	48.5	8.5	100.0
Norway	15.1	41.2	10.7[b]	33.0[b]	100.0
Sweden	13.6	36.2	49.8	0.5	100.0
Switzerland	10.4	39.5	49.7	0.3	100.0
United Kingdom	8.9	27.9	49.9	13.3	100.0
United States	7.6	27.5	50.0	14.9	100.0

| | Absolute poverty rate among elderly persons living | | | | |
| | Alone | | In married | Other | |
Country	Male	Female	couples	combinations[a]	Total
B. *Poverty*					
Australia	40.1	48.0	6.1	2.9	19.2
Canada	6.2	9.4	1.6	5.5	4.8
Germany, F.R.	18.6	24.0	9.3	10.3	15.4
Norway	32.3	31.0	0.4	3.1	18.7
Sweden	6.8	3.0	0.2	0.6	2.1
Switzerland	8.7	11.4	1.1	0.0	6.0
United Kingdom	55.1	69.5	24.1	5.2	37.0
United States	25.7	30.7	8.2	11.1	16.1

Source: Same as table 5.1.
a. "Other combinations" include all elderly not living alone and not living in (married) couples.
b. The Norwegian data file lists two elderly adults living together as couples only if they are married; but, because living together unmarried is customary in Norway, even for couples who have been living together for several decades, other combinations and couples are hard to distinguish.

the 65- to 74-year-old group. Moreover, in every country studied, the majority of very elderly poor were single women living alone.

Thus it is the situation of young single women and their children and very old single women that characterizes social disadvantage in industrial societies, particularly in the United States. The poverty of our very old single women we share with other countries; the poverty of our families with children, however, is considerably higher than in any other country but Australia.

Table 5.9   POVERTY RATES AMONG SELECTED SUBGROUPS IN NATIONAL
POPULATIONS (percentage)

	Children	Elderly
Australia, total	16.8	19.2
Native	17.1	19.7
Foreign	16.3	17.4
Canada, total	9.6	4.8
Native	9.6	4.8
Foreign	9.6	4.6
(Arrival after 1971)	(10.4)	(17.6)
Switzerland, total	3.8	6.0
Native	5.6	5.1
Foreign	2.6	25.5
United States, total	17.1	16.1
Blacks	40.5	36.7
Hispanics	28.9	27.0
White (nonblack and non-Hispanic)[a]	11.4	14.0

Source: Same as table 5.1
Note: Absolute measure includes all persons with adjusted incomes below the
official U.S. Government three-person poverty line converted to other currencies
using OECD purchasing power parities, where adjusted incomes are computed
using the U.S. poverty line equivalence scales.
a. Poverty rates for U.S. whites and others, including Hispanics, are 13 (children)
and 14.3 (aged). Because Hispanics may also be either black or white, the easiest
way to separate U.S. minorities from the U.S. majority is to calculate the nonblack
and non-Hispanic poverty rate. We call this the "white" poverty rate in this
chapter.

■ HETEROGENEITY OF POPULATION

If poverty rates vary by race or ethnic groups, as they do in the
United States, countries with a more diverse population may have
higher poverty rates than more ethnically homogeneous countries.
Among the nations compared in this chapter, four—Australia, Canada, Switzerland, and the United States—have populations that are
culturally diverse enough to separate minority subgroups. Norway,
Sweden, and the United Kingdom do not differentiate. The West
German data set excludes foreign-born heads of households. In the
United States, black families with children are particularly economically disadvantaged relative to comparable white (nonblack and
non-Hispanic) families (table 5.9). The low-income and poverty rates
among black children are almost four times as high as the rates
among white children; the same rates for the black elderly are more

than two-and-one-half times the rates for white elderly. Hispanic poverty rates for children and the elderly are double the rates for nonblack non-Hispanics.

Analysts have speculated that the U.S. poverty rates are high because of our diversity. If this speculation were correct, the poverty rates of whites in the United States relative to whites in other countries would be much more similar than the overall rates. But this turns out not to be the case. When the poverty rates of the nonminority populations in the other countries with data are compared, the poverty rates for young and old American whites are still high compared with two of the three other countries. Native Canadians, both young and old, have lower poverty rates than whites in the United States. So do the native Swiss. And the poverty rate among white American children is higher than the minority or majority poverty rates for these other countries (see table 5.2 presented earlier).

Heterogeneity does matter; poverty rates are different for different populations, and poverty rates in the United States are high in part because of its social and ethnic diversity. But this diversity does not fully explain the broad differences in poverty among nations in general and the high poverty of American children in particular.

■ *WIVES' INCOME AND THE REDUCTION OF POVERTY*

The "traditional" income redistribution model starts with a family's traditional income (husband's earnings and assets) before taxes and transfers. This is often described as "original income," implying that the state has played no important role in shaping the level or distribution of this income. The state enters the redistributive process only at the second stage when it taxes (reduces incomes of some) and transfers (adds to the resources of others).

One of the important recent changes in family income is that families no longer live on what has been traditionally defined as family incomes. In particular, families are more dependent on the earnings of wives than ever before. Women have always worked, but only in recent years has the income of wives become an important income source for families.

Different earnings patterns among wives may contribute to our understanding of different poverty patterns among families in different countries. Taking wives' earnings into account, however, poses a conceptual problem, because we are not clear about when in the process of generating family income wives' earnings comes

Table 5.10   CONTRIBUTION OF WIVES TO REDUCING POVERTY AMONG
POOR FAMILIES WITH CHILDREN

Country	Percentage distribution of wives in poor families			
	No wives' earnings	Wives' earnings less than the poverty gap	Wives' earnings greater than the poverty gap	Total
Australia	71.8	6.8	21.4	100
Canada	47.4	8.7	43.9	100
Germany, F.R.	57.1	4.3	38.6	100
Norway	22.0	12.3	65.6	100
Sweden	20.5	4.5	75.0	100
Switzerland	29.7	—	70.3	100
United Kingdom	62.4	5.6	32.0	100
United States	41.0	15.7	43.3	100

Source: Same as table 5.1.
Note: Poor families include only those with two parents and one or more children.
Poverty is computed by taking disposable income and subtracting wives' earnings
and means-tested transfer benefits.

into play. Wives' earnings potentially can substitute for any of
several income sources—in particular, the earnings of other family
members or means-tested benefits. A theory of income-generating
dynamics and substitution is needed to fully disentangle the story.
Such a theory is beyond the scope of this chapter. Fortunately, when
we tried several different scenarios of where wives' income enters
the process, we found that it makes much less difference to the basic
story than we had expected.

In this analysis we assume that wives' earnings come next to last
in the income-generating process of families, with means-tested
welfare as the income of last resort. Thus, we counted all income
sources *except* wives' earnings and means-tested benefits. Then we
computed the number of families in poverty and the poverty gap
for three different earnings positions of wives living in families with
children: wives without earnings, wives whose earnings were larger
than the poverty gap, and wives who earned less than the poverty
gap (table 5.10). Three patterns emerge: countries in which about
two-thirds or more of the wives do not work (Australia, the United
Kingdom), countries in which roughly half the wives work, (Canada,
the United States, West Germany), and countries in which more
than two-thirds of the wives work (Norway, Sweden, and Switzerland). The pattern is relatively consistent across countries: the higher

the proportion of wives who work, the higher the proportion of wives whose earnings move their family out of poverty.

These findings indicate that, for the two-thirds of children who live in families with two parents, wives' work behavior can play an important role in prevention of poverty for the children. Of course, we do not know what the economic position of the family would be if the wife did not work. It seems likely that some of the families would have turned to means-tested benefits. But in cases where such substitution occurs, countries may differ in the extent to which these benefits move a family out of poverty, as discussed later in the chapter.

■ *INCOME INEQUALITY*

Poverty may occur not only when average incomes are low, but also when incomes are unequal. How well does the proportion of poverty in a country correlate with the degree of inequality? Our evidence indicates that the relationship is not strong. We measured the distribution of incomes for various groups within a population as well as overall for the eight countries in our study (using the Gini coefficient as our measure).[7] In all countries except Sweden, incomes were less equal among the elderly than among families with children. And in all countries but Sweden and Norway, inequality among single-parent families was higher than among the elderly. Income inequality among all groups was higher in the United States than in any of the other countries, with Canada next on the list.

The level of income inequality among families with children is only somewhat related to their poverty rates. The United States, which had the highest levels of overall inequality, for example, had the highest child poverty rates; Sweden had the lowest levels of inequality and lowest child poverty. However, child poverty rates are the same in Switzerland as in Sweden, despite significantly higher overall levels of inequality among families with children in Switzerland. And the child poverty rate is much higher in Australia than in Canada and West Germany, despite similar or lower overall inequality levels among families with children in Australia.

This direct relationship is even weaker for the elderly. The United States and Canada, which have the highest inequality, have the fourth and second lowest poverty rates. Inequality among the British elderly is (tied with Switzerland) third lowest of the eight countries, but absolute poverty rates are by far the highest in the United Kingdom among the countries studied. The wage replacement ratio of the British social pensions for the elderly is similar to the wage replacement ratios of Canada and West Germany (Smeeding and Torrey 1986). But the wages themselves were sufficiently low that, even with a relatively low degree of inequality, the average elderly family in the United Kingdom had a relatively low income and therefore more poverty.

■ *THE INCOME SUPPORT SYSTEM*

The income support system, as already noted, helps explain different poverty patterns across countries. Government programs among the eight countries studied vary considerably in how much they provide to their poverty populations and through which mixes of programs, and comparisons of the roles of these various government programs suggest that different social philosophies are embedded in the transfer programs of the industrialized countries studied.

These different social philosophies can be divided into three types: (1) *selective strategies*, which seek target efficiency through categorical, income, and asset-tested standards of eligibility; (2) *social insurance*, under which entitlement is based on the past contribution of employer, employee, or both, thus depending on a history of attachment to paid employment and linked not to need but to work; and (3) *universal entitlement programs*, based on common citizenship in society, of which children's allowances are the prototype.[8]

Alongside this system of benefits is the structure of taxation. Countries differ enormously in how much the structure of taxes affects poverty. For example, the tax system increases poverty among families with children in Canada by less than 1 percent, in Sweden by as much as 12 percent. The role of transfers can only be assessed appropriately in combination with the role of taxes.

Social insurance benefits are not means-tested and therefore go to both poor and nonpoor. The tax systems in every country studied, however, are related to overall incomes. For this reason, the countries that rely heavily on social insurance programs to help the poor also have higher effective tax rates, even among the poor, to recover some of their broadly distributed benefits. The United States, for example, which provides most of its income support to poor families through income- and means-tested programs, and much less via social insurance (which in turn is not heavily taxed), has one of the lowest effective tax rates on poor families. In this section we assess the role of specific types of transfers in filling the poverty gap—the difference between resources before taxes and transfers and needs, as measured by the absolute poverty line adjusted for family size.

Table 5.11   ROLE OF PUBLIC TRANSFERS IN REDUCING THE POVERTY GAP
AMONG CHILDREN AND THE ELDERLY

Family type and country	Poverty gap reduction rate[a]	Percentage of total poverty gap reduction			
		Social insurance	Means-tested program	Child allowances	Total
Families with children					
Australia	0.71	—	87	13	100
Canada	0.85	38	48	14	100
Germany, F.R.	1.06	68	11	21	100
Norway	1.05	86	3	11	100
Sweden	1.76	52	37	11	100
Switzerland	0.91	93	7	—	100
United Kingdom	1.17	38	38	24	100
United States	0.65	29	71	—	100
Single-parent families					
Australia	0.71	—	88	12	100
Canada	0.75	19	69	12	100
Germany, F.R.	0.84	67	16	18	100
Norway	1.13	83	4	13	100
Sweden	2.03	45	45	10	100
Switzerland	0.78	92	8	—	100
United Kingdom	0.90	15	63	22	100
United States	0.58	7	93	—	100
Elderly families					
Australia	1.30	—	100	—	100
Canada	1.61	94	6	—	100
Germany, F.R.	1.56	99	1	—	100
Norway	1.24	99	1	—	100
Sweden	2.42	94	6	—	100
Switzerland	1.92	95	5	—	100
United Kingdom	1.10	91	9	—	100
United States	1.48	93	7	—	100

Source: Same as table 5.1.
a. This rate is calculated by dividing total public transfers to the pretax/pretransfer poor by the total poverty gap.

The relative effectiveness of the transfer systems of the eight countries in filling their poverty gaps for children and the elderly is shown in the first column of table 5.11. All countries more than fill the poverty gap for elderly families, but the United Kingdom does least well in this respect. The United States is in the middle of the group. All countries do less well in filling the poverty gap for families with children than they do for the elderly, and four of the eight do not fill the entire gap. The United States is conspicuously at the bottom of the list, filling less than two-thirds of the gap—even below Australia, which is a considerably poorer country. For single-parent families all except the two Scandinavian countries do worse than for all families with children. The United States is again at the bottom, and again below Australia.

One can gain further insight into the differences by looking at the main categories of transfer by family type (the rest of table 5.11). For the elderly in all countries except Australia, the vast majority of the transfers are social insurance. For families with children, however, countries differ. In four of the eight countries (Norway, Sweden, Switzerland, and West Germany) non-means-tested social insurance benefits provide considerably more income than means-tested welfare benefits for all families with children, and in three of the four (Norway, Switzerland, and West Germany) the same is true for single-parent families.

The two countries that fill least of the poverty gap for all families with children (Australia and the United States) depend much more heavily on means-tested benefits than the other six countries. And four of the six countries that fail to fill the poverty gap for single-parent families rely more heavily on means-tested than on social insurance benefits for that group. Only Switzerland and West Germany of the countries that fail to fill the poverty gap for this group depend primarily on social insurance.

Perhaps the most interesting finding from table 5.11 is the critical role that social insurance programs play relative to children's allowances in reducing the poverty gap. It might be expected that, in countries that have them, child-related benefits such as child allowances and maternity grants would be an important source in filling the poverty gap for families with children. In fact, social insurance benefits (which are primarily employment-related) are overwhelmingly more important in every country with both kinds of benefits save for U.K. single parents with children.

The proportions of families in poverty before taxes and transfers, after taxes, and after taxes and transfers provide additional insight into the differences among countries. These are shown in table 5.12, along with the overall poverty reduction rates. Note that a poverty reduction rate can be low either because initial poverty was low (see Switzerland for all families with children) or because the system is not very effective (see the United States for single-parent families).

Table 5.12 ROLE OF PUBLIC TRANSFERS IN REMOVING FAMILIES FROM
POVERTY, CHILDREN AND THE ELDERLY

Family type and country	Proportion of formerly poor families			Overall poverty reduction rate
	Pretax/ pretransfer	Pretransfer/ posttax	Posttax/ posttransfer	
Families with children				
Australia	17.6	19.9	15.0	14.8
Canada	13.6	14.4	8.6	36.8
Germany, F.R.	7.9	15.0	6.9	12.7
Norway	12.1	15.9	6.4	47.1
Sweden	10.4	22.5	4.4	57.7
Switzerland	4.4	6.2	4.1	6.8
United Kingdom	14.1	20.6	8.5	39.7
United States	16.6	18.0	13.8	16.9
Single-parent families				
Australia	67.6	71.2	61.4	9.2
Canada	48.0	49.1	35.3	26.5
Germany, F.R.	37.2	47.1	31.9	14.2
Norway	35.2	40.8	17.6	50.0
Sweden	33.1	49.4	7.5	77.3
Switzerland	14.5	17.9	11.9	17.9
United Kingdom	53.1	59.6	36.8	30.7
United States	49.3	51.4	42.9	13.0
Elderly families				
Australia	72.2	74.1	23.8	67.0
Canada	56.8	57.6	5.9	89.6
Germany, F.R.	80.6	82.2	17.1	78.8
Norway	76.6	81.3	19.6	74.4
Sweden	87.9	98.1	2.6	97.0
Switzerland	59.8	65.6	7.3	87.8
United Kingdom	77.6	80.8	40.9	47.3
United States	59.0	59.8	18.7	68.3

Source: Same as table 5.1.

Comparing the first two columns of table 5.12 provides an indication of how much the tax systems in the various countries take
from the poor. As already noted, the big effects are going to be seen
for the countries that depend most heavily on non-mean-tested
transfers. Australia, Canada, and the United States have the lowest
tax bite on all families with children and on single-parent families
(the smallest differences between the first two columns). The tax
system also takes more from families with children and single-
parent families in all countries than from elderly families.

Table 5.13   AVERAGE POVERTY GAP OF FAMILIES WHO WERE STILL POOR
AFTER TAXES AND TRANSFERS

	Type of household	
Country	Families with children	Elderly families
Australia	31.6	12.6
Canada	31.4	22.7
Germany, F.R.	24.1	26.5
Norway	25.4	18.8
Sweden	28.4	3.0
Switzerland	28.8[a]	19.8[a]
United Kingdom	21.4	16.4
United States	37.7	29.3

Source: Same as table 5.1.
Note: The poverty gap is the difference between the average income of the poor
and the poverty line divided by the poverty line.
a. Some Swiss families who are poor after taxes and transfers have little net
income because of large tax losses. These anomalies have been eliminated from the
Swiss data.

The proportion of families left poor after taxes and transfers is
shown in the third column of table 5.12. The ranking is consistent
with the findings on the poverty gap reductions of the previous
table. The United States again leaves more families with children
and more single-parent families poor than any other country. And
its poverty reduction rate for those two groups is lower than the
rates for all countries except Australia (which is poorer than the
United States) and Switzerland (which has relatively little pretax-
pretransfer poverty).

Pretax-pretransfer poverty is much higher for the elderly in all
countries than it is for all families with children and somewhat
higher than for single-parent families. This is to be expected because
most pretransfer income comes from earnings. The overall poverty
reduction rate is also invariably much higher than for the other
groups. Even so, only Sweden virtually eliminates poverty among
the elderly, and the United States does less well than four other
countries (Canada, Sweden, Switzerland, and West Germany).[9]

It remains to look at how far into poverty the families who are
left in poverty sink in the different countries. This can be measured
by the average poverty gap after taxes and transfers (table 5.13). The
poor performance of the United States with respect to families with
children is as conspicuous here as in earlier tables; no other country
has a larger poverty gap for those families after taxes and transfers.

With the exception of West Germany, families with children are in deeper poverty than elderly families. In the United States, for example, the poverty gap for families with children is over one-quarter larger than the gap for elderly households. However, the posttax-posttransfer poor elderly in the United States are worse off than the comparable group in other countries.

CONCLUSIONS

In the United States over the past decade (1976–86), the official poverty rates for the elderly and for children have diverged considerably, with child poverty rising from 15.8 percent to 19.8 percent and elderly poverty declining from 15.0 percent to 12.4 percent. If noncash transfers in the form of food, housing, or medical care were included in the income definition for determining poverty, the differences between poverty among the elderly and among children would be even wider (U.S. Bureau of the Census 1985). Other chapters in this volume have made these points as well. The contribution of this chapter is to compare poverty rates and incomes of children and elderly in the United States with those in several other nations.

The patterns of income and poverty described here suggest more diversity among eight modern Western industrial nations than generally suspected. The relative economic status of the young and old varies considerably by country. There is, however, more similarity in the economic status of the elderly in the eight countries than of families with children, largely because of the similarity of government programs for the elderly, and the levels of benefits provided through the income tax and transfer systems in general, and the social insurance systems in particular. The economic status of children varies much more than the status of the elderly; so does the variety of transfer approaches and level of benefits provided to poor families.

The poverty of American children contrasts glaringly with the poverty of the young in every other country but Australia (the country with the lowest adjusted median family income among the eight included in the comparison). The poverty rate for American children was 70 percent higher than the rate for children in Canada, our closest neighbor. In fact, American children are not only at a disadvantage relative to American elderly; they are at a disadvantage relative to their peers in all the other countries examined here, except Australia. The reasons for this relative disadvantage seem straightforward:

□ The high U.S. rates of poverty and low income for children are due neither to an inordinately high proportion of children in the population share, nor to a measurement quirk (for example, choice of equivalence scales or low-income or poverty measure), nor to overall levels of income inequality.

□ Neither poor minority populations nor a preponderance of single-parent families adequately explains high U.S. poverty rates for children. Our minorities do have higher poverty rates than the white majority, but so do minorities in other countries. Our poverty rate for majority families with children is still second highest among the countries studied.

□ Although the United States has proportionately more single-parent families than several of the other countries have, the American families are economically much more vulnerable. They have both more income inequality and more poverty than similar families elsewhere.[10]

□ The income transfer system for families with children in the United States seems to be the main reason for these high poverty rates. It relies on categorical means-tested programs much more than do other countries (with the exception of Australia) to provide benefits to poor children. Despite their presumably more effective targeting, countries that rely on means testing seem politically unable or unwilling to raise benefits high enough to be as effective in moving children out of poverty as universal and social insurance approaches. This situation is particularly glaring in the United States, where the level of benefits in comparison to the poverty line is lower than for all countries except Switzerland.

□ The ineffectiveness of the U.S. system is further exacerbated by its categorical nature, which excludes most poor two-parent families with children from public support. Even Australia has a modest universal child allowance program.

The social welfare programs of each country can be seen as a reflection of its social philosophy. Some national programs implicitly favor one group over another. Some programs are considered a right of the beneficiaries (social insurance) or a right of all citizens (universal programs); others are considered a favor (means-tested). Some programs and philosophies may be transferable across borders; others, almost certainly, are not. In particular, the lack of U.S. commitment (through the transfer system) to securing minimum decent standards for poor children stands in sharp contrast to the commitment of other countries studied here. Although the U.S. public safety net does an average-to-above-average job for the otherwise needy elderly, many poor families with children in the United States are largely excluded from the safety net, and those who are not excluded receive inadequate benefits.

This chapter has focused on economic status under the social programs of eight countries in operation about three-quarters of the way through the twentieth century. In this context, the situation of American children is comparatively bleak. Although any changes in social welfare programs must be made in the context of the social philosophy of the country concerned, international comparisons of social systems and their economic consequences help define a range of options available to national policymakers. These comparisons also provide encouragement for improvements, because no economic outcome seems either immutable or inevitable in our modern industrial societies.

Notes

1. The West German data set excludes households with foreign-born heads, as well as the homeless and the institutionalized; the Swiss data set excludes nonresident foreigners.

2. The reader may wonder about the sensitivity of these estimates to choice of equivalence scales and income concepts. Tables identical to table 5.1 using the LIS equivalence scale indicate virtually the same pattern as that shown here. Unadjusted incomes indicate a lower income for the elderly but, in general, a higher income for younger childless couples than for younger families with children. Per capita incomes (household income per family member) indicate a higher relative income for the elderly in all countries.

3. Some data sets are for 1981 and some for 1979; the U.S. poverty line and OECD purchasing power parities for the correct year were used in each case. The 1979 and 1981 U.S. poverty lines differ only by the change in the Consumer Price Index over that period. For Switzerland (1982 data) and Australia (1981–82 data), adjustments were made for the appropriate year using the same procedure.

4. For example, Swiss and U.S. median incomes (in 1979 U.S. dollars) are virtually identical. The poverty line in both countries (using the U.S. standard) is also the same proportion (42 percent) of median income. However, the Swiss poverty rate is 47.4 percent below its low-income rate, whereas the U.S. poverty rate is 33 percent below its low-income rate. In summary, changes in the poverty rate depend on a host of factors including equivalence scales, overall inequality, and group incomes, not just the relationship between half of the median income and the U.S. poverty line. Tables 5.3 and 5.4 are designed to illustrate this sensitivity.

5. If the British supplemental benefit and housing allowance levels are added together to construct a British "poverty measure," the poverty rate among the British elderly drops to 2.6 percent.

6. Standardizing poverty rates among the elderly as was done for children in table 5.7 did not much affect the results in table 5.8, so these figures are not shown here.

7. The Gini coefficient measures the deviation of the actual distribution of income from perfect equality. It ranges from zero to one, with numbers closer to one indicating more inequality.

8. In practice these social philosophies are often mixed. Sweden's housing allowance provides an excellent example. It is based only on a test of income; assets such as property and savings are not taken into account. Moreover, it is an income-tested program that reaches more than half of all families with children and thus goes a long way toward being a universal program. Comparing income-tested Swedish housing allowances with American style means-tested AFDC—which reaches less than 20 percent of poor families with children—can therefore be misleading, even though both are selective programs based on a test of need. This reservation notwithstanding, the threefold classification effectively captures the philosophical differences among countries and the resulting differences in patterns of poverty alienation.

9. The high West German and Swedish social insurance and taxes on the elderly are part of the same package. In these countries, means testing of transfers is accomplished largely through the income tax system, which includes virtually all social insurance and other public transfers in the tax base.

10. Australia is the only country of the eight that has higher poverty among single-parent families than the United States. Even so, Australia has a smaller posttax-posttransfer poverty gap for these families (26.5 percent) than does the United States (32.2 percent).

References

Achdut, Lea, and Yosi Tamir. Forthcoming. "Comparative Economic Status of the Retired and Nonretired Elderly." In *Poverty, Inequality and the Distribution of Income in an International Context: Initial Research from the Luxembourg Income Study (LIS)*, edited by T. Smeeding, M. O'Higgins, and L. Rainwater. London: Wheatsheaf Books.

Organization for Economic Cooperation and Development (OECD). 1985. *Social Expenditure 1960–1990*, OECD Social Policy Studies Reports. Paris: OECD.

Preston, Samuel. 1984. "Children and the Elderly: Divergent Paths for America's Dependents," *Demography* 21:435–57.

Rein, Martin. 1970. "Problems in the Definition of Measurement of Poverty." In P. Townsend, *The Concept of Poverty*. London: Heinemann Education Books, Limited.

Smeeding, Timothy, Gunther Schmaus, and Serge Allegreza. 1985. "An Introduction to LIS." Luxembourg Income Study-CEPS Working Paper no. 1, presented to the First LIS Research Conference, Luxembourg, July.

Smeeding, Timothy, and Barbara Boyle Torrey. 1986. "An International Perspective on the Income and Poverty Status of the U.S. Aged: Lessons from LIS and the International Database on Aging." LIS-CEPS Working Paper no. 9, December.

Torrey, Barbara Boyle, and Timothy Smeeding. 1988. "Poor Children in Rich Countries." Paper presented to the Population Association of America, New Orleans, April 21–23.

U.S. Bureau of the Census. 1987. "Monthly Income and Poverty Status of Families and Persons in the U.S.: 1986." *Current Population Reports*, series P-60, no. 157. Washington, D.C., July.

————. 1985 "Estimates of Poverty Including the Value of Noncash Benefits: 1984." Technical Paper no. 55. Washington, D.C., August.

Part Two

OTHER RESOURCES AND MEASURES OF WELL-BEING

Chapter Six

RELATIVE WEALTH HOLDINGS OF CHILDREN AND THE ELDERLY IN THE UNITED STATES, 1962–83

Daphne T. Greenwood and Edward N. Wolff

The wealth of a nation has long been a topic of interest to national leaders and the distribution of that wealth to social reformers. The difficulty of collecting comprehensive and accurate data on wealth has restricted the information available on family wealth in the United States, and even less data are available in most other industrial countries. Recent evidence does indicate sharp declines in the inequality of the distribution of personal wealth among families in several of the other industrial countries (see Shorrocks 1987, and Spant 1987, for example). Data for the United States show that inequality in the distribution of wealth declined from the early 1920s through the late 1940s (Smith 1987, Wolff and Marley forthcoming). Since that time wealth inequality has remained relatively stable, except for cyclical fluctuations. Comparisons of the distribution of wealth during the past two decades indicate declines in most measures of inequality during the decade of the 1970s, followed by increasing inequality in the early 1980s (Wolff 1987a). Indeed, the level of overall wealth inequality in 1983 appears to be little changed from that of 1962.

In this chapter we consider whether there has been any major change in the relative wealth holdings of the elderly and the young in this country from 1962 to 1983. We present data on wealth holdings by age and by families with and without children for 1962, 1973, and 1983, and we analyze the available evidence on trends in inequality between and within these groups.[1] Where possible, comparisons are made with other industrial countries.

WEALTH AND WELL-BEING

It is useful to consider the stock of wealth as well as the flow of income available to the various age groups when evaluating their relative well-being. Income statistics in the United States are generally based on census data (or on the annual *Current Population Survey* for noncensus years). Although coverage of wage and salary income and of transfer income is relatively good, these data substantially understate property income such as dividends and interest. In some years, reported income is less than half of what the national balance sheets indicate it should be. It is therefore wholly inadequate to use conventional income statistics to represent the distribution of asset income in this country.

In addition, it has been shown that rates of return on various types of wealth vary widely between years and within any one year (Steuerle 1984). Even well-reported asset income numbers would yield an incomplete picture of the wealth from which they flow. Other types of wealth may yield no income at all in any one year. Wealth and income are positively correlated, but in a recent attempt to explain variations in wealth holdings by various factors, census money income raised the amount of variation explained only from 6 percent to 17 percent (Greenwood 1987). Age explains part of the variation in the wealth-income ratio, but much remains unexplained (see also Radner and Vaughan 1987). As a result of this unexplained variability, wealth as an indicator of relative well-being gives a different ranking, in both ordinal and cardinal terms, than does income.

A family's current holdings of wealth depend on four factors. The first is the accumulated value of family members' labor earnings and transfers received from the start of their working lives to the present. The second is the amount of savings from income, and the third is the rate of return realized on the value of family assets. The fourth is the amount of gifts and inheritances the family has received to date (less the gifts and transfers made to others). It is apparent that wealth will depend, in part, on age because older families will tend to have more accumulated work experience. Moreover, wealth and income will be more highly correlated for families in the same age group than for the population as a whole, because current labor earnings are highly correlated with past labor earnings and property income is a direct function of wealth holdings. There is still substantial variation in this relationship, however, because savings rates, asset yields, and—most important—gifts and inheritances received may differ greatly among families of the same age and with the same income.

Family wealth is also a source of well-being, independent of the financial income it provides. There are three reasons for this. First, certain assets, most notably owner-occupied housing, provide services directly to their owner. This is true also for consumer durables, such as automobiles. Such assets can substitute for income in satisfying economic needs. Families that receive the same money income but differ in the stock of consumer durables and housing that they own will enjoy different levels of well-being.[2] This factor is particularly important in assessing the well-being of children, who benefit directly from the services that housing supplies. Indeed, failure to consider owner-occupied housing in comparisons between the elderly and the young may introduce bias, because more than three-fourths of the elderly own their own homes, a much higher proportion than is true for younger families.

Second, wealth is a source of consumption, independent of the income it provides. With the possible exception of consumer durables, assets can be converted directly into cash and thus provide for consumption needs. This is true for the equity in owner-occupied housing, for example, because second mortgages are a relatively available source of credit. This additional dimension to consumption possibilities is also important in evaluating the well-being of children, for whom family wealth may be the primary source for financing educational expenses.

Third, other financial and business assets can provide a cushion of safety for medical bills or other large expenses that arise or for periods of unemployment. In this sense, wealth is a source of economic security for the family over and above the income it receives.[3]

MEASUREMENT OF WEALTH

Wealth refers to the net value of a stock of assets held at any one time, in contrast to *income*, which refers to a flow of dollars over some period of time. Here we use the term wealth to represent the current value of all marketable or fungible assets (such as stocks and bonds, real estate, bank accounts, unincorporated businesses, and other personal possessions) less the current value of debts. We also call this *net worth*. Technically, our definition of wealth is the difference between total family assets and total family liabilities or debt. Total assets are the sum of the value of owner-occupied housing; other real estate owned by the family; cash, demand deposits, time and savings deposits, certificates of deposit, and money market funds; government bonds, corporate bonds, foreign bonds, and other financial securities; the cash surrender value of life insurance plans; the cash surrender value of pensions; unincorporated farm and nonfarm business equity; corporate stocks; and equity in trust funds. Total liabilities are the sum of mortgage debt, consumer debt, and other debt.

We use this measure of wealth because we are interested primarily in wealth as a store of value and hence a source of potential consumption. We believe that this is the concept that best reflects the level of well-being associated with family assets. Thus, we include only assets that can be readily converted to cash (that is, "fungible" ones). As a result, we exclude two kinds of assets that are normally included in broader concepts of wealth: consumer durables and retirement wealth.

Consumer durables are automobiles, television sets, family appliances, furniture, and the like. Although these items provide consumption services directly to the family, they are not easily marketed. Indeed, the resale value of these items usually far understates the value of the consumption services they provide to the family. Retirement wealth includes pensions and Social Security. Pension wealth is usually defined as the present value of the future stream of pension benefits a worker receives following retirement. Social Security wealth is usually defined as the present value of Social Security benefits received following retirement. As is immediately apparent from these definitions, such wealth is not fungible or marketable, because people cannot convert these assets into cash. The only exceptions are certain forms of pension plans that allow workers to convert their accumulated pension contributions into lump-sum payments for immediate use upon retirement. This so-called cash surrender value of pensions represents a small fraction of the total value of pension wealth, and it is included in the concept of net worth that we are using here. Because Social Security and pension wealth have received considerable attention in the literature in recent years (see Feldstein 1974, Wolff 1988), we comment about them further in the conclusion.

Information on wealth is less readily available than information on income for a variety of reasons. Most countries collect income statistics for tax purposes or through surveys on an annual basis. But systematic procedures for collecting information on assets are rare; and in countries where such data exist, they do not typically cover all types of assets and hence do not measure total family wealth. Wealth is difficult to measure because it requires the valuation of many types of assets, some of which may not be frequently traded (land, antiques, etc.). In addition, response rates on voluntary surveys of wealth are typically quite low.

Our analysis covers three years: 1962, 1973, and 1983. For 1962 and 1983 we use the extensive surveys conducted under the auspices of the Federal Reserve Board, the *1962 Survey of Financial Characteristics of Consumers* (SFCC), and the *1983 Survey of Consumer Finances* (SCF). Both samples included high-income supplements and asked detailed questions regarding assets and debts of the respondents.[4] For 1973 we use a merged data set of income tax returns and census data that oversampled high income families to which net wealth has been imputed (see Greenwood 1983 for a description).[5] For consistency, the asset and liability figures for each of the three years have been aligned to national balance sheet totals for the family sector provided in Ruggles and Ruggles (1982). Dollars have been converted to 1985 levels using the Consumer Price Index for all items.

DISTRIBUTION OF WEALTH BY AGE, 1962–83

For each of the three years, our data contain net worth by family, with information on the number of adults and children in the family and the age of the family head. In the tables that follow, we examine the distribution of wealth among and between the elderly, children, and other adults in several different ways. First, we look at the distribution of wealth among families by age group. Second, we look at the distribution of wealth among families with and without children, also by age group. Third, we examine the distribution of wealth among individuals by age group when family wealth is adjusted by an equivalence scale measure to account for economies of consumption that occur in larger families.

In addition to looking at the average and relative wealth of each of these groups, we examine the distribution of wealth within each group and the degree of wealth inequality (defined later). These measures of distribution of wealth are as important as the comparisons of averages because the distribution of wealth varies a great deal within every group, so the average is not representative of the "typical" individual or family.

Wealth by Age Group

Differences in age have often been cited as one reason for the high degree of inequality in the distribution of wealth consistently found in the United States, the United Kingdom, and all industrial countries for which data are available. The most common explanation is based on the life-cycle theory of wealth accumulation, first developed by Modigliani and Brumberg (1954). According to the life-cycle model, the primary motivation for family saving is to provide for consumption expenditures during retirement years. Thus, families will typically accumulate savings during their working years. When they retire, families will start to draw down their accumulated wealth to pay for consumption needs. The model thus predicts what is called the hump-shaped or inverted U-shaped wealth profile by age. Wealth should rise with age until at or near retirement age, which is typically 65 in the United States, and then decline. In the crudest form of the model, net worth should fall to zero at time of death.

Considerable empirical work has been done to verify or disprove the life-cycle model, which we shall not review here.[6] Our own results from table 6.1 follow the expected hump-shaped profile, with mean wealth (in constant 1985 dollars) at its highest for families headed by persons between the ages of 55 and 59 in 1962 and for families headed by persons ages 65 to 69 in 1973 and 1983. However, if we were to follow each of these groups across the three decades, we would not find a systematic life-cycle pattern for all groups, with accumulation of family wealth followed by a drawing down of wealth after a certain age. Economic growth generally causes succeeding groups to be better off than their predecessors and tends to bias cross-sectional data toward the life-cycle pattern. Conversely, higher mortality rates among the poor may cause average wealth among surviving elderly to be higher than it would have been had there been no correlation between wealth and longevity. A more detailed analysis of these effects and of the degree of validity of the life-cycle model is beyond the scope of this chapter.[7]

In 1962, mean family wealth was lower than average for the youngest three age groups, about average for the 45- to 54-year-old group, greater than average for groups between 55 and 79 years of age, and about average for the 80-and-older age group. Mean family wealth increased with age from a low of 12 percent of the average for the youngest age group to a peak of 83 percent above average for those ages 55 to 59. The differential fell to 33 percent for those ages 60 to 64 and then rose to 73 percent for those ages 65 to 69. Then

Table 6.1 HOUSEHOLD WEALTH BY AGE GROUP, 1962–83 (1985 dollars)

Age group	1962		1973		1983		Ratio of mean values			1983 to 1962 Ratio of means ÷ ratio of overall means
	Mean value	Ratio to overall mean	Mean value	Ratio to overall mean	Mean value	Ratio to overall mean	1973–62	1983–73	1983–62	
Under 65	90,770	0.88	86,481	0.85	133,820	0.89	0.95	1.55	1.47	1.02
Under 25	12,244	0.12	25,707	0.25	14,447	0.10	2.10	0.56	1.18	0.81
25–34	34,674	0.34	59,624	0.59	49,046	0.33	1.72	0.82	1.41	0.97
35–44	79,162	0.77	92,186	0.91	123,471	0.83	1.16	1.34	1.56	1.07
45–54	106,779	1.04	108,615	1.07	235,478	1.57	1.02	2.17	2.21	1.52
55–59	188,943	1.83	118,617	1.17	247,456	1.65	0.63	2.09	1.31	0.90
60–64	136,633	1.33	124,786	1.23	262,863	1.76	0.91	2.11	1.92	1.33
65 and over	156,397	1.52	161,051	1.59	227,464	1.52	1.03	1.41	1.45	1.00
65–69	177,879	1.73	169,366	1.67	321,562	2.15	0.95	1.90	1.81	1.25
70–74	158,984	1.54	164,091	1.62	196,863	1.32	1.03	1.20	1.24	0.85
75–79	147,920	1.43	136,022	1.34	185,291	1.24	0.92	1.36	1.25	0.86
80 and over	111,747	1.08	168,441	1.66	143,351	0.96	1.51	0.85	1.28	0.88
All	103,108	1.00	101,293	1.00	149,659	1.00	0.98	1.48	1.45	1.00

Sources: Computations by authors from the 1962 Survey of Financial Characteristics of Consumers; the 1973 Census/Tax File Merge; and the 1983 Survey of Consumer Finances.

came a steady decline of mean wealth with age group, with families headed by persons age 80 or over at average wealth. Overall, the mean wealth of elderly families (those age 65 and over) was 52 percent greater than average, whereas mean wealth of the nonelderly families was 12 percent below average.

In 1973 the youngest three age groups had lower-than-average wealth, as they did in 1962. However, the relative position of each group improved, compared to 1962. The relative wealth of the youngest group increased from 12 percent to 25 percent of the average of the respective years; that of the 25-to-34 age group increased from 34 percent to 59 percent of average; and that of the 35-to-44 age group from 77 percent to 91 percent of average. The relative position of the 45-to-54 age group remained almost unchanged between 1962 and 1973, whereas the relative standing of all the older age groups declined over the period, with the exception of the 70-to-74 age group and those age 80 and older. In 1973 the highest wealth level—67 percent above average—was achieved by the 65-to-69 age group. This is the same group who were between the ages of 55 and 59 in 1962 and had the highest mean wealth of any group (83 percent above the overall mean) in that year. The elderly as a whole achieved average wealth holdings 59 percent higher than the overall mean in 1973, slightly higher than the 52 percent advantage a decade earlier. The mean wealth of families with heads under 65 years old was 85 percent of average wealth, slightly below the corresponding figure for 1962.

As in 1962 and 1973, the youngest three age groups in 1983 had below-average wealth. Moreover, the relative positions of the three groups in terms of wealth were almost identical to the 1962 rankings. The mean wealth of the 45-to-54 age group was 70 percent above average, compared with 4 percent above average in 1962 and 7 percent above average in 1973. The average relative wealth holdings of families in the 55-to-69 age range were all greater in 1983 than in 1973, while the relative wealth position of families age 70 and older declined between 1973 and 1983. The highest wealth was achieved by the 65-to-69 age group, as it was in 1973, but the peak was much higher in 1983, more than double average wealth. The mean wealth of the nonelderly stood at 89 percent of the overall mean in 1983, slightly greater than in 1973 but almost identical to the figure for 1962. Moreover, the mean wealth of the elderly was 52 percent above the overall mean in 1983, slightly less than the 59 percent differential in 1973, but identical to that of 1962.

All age groups showed gains in real net worth per family between

1962 and 1983. During this period, overall mean net worth per family grew by 45 percent—an average growth rate of 1.9 percent per year. During the first decade (1962–73), an absolute decline in stock prices and other financial assets caused a 2 percent decline in real mean net worth per family. During the subsequent decade (1973–83), the average growth rate per year increased to 3.9 percent, and the declines in real wealth were more than compensated. Rapidly rising real estate values in the late 1970s, the recovery of the stock market, and extremely high rates of interest occurred during this period.

All age groups gained over the 20-year period; however, gains were concentrated in the first decade for the two youngest and the oldest (age 80 and older) age groups. In contrast, most of the gains of families headed by persons between the ages of 35 and 79 occurred in the latter decade. These differentials by age group are probably related to the changes in portfolio composition associated with age. For younger families owning a home represents a large percentage of wealth on average. Older families typically hold a larger share of wealth in financial assets. As a result, changes in relative asset prices can substantially affect the distribution of wealth by age across time.

Families headed by persons between the ages of 45 and 54 in 1983 had more than double the real wealth that the same age group had in 1962, although overall wealth per family was 145 percent of what it had been in 1962. All other groups shared in the growth in real wealth generated by the U.S. economy over the two decades, but for some the share in growth was much less. There were relative gainers and losers among both the elderly and nonelderly, resulting in almost no net change in the relative position of either group over the 21-year period. The breakdown into 10-year age groups in table 6.1 indicates a shift in the distribution of wealth away from those under 35 years of age and those 70 and over, to families headed by persons in their mid-30s to their 60s.

This shift in relative well-being was due to two opposing trends. In the first half of the period, until 1973, it was the young families (those under age 55) and the very old (those 80 and over) who gained relatively and absolutely, while those families with heads between age 55 and 79 lost both absolute and relative ground. This pattern of relative winners and losers was almost exactly reversed in the second half of this period. Moreover, the latter trend considerably outweighed the former, leading to a fairly strong overall shift in wealth to families between 35 and 69 years of age.

Wealth of Families with and without Children

To determine the effect of this shift of wealth toward the middle-aged on the well-being of children, we must differentiate between young families that include children and those that do not. Because more than 25 percent of women have had their first child by age 20 and more than 60 percent by age 25, many families with children are likely to be headed by young adults under the age of 35 who have very low wealth holdings.

Table 6.2 shows the results for the mean wealth of each group. As already noted, the elderly held greater than average wealth in each of the three observation years over the 1962–83 period and showed no net change over the period as a whole. Families with children had below-average wealth in each of the three years. This is mainly because these families are young and have not had time to accumulate much wealth.

The most striking result is that the relative wealth position of families with children declined over the period from 78 percent of average in 1962 to 71 percent of average in 1983. In real terms, average wealth for families with children grew by 32 percent, compared with 45 percent overall; all the relative deterioration occurred after 1973. This is consistent with our earlier finding that the relative wealth holdings of younger families increased over the first decade of the 1962–83 period and declined over the second decade. Nonelderly families without children had mean wealth slightly above the overall mean in 1962 and 1983 and slightly below in 1973. Their average wealth in 1985 dollars was 40 percent higher at the end of the two decades than at the beginning, slightly below the average overall gain.

Wealth, like income, tends to be unevenly distributed among the population. This is true for each age group in the population, as well as for the three categories of families we are examining. In table 6.3, we present three measures of wealth inequality for each of these groups, as well as for the full population.

The ratio of median wealth to mean wealth as a measure of inequality is shown in the first three columns. Because of the unevenness of the wealth distribution, median family wealth is considerably less than mean family wealth. In 1962 median family net worth for the full population was 26 percent of mean family net worth; in 1973 it was 29 percent; and in 1983 it was 27 percent. Moreover, changes in median net worth will generally differ from those in mean net worth if the shape of the wealth distribution

Table 6.2 HOUSEHOLD WEALTH BY HOUSEHOLD STATUS, 1962–83

Age group	Mean wealth (1985 dollars)			Ratio to overall mean			Ratio of mean values		
	1962	1973	1983	1962	1973	1983	1973–62	1983–73	1983–62
65 and over	156,397	161,051	227,464	1.52	1.59	1.52	1.03	1.41	1.45
Under 65									
Without children	115,033	93,559	160,980	1.12	0.92	1.08	0.81	1.72	1.40
With children	80,649	82,051	106,487	0.78	0.81	0.71	1.02	1.30	1.32
Overall	103,108	101,293	149,659	1.00	1.00	1.00	0.98	1.48	1.45

Source: Same as table 6.1.

Table 6.3 WEALTH INEQUALITY WITHIN HOUSEHOLD GROUPS, 1962–83

Age group	Ratio of median to mean			Gini coefficient			Share of top 5 percent of households (percentage)		
	1962	1973	1983	1962	1973	1983	1962	1973	1983
65 and over	0.27	0.36	0.28	0.78	0.68	0.77	55.4	42.3	53.3
Under 65									
Without children	0.30	0.18	0.22	0.78	0.82	0.81	51.4	56.5	57.6
With children	0.22	0.24	0.27	0.79	0.81	0.78	54.5	59.2	48.8
Overall	0.26	0.29	0.27	0.80	0.79	0.80	55.0	54.8	54.7

Source: Same as table 6.1.

changes. In particular, if inequality increases, median wealth will increase less than mean wealth; if inequality declines, the opposite will be the case. Therefore, the ratio of median net worth to mean net worth is an indicator of the degree of inequality: the greater the ratio, the smaller the inequality.

The Gini coefficient as a measure of inequality is shown in the second three columns. It measures the deviation of the actual distribution of wealth from perfect equality. It ranges from zero to one in value, with numbers closer to one indicating more inequality.

There was almost no change in the degree of wealth inequality among the full population between 1962 and 1973 or between 1973 and 1983. For the elderly there was a sharp decline in inequality between 1962 and 1973, with the Gini coefficient falling from 0.78 to 0.68 and the share of the top 5 percent declining from 55.4 percent of total wealth to 42.3 percent. This decline in inequality was almost exactly reversed in the subsequent decade. As a result, there was almost no net change in wealth inequality among the elderly between 1962 and 1983.

For nonelderly families without children, there was a moderate rise in wealth inequality between 1962 and 1973, with the Gini coefficient increasing from 0.78 to 0.82 and the share of the top 5 percent from 51.4 percent to 57.6 percent. In the subsequent decade there was almost no change in the degree of inequality within this group.

For families with children the results differ according to the measure. The ratio of the median to mean indicates declining inequality between 1962 and 1973 and again between 1973 and 1983; the other two measures, in contrast, show increasing inequality in the first decade followed by declining inequality in the second. For the period as a whole, two of the measures indicate a fairly significant decline in inequality; but the Gini coefficient shows almost no net change between 1962 and 1983.

Thus, over the two decades, the elderly have remained at roughly the same—higher-than-average—wealth position relative to the rest of the population in the United States. Their absolute wealth has risen sharply, but their relative position and the degree of inequality within the group have remained stable. Nonelderly families without children have a slightly lower relative wealth position than 20 years ago; there is also somewhat higher inequality among them. Families with children now have average wealth holdings that are 32 percent higher than in 1962, but their *relative* wealth position is lower in comparison to the rest of the population. On balance, inequality seems to have fallen slightly within this group.

Table 6.4   INDIVIDUAL WEALTH OF CHILDREN, THE ELDERLY, AND OTHER
ADULTS, 1962–83

Age group	1962		1973		1983	
	Mean	Ratio to overall mean	Mean	Ratio to overall mean	Mean	Ratio to overall mean
Under 18	4,072	0.51	59,297	0.53	74,946	0.52
18–64	93,076	1.08	90,196	0.81	151,194	1.05
65 and over	215,203	2.51	217,534	1.96	326,382	2.26
Overall	85,867	1.00	111,105	1.00	144,411	1.00

Source: Same as table 6.1.
Note: Calculated using equivalence scale factors to adjust for differences in family
size.

In sum, elderly families have maintained the same relative wealth
position over the period, whereas nonelderly families have experienced a worsening in their relative position. If some groups are
relatively worse off, do other groups have to be better off? In this
case, the answer is no. Each group is being compared with the mean
wealth of all families. Because elderly families as a group have
higher-than-average wealth holdings, and because the proportion of
elderly families in the population has been growing during the past
two decades, the average level of family wealth has risen. Nonelderly
families appear somewhat worse off in relation to this average than
they did 20 years ago, whereas elderly families have maintained the
same relative position.

Wealth of Individuals: Children, Adults, and the Elderly

We convert our data on family wealth into a measure of individual
wealth by using an equivalence scale to adjust for economies of
consumption due to age and family size. We choose the poverty line
equivalence scale and divide family wealth by the appropriate factor
to yield "equivalence scale" wealth.

Children under age 18 have significantly lower access to wealth
on average than do adults 18 to 64 or the elderly (table 6.4). In all
three years, their equivalence scale level of wealth was half the
overall average. There are two reasons for this, both discussed earlier.
First, children tend to be found in large families. Second, children
tend to be found in families with below-average wealth, largely
because their parents are young.

The individual wealth of nonelderly adults was about average in all three years. In contrast, the elderly were more than twice as rich in terms of individual wealth as the average individual, and four to five times as rich as children. This is because the elderly are found in wealthier families, and their family size is typically small.

The relative position of children showed almost no change over the 1962–83 period, because of two counteracting trends. First, as shown in table 6.2 presented earlier, the average wealth of families with children declined over the period. Second, average size of families with children also declined. As a result, the average equivalence scale wealth of children remained almost unchanged. For nonelderly adults the trends were different but the net results the same. Their relative wealth position declined sharply between 1962 and 1973 and then increased sharply in the subsequent decade. The net result was no change in their relative wealth position. For the elderly, the directions of change over the two decades were the same as for nonelderly adults. However, in this case, the net change was a slight decline, from a level 2.5 times greater than average in 1962 to one 2.3 times greater than average in 1983.

A summary comparison of the degree of inequality in individual wealth distribution among children, adults, and the elderly is shown in table 6.5. It is notable that in 1962 the overall inequality in individual wealth was slightly higher than that in family wealth, whereas in the other two years the two were almost identical. Moreover, overall inequality in individual wealth declined between 1962 and 1983, with the Gini coefficient falling from 0.83 to 0.80. For the elderly, as with family wealth, the degree of inequality in individual wealth declined slightly between 1962 and 1983. The same was true for nonelderly adults over the period. However, among children, there was a substantial decline in the inequality of individual wealth over the period, with the Gini coefficient falling from 0.85 to 0.79 and the share of the top 5 percent from 59 percent to 47.5 percent.

Thus, the results based on individual data differ from those based on family data. Children as individuals have substantially less wealth than families with children; conversely, the elderly as individuals have substantially more wealth than elderly families. However, the individual measures indicate a 70 percent increase in real wealth for children, no change in the *relative* wealth position of children over the two decades, and a sharp decline in inequality among them. The elderly experienced a 52 percent increase in real wealth, a moderate decline in their relative wealth position, and a slight decrease in inequality.

Table 6.5   WEALTH INEQUALITY WITHIN INDIVIDUAL AGE GROUPS, 1962–83 (equivalence scale adjusted)

Age group	Gini coefficient			Ratio of median to mean			Share of top 5 percent of wealthholders (percentage)		
	1962	1973	1983	1962	1973	1983	1962	1973	1983
Under 18	0.85	0.82	0.79	0.19	0.24	0.26	58.9	59.8	47.5
18–64	0.82	0.81	0.80	0.23	0.25	0.24	55.3	57.6	55.1
65 and over	0.77	0.80	0.76	0.27	0.12	0.29	55.7	55.8	52.6
Overall	0.83	0.80	0.80	0.22	0.24	0.24	57.7	55.8	55.5

Source: Same as table 6.1

Table 6.6   SHARES OF HOUSEHOLD WEALTH, SELECTED COUNTRIES, BY AGE OF HOUSEHOLD HEAD, SELECTED YEARS, 1962–83

United States			Canada		Australia	
Age group	1962	1983	Age group	1977	Age group	1967
Under 25	0.01	0.02	Under 45	0.35	Under 30	0.05
25–34	0.07	0.09	45–64	0.47	30–39	0.17
35–44	0.17	0.16	65 and over	0.18	40–49	0.27
45–54	0.22	0.23	All	1.00	50–59	0.24
55–64	0.27	0.24			60 and over	0.27
65 and over	0.26	0.26			All	1.00
All	1.00	1.00				

Sources: U.S.: Computations by authors based on traditional net worth concept, including consumer durables and household inventories; Canada: Oja (1983); Australia: Podder and Kakwani (1976).

INTERNATIONAL COMPARISONS OF THE DISTRIBUTION OF WEALTH AMONG FAMILIES BY AGE

For countries other than the United States, the information on the distribution of wealth is limited, is generally not available for comparable years, and does not include strictly comparable definitions of wealth across countries. In some cases, it has been compiled by age groups but in no case by families with children and without. However, we can look at the share held by elderly families relative to that held by nonelderly families (and particularly those with heads under age 45) to get a general idea of how the young are faring relative to the elderly.

Our comparisons are limited to countries for which wealth by age group is available: Canada, Australia, and Japan. Table 6.6 shows the share of wealth held by age group, and table 6.7 shows the Gini measure of inequality within age groups. As can be seen, our comparisons are further limited by differences in age categories that researchers in other countries have used.

The share of wealth held by those under age 45 is much higher in Canada (35 percent) and Australia (45 percent) than in the United States for any of the years studied, according to table 6.6. The share of the elderly is correspondingly lower: 18 percent for those age 65 and older in Canada and 27 percent for those age 60 and older in Australia, compared with 26 percent for those 65 and older in the United States. This situation is attributable in part to differences in

Table 6.7   HOUSEHOLD WEALTH INEQUALITY WITHIN AGE GROUPS, SELECTED COUNTRIES AND YEARS (Gini coefficients)

United States			Canada		Australia		Japan	
Age group	1962	1983	Age group	1977	Age group	1967	Age group	1974
Under 25	0.38	0.52	Under 45	0.75	Under 30	0.52	Under 30	0.76
25–34	0.68	0.60	45–64	0.61	30–39	0.52	30–39	0.65
35–44	0.66	0.62	65 and over	0.59	40–49	0.47	40–49	0.59
45–54	0.66	0.73	All	0.69	50–59	0.49	50–59	0.51
55–64	0.68	0.70			60 and over	0.49	60 and over	0.59
65 and over	0.74	0.70			All	0.52	All	n.a.
All	0.72	0.73						

Source: Same as table 6.6
n.a. Not available.

the proportion of elderly in the population in the countries compared here. Australia, in 1967, had only 4.5 percent of elderly families in the population, in comparison with 9.5 percent in the United States in 1962. Canada also had a somewhat smaller proportion at 8.8 percent in 1977. Japan, in contrast, had the highest proportion of the elderly for comparisons in the mid-1970s, with around 11.5 percent of the population over age 60. Differences in the age distribution and the living arrangements of the elderly in Australia, Canada, Japan, and the United States suggest that these data should be interpreted with caution until they can be put on a more strictly comparable basis. In addition, there are some differences in survey coverage from country to country.

Wealth concentration as measured by the Gini coefficient is compared in table 6.7. (As noted, higher numbers indicate greater inequality.) In Canada in 1977 the Gini coefficient was 0.69, slightly lower than the 0.72 figure for the United States in 1962 and 0.73 in 1983. In Australia in 1967 the Gini inequality coefficient was only 0.52, very low for wealth distribution. Inequality coefficients of the various age classes are somewhat above the overall Gini for the youngest age groups and below the average for the upper age groups for both countries. In Japan the Gini coefficients by age group are high for the younger age groups (0.76 for families with heads younger than 25 and 0.65 for those with heads between the ages of 30 and 39), with declines to 0.51 and 0.59 for upper age groups.

These comparisons indicate that wealth inequality among the elderly is higher in the United States than in Australia, Canada, or Japan. In addition, the share of wealth held by the elderly as a group is higher in the United States than in other countries.

SUMMARY AND CONCLUSIONS

Between 1962 and 1983 families with heads under 35 years of age lost ground in relative terms. The evidence indicates a fairly substantial shift in family wealth away from those under age 35 and over age 69 to those between 35 and 69. This shift is a result of two opposing trends. In the first half of the period, families headed by persons under age 55 and over age 80 gained in relative and absolute terms. However, a reversal of this trend in the latter half of the period was strong enough to outweigh the initial gains of the young and the very old. Changes in the relative prices of corporate stock and real estate and interest rate increases may be responsible for these differential trends, because younger families tend to carry more debt and invest a larger proportion of their wealth in real estate, whereas older families own more corporate stock and interest-earning assets.

The downturn in mean wealth by age that has been observed to occur for the elderly in numerous cross-section studies is apparent in our data also; it is likely to be due in part to group effects. As successive groups have higher incomes during their lifetime and better pension systems to look forward to upon retirement, this downturn may not occur. But the negative effects of the labor force bulge of the baby boomers and of prohibitively high housing prices and interest rates for first-time buyers during the latter part of the 1970s may have a lifetime effect on the wealth profiles of the future elderly. Although we expect some trend among successive groups of the elderly to higher and more equally distributed wealth, the extremely favorable position of many of today's elderly may not be replicated.

When we group families into three categories—families with children, nonelderly families without children, and the elderly—it becomes clear that families with children have lost ground. Between 1962 and 1983 their relative wealth position declined by 9 percent. But wealth is now distributed somewhat more equally among this group than it was a generation ago. The elderly have changed neither in their relative position with regard to family wealth nor in the degree of wealth inequality within the group. Nonelderly families without children have a slightly lower relative wealth position and increased inequality within the group.

The relatively small gains in real wealth for young families with children compared with other groups reflect some negative group effects associated with reduced economic opportunity and greater tax burden in the 1970s. The sharp increase in housing prices and mortgage rates benefited those who owned homes in the 1970s but caused real difficulties for potential first-time buyers. The decreased real value of the personal exemption on the federal income tax caused families with children to be taxed at relatively higher rates than in earlier decades. In addition, the simultaneous entry into the labor force of the baby boom generation along with sharply higher participation rates for married women depressed wages and salaries for these people. Indeed, this group lost ground in terms of family wealth over the 1962–83 period relative to other groups despite the fact that there were many more two-earner families in this group in 1983 than in 1962.

The wealth patterns of various age groups change somewhat when we convert our figures to an individual wealth measure based on an equivalence scale. Real wealth has grown on average for all groups. In addition, the relative wealth position of children has not changed over the two decades. Although the average wealth holdings of families with children rose by less than the holdings of other groups, and thus their relative position was worse at the end of the period, the average size of families with children declined in corresponding fashion. The net effect was that the relative position of children with regard to individual wealth holdings remained unchanged over the period. Somewhat surprisingly, our measures of inequality indicate substantial increases in the equality of distribution among children during this period.

The elderly have experienced a moderate decline in their relative wealth measured on an individual basis and a slight decrease in inequality during this same period. However, on the basis of the limited international data we have been able to examine, we find that the share of wealth held by the elderly is lower in Australia and Canada than in the United States and that inequality among the elderly is also substantially lower in these countries and in Japan than in the United States.

Although there is no noticeable trend toward increasing wealth inequality—and, indeed, among children there has been a decline in wealth inequality over the past 25 years or so—the overall level of wealth inequality is still extraordinarily high in the United States.

This high level of wealth inequality in the United States is found within subgroups of the population as well. For the elderly, for example, the results suggest that some subgroups have particularly benefited from the increasing wealth of the elderly as a group. As the size of the elderly population grows and the average life span lengthens, recognition of diversity within this group becomes more important in assessing well-being and formulating social and economic policies that affect the elderly. Some of this diversity is captured by distinguishing between the "old old" and the "young old," because, by most measures, mean wealth declines from age 70 on. However, much of the variation in the wealth of the elderly is not due to age differences within the group but to other factors, such as lifetime earnings history, savings rates, and rates of return. Added to these factors is the incidence of inheritance, which generally occurs when the recipients themselves are no longer young. The cumulative effect is to produce a group in which those who "did well" earlier in life continue to have relatively high wealth and those who were always "getting by" have little or no wealth.

Despite the large wealth holdings of elderly Americans, inheritances are not likely to effect any major changes in distribution of wealth by age group in coming decades. A recent study that explored changes in inheritance patterns in the United States (Shammas, Salmon, and Dahlin 1987) found that an ever larger share of inheritances is left to the spouse (who is generally also elderly) rather than to younger family members. When children do inherit, they themselves tend to be in their 50s and 60s (see also Projector and Weiss 1966). Young children in large numbers are not likely to benefit from these bequests. Indeed, in future years the median age of inheritance is likely to rise because of increasing longevity, particularly among the wealthy. This study concluded that, although state probate laws favor bequests to spouses or children, the elderly are showing an increasing tendency to commit to life-care contracts with nursing homes. As a result, children may have smaller inheritances from the life savings of parents.

The effect of inheritances on the distribution of wealth is also small. Studies indicate that at most 20 percent of current holdings of wealth can be attributed directly or indirectly to inheritances (Modigliani 1975, Kessler 1987). All evidence to date is that the bulk of inheritances pass from the rich to those who are already well-off (see Menchik 1979 and Menchik and David 1983 for the United States; Harbury 1962, and Wedgwood 1929, for the United Kingdom). Thus, it is unlikely that the average nonelderly person benefits much from inheritances.

If we include imputations for Social Security and pension wealth as part of family wealth, it is likely that the elderly will appear substantially better off and younger adults (particularly children) worse off. It is also likely that the wealth position of young adults and children relative to that of the elderly would show a marked deterioration over the period from 1962 to 1983, because of the enormous growth of both Social Security and pension wealth (Wolff 1988). The imputation of Social Security and pension wealth is a controversial subject and requires many accounting assumptions that are beyond the bounds of this chapter. However, almost all imputation procedures tend to increase the wealth position of the elderly, who are current recipients of retirement income, more than that of young families, who must continue to contribute to retirement plans and whose future expected retirement benefits must be discounted to obtain a present value.

Finally, economic policies, particularly in the area of income and wealth taxation, influence the ability to amass and to retain wealth.

Equity considerations may lead us to reexamine preferences that favor the elderly over the young if the trend toward wealth concentration appears to be correlated with relative gains by the elderly at the expense of younger families. Just as economic policies can affect the distribution of income through taxes, transfers, and expenditures on in-kind benefits, they can also affect the distribution of wealth among the population through such policies as direct and indirect subsidies for housing, taxes on capital gains, and inheritance taxes. In assessing the impact of economic policies on various age groups in the U.S. population, it is important to examine the ways in which they affect wealth accumulation as well as income flows.

Notes

1. Our definition of family is close to the Census definition of an independent household; that is, there may be single-person "families" as well as multiperson families.

2. The National Income and Product Accounts attempt to capture this important source of material well-being by imputing rent to owner-occupied housing. There has also been frequent discussion of imputing "rent" to stocks of consumer durables in the national accounts.

3. It is possible also to argue that families with identical earnings histories may differ in their current level of wealth because of differences in their savings behavior. Insofar as families make different savings decisions because of dissimilar time preferences, differences in wealth holdings attributable to this cause would not reflect variations in well-being. Rather, they would reflect only dissimilarities in taste. We do not disagree with this point of view, although the evidence on it is rather scant; however, we believe that differences in savings behavior account for only a small part of the variation in wealth among families.

4. See Projector and Weiss (1966) for a description of the 1962 SFCC and Avery, et al. (1984) for a description of the 1983 SCF. In both cases, imputations were performed for missing values.

5. Results reported here for 1973 differ somewhat from those in Greenwood (1983), because of new imputations for the real estate holdings of elderly families who did not file a tax return in that year. These imputations have increased the real estate estimates for 1973, so that the number of elderly families reporting homeownership corresponds to that reported by the U.S. Census Bureau and the total dollar value of real estate wealth owned by the family sector corresponds to the figure in the national balance sheets.

6. See Wolff (1988) for a recent review of this literature.

7. So-called cohort effects may account for the dips observed in the 1962 and 1973 age-wealth profiles. Particular cohorts may have had economic advantages or dis-

advantages because of the time period in which they developed their human capital resources. If large enough, these effects may dominate whatever life-cycle patterns exist. The age cohorts that show these dips were both born around 1900. They may have been particularly disadvantaged, because they reached the age of family wealth accumulation around the time of the Great Depression. Additional analysis of this cohort is beyond the scope of the present chapter. However, a similar "dip" was observed by Masson (1986) based on French family wealth data.

References

Avery, Robert B., Gregory E. Elliehausen, Glenn B. Canner, and Thomas A. Gustafson. 1984. "Survey of Consumer Finances, 1983." *Federal Reserve Bulletin* (September):679–92.

Feldstein, Martin S. 1974. "Social Security, Induced Retirement and Aggregate Capital Accumulation." *Journal of Political Economy* 82 (October):905–26.

Greenwood, Daphne T. 1983. "An Estimation of Family Wealth and Its Distribution from Microdata, 1973." *The Review of Income and Wealth* (March):23–44.

———. 1987. "Age, Income, and Household Size: Their Relation to Wealth Distribution in the United States." In *International Comparisons of the Distribution of Household Wealth*, edited by Edward N. Wolff. New York: Oxford University Press.

Harbury, C. D. 1962. "Inheritance and the Distribution of Personal Wealth in Britain." *Economic Journal* 72 (December):845–68.

Kessler, Denis. 1987. "Comment on M. Hurd and G. Mundaca, 'The Importance of Gifts among the Very Wealthy.'" Paper presented at the Conference on Income and Wealth, Baltimore, March.

Masson, Andre. 1986. "A Cohort Analysis of Age-Wealth Profiles Generated by a Simulation Model of France (1949–1975)." *Economic Journal* 96:173–90.

Menchik, Paul L. 1979. "Intergenerational Transmission of Inequality: An Empirical Study of Wealth Mobility." *Economica* 46 (November):349–62.

Menchik, Paul L. and Martin David. 1983. "Income Distribution, Lifetime Saving and Bequests." *American Economic Review* 73 (September):672–90.

Modigliani, Franco. 1975. "The Life Cycle Hypothesis of Saving, Twenty Years Later." In *Contemporary Issues in Economics*, edited by M. Parkin. Manchester: Manchester University Press, 2–36.

Modigliani, Franco, and Richard Brumberg. 1954. "Utility Analysis and the

Consumption Function: An Interpretation of Cross-section Data."
In *Post-Keynesian Economics*, edited by K. Kurihara. New Brunswick, N.J.: Rutgers University Press.

Oja, Gail. 1983. "The Distribution of Wealth in Canada." *Review of Income
and Wealth* 29 (June):161–73.

Podder, N. and N.C. Kakwani. 1986. "The Distribution of Wealth in
Australia." *Review of Income and Wealth* 22 (March):75–92.

Projector, Dorothy, and Gertrude Weiss. 1966. "Survey of Financial Characteristics of Consumers." Federal Reserve Technical Papers. Washington, D.C.

Radner, Daniel B., and Denton R. Vaughan. 1987. "Wealth, Income and the
Economic Status of Aged Families." In *International Comparisons
of the Distribution of Household Wealth*, edited by Edward N.
Wolff. New York: Oxford University Press.

Ruggles, Richard, and Nancy Ruggles. 1982. "Integrated Economic Accounts
for the United States, 1947–1980." *Survey of Current Business* 62
(May):1–53.

Shammas, Carol, Marylynn Salmon, and Michel Dahlin. 1987. *Inheritance
in America from Colonial Times to the Present*. New Brunswick,
N.J.: Rutgers University Press.

Shorrocks, A.F. 1987. "U.K. Wealth Distribution: Current Evidence and
Future Prospects." In *International Comparisons of the Distribution
of Household Wealth*, edited by Edward N. Wolff. New York:
Oxford University Press.

Smith, James D. 1987. "Recent Trends in the Distribution of Wealth in the
U.S.: Data, Research Problems, and Prospects." In *International
Comparisons of the Distribution of Household Wealth*, edited by
Edward N. Wolff. New York: Oxford University Press.

Spant, Roland. 1987. "Wealth Distribution in Sweden." In *International
Comparisons of the Distribution of Household Wealth*, edited by
Edward N. Wolff. New York: Oxford University Press.

Steuerle, C. Eugene. 1982. "The Relationship Between Realized Income and
Wealth." OTA Paper no. 50. Washington, D.C.: U.S. Department of
Treasury, December.

————. 1984. "Realized Income and Wealth for Owners of Closely Held
Farms and Businesses: A Comparison." *Public Finance Quarterly*
12 (October):407–24.

Survey Research Center. 1983. "1983 Survey of Consumer Finances, Ques-
tionnaire Form." Survey Research Center, University of Michigan.
Mimeo, July.

Takayama, Noriyuki and Mitsutaka Togashi. 1980. "A Note on Wealth Distribution in Japan." *Philippine Economic Journal* 19, no. 2: 163–87.

Wedgwood, Josiah. 1929. *The Economics of Inheritance*. London: Routledge.

Wolff, Edward N. 1988. "Estimates of Household Wealth Inequality in the
U.S., 1962–1983." *Review of Income and Wealth* 33 (September):231–56.

————. 1987. *International Comparisons of the Distribution of Household Wealth*. New York: Oxford University Press.

————. 1988. "Social Security, Pensions, and the Life Cycle Accumulation of Wealth: Some Empirical Tests." *Annales d'Economie et de Statistique* (April).

Wolff, Edward N., and Marcia Marley. forthcoming. "Long-Term Trends in U.S. Wealth Inequality: Methodological Issues and Results." In *The Measurement of Saving, Investment, and Wealth*. Studies of Income and Wealth 52, edited by Robert E. Lipsey and Helen Stone Tice. Chicago: Chicago University Press.

Chapter Seven

DISPARITIES IN WELL-BEING AMONG U.S. CHILDREN OVER TWO DECADES: 1962–83

Robert Haveman, Barbara L. Wolfe, Ross E. Finnie,
and Edward N. Wolff

Children's well-being has important life-cycle consequences. The productivity and attainments of adults rest on their well-being as children and on the investments that their parents—and society generally—have made in them during their formative years. This productivity and economic success, of course, determine the rate of economic progress and, in turn, the resources available both for the retirement years of the current generation and for the well-being of the next generation's children.

In addition to the connection between children's well-being and success and future economic growth, there are other reasons for studying children's well-being and changes in it over time. First, there is accumulating evidence that some of today's children have inadequate family and social support available to allow for healthy and normal development of their intellectual and physical endowments. The incidence of child poverty has been increasing since the mid-1970s. Many of today's children have fewer resources available to them than did the previous generation of children.

Second, there have been major changes in family structures, lifestyles, and economic conditions over the past decades, several of which appear to affect adversely the well-being of children and their life chances. The rising incidences of marital break-ups, single-parent families, and out-of-wedlock births come immediately to mind. The revolution in women's work patterns with the associated changes in child-care arrangements is another change with potentially negative effects. The long-term upward trend in the aggregate unemployment rate, and the wide variations over time and across geographical areas in public support for children and their families, also cause concern about the conditions in which today's children live and invite speculation over the direction of changes in these conditions.

Third, underlying recent writings of economists and demographers is the implicit judgment that the well-being, environment, and nurture of children have an important effect on their achievements and their success when they become adults. Preston (1984) made a powerful case that society's concern for its children has deteriorated substantially over recent decades, at least as reflected in the public support devoted to children relative to other dependent groups, especially the elderly. Public spending on the elderly through Social Security and Medicare has risen dramatically, but spending targeted toward children—primarily through education and welfare—has stagnated or fallen. As a result, wages of highly trained professionals serving the elderly population (health professionals, for example) have risen, while those of teachers and others caring for children have not. Presumably, the quality and skill levels of these groups of professionals have followed their relative wages.

Although Preston's case regarding public sector support for children seems correct, that finding does not imply that the aggregate level of support for—and well-being of—children has deteriorated. Indeed, Easterlin (1985) argues that children's overall well-being has increased, despite changes in family structure, parental time available to children, and economic conditions that imply some deterioration. Easterlin's argument and data rest on the observed decline in the size of cohorts of children in recent decades. With smaller family sizes, the per child level of support and well-being— as reflected in income, assets, and parental time—may well have increased, overriding the effects of other changes that have tended to erode children's well-being.[1]

Finally, Danziger and Gottschalk (1986) have measured the changes over time in the level of income of families with children, and compared these changes with those of other families, including the elderly. Overall, families with children have fared less well than the other groups, as evidenced by a variety of indicators of family income. Moreover, certain groups of families with children—for example, mother-only families—have dropped behind both the remainder of families with children and the remainder of the population.

The picture that emerges from these studies is a complex one. Some components of children's well-being appear to reflect deterioration, while others seem to favor children's status. Yet, although the overall picture is cloudy, the picture for certain groups is not. As chapter 4 makes clear, children in mother-only families and black children are far below other children in terms of well-being and support.

There are several reasons for the cloudy picture presented by these studies. First, the indicators of status used in the studies differ, and none is a comprehensive indicator of well-being. The studies rely heavily on the income of the families of the children; in some cases, family income is expressed in per capita terms. No studies have considered broader indices of the opportunities available to families or more permanent indicators of economic well-being (such as earnings capacity or wealth). Second, in most of the studies the family unit is the object of investigation, not the child. Third, although no one knows for certain how the time that parents have available for children affects the well-being of the children, few are willing to argue that the availability of parental time is an unimportant component of children's well-being. Changes in this indicator have seldom been studied, however, despite recent changes in the level and patterns of women's work. Finally, none of the previous studies has examined several of the indicators together in an effort to develop a richer understanding of how various aspects of children's well-being have changed over time and to identify which areas in children's lives appear to be in greatest need of supplementation either by families or by the public sector.

In chapter 6 Daphne Greenwood and Edward Wolff examine the wealth of children in the United States. Their basic purpose is to compare trends in wealth for children and the elderly over the last two decades. They find that the wealth of the young relative to that of the elderly remained essentially the same. They also found that the average real wealth of children (as well as the elderly) increased substantially. The increases were not shared equally by all children, however, and the increase in the median wealth of children was often much smaller than the increase in the averages.

Our purpose in this chapter is to pursue the issue of the well-being of children in the United States another step by widening the definition of well-being to include not only a variety of indicators of financial resources, but also parental time. We first document the changes in the number and family composition of children over the two decades from 1962 to 1983. With this as a base, we examine how groups of children have fared over this period, using a variety of indicators of well-being. Within each group, we identify the changes in these indicators for children living in a variety of family arrangements. Our measures of financial resources are equivalent income and three measures of equivalent assets or the service flows from them (all measured in constant 1985 dollars);[2] we measure parental time both as the total time of parents available to the children in a family and as time available per child. In addition to distinguishing changes in these indicators by race, we also identify changes by family type: (1) two-parent households where only one parent works; (2) two-parent families where both parents work; and (3) single-parent families. This chapter, then, is a first effort to develop a multidimensional picture of the well-being of children as well as changes in this picture over time.

Before we present our findings, several caveats are in order. First, we are examining measures of the well-being of children as reported by families on two cross-sectional surveys, one for 1962 and the other for 1983. They have all the usual biases of such self-reports, except that the data for both years have been adjusted to reflect the aggregate levels of the relevant economic variables as recorded in the U.S. national balance sheets. Second, we examine only the amount of these indicators of children's well-being adjusted for family composition; we have no way of knowing the actual distribution of income, assets, or parental time within a family. Third, some of the subgroups we identify have small sample sizes; we present evidence only on those categories with 25 or more observations. Fourth, observations with missing data for important variables—rental value of housing, education, and work time— have had values imputed from regression estimates. Fifth, we include private sources of children's well-being and public income transfers (such as Aid to Families with Dependent Children—AFDC); we do not count nonincome public sources such as education or health care.

MEASURES OF THE WELL-BEING OF CHILDREN

The traditional measure used to capture the economic well-being of children is current family (household) income. The basic idea is that this income is available for the purchase of goods that contribute to the well-being of children in the family, such as books, health care, shelter, and food. Although family income does not capture the value of the specific goods and services that provide well-being to children, it is taken to be highly correlated with the value of children's consumption. Some family goods purchased with family income are "public" goods, such as shelter, heat, and sanitation. The benefits from these are indeed likely to be highly correlated with family income. However, the benefits of other goods and services purchased with family income may be privately appropriated by other members of the family and hence do not convey well-being to children at all. However, to the extent that the composition of family spending among the public components (such as housing), the amounts directly spent on children, and the amounts devoted to the private consumption of parents remains constant both over time and over individual families, current family income can serve as a proxy for the changes in the well-being of children across children and over time.

Family net financial assets reflect the resources that may be available to the child for future investments in health care, education, or training, or for future consumption. An alternative measure, fungible assets, includes the net value of both financial assets and real assets (such as housing) that can be readily transformed into cash. A third asset concept, "assets yielding service flows," captures the gross value of services or consumer durables such as housing and automobiles that are available to the child.

These wealth-related indicators reflect an important element of child nurture: security. Such measures also do better than current income at capturing the permanent economic status of the family in which children live. Finally, to the extent that family contacts, acquaintances, and influence contribute to the ultimate economic success of children, wealth-related indicators are likely to reflect these advantages better than does income. Again, issues of public versus private appropriation within the family arise; but under the same assumptions noted for the use of family income as a proxy for the well-being of children, such asset-related variables convey important aspects of the well-being of children. The value of these nonhuman resources forms an important alternative measure of the economic well-being of children.

The amount of parental time available to a child is the final measure of child well-being that we use. To the extent that parents spend time with their children, they can be considered as investing in their children's current and future well-being. Thus, in addition to measuring total quantity of parental time available for children, we identify both the amount of nonwork time parents actually devote to activities with potential benefit to their children and allocate it among the children. Of course, the number of children in a family is relevant here, as well as birth order. We treat parental time both as a "public good" (assuming that the total parental time is available to all the children in a family) and as a private good divided equally among the children.

THE DATA

We use two data sets developed under the auspices of the Federal Reserve Board for our estimations. One is the *1962 Survey of Financial Characteristics of Consumers* (SFCC), which contains information on 2,557 family units; the second is the *1983 Survey of Consumer Finances* (SCF), which contains information on 4,262 family units. Detailed measures of family socioeconomic characteristics are available on the files, as well as information on income, assets of a variety of types, and the amount of work time by the adults in the family unit. The data are weighted to represent national totals, and egregious inconsistencies have been eliminated. The 1962 and 1983 data have been adjusted to conform with aggregates in the U.S. national balance sheets.[3] To these data we have added a housing value for rental units and estimated the annual parental time available by subtracting hours worked from 16 hours per day times 365 days.

RESULTS

An overview of the population of children whose well-being we are examining appears in table 7.1. Here and throughout the chapter we define children as all household members under 19 years of age. Several changes over time are noteworthy. First, between 1962 and 1983 the total number of children in the United States fell from almost 71 million to less than 62 million, a decrease of nearly 13 percent. Second, the proportion of children who are nonwhite (black and Hispanic) rose from 14 percent in 1962 to more than 25 percent in 1983. Third, there have been major shifts of children among the various family types over the two decades, particularly among white families. In 1962 7 percent of white children and 39 percent of nonwhite children lived in single-parent families; by 1983 these percentages had increased to 14 percent and 43 percent, respectively. Fourth, within the category of two-parent families, there has been a shift away from the traditional family in which the mother does not work outside the home to families in which both father and mother are workers. For whites in 1962, for example, 72 percent of children in two-parent families lived in such traditional one-worker families; by 1983, the percentage had fallen to 52. Finally, the number of children per family has declined over the period by 23 percent

Table 7.1   NUMBER OF CHILDREN AND COMPOSITION AND TYPE OF FAMILY STRUCTURE BY RACE, 1962 AND 1983

	1962				1983			
	Number (in millions)	Percentage of total	Percentage of race	Children per family	Number (in millions)	Percentage of total	Percentage of race	Children per family
All children	70.9	100	—	—	61.8	100	—	—
Whites	61.0	86.1	100	2.46	46.0	74.4	100	1.90
Two parents, wife home	40.6	57.3	66.6	2.18	20.6	33.3	44.8	1.83
Two parents, wife works	16.0	22.6	26.2	2.11	18.8	30.4	40.9	1.96
Single parent	4.4	6.2	7.2	2.13	6.6	10.7	14.3	1.62
Nonwhites	9.9	14.0	100	3.21	15.7	25.6	100	2.13
Two parents, wife home	3.1	4.4	31.3	3.22	4.7	7.6	29.7	2.30
Two parents, wife works	2.9	4.1	29.3	2.75	4.2	6.8	26.6	1.93
Single parent	3.9	5.5	39.4	3.69	6.8	11.0	43.0	2.17

Sources: Computations by authors from the *1962 Survey of Financial Characteristics of Consumers*; and the *1983 Survey of Consumer Finances*.
Note: Detail may not add to totals because of rounding. Children are the unit of observation throughout the table.

among white families and 34 percent among nonwhite families. Among both groups the largest percentage decline was for single mothers. And among nonwhites, two-parent families with an employed wife had the smallest average number of children in both 1962 and 1983.

We use five indicators of the well-being of children: (1) current family income; (2) net financial wealth; (3) fungible wealth, which includes both net financial assets and the net value of housing; (4) assets yielding service flows, which includes the gross value of housing and other consumer durables; and (5) parental time, which is defined as 16 hours per day less the time spent working. All the indicators use children as the unit of observation. The value for each dollar measure is adjusted for family composition using an equivalence scale and is then assigned to each child in the family. The values are reported in 1985 dollars.

Table 7.2 presents results for all children and for all white and all nonwhite children. In addition, estimates of similar values for the elderly population are presented to allow for some rough comparisons. As expected, and consistent with Easterlin's (1985) analysis of cohort size, average equivalent children's income (mean and median) indicates an increase in average levels of well-being over the past two decades. In real terms, the increase over the two-decade period is 45.7 percent. This is true for all children, but the pattern differs by race. The average income available to nonwhite children has increased at a faster rate than that for white children over the period, yet the average income available to nonwhite children is still only about 53 percent of that available to white children.

Our second and third measures of well-being, financial wealth and fungible wealth, tell a similar story. On average (using the mean), the availability of financial resources for all children has increased somewhat more than income over the two decades—by about 55 percent. The percentage increase for nonwhite children was more than twice that for white children. Nevertheless, nonwhite children have access to substantially less wealth—financial or fungible—than do white children. For financial wealth in 1983, the white-nonwhite ratio stands at 5.6 to 1; for fungible wealth, the ratio is 4.5 to 1. The comparable ratios in 1962 were 9.0 and 8.6 to 1. Although progress in reducing this differential has been made, the ratio is still enormous and the absolute gap has widened.

Our fourth measure of the economic well-being of a child is the value of real assets yielding service flows. This indicator suggests a smaller improvement in well-being than does the income indicator: an increase of 32 percent compared with 46 percent. The percentage increase in this indicator over the period is smaller for nonwhites than for whites. As a result, the white-nonwhite ratio has increased over the period from 1.4 to 1.5.

Our final measure of children's well-being, available parental time, moves in the opposite direction to the income and asset indicators, a pattern that further fuels concerns raised by Preston (1984). On average, children living in 1983 had 9 percent less parental time available to them than did children 20 years earlier. The time available to nonwhite children decreased; that for white children increased. This change is primarily the result of the shift to single-parent families and the substantial increase in working mothers, both of which reduce the time available to children.[4]

Simple comparisons of these indicators of well-being, then, suggest rather different trends. The income indicator suggests that, on average, children were better off in 1983 than two decades earlier, and that the income ratio between white and nonwhite children has been reduced. Nevertheless, the income level of nonwhite children remains far below that of white children. The two financial-asset indicators suggest a substantial increase in mean assets among both white and nonwhite children. In relative terms, the increase is greater for nonwhites than whites; in absolute terms, white children were the larger gainers. By contrast, the indicator reflecting available parental time suggests a substantial drop in nonwhite children's well-being over time. The measure of assets yielding service flows indicates that children are better off today than two decades ago, but black children are even further below white children.

To get another perspective on how well children have been doing over this period, table 7.2 shows income and wealth data for the elderly.[5] These averages suggest that the elderly of today are much better off economically than those of two decades ago. Equivalent income for elderly households increased by about 73 percent in real terms, a larger increase than any other income increase recorded in the table. Real financial and fungible wealth increased by 41 percent and 52 percent, respectively—increases that are somewhat lower than those recorded for children. The financial assets indicators, however, show that the elderly have substantially more assets at their disposal than do children (even allowing for the household base of the wealth data for the elderly). The fungible asset value for elderly households ($326,400) is a strikingly large number. On average, children had 19 percent and 21 percent of the elderly

Table 7.2   INDICATORS OF THE WELL-BEING OF CHILDREN, 1962 AND 1983 (thousands of 1985 dollars)

	1962		1983		Percentage change 1962–83	
	Mean	Median	Mean	Median	Mean	Median
All children						
Income	16.4	13.2	23.9	19.1	45.7	44.7
Financial wealth	34.5	0.6	53.4	4.3	54.8	617.0
Fungible wealth	44.3	8.2	74.9	20.0	69.1	143.9
Assets yielding service flow	50.8	49.8	67.0	59.6	31.9	19.7
Parental time (thousands of hours/year)	8.7	9.3	7.9	8.1	-9.2	-12.9
All white children						
Income	17.5	17.4	27.2	21.2	55.4	21.8
Financial wealth	39.7	2.2	67.1	8.7	69.0	295.5
Fungible wealth	50.5	11.5	92.8	32.3	83.8	180.9
Assets yielding service flows	54.5	51.1	72.7	60.3	33.4	18.0
Parental time (thousands of hours/year)	9.0	9.3	9.0	9.5	0	2.2
All nonwhite children						
Income	8.9	7.3	14.4	11.9	61.8	63.0
Financial wealth	4.4	0.02	12.0	0	172.7	-X
Fungible wealth	5.9	0.1	20.8	1.2	252.5	+X
Assets yielding service flows	38.6	34.4	50.3	40.4	30.3	17.4
Parental time (thousands of hours/year)	7.6	8.0	7.3	7.3	-3.9	-8.8

All elderly

Income	19.6	11.0	33.9	15.4	73.0	40.0
Financial wealth	181.8	26.6	256.9	33.3	41.3	25.2
Fungible wealth	215.2	58.7	326.4	94.8	51.7	61.5

Sources: Same as table 7.1.

Notes: Children are the units of observation except for figures for the elderly. Values are adjusted using equivalent value scale, except for parental time variables, which are parental time for the family unit with no adjustment for family size or composition. Parental time is an estimate of parental time potentially available to a family's children, calculated as [(16 multiplied by 365) minus hours worked per year], summed over one or two parents depending on family structure. Financial wealth is net real estate investments, value of cash, checking and saving accounts, value of bonds, other financial securities, stocks, trusts, unincorporated business, and the cash surrender value of life insurance and private pensions minus nonmortgage debt. Fungible wealth is financial wealth plus the net value of owner-occupied housing. Except for financial wealth, observations missing the race variable are omitted from the calculations. Where included, they are in the white category. Assets yielding service flows equals the gross value of family-owned housing or the gross value of any rental housing the family occupies plus the gross value of cars and trucks owned. All dollar values are in 1985 dollars. The symbols −X and +X are used to indicate direction of change when a precise percentage change cannot be calculated.

Table 7.3 INCOME, NET FINANCIAL WEALTH, FUNGIBLE WEALTH, AND
PARENTAL TIME, BY RACE AND FAMILY TYPE, 1962 AND 1983
(thousands 1985 dollars)

	1962		1983		Percentage change 1962–83	
	Mean	Median	Mean	Median	Mean	Median
White Children by Family Type						
Two parents, wife home						
Income	17.1	12.9	27.8	18.6	62.6	44.2
Financial wealth	43.2	2.2	81.5	8.3	88.7	277.3
Fungible wealth	54.2	10.7	109.7	28.5	102.4	166.4
Total parental time	9.6	9.2	9.6	9.2	0	0
Per child parental time	3.7	3.2	4.8	4.7	29.7	46.9
Two parents, wife works						
Income	19.9	18.6	30.5	26.6	53.3	43.0
Financial wealth	29.9	1.0	66.2	14.4	121.4	1,340.0
Fungible wealth	42.8	10.8	91.9	38.5	114.7	256.5
Total parental time	8.5	8.0	7.9	7.8	−7.1	−2.5
Per child parental time	4.0	3.6	4.5	3.5	12.5	−2.8
Single mothers						
Income	12.7	8.4	16.9	17.5	33.1	108.3
Financial wealth	19.9	0.02	26.2	1.9	31.7	+X
Fungible wealth	30.5	1.0	44.6	12.1	46.2	1,110.0
Total parental time	5.0	6.0	4.4	4.7	−12.0	−21.7
Per child parental time	2.3	1.6	2.7	2.3	17.4	43.8

household's net financial and fungible assets, respectively, available to them two decades ago compared with 21 percent and 23 percent on average today.

The role of changes in family composition and changes in women's labor force participation over these two decades should be noted. In particular, because of the increase in single-parent families (see table 7.1 presented earlier), today's children, on average, have less access to parental time than previous generations of children. Because of the increased propensity of women to work, today's children may have higher family income and assets, but less available parental time.

To examine these possibilities further and to increase our understanding of child well-being, we divide the population of children into three types of families and measure the income, assets, and parental time indicators of well-being for each of these types.[6] We

	1962		1983		Percentage change 1962–83	
	Mean	Median	Mean	Median	Mean	Median
Nonwhite Children by Family Type						
Two parents, wife home						
Income	10.8	9.4	14.0	11.8	29.6	25.5
Financial wealth	7.6	0.1	17.7	0	132.9	−X
Fungible wealth	9.8	0	26.5	1.8	170.4	+X
Total parental time	9.7	9.1	10.1	9.0	4.1	−1.1
Per child parental time	3.0	2.3	4.4	3.9	46.7	69.6
Two parents, wife works						
Income	13.2	14.5	24.0	21.0	81.8	44.8
Financial wealth	6.0	0	16.1	1.9	168.3	+X
Fungible wealth	8.2	0.4	30.1	9.7	267.1	2,325.0
Total parental time	8.8	9.0	7.9	7.1	−10.2	−21.1
Per child parental time	3.1	2.0	4.1	3.7	32.3	85.0
Single mothers						
Income	4.2	4.7	8.9	6.3	111.9	34.0
Financial wealth	1.1	0.1	6.0	0.1	445.5	0
Fungible wealth	1.8	0.1	10.9	0.1	505.6	0
Total parental time	5.2	5.9	5.0	5.9	−3.8	0
Per child parental time	1.5	1.2	2.2	1.5	46.7	25.0

Sources: Same as table 7.1.
Note: Figures in table 7.3 do not aggregate to those in table 7.2 because groups with small numbers are omitted here. Income and wealth are in dollar values using equivalence scales applied to each child in each family. Time measures are in thousands of hours. See note to table 7.2 for definitions.

do so for each of the racial subgroups because, as indicated in table 7.1, the changes in family structure and women's work patterns appear to differ substantially between the two groups.

Table 7.3 presents these calculations. Numerous patterns can be observed in the table. We summarize the main ones in catalogue form, relying primarily on the mean values:

□ In 1983 equivalent income for children in white, two-parent families in which the mother was employed exceeded $30,000, substantially greater than for any other group.
□ The growth in equivalent income was the greatest for children in

nonwhite families headed by a single woman—a 112 percent increase in real income over the period. The 1962 base income of such families was very low ($4,200), however. The equivalent income growth for nonwhite children in two-parent families in which the mother was employed was also very large—82 percent.

□ Within each racial category, the equivalent income of children in families headed by single women was substantially lower than that for children in two-parent families. For nonwhites, the level of 1983 equivalent income in such families was only 37 percent of the level for children in two-parent families in which the mother was employed; for whites, it was 55 percent.

□ For the average child living in a white, two-parent family, financial wealth approximately doubled over the 1962–83 period. For the average child in a nonwhite, two-parent family, the increase was substantially greater. For nonwhite children in two-parent families in which the mother was employed, financial wealth increased about 1.75 times. Wealth levels—either financial or fungible—for mother-only families were less than one-half of those for two-parent families for both racial groups.

□ For all white families, financial assets were substantially greater than annual income. However, for nonwhite families, financial assets did not exceed family income in two out of three family categories.

□ For all families, fungible assets exceeded annual income. For all types of white families, the ratio of fungible assets to income exceeded 2.5 in 1983. For nonwhites, the ratio ranged from 1.22 to 1.9 to 1.

□ For all families other than those in which the mother was not employed (two-parent families with an employed wife and female-headed families), total parental time decreased over the two decades. The reductions ranged from 12 percent (white, female-headed families) to 7 percent (white, two-parent families in which the wife was employed). Parental time per child, however, increased for all families, reflecting the substantial reduction in average family size over the period.

The following points summarize the main patterns of children's well-being and changes in it over the period.

□ For white children, the income indicator suggests rather high and growing levels of well-being for those in two-parent families. Those in mother-only families have significantly lower levels of well-being than two-parent families and have experienced slower income growth.

□ For white children, equivalent wealth measured in 1985 dollars has grown even more rapidly than income over the period. Again, the lowest growth was recorded for mother-only families.
□ For nonwhite children, well-being as indicated by the income measure was substantially lower than for whites, but showed far larger increases over the period for most of the family types.
□ For nonwhite children, the indicator based on the wealth measures recorded very low levels of child well-being relative to whites, although asset growth was very large in percentage terms.[7]
□ For both white and nonwhite children, total available parental time decreased in all types of families except two-parent families with a nonworking spouse. The percentage decreases were largest for children in white, single-mother families and black, two-parent families with a working spouse.[8]
□ Parental time measured on a per child basis increased over the two decades.

Our discussion to this point has focused on average levels of well-being of children living in various family types and changes in these levels, using a variety of indicators of well-being. The story is not straightforward. Changes in equivalent income and in all the asset measures suggest improvements in child well-being for both whites and nonwhites, but the indicator based on total available parental time paints a picture of stagnant or declining levels of well-being. Available total parental time has decreased substantially in mother-only families and two-parent families in which the mother is employed, but changes in family composition—in particular, the major decrease in average family size—have led to an opposite trend in the available parental time per child.

A related question is the level of inequality in well-being among children and changes in it over time. Table 7.4 presents our estimates on this issue. It shows Gini coefficients based on income, net financial wealth, fungible wealth, and both indicators of parental time for a variety of family types in 1962 and 1983.[9] The story told by these data is also mixed: for all children—and for children distinguished by race and family type—the level of inequality as measured by income has increased over the 1962–83 period. This growing inequality among children has occurred in the aggregate—where the Gini coefficient on income has increased by 23 percent—as well as within the groups by race and family type. Among the family types, the gap has widened most within two-parent families. For nonwhite families of this type in which the mother is not employed, income

Table 7.4   MEASURES OF INEQUALITY FOR INCOME AND NET FINANCIAL WEALTH, 1962 AND 1983 (Gini coefficients)

	1962					1983				
	Income	Total parental time	Parental time per child	Financial wealth	Fungible wealth	Income	Total parental time	Parental time per child	Financial wealth	Fungible wealth
All families with children	0.35	0.10	0.32	0.93	0.85	0.43	0.15	0.31	0.88	0.79
All white families	0.34	0.09	0.31	0.93	0.84	0.40	0.13	0.28	0.85	0.75
Two parents, wife home	0.34	0.04	0.30	0.93	0.84	0.46	0.03	0.26	0.85	0.77
Two parents, wife works	0.30	0.07	0.30	0.83	0.82	0.32	0.06	0.26	0.80	0.67
Single mothers	0.38	0.13	0.35	0.90	0.80	0.38	0.12	0.27	0.93	0.77
All nonwhite families	0.39	0.18	0.38	—	0.99	0.43	0.19	0.35	—	0.91
Two parents, wife home	0.25	0.03	0.28	—	0.93	0.39	0.05	0.30	—	0.91
Two parents, wife works	0.31	0.09	0.33	—	0.91	0.31	0.06	0.28	0.97	0.76
Single mothers	0.37	0.09	0.30	—	—	0.39	0.11	0.35	—	0.94

	Income	Total parental time	Parental time per child	Financial wealth	Fungible wealth
		Percentage change 1962–83			
All families with children	22.9	50.0	-3.1	-5.4	-7.1
All white families	17.6	44.4	-9.7	-8.6	-10.7
Two parents, wife home	35.3	-25.0	-13.3	-8.6	-8.3
Two parents, wife works	6.7	-14.3	-13.3	-3.6	-18.3
Single mothers	0	-7.7	-22.9	3.3	-3.8
All nonwhite families	10.3	5.6	-7.9	—	-8.1
Two parents, wife home	56.0	66.7	7.1	—	-2.2
Two parents, wife works	0	-33.3	-15.2	—	-16.5
Single mothers	5.4	22.2	16.7	—	—

Sources: Same as table 7.1.
— indicates either that sample has negative values so it was not possible to calculate Gini coefficients, or that sample size was too small.

inequality has increased by 56 percent; for white families of this type, the increase is 35 percent.

Inequality in terms of wealth, especially financial wealth, is very high. For the aggregate, the Gini coefficient was 0.88 in 1983 compared with 0.93 in 1962. It was higher among nonwhite families in 1983 than white families, but the reverse was true two decades earlier. Fungible wealth is also unequally distributed—in the aggregate, the Gini coefficient was 0.79 in 1983 versus 0.85 in 1962. Inequality based on wealth has decreased over the two-decade period, although it remains high. The decrease holds across all family types for fungible wealth, but only among white families for financial wealth.

The picture for parental time is more mixed, but the Gini coefficients provide evidence that parental time is more equally distributed than the other indicators. In the aggregate, there has been an increase in inequality in terms of total parental time. This increase in inequality is also recorded for each of the racial groups. However, within the family types by race the changes vary. Inequality fell for all of the white family types but increased for black single mothers and black two-parent families in which the mother is not employed.

In the aggregate and for both racial groups, there have been decreases in the measured inequality of parental time per child. However, this is not the case for nonwhite children living in two-parent families with a single earner or for those living with a single mother. For children in these two groups, inequality in terms of parental time per child has increased.

CONCLUSIONS, CAUTIONS, AND CAVEATS

The main conclusion of this empirical exploration is that the measurement of the economic well-being of children is not a straightforward exercise. The picture obtained of the relative levels of well-being of children of various racial and family categories, and of changes in these levels, depends on the indicator of well-being on which one relies. The sizable increases in well-being that are recorded when income is used as the indicator are substantially tempered when less transient indicators, such as parental time, are employed. However, they are significantly increased when assets are used as the indicator of well-being. Hence, by employing a variety of indicators of well-being, a richer, more diverse, and more complicated picture of the gaps in well-being among various groups of children, and of changes in their well-being over time, emerges. We have described a number of these patterns and changes.

We began our discussion by recalling the results of previous studies of the well-being of children—those by Preston (1984), Easterlin (1985), and Danziger and Gottschalk (1986). How do our results compare with theirs? Preston's conclusion regarding the increasing gap between children and the elderly is largely confirmed by our results. When one looks at income, the increase in children's economic well-being has been substantially less than that of the elderly over the past two decades. The increase in assets is similar for both age groups, although the absolute difference remains nearly five to one.

Easterlin's results are also supported by ours. On an equivalent basis, children as a group have improved their level of well-being, whether the relevant indicator is income or assets. The conclusion of Danziger and Gottschalk that there has been an increase in inequality among families with children is borne out when children themselves rather than their families are used as the unit of observation, but only when either income or total parental time is used as the indicator of well-being.

Finally, our result on the substantially increased level of income inequality among children is consistent with the increase in the incidence of measured poverty among children during the past decade. But our finding that the increase in inequality is based primarily on increased within-group inequality (especially among two-parent households with a single earner), rather than an increase in the number of single-parent families or the number of families in which mothers are employed, is inconsistent with much conventional wisdom.

At this stage, these results should be viewed as preliminary. The data for 1962 need further refinement and the 1983 results await a final tape to be provided by the Federal Reserve Board. We have had difficulties with missing data for several important variables and have omitted observations with such missing-data problems. Alternative estimates with imputed values do not substantially change the picture, however.

Moreover, if we wish ultimately to characterize fully the "economic environment" in which children live, we need to measure, even if crudely, a number of aspects of well-being that we have not dealt with here. Several come immediately to mind: schooling services and their quality; the availability of health care services; the actual time that parents spend with their children and the "nurturing" value of that time to the children; and the presence in the family unit of adults other than parents whose time with children might substitute for that of parents. If it proves feasible to estimate these aspects of children's well-being, the joint distribution across children of all of them should be estimated. Such an approach would lead to a rather comprehensive definition of children's well-being based on an appropriately weighted aggregation of the components of well-being.

Another important issue that needs to be addressed in a more full-blown analysis of children's well-being is the pattern in which the resources of the family are shared among its members. In this chapter, we have employed a rough equivalence scale to adjust family aggregates for differences in family size and structure. Although this procedure implicitly assumes some sharing, there is little to indicate that actual sharing arrangements follow this pattern. To obtain reliable estimates of true sharing arrangements within families is probably impossible given the limitations of existing data bases. Nevertheless, it should be possible to show the effect of a range of plausible sharing arrangements on the results of the analysis.

These calculations and measures are important in and of themselves because current policy is based primarily on measures of current income, which may provide only a limited view of the well-being of children across family type and across time. The significant differences in patterns using current income and these other indicators suggests that current income as a basis for income transfers and other social policies is less than satisfactory.

Notes

1. Easterlin's results are, in part, due to his methodology. First, he calculates the ratio of children's needs to adults' needs using an equivalence scale. The ratio is then multiplied by family income to get family income devoted to children. Then the product is divided by the number of children to get a per child family income value. Because equivalence scales generally give smaller values to the younger children in a family (reflecting economies of scale), a declining number of children per family will lead to an increase in the per child family income value for this reason alone. See also Easterlin (1983).

2. The expression of the income and wealth variables in equivalent units is an

attempt to control for differences in family size and composition in the estimates. For example, a family income of $20,000 means far less well-being for each member if there are 10 people in the family than if there are but 2. The adjustment is based on estimates of the "income needs" of families of various sizes and compositions required to achieve the level of well-being equivalent to that of some "norm" family (say, a family with 2 adults and 2 children) with some base income level (say, $15,000). The equivalence scale used here is the U.S. Census Bureau scale for estimating the size and composition of the poverty population.

3. See Wolff (1987) for a detailed description of the adjusted procedure for the wealth components. According to Wolff and Marley (forthcoming), the fungible and financial net worth measures of inequality are quite insensitive to adjustment procedures, and so the different treatment should not affect the inequality measures reported below. The 1962 values for owner-occupied housing and other real estate and the 1983 values for tangible assets, unincorporated business equity, and trust fund equity require no adjustment.

4. The true reduction in available parental time from 1962 to 1983 is likely to be understated by these calculations. The unemployment rate was substantially greater in 1983 (9.5 percent) than in 1962 (5.3 percent); this increase in unemployment will be recorded as an increase in nonwork time and, hence, as an increase in the parental time variable.

5. These data are also adjusted by equivalence scales and hence reflect changes in family size and composition.

6. Children living with never-married mothers or single fathers are excluded from much of the subsequent analysis because of small sample sizes.

7. For two-parent white families, equivalent fungible assets averaged about $109,000 in 1983, compared with $26,500 for nonwhite families; for children in white single-parent families, mean asset levels were less than $45,000, compared with $11,000 for nonwhite families. One-half of the white children in these two family-type categories had access to equivalent fungible assets of $12,000 or less; the comparable figure for nonwhite children was $100 or less.

8. These decreases would have been even larger had adjustments been made for the increase in unemployment rates and the decrease in the average work week over the two decades.

9. The Gini coefficient measures aggregate income inequality, with zero indicating complete equality and one indicating complete inequality.

References

Danziger, Sheldon, and Peter Gottschalk. 1986. "How Are Families with Children Faring?" Discussion Paper no. 801-86. Madison, Wis.: Institute for Research on Poverty, University of Wisconsin.

Easterlin, Richard. 1983. "The Impact of Demographic Factors on the Family Environment of Children, 1940–1995." In *American Families and the Economy*, edited by R. R. Nelson and Felicity Skidmore. Washington, D.C.: National Academy Press.

————. 1985. "The Struggle for Relative Economic Status." Los Angeles: University of Southern California. Processed.

Preston, Samuel. 1984. "Children and Elderly in the U.S." *Demography* 21, no. 4 (November):435–57.

Wolff, Edward N. 1987. "Estimates of Household Wealth Inequality in the U.S., 1962–1983." *Review of Income and Wealth* 33 (September): 231–56.

Wolff, Edward N., and Marcia Marley. Forthcoming. "Long-term Trends in U.S. Wealth Inequality: Methodological Issues and Results." In *The Measurement of Saving, Investment, and Wealth.* Studies of Income and Wealth 52, edited by Robert E. Lipsey and Helen Stone Tice. Chicago: Chicago University Press.

Chapter Eight

HEALTH CARE SPENDING ON CHILDREN AND THE ELDERLY

Jack A. Meyer and Marilyn Moon

The vast difference in public spending on health care between children and the elderly in the United States at first glance lends credence to the argument that, in health policy, our oldest citizens fare much better than our youngest ones. Conclusions about the size and direction of any imbalance, however, require much closer examination. Sources of payment for health care, health status, and need for care differ dramatically. Thus, comparisons between these two age groups must be made with caution. Nonetheless, such contrasts are inevitable and a careful understanding of their implications can help in the development of more balanced approaches to public policy.

The purposes of this chapter are to analyze differences in access to health care among the young and the elderly and to explain those differences in terms of the policy and institutional framework for delivery and financing of health care. We conclude that casual comparisons of health care spending overstate the well-being of elderly persons relative to children, but that an imbalance does persist, particularly for children in families with low incomes. One source of this imbalance is the basic asymmetry in our public policy toward the young and the elderly. We also note some basic imbalances and inefficiencies in the health care financing system that affect both young and old. A reordering of spending priorities and policy reforms in the public and the private sectors could aid children and the elderly by better targeting dollars to areas of need.

A major goal of public policy should be to assure that everyone has access to health care. In the United States providing such access will require some combination of public and private sector measures to extend health insurance coverage. An additional goal is to reduce waste and inefficiency in the purchase of health care services. Paying more than is necessary for health care ties up resources that have more efficient alternative uses.

A key challenge involves reconciling the potential conflict between the goals of equity and efficiency. As prudent purchasing and market pressures are applied increasingly to health care, it becomes more difficult for health service providers to offer services to the millions of Americans who lack the means to pay for them. Efforts to squeeze "unnecessary" payments and procedures out of the health system in the United States will erode the implicit subsidies paid by providers—and ultimately purchasers—that have financed care for many of the uninsured in the past. Thus, the drive for efficiency in the organization, delivery, and financing of health services should be accompanied by efforts to extend coverage directly to those who lack it.

Children and working-age adults are the groups who often lack insurance in the United States. But although virtually all the elderly are covered by Medicare and many have some supplemental coverage, the elderly as a group pay about one-third of their health expenses out-of-pocket, and these expenses amount to a substantial portion of income for the neediest among them. Providing needed coverage for children in the United States by scaling back coverage for the elderly would simply exacerbate this burden.

The first part of the chapter examines cross-national, cross-age, and cross-time comparisons in health care spending. A second major section examines some reasons for these differences, focusing on coverage by third parties, on the links between health spending and health status, and on the danger of ignoring the complexities of comparative access to health care between the two groups. We conclude by presenting a few options to redress the imbalances we find.

EXPENDITURES ON HEALTH CARE

The section begins by making comparisons of health care expenditures among countries. It then looks at comparisons among groups in the United States.

International Comparisons

Health spending has increased sharply as a percentage of gross domestic product (GDP) in all industrialized nations since 1960, but the increase has been much more substantial in some countries than in others. As of 1960 the Organization for Economic Cooperation and Development (OECD) countries as a group were spending 4.2 percent of GDP on health care. Moreover, the variance around this average was rather small; of the 23 countries reporting data, 15 were within one percentage point of the 4.2 percent average, and the proportions ranged from 2.9 percent (Greece) to 5.7 percent (Iceland). Health care accounted for 5.3 percent of GDP in the United States in 1960, a little below the corresponding figure for Canada, 5.5 percent (OECD 1985).

In 1984 the proportions of GDP allocated to health care ranged from 4.6 percent (Greece) to 10.7 percent (U.S.). Only Sweden (9.4 percent) and France (9.1 percent) were close to the U.S. figure; in both these nations, as in the United States, health spending had more than doubled as a share of output (see table 8.1). Other nations were spending some four to five percentage points less than the United States, including the United Kingdom (5.9 percent), Belgium (6.2 percent), and Finland (6.6 percent). Canada, which was so close to the United States in spending in 1960, spent only 8.4 percent of its GDP on health in 1984 (Schieber and Poullier 1986).

In recent years the health care share of GDP in the United States has leveled out, remaining just under 11 percent between 1982 and 1986. Moreover, in most OECD countries, the elasticity of health expenditure to GDP (that is, the dollar increase in spending on health from a one-dollar rise in GDP) has tapered off since 1975. In the United States this elasticity fell from 1.9 over the 1960–75 period to 1.4 over the 1975–82 period. The corresponding figures for the United Kingdom were 2.3 and 1.2, and for West Germany, 1.6 and 0.8. (In a few countries such as Belgium and Sweden, the change in elasticity went the other way in the second period; see OECD 1985.)

The fact that a country increases the *proportion* of GDP it spends on health care does not necessarily mean that it is spending *too much* on health care. First, if a greater proportion of output devoted to health care leads to a greater *rate of growth* in output by contributing to a healthier work force, the investment could make more resources available for the purchase of all goods and services (including health care). In this sense, an increase in the share of output devoted to health care would have to yield only a small increase in labor productivity and economic growth in order to pay for itself. For this to occur, however, the additional resources devoted to health care must be spent on people who are in a position to contribute to output growth.

In the health care context, obviously, a zero-sum game framework,

Table 8.1 PUBLIC HEALTH AND TOTAL HEALTH EXPENDITURES, 1960 AND
1984

| | 1960 | | 1984 | |
| | Public expenditures as percentage of total | Total health | Public expenditures as percentage of total | Total health |
Country	expenditures	expenditures as percentage of GDP	expenditures	expenditures as percentage of GDP
Australia	47.6	5.2	84.5	7.8
Austria	65.3	4.4	60.9	7.2
Belgium	61.6	3.4	91.6	6.2
Canada	43.1	5.5	74.4	8.4
Denmark	88.7	3.6	83.4	6.3
Finland	54.5	4.1	78.8	6.6
France	57.8	4.3	71.2	9.1
Germany, F.R.	67.5	4.7	78.2	8.1
Greece	57.9	2.9	79.3	4.6
Iceland	40.0	5.7	82.7	7.9
Ireland	76.0	4.0	86.9	8.0
Italy	83.1	3.9	84.1	7.2
Japan	60.4	3.0	72.1	6.6
Luxembourg	—	—	—	—
Netherlands	33.3	3.9	78.3	8.6
New Zealand	—	—	78.4	5.6
Norway	77.8	3.3	88.8	6.3
Portugal	—	—	71.1	5.5
Spain	—	—	72.3	5.8
Sweden	72.6	4.7	91.4	9.4
Switzerland	—	3.3	—	—
United Kingdom	85.2	3.9	88.9	5.9
United States	24.7	5.3	41.4	10.7
Mean	61.0	4.2	78.7	7.5
Standard deviation	18.2	0.8	12.2	1.5

Source: Scheiber and Poullier (1986).

in which one group's gain comes only at the expense of another group, is inappropriate. The point is not to deny care to the nonproductive in order to target benefits only to those who are at peak productivity. Rather, it is important for a society to "invest" in coverage for its youth not only because it is humane to do so, but also because better health, like better education, will enhance the productive capacity of youth as they reach adulthood. This enhanced productivity will help today's elderly by making the working-age population better able to finance benefits for everyone in need. Moreover, when workers are able to participate actively in the labor force, they invest in their own old age through making social insurance contributions or putting money aside for themselves in later years. Simply stated, health coverage fosters productive work, productive work generates a larger economic pie, and a larger economic pie benefits everyone, young and old alike.

Second, if spending a higher proportion of GDP for health care purchases better health outcomes, it could certainly be viewed as justifiable. A society, particularly a wealthy one, may make a conscious choice to spend more on health care to relieve discomfort or expand life expectancies. These consumption uses for health care are certainly as valid as spending on better transportation or housing, for example.

By contrast, if a country is spending relatively more on health care as a result of unnecessarily high payments to those who provide health services or inefficiencies in the way health care is provided and paid for, the "excess" outlays would not seem to be justified. If physicians are paid more than is necessary to call forth an adequate supply of high-quality services or the health care payment system leads to excessive tests, medical procedures, and rates and length of hospitalization, a country could be judged to be better off by bringing down spending attributable to these factors and freeing up resources for other uses.

We shall return later to an examination of whether these expenditures can be justified. First, however, we need to focus on how these services are distributed across the population.

Differences in the Use of Health Care in the United States

The very high level of spending on health care in the United States relative to its GDP is not evenly spread across the population. For reasons to be described later, use of health care services and associated expenditures in the United States vary enormously by age, income, and health status.

The widest—and most distorted—view of the differences in spending on the two dependent groups emerges from a comparison of public sector spending. In 1978, the most recent year for which data are available, per capita health care spending through the public sector was 15.6 times as high for the elderly as the young. In 1986 about three-fourths of the $100 billion spent on health care by the federal government aided persons ages 65 and older, whereas only about 5 percent of the total was spent on children.

Before jumping to unwarranted conclusions about differential access to care, a closer look is needed. First, public spending comparisons must be placed in the proper policy context. Sources of payment for our elderly citizens are quite different from those for children. The elderly rely disproportionately on the government, while children's expenditures are paid from several private and public sources. The passage of Medicare and Medicaid in 1965 increased dramatically the government's role in paying the health care costs of persons ages 65 and older. Thus, comparisons of public spending on health care necessarily lead to an exaggerated imbalance in the amounts of health expenditures directed at the two groups.

Moreover, the tax subsidies that help encourage private employers to offer health insurance to workers ought to be factored in when calculating government's role. Such an adjustment would change considerably the ratio of "spending on the old relative to the young." Furthermore, the blend of public and private financing of health care in the United States inherently puts most of the burden for aiding the elderly on the government, while limiting the public sector's responsibility for children to a portion of those children who live in poverty and are covered through Medicaid and another portion whose families benefit from a tax subsidy. This asymmetry makes valid comparisons more difficult. (Nonetheless, for those children who do not have coverage and thus may lack access to care, the question of whether the government should expand in this area is appropriate.)

If, instead of focusing solely on public expenditures, we also recognize the role of private insurance and look at overall spending, the ratio of expenditures on the elderly to those on the young drops. In 1978 total health care spending in the United States for elderly persons was 7.1 times higher than for children. If outlays for nursing home care are omitted from these figures, the ratio of spending by the elderly to spending by younger families drops even further, from 7.1 to 1 to 5.3 to 1 in 1978. Because the elderly are the major users of nursing home care and children are seldom institutionalized in the United States, these acute care comparisons may be more valid in assessing relevant differences between the two groups.

The spending differentials between the elderly and children do not represent a new phenomenon. Even before the introduction of Medicare and Medicaid—the major government programs providing health care services—spending on health care was heavily skewed

Table 8.2 TOTAL SPENDING ON HEALTH CARE AND RATES OF GROWTH IN
SPENDING FOR CHILDREN AND THE ELDERLY, SELECTED YEARS,
1965–84

Year	All persons	Children (under age 19)	Elderly (age 65 and older)
Total spending (dollars)			
1965	188	83	472
1970	315	138	852
1978	753	286	2,026
1984	1,595	n.a.	4,202
Rates of growth (percentage)			
1965–70	67.4	65.8	80.8
1970–78	138.8	107.8	137.3
1978–84	111.8	n.a.	107.4

Sources: Waldo and Lazenby (1984); Fisher (1980).
n.a. Not available.

towards older Americans (see table 8.2). In 1965, for example, persons over age 65 consumed 5.7 times more health care than did children under age 19. Moreover, although the gap has continued to widen somewhat, this change occurred largely between 1965 and 1970. In fact, between 1970 and 1978, public spending on children grew faster than public spending on the elderly (albeit from a small base). And since that time, overall per capita spending has increased slightly faster than such spending for persons over age 65.

International comparisons also show the elderly using more services in systems where all age groups have equal access to care. In Canada, for example, relative differences in the number of physician visits for persons ages 65 and older as compared with those for children under age 17 increased after the introduction of the national health insurance program (Enterline et al. 1973).

Major differences in use of services also occur within the broad categories of the elderly and children. Among the elderly, the use of health services, particularly services associated with long term or chronic care needs, rises progressively with age. Table 8.3 shows the major difference in use of skilled nursing and home health services for persons age 80 and older compared with those ages 65 to 69. The oldest old are nearly twice as likely to be hospitalized as younger elderly (HCFA 1986).

Children also show differences in health care use. For example,

Table 8.3 RATIO OF MEDICARE SERVICE USE BY PERSONS AGE 65–69, 1981

| Type of service | Ratio of elderly persons served per 1,000 enrollees by age: (age 65–69 = 1) | | | |
	70–74	75–79	80–84	85 and older
Skilled nursing facility	2.04	4.00	7.31	11.65
Home health care	1.64	2.51	3.62	4.60
Inpatient hospital	1.18	1.41	1.65	1.82
Physician services	1.08	1.16	1.22	1.29
Outpatient services	1.06	1.12	1.17	1.23
Average Medicare reimbursements[a]	$1,175	$1,404	$1,640	$1,777

Source: Health Care Financing Administration (1986).
a. The average reimbursement level in 1981 for persons age 65–69 was $958; the overall average was $1,262.

children age 6 or younger have more visits to physicians and use more prescription drugs than older children (see table 8.4). They also are more likely to have a hospital stay (U.S. Public Health Service 1986). But in terms of overall health expenditures, there is little variation between these two age groups.[1]

Table 8.4 also highlights another source of variation in health care expenditures, and one that particularly affects children. Lack of protection from a public program or from private health insurance can limit access to needed care. The data shown focus on children with 15 or more days of restricted activity per year, shown by poverty status and access to Medicaid. Children who are not poor and those who have Medicaid coverage used about the same level of physician services on average; poor children ineligible for Medicaid had fewer such visits. Use of prescription drugs was also lower for poor children who lacked access to Medicaid.

Thus far we have raised more questions than we have answered concerning the role of health care financing in improving the status of the young and the elderly. We explain the source of some of this variation in the next section.

UNDERSTANDING THE VARIATION IN HEALTH CARE SPENDING

Although we have noted many factors affecting the variation in health care spending between the two groups, we focus here on two

Table 8.4   USE OF HEALTH SERVICES BY PERSONS UNDER AGE 18 WITH 15
OR MORE RESTRICTED-ACTIVITY DAYS, 1980

Age group	Physician visits (mean)	Number prescribed drugs (mean)
Under 6 years		
With Medicaid	7.3	5.2
Without Medicaid		
Poor	6.7	4.8
Nonpoor	7.4	5.5
6–17 Years		
With Medicaid	6.2	3.2
Without Medicaid		
Poor	5.4	2.8
Nonpoor	6.3	3.9

Source: Health Care Financing Administration (1986).

broad concerns: the extent of third-party payer coverage and the complicated issue of the link between need for health care services and actual expenditures.

The Gaps in Health Insurance in the United States

Despite the U.S. position at the top of all OECD nations in terms of the share of GDP devoted to health care, the U.S. public-private health insurance system has three major gaps. First, an estimated 31 to 37 million people, about 1 in 7 Americans, lack health insurance altogether. Particularly troubling is the substantial number of children among this group—11.1 million in 1985. Of this group, 4.3 million lived in poverty and another 3.6 million lived in households with incomes between the poverty threshold and twice that level (Chollet 1987). Moreover, of the 11 million children who lacked health insurance in 1985, 3.2 million lived in a household where the household head had employer-based health insurance. This situation reflects the phenomenon of employers offering insurance to workers but not their dependents. Thus, even when a child lives with a parent or other relative who is part of the work-based insurance system, the child may still be at risk.

Second, a substantial number of people in the insured working population are underinsured; often, their insurance policies lack protection against catastrophic illness.

Third, although all the elderly are covered by Medicare, this program covers only half of all health outlays. That is, Medicare protection, even for acute care, is generally less comprehensive than private health insurance held by the working-age population (U.S. Congress, Congressional Budget Office 1983). About two-thirds of the elderly have private supplemental insurance, but a significant group fall through the cracks between this type of insurance and Medicaid, which pays for out-of-pocket costs for only a little over one-third of the elderly poor.

Publicly subsidized health coverage for the nonelderly poor in the United States tends to be *deep but not widespread*; it is "all or nothing." About half the poor have Medicaid; and for this group coverage is generally comprehensive, although covered services vary from state to state. Some of the poor have private coverage; but many, particularly children and young adults, are totally uninsured. By contrast, among the elderly insurance coverage is *broad but not deep*. Everyone is covered, but older Americans remain vulnerable to long-term care expenses and outlays for such items as prescription drugs that are not covered by Medicare. In addition, even covered services require substantial copayments, deductibles, and premiums (U.S. Congress, Congressional Budget Office 1983).

The U.S. health insurance system for working-age persons and their families has two major components—a *work-based* system providing generally, but not always, adequate private health coverage and a *welfare-based* public assistance system in which health care aid is tied to welfare. People fall out of this system if they are poor but ineligible for welfare and if they are unemployed or working at one of the many U.S. jobs that do not include health insurance coverage. Indeed, in 1985 a little over two-thirds (69 percent) of the uninsured lived in families of full-time, full-year workers (people who worked or sought work 35 weeks or more and worked 35 hours or more per week (Chollet 1987).

The U.S. health care system varies in many important ways from the systems in the rest of the world, but perhaps the greatest differences occur in the way the system is financed. The United States stands alone among the OECD countries in the large share of health care financed by private resources. (See table 8.1 presented earlier.) In 1984 41.4 percent of U.S. health care was financed through the public sector; the mean for OECD countries was 78.7 percent (Schieber and Poullier 1986). After the United States, Austria obtains the smallest share from the public sector: 60.9 percent. At least some of the variation in spending between the young and the elderly stems from this unique health care finance system. It is worth noting, however, that a mixed public-private system per se need not lead to gaps in coverage if each sector's coverage is complete and the two systems mesh well.

The Problem of Segmentation

The United States stands virtually alone among industrial nations in segmenting its youth population for purposes of health care assistance. Although there are some children in all countries who do not get needed care (the homeless, for example), only the United States excludes a major segment of children on a systematic basis. Other countries take a more universal approach to cash assistance (indeed, often providing child allowances for all children, regardless of income, see chapter 14 of this volume) and also treat health insurance protection for children as part of a universal system. Some countries, such as West Germany, use a payroll tax model; others, like Sweden, use a national health plan.

Thus, one basic difference in U.S. public health policies toward children and the elderly is that the United States uses a *categorical* approach for children and a *universal* approach for the elderly. The disparate treatment of the young and the elderly in health care is a microcosm of a much broader disparity in U.S. social policy. Virtually all the programs assisting the elderly in the United States transcend income lines, providing universal benefits. With the important exception of public education, however, programs for children are typically means-tested and, within the lower-income group, sliced up again in ways that exclude large numbers of impoverished children.

American children are the victims of social policy that distinguishes between "deserving" and "undeserving" recipients of aid. Although most Americans consider children as deserving of assistance, assistance for children is contingent on public judgments of the worthiness of their parents to receive government aid. By contrast, U.S. policymakers have never applied notions of "benefit worthiness" to the health care of the elderly, all of whom are judged deserving.

Implementation of the Supplemental Security Income (SSI) program in 1974 brings the contrast between treatment of children and the elderly into high relief. At the same time that welfare reform plans featuring a federal minimum for adults and children were foundering, SSI established a national standard for the elderly and disabled. The United States made a decision that it was simply unwilling to let states set cash assistance benefits for the elderly and the disabled at any level they pleased. Yet even today, states set their own benefit levels under Aid to Families with Dependent Children (AFDC), resulting in severe regional disparities.

It would be a mistake, however, to think of the United States as having a subsidized public system and an unsubsidized private system. The tax preference regarding the exclusion by workers of the full value of employer contributions amounts to roughly $40 billion in forgone revenue.[2] This amount compares with $78 billion projected for Medicare in fiscal 1988 (current services) but exceeds the federal share of Medicaid, which is estimated at $26.9 billion in fiscal 1988 (Office of Management and Budget 1987). This tax preference has undoubtedly contributed to the spread and comprehensiveness of employer-based health coverage; but it may also have contributed to higher costs and the maldistribution of coverage, because excluding this fringe benefit from taxation benefits higher-income employees disproportionately.

Factors Affecting Health Coverage for Children

The extent to which health care for children is covered in the United States depends on several factors—including whether their parents are employed, where their parents are employed, and the state in which they live.

Children's coverage depends first on whether their parents have a job with employer-provided health coverage. In certain industries and occupations, lack of health coverage is widespread. In 1985, for example, 52 percent of all uninsured workers were employed in either retail trade or services (Chollet 1987). Of women working full time in 1984 in jobs paying less than $10,000 per year, 57 percent lacked job-related health insurance; of women working part-time in such jobs, 87 percent lacked group health coverage (Reischauer 1987). Most of these working women also are not receiving Medicaid.

Thus, many children whose parents are in the work force are still *outside* the work-based health system. Their next shot at coverage is to qualify for the welfare-based system. But the United States has made it very difficult for even minimum-wage workers to qualify for Aid to Families with Dependent Children (AFDC)—and therefore Medicaid. In fact, in 1985 only 50.5 percent of poor children in the United States were covered by Medicaid (U.S. Congress 1987).

States base AFDC and Medicaid eligibility on both need standards

Table 8.5   AFDC MONTHLY NEED AND PAYMENT STANDARDS FOR A FOUR-PERSON HOUSEHOLD, JANUARY 1987 (dollars)

State	Need standard	Payment standard (maximum benefit)	Payment standard as a percentage of federal poverty line[a]
Alabama	480	147	16
California	734	734	79
Illinois	778	386	41
Kentucky	246	246	26
Louisiana	750	234	25
Vermont	963	642	69
Wisconsin	764	649	70
Median state	515	415	44

Source: U.S. Congress, House Committee on Ways and Means (1987), 408–12.
a. Four-person poverty line in 1986.

and payment standards. The need standard is the amount of money determined to be necessary for a family to meet basic subsistence needs. A household is eligible today for AFDC only if its gross income is less than 185 percent of the need standard in the state. Although at first glance this might seem generous, most state need standards are well below the official federal government poverty line. Table 8.5 illustrates the seriousness of this problem and shows the importance of considering both payment and need standards. For example, Kentucky has the lowest need standard in the country—$246 per month for a family of four in 1987, or $2,952 per year. This amount is only about one-fourth of the federal poverty line for a four-person family. Thus families with annual incomes as low as half the federal poverty line would be ineligible in Kentucky. By contrast, in California the 1987 AFDC need standard is $734 per month, or $8,808 per year. A person could have a gross income of up to $16,295 per year and make it through this screen. The median state has a need standard of $515 a month, or $6,180 per year.

In fact, AFDC eligibility is even more stringent than these numbers suggest. In addition to the 185 percent limit on gross income, AFDC also requires that countable income or net income after work-related expenses be less than a state's payment standard. The payment standard is the maximum benefit a state will actually pay, and it may be set at some fraction of the state's own need standard. For example, in Alabama the AFDC payment standard—maximum benefit—is $147 per month for a family of four in 1987, or $1,764 per year. This amount is only 16 percent of the corresponding federal poverty line. Families of four in Alabama with incomes above this line are ineligible for AFDC and will therefore typically also be denied Medicaid.[3]

The importance of the state disparities for the health care of children is that many poor children in the United States find themselves without Medicaid even though they live in households with incomes as low as 30 to 50 percent of the official poverty line. Many of these children live in categorically eligible households. But it is not enough for their household to be poor in order to get assistance; they must be pathetically poor in some regions to get help. Clearly, where poor children happen to live affects their chances of getting help.

This problem has been getting worse in recent years. The real value of AFDC maximum benefits has fallen over the 1970–1986 period in all but three states (California, +$17 per month; Maine, +$8 per month; Wisconsin, +$10 per month). When we examine the situation of heads of four-person households *earning* three-fourths of the poverty-level of income in 1986, we find that only eight states added enough in AFDC and food stamps benefits to carry the household over the poverty line. In 1976, by contrast, 44 states did so (U.S. Congress, unpublished data).

For children without third-party health insurance coverage, receipt of services is likely to be spotty (again, see table 8.4). When families must depend on charity care, they are likely to wait until problems are severe before seeking treatment, thereby exacerbating their health problem and increasing the cost of treatment.

The Elderly Poor and the Disabled

Many lower-income senior citizens and disabled persons need help with uninsured health outlays. The special problems of the elderly and disabled poor are supposed to be dealt with through Supplemental Security Income (SSI) and Medicaid. The latter program has an arrangement (called "buy in") that enables it to cover copayments, deductibles, and other medical expenses under Medicare for the poor, and to cover nursing home expenses for persons who have depleted their assets.

Only about one-third of the elderly poor actually receive Medicaid benefits. There are several reasons for this. First, only about 50 percent of the eligible elderly poor participate in SSI, and SSI participation triggers Medicaid eligibility. Second, maximum SSI benefits are more generous and consistent than AFDC, but they do not provide a poverty-line income. In 1986 maximum SSI benefits were 76 percent of the one-person poverty line for individuals and 90 percent of the two-person poverty line for couples. Thus, poor people with incomes *between* maximum benefits and the poverty line often cannot get Medicaid because they cannot qualify for SSI.

Finally, states have some flexibility in establishing the link between SSI and Medicaid. They can set criteria for Medicaid eligibility that are more restrictive than for SSI (14 states exercise the so-called 209b option). And the extent of actual buy-in arrangements (and therefore, the proportion of health costs not covered by either Medicaid or Medicare) varies from state to state.

Medicaid's medically needy program does serve some elderly who do not get SSI but whose resources after spending on health care place them within the eligibility range. A number of states have no medically needy program, however, and in others the net income limits are very restrictive. A large share of those in the medically needy program are receiving support for nursing home care.

The Link between Health Status and Expenditures

Expenditures on health care are often used as a proxy for better health. If it is true that more spending on care improves health, a rising share of a country's resources spent on care could be readily justified as legitimate spending, and discrepancies between age groups might reflect unwarranted preferential treatment. But persons with worse health might require more health care expenditures to leave them equally well off in terms of health—assuming that expenditures and needs can be linked in any reasonable way. Assertions about the relationship between health care spending and better health are made without much evidence to back either claim, however. The issues are complex and multifaceted. Trying to make sense of the relationship requires that we look at (1) how health status is measured, (2) whether medical care improves health status and whether improvements are constant across different types of individuals, and (3) whether actual health care expenditures are correlated closely with efficacious treatment.

■ *DIFFERENCES IN HEALTH STATUS*

At least some of the long-standing disparity in acute care spending between the elderly and the young reflects not simply a preference for more physician visits and other use of health care or greater financial ability to purchase such services. Rather, various age groups display large differences in health status. Like so many other measures in the area of health care, however, health status measures have many limitations.

Unfortunately, development of accurate measures of health status remains in its infancy. At the crudest level, we can measure changes in mortality rates over time to gauge one type of improvement in health status. Obviously, this ultimate measure tells us little about the condition of the living population; for example, great strides could be made in improving functioning and reducing suffering with no visible change in mortality figures.

A variety of indicators have been developed to try to fill these gaps. For example, selected mortality figures are sometimes used to examine changes in health status associated with particular diseases. The decline in mortality due to heart disease in recent years has often been cited as one indicator of improved health status.

Some strides have also been made in developing indicators to quantify functional disability. Perhaps the best known of these are the ADL (activities of daily living) and IADL (instrumental activities of daily living) indicators, which are used particularly to measure the severity of functional impairments among the elderly. The ability to dress oneself, for example, is one of the ADL. Although these functional indicators can generally be measured objectively, ADL and IADL are mainly used to assess need for long-term care. These functional indicators can generally be measured objectively, but because of the many differences in activities of the young and old, comparisons across age groups would be troublesome.

Another major indicator of health status is obtained from a self-rating system, in which respondents compare their health with the health of others of the same age (or in otherwise similar settings). Respondents are sometimes also asked to indicate how often they were unable to work outside the home or do housework, or how many "bed disability days" they had. These relative status measures also are best used to highlight contrasts among persons who are otherwise quite similar; again, comparisons between the young and the elderly may be troublesome.

Finally, use of preventive health services is sometimes chosen as a proxy for health status, on the assumption that such care is efficacious. Immunizations and prenatal care are input measures that reflect access to services proved effective in enhancing health status. These particular indicators are important for children's well-being.

As yet there are no good indicators of more subtle differences in health status, such as presence of pain or other subtle measures of discomfort. We are probably many years away from the development of such measures, particularly from developing ones that could be used to evaluate status variations across disparate population categories such as age.

Nonetheless, crude measures do allow us to discern a few trends over time and differences at points in time in health status. For example, improvements in life expectancy have come more rapidly for persons over age 65 than for the population as a whole since 1970 in the United States. Between 1970 and 1984, life expectancy at age 65 increased by 10.5 percent, whereas the increase across the entire lifespan has only been 5.4 percent (U.S. Public Health Service 1986).

These indicators are also often used to make international comparisons. For example, although steady progress has been made in reducing infant mortality since the 1960s, the United States continues to rank below many other developed countries on this indicator. In 1983, for example, the United States ranked 15th among OECD countries on infant mortality. In overall life expectancy, the United States was 14th for women and 18th for men in 1980. The U.S. record for life expectancy at age 60 improves somewhat; in 1980, the United States tied for 5th for women and 10th for men (OECD 1985).

Disease-specific mortality rates also indicate that some of the most striking improvements have come in conditions that affect older persons. For example, death rates from heart disease have fallen from 254 per 100,000 residents in 1970 to 189 in 1983. And an even more dramatic decline has occurred in cerebrovascular disease—from 66 per 100,000 to 34 over the same time period (Andersen, Aday, and Chen 1986).

It appears from these various mortality statistics that improvements in mortality have come at the upper end of the age distribution. Although it is not known whether this drop in the mortality rates can be linked directly to higher spending on the elderly, the converse argument—linking infant mortality and lack of spending on health care for children—is often made. The importance of other factors such as incomes of families with newborns also needs to be considered, however (Andersen, Aday, and Chen 1986).

As already mentioned, ADL and IADL indicators are used mainly to rank the older population; in part, this reflects their much greater degree of functional impairment. For instance, more than 8 million

Table 8.6   SELF-ASSESSMENT OF HEALTH STATUS BY AGE, 1981
AND 1983

Age group	Percentage of persons		
	With limitation of activity (1981)	In excellent health (1983)	In fair or poor health (1983)
Under 17	3.7	52.5	3.1
Under 6	2.5	53.4	2.8
6–16	4.3	52.0	3.2
17–44	8.9	44.0	6.1
45–64	24.3	26.5	20.0
65 and over	45.4	16.5	33.1

Source: U.S. Public Health Service (1986).

persons in the United States are estimated to need assistance with personal care, two-thirds of whom are elderly. Moreover, among those over age 65, these needs are highly correlated with age. Just 2.6 percent of persons ages 65 to 69 have functional limitations, whereas 31.6 percent of those age 85 and older require assistance with personal care (Doty, Liu, and Wiener 1985).

The health indicators based on use of services also show some progress for children in terms of access to care in the United States. The proportion of mothers who did not seek prenatal care until after the first trimester of pregnancy has declined from 32 percent in 1970 to 24 percent in 1983. Women have had greater access to such services over time. Improvements have also occurred in the proportion of children immunized against rubella, measles, and mumps, although more than a third of children ages 1 to 4 remain unimmunized (Andersen, Aday, and Chen 1986).

Finally, as people age, they consistently rate themselves in poorer health, as indicated in table 8.6. More than half of all children in the United States are listed in excellent health in 1983, but only one-sixth of the elderly persons place themselves in this category (U.S. Public Health Service 1986). Less than 4 percent of children were reported to have limitations of activity, compared with more than 45 percent of persons over age 65. These statistics have remained quite stable over a seven-year period.

■ THE LINK BETWEEN TREATMENT AND HEALTH STATUS

Consider first the most straightforward comparison—between persons who have the same health problems. Will medical treatment prolong life, control disease, or reduce suffering? The answer seems to be a resounding "probably, at least in some cases."

Many researchers have worried about the link between health care utilization and health status. In a recent article in *Health Affairs*, Andersen, Aday, and Chen (1986) discuss the importance of environmental factors and life-style in health promotion as well as the preventive, curative, and palliative aspects of using health services. The authors note that there have been many measurable improvements in health status, that the rates at which people use the health care system have gone up, and that people are becoming increasingly aware of the need for environmental protection and healthier lifestyles. Because all these factors are changing simultaneously, the direct causal links are more difficult to establish.

Results from the Rand Corporation's massive experimental study of health insurance in the United States suggested that health care spending differences at the margin had only small effects on health status (Brook and Lohr 1986). In hypertension and in dental problems, some differences were observed between persons who received more or less care.

When the stakes are higher, however, the consequences have been more visible. For example, a recent follow-up study of 186 patients who lost eligibility for Medi-Cal benefits (California's Medicaid program) indicated a decline in health status as compared with the status of a control group of patients who remained eligible (Lurie et al. 1986). The authors found not only that the ineligible had more problems of access to care and a general decline in health status, but also that four deaths over the year could be linked to problems of access to care. Because these patients had low incomes, they may have been particularly vulnerable to health problems arising from denied access.

Finally, Hadley (1982) attempted to answer directly the question in his book's title, *More Medical Care, Better Health?* Hadley used a variety of statistical techniques to hold fixed the effects of a number of sociodemographic, behavioral, and environmental factors so he could determine whether higher expenditures significantly lowered mortality rates. His answer is an unambiguous yes.

But Hadley went even further, to ask whether there were systematic differences in the effectiveness of expenditures by age group. Thus, he addressed the second issue raised earlier about the degree to which the effectiveness of health care treatment varies with patient characteristics. Here he concluded that devoting more expenditures to the elderly had the greatest possible impact on reducing death rates. Factors other than medical treatment were relatively more important in affecting mortality of other age groups, such as infants. These results were limited to the mortality indicator of health status, and as such, certainly leave out a number of other possible reasons for redirecting health resources, as already discussed. Nonetheless, they offer interesting reading to those thinking about the debate over whether too many health resources are directed at the elderly.

Earlier in this chapter, we examined what various measures indicated about relative health status across age groups. Certainly there are striking differences in self-reported health status by age, although a large share of the difference seems to relate to problems of disability and functional limitation. Is health care more effective in alleviating poor health arising from a chronic condition associated with aging or in treating a child with a totally different acute care problem? Again, the great differences between the young and the elderly and the relative crudity of our measures for assessing treatment effectiveness hamper conclusions. Yet, this critical question is central to the problem of determining how much care should appropriately be directed at a particular age group.

■ THE RELATIONSHIP BETWEEN EXPENDITURES AND NEEDED CARE

Before considering whether health *expenditures* can be used as an indicator for access to improved health status, or what variations in spending are justified, we must examine the third issue—whether more money buys better care. This issue can in turn be further subdivided to look both at the extent to which care received is appropriate and the extent to which higher-priced care (both over time and at a point in time) reflects differences in quality.

The Rand Corporation health insurance experiment provides detailed information about use of services across the nonelderly population. One particularly intriguing finding, as noted, was the large proportion of medically ineffective care consumed by the sample population. Furthermore, the study found that cost sharing— requiring insured persons to bear part of the costs of the services— discouraged use of all services, effective and ineffective (Brook and Lohr 1986). That is, when persons in like situations chose to consume less care, they were not able to discriminate so that they used only the most efficacious services. These findings suggest that the U.S. population probably consumes more health care than necessary, but that the problem is likely to exist across the board, among high spenders and low spenders alike.

Part of the high cost of care in the United States arises from what we pay providers. Physicians earned an average of $113,200 in 1985, more than seven times the 1985 average earnings for all occupations taken together. This ratio is higher than for virtually all other nations. And the open-ended reimbursement system (now rapidly changing) that prevailed throughout the period when health costs exploded has contributed not only to the higher fees and charges, but also to a tremendous increase in the quantity of inputs into the health care sector—an increase that probably far outpaced improvements in health care outcomes, as hard as those are to measure accurately.

Another troubling aspect of making comparisons on the basis of health dollars spent arises from the tremendous differences in the costs of care across the country—and sometimes even within the same location and for the same types of providers. There have always been major variations in the costs of care in the United States, particularly between rural areas and the West Coast or eastern urban centers in New York or Massachusetts. (There are likely to be wide variations in the norms of treatment around the country as well.) The rise of health care competition and the emphasis on groups with market power bargaining for preferential rates means that some patients—backed by a powerful employer, for example— would spend less for inpatient care delivered in the same hospital than another patient whose insurance company did not receive a "discount" price.

Comparisons of health care expenditures over time may prove problematic even within a single population group because of the tremendous increases in the price inflation of medical care. The ever-rising dollar values of health care benefits increasingly overstate the extent to which needs are being met. When medical inflation rises faster than the general rate of inflation (as it has consistently done for the past 15 or more years), health care costs rise relative to other consumption items even if there are no improvements in services or benefits.

Thus, reliance on health care spending as a proxy for health care service use creates additional biases and strains on any comparisons. Some of these biases may cancel each other out—for example, geographic variations may not much influence the ratio of spending for the young compared with spending for the elderly. Moreover, if the differences are great enough, as seen in the case of the Medi-Cal beneficiaries taken off the rolls in California, lower health care spending can indeed lead to a lowering of health status (Lurie et al. 1986). If deprivation of health care services could be studied over a longer period of time, the results might be even more dramatic. Even so, we cannot make the link between health status and health care dollars with great confidence.

Nonetheless, comparisons in spending levels are often made in the media and in policy discussions. Because these comparisons will undoubtedly continue, in the next section we try to make sense of the numbers and suggest some simple adjustments that may improve comparisons.

EVALUATING HEALTH CARE SPENDING

Three issues remain unresolved. First, should we be concerned about the high level of overall health care spending in the United States compared with spending elsewhere? Second, should the U.S. spending be reordered between the young and the elderly? Third, and closely linked to the second, how does health care spending contribute to well-being, and does variation in such spending differentially benefit some groups more than others? The second and third issues are considered together in the paragraphs that follow.

Evaluating the Level of U.S. Health Care Spending

As indicated earlier, the United States spends a greater proportion of GDP on health than any other nation. We now turn to the question that we raised at the outset: Can such a high proportion be justified by factors such as an improvement in productivity and economic growth or by improved health outcomes?

A disproportionate share of the U.S. public investment in health care over the past two decades has gone to the elderly. In addition to the rapid growth in Medicare outlays, Medicaid has tilted toward a program for the elderly in recent years. In 1982 children constituted 48 percent of all Medicaid recipients, but only 13 percent of all payments went for children's care (National Study Group on State Medicaid Strategies 1983). This may be a compassionate approach to the distribution of public sector health care resources, but it cannot be described as one that is targeted toward maximizing the productive capacity of our economy. Indeed, we provide no government help with health care outlays to many low-income workers who are on the edge of falling back on welfare. And the fact that we do not make basic preventive care available to many youth undoubtedly raises the odds against their later success in the labor market.

As mentioned earlier, the government's tax preferences for health care have encouraged the spread of employee group health insurance and probably contributed to its comprehensiveness. To the extent that group health insurance has enhanced access to health care among active workers, it has probably reduced absenteeism and enhanced the health status and productivity of the labor force. This tax preference, however, is worth more to higher-paid workers than to lower-paid workers (because its value depends on the marginal income tax rate), so that workers who need the most investment in human capital may often receive the least help. In addition, as noted earlier, many workers—particularly lower-wage workers—do not have employee group health insurance and therefore do not benefit from the ability to exclude employer contributions from taxable income.

The 1965–85 period represents an era of explosive growth in health care costs. The beginning of this period was marked by a time of steady and significant economic expansion, when economic growth was projected at 3.5 percent to 4.0 percent per year. In contrast, actual growth of output in the United States from 1965 to 1985 averaged 2.7 percent. If 4 percent growth had been experienced over these two decades, GNP would have been $5 trillion instead of the just under $4 trillion actually achieved, and health care expenditures of somewhat over $400 billion in 1985 would have been 8.3 percent of GNP instead of the 10.7 percent that we actually experienced (Makin 1987). At 8.3 percent, we would have been in the middle of the pack of the other OECD countries; of course, their economies generally also fell short of pre-1965 experience during the past two decades.

Productivity gains in the United States, which averaged 3.0 percent per year from 1947 to 1973, averaged only 0.9 percent per year over the 1973–85 period. Thus, the U.S. economic performance over the period during which health care costs exploded does not seem to reflect a successful strategy of productivity-enhancing investments in areas such as the health and education of our work force. Other factors, such as demographic trends, the fall-off in research and development expenditures increases, and the OPEC oil price shocks, influenced productivity trends and may well have masked some true health-related productivity gains. But other countries also experienced these trends and had better productivity gains than the United States.

Although it is difficult to sort out all these factors, it appears that the relatively high position of the United States in terms of health spending does not reflect a conscious strategy to target extra resources on health care in ways designed to maximize our productivity. Other factors—such as the decision to invest heavily in access to health care among the elderly, clear inefficiencies in the way health care has been paid for, and the relatively high pay of physicians in the United States—seem to explain the gap between the United States and other countries. One can argue that the first of these factors yields benefits—the life expectancy of the elderly has increased. The third factor, higher pay of doctors, may also be instrumental in attracting talent to this profession (and away from other countries) and encouraging high-quality care in the United States. The second factor—allocative inefficiency that devotes unnecessarily large amounts of resources to health care—surely cannot be justified.

As we have already seen, there have been a number of gains in health status in recent years, justifying at least some higher spending on health as a consumption good. Longer life expectancies, lower infant mortality, and advances against some diseases attest to the benefits of more health expenditures. The efficacy of specific treatments for some groups versus others and improved efficiency in spending deserve further study.

Given the basic imbalances in the distribution of resources—fully comprehensive coverage for some people versus absolutely no coverage for others—there appear to be opportunities to redirect some of the already large total amount of resources devoted to health care in the United States. Moreover, the inefficiencies in the U.S. health system are being corrected to a large degree by the much more aggressive and competitive purchasing practices of both the U.S. government and private employers. As these large buyers of health services continue to whittle down the inefficiencies in the system, however, they will also continue to erode the hidden subsidies to the poor that have long been embedded in the U.S. health financing system. Thus, as the "excess" spending in the United States begins to taper off or decline, the vulnerability of people outside the social protection system—particularly, children—will increase.

UNDERSTANDING SPENDING DIFFERENCES BETWEEN THE YOUNG AND THE ELDERLY

We began by examining some of the gross differences in health care spending between the young and the elderly in the United States.

Table 8.7   SPENDING ON HEALTH CARE FOR CHILDREN AND THE ELDERLY
BY INSURANCE STATUS, 1980 (dollars)

Population and age group	Spending levels (mean)	Spending levels (median)
65 and older	1,904	396
All children with insurance coverage	342	128
6 or younger	253	108
7–18	370	136
Spending on children as a proportion of spending on the elderly	0.176	0.323

Source: Computations from the National Medical Care Utilization and Expenditure Survey (1980).

Such differences may affect the health and economic status of Americans, but firm conclusions depend on a number of factors already discussed. What, then, should we conclude? Certainly some differences in spending are justified, and merely adding spending by third parties such as government and employees to the income of various groups would distort rather than improve measures of economic well-being.

We have suggested two major sources for the differential in health care spending on the young and the elderly that may require adjustments. The first of these—access to care by virtue of ability to pay—surely constitutes an unacceptable source of variation. If children (or others) are denied care because they cannot afford it, a true problem exists. The second source—variation in the need for services—provides a legitimate justification for differences.

As already discussed, some persons do not receive the health care they need; medical care is expensive and not all families and individuals have enough resources, or access to programs such as Medicare and Medicaid, to ensure that they receive adequate treatment. As a first step, we compare expenditures on health care by all the elderly (who at least have coverage under Medicare) with expenditures on health care for children with either private health insurance or Medicaid.[4] Average (mean) expenditures in 1980 for the elderly were $1,904, and for insured children, $342; thus expenditures for children were roughly 18 percent of the level for the elderly (see table 8.7). Somewhat surprisingly, the figure for insured children is only slightly higher than for all children ($336). Whether this suggests little problem with aggregate access or whether the data source is not sensitive enough to capture real differences is unclear. For example, if poor uninsured children eventually get access to care when they are faced with catastrophic problems, averages might be deceptive.

For this reason, we also present the ratio based on median spending levels. Because the median for persons ages 65 and older is much smaller than the mean for that group, spending on children with health insurance represents a greater proportion compared with those over age 65—32 percent. If median spending on the elderly were compared with that for all children (even those with insurance), the proportion of that for the young to that for the old would be 29 percent. When medians are used, it does make a difference if children who lack insurance are excluded—although to a relatively modest degree.

Figures on *public* expenditures for all children indicate that they received only 6.4 percent as much as the elderly in 1978. Thus, if the 18 percent figure (the average overall spending differential for those with insurance) is used as the benchmark for evaluating public spending differentials, a very different estimate emerges of how close public spending on children comes to offering "equivalent" benefits. If the goal is to cover a proportional amount of the needs of the young, spending would need to triple rather than to rise by a factor of 15.

As already described, however, we might wish to add employer-provided health insurance to the public spending figures for both the young and the old to account for differences in the source of payment of health care. We know that the proportion of children who have insurance coverage paid for by their parents' employer is higher than the proportion of the elderly who have comparable employee or retiree supplemental health benefits.

Contributions by government for health care thus exacerbate the imbalance in overall spending between the two groups, but the amount is not so high as when public spending levels are contrasted without any adjustments. The unadjusted 15 to 1 differential in spending is too high; after accounting for legitimate differences in use, the imbalance in terms of public spending is more in the range of 3 to 1. And that ratio would be somewhat smaller if the private employer-provided insurance contributions on behalf of children also were incorporated.

The second type of adjustment (recognizing differences in needs) is considerably more problematic. The evidence on health status and the efficacy of treatment suggest that the needs are greater for the elderly and that treatment can be effective in prolonging life expectancy. The magnitude of any justifiable difference is, however, not quantifiable.

What we do know is that, inasmuch as needs differ, it is misleading simply to add expenditures to income. Expenditures on medical services do not, of course, directly buy good health. But, if everyone received the level of health spending they required, there would be a *negative*—not a positive—correlation between high expenditures and well-being. Medical expenditures, to some extent, reflect the lack of health of individuals; and in a world of perfect access, overall spending might be used as a proxy for need, not for improved well-being.

In sum, there are legitimate reasons for the differential spending levels between the elderly and the young. However, the evidence suggests that access problems may have led to a greater differential than justified, and public spending on health care may be somewhat at fault. The lack of a quantifiable link between health status and health care expenditures makes it impossible to suggest the proper differential. Finally, because health care spending is a result of poor health at least to some degree, it is not reasonable to treat higher spending levels on health care as synonymous with greater well-being.

CONCLUSIONS

We have documented a number of concerns about the U.S. health care system. Although the United States spends an extraordinary amount on health care, a substantial minority of Americans have problems of access to care. Payments to providers are high, and people often consume inappropriate care. Nonetheless, many of the nation's poor lack access to services; there are significant gaps in the protection offered by our mixed private-public financing system. And for people who do have some protection, vital services such as long-term care remain uncovered by any third-party payer.

Although much of our attention has centered on describing these problems, we believe there are solutions. In conclusion, we suggest some general approaches, most of which build on the mixed private-public system that seems to be so uniquely American.

First, it is critical to address the important gaps in health care coverage for the poor and near-poor. A variety of approaches are possible, ranging from refundable tax credits or sliding-scale vouchers to a major revamping of the Medicaid program. Improved health care protection for people with low incomes should go hand in hand with better *income* protection as well. Coverage for both AFDC and SSI needs to be improved.

Private employers may also be encouraged to expand their role in the health care system. Employers could be required to provide health insurance to full-time workers, and state-level risk pools could allow small employers more affordable access to insurance.

We should also consider revamping the protection offered by both the private and the public sectors to encourage preventive care and to offer some protection against long-term care costs. Moreover, third-party payers must become more prudent buyers of care to ensure that everyone gets the best value for the health care dollar.

All these activities could improve the balance among recipients of health care benefits in the United States and yield greater benefit from the resources that the United States devotes to health care.

Notes

1. Unpublished data from the National Medical Care Utilization and Expenditure Survey, provided by Katherine Swartz.

2. The exact amount depends on factors such as the amount of the employee's share of health insurance premiums that is sheltered from taxation through various salary reduction plans, added to the full amount of employer contributions to health insurance that the worker may exclude from taxation. This estimate also includes forgone payroll taxes.

3. About 30 states have medically needy programs that provide Medicaid assistance to households with incomes up to 133 percent of the state's payment standard if the household has unusually large medical expenses and "spends down" into the eligible category. Likely passage of the Catastrophic Health Insurance bill in 1988 would help expand Medicaid coverage to mothers, children, and the elderly.

4. Some insurance coverage (for both groups) is inadequate. Nonetheless, we are offering these adjustments as indicative of how we might develop different measures.

References

Anderson, Ronald, Lu Ann Aday, and Meei-shia Chen. 1986. "Health Status and Medical Care Utilization." *Health Affairs* (Spring):154–72.

Brook, Robert H., and Kathleen Lohr. 1986. *Use of Medical Care in the Rand Health Insurance Experiment.* Santa Monica, Calif.: Rand Corporation (December).

Chollet, Deborah. 1987. "Uninsured in the U.S.: The Nonelderly Population Without Health Insurance." Washington, D.C.: Employee Benefits Research Institute (March 4).

Doty, Pamela, Korbin Liu, and Joshua Wiener. 1985. "An Overview of Long-Term Care." *Health Care Financing Review* 6 (Spring):69–78.

Enterline, Philip, Vera Salter, Alison MacDonald, and J. Corbett MacDonald. 1973. "The Distribution of Medical Services before and after 'Free' Medical—The Quebec Experience." *New England Journal of Medicine* 289:1174–78.

Fisher, Charles. 1980. "Differences by Age Groups in Health Care Spending." *Health Care Financing Review* 2 (Spring):65–85.

Hadley, Jack. 1982. *More Medical Care, Better Health?* Washington, D.C.: The Urban Institute Press.

Health Care Financing Administration (HCFA). 1986. *Medicare and Medicaid Data Book.* Baltimore: HCFA, June.

Lurie, Nicole, Nancy B. Ward, Martin F. Shapiro, Claudio Gallego, Rati Vaghaiwalla, and Robert H. Brook. 1986. "Termination of Medi-Cal Benefits: A Follow-up Study One Year Later." *New England Journal of Medicine* 314:1266–8.

Makin, John. 1987. "Economic Growth and the Health Care Budget." Washington, D.C.: American Enterprise Institute. Photcopy.

National Study Group on State Medicaid Strategies. 1983. *Restructuring Medicaid: An Agenda for Change.* Washington, D.C.: Center for the Study of Social Policy.

Office of Management and Budget. 1987. *Budget of the United States Government, Fiscal Year 1988.* Washington, D.C.

Organization for Economic Cooperation and Development (OECD). 1985. *Measuring Health Care, 1960–1983.* Paris: OECD.

Reischauer, Robert. 1987. Testimony before the Subcommittee on Social Security and Family Policy, Committee on Finance, U.S. Senate (February 23, 1987).

Schieber, George J., and Jean-Pierre Poullier. 1986. "International Health Care Spending." *Health Affairs* (Fall):111–22.

U.S. Congress. 1987. House Committee on Ways and Means. *Background Material and Data on Programs within the Jurisdiction of the Committee on Ways and Means,* 1987 edition. (March 6):408–12.

U.S. Congress, Congressional Budget Office (CBO). 1983. *Changing the*

Structure of Medicare Benefits, Issues and Options. Washington, D.C. (March).

U.S. Public Health Service. 1986. *Health United States 1985*. Washington, D.C.

Waldo, Daniel and Helen Lazenby. 1984. "Demographic Characteristics and Health Care Use and Expenditures by the Aged in the United States: 1977–1984," *Health Care Financing Review* 6 (Fall):1–29.

Chapter Nine

THE ALLOCATION OF PUBLIC RESOURCES TO CHILDREN AND THE ELDERLY IN OECD COUNTRIES

Michael O'Higgins

This chapter tracks the trends in government spending on the elderly and on children in ten economically developed countries. It distinguishes spending in programs with different client groups and, to the extent possible, spending for beneficiaries of different ages. The chapter thus compares the ten governments' contribution to the economic welfare of children and the elderly, the extent to which the spending priority accorded to each group has changed over the years, and the degree to which any such changes are due to demographic pressures or to political choices about benefit generosity or service quality.

It becomes clear that pensions have received priority over other social programs in each country—not only because of demographic pressures, but also because of policy decisions. Countries vary in the generosity of their family benefits, but even in the most generous cases, family benefits are much less important to the well-being of children than are public expenditures on education. Thus, although the provision of pensions may be an important factor in explaining differences among countries in the economic welfare of the elderly versus other population groups, the same is not true of family benefits.

DATA, TIME PERIOD, AND COUNTRIES

This section discusses the available data, the choice of countries, and the time frame for the analysis. An understanding of the strengths and limitations of the data base is important for interpeting the findings.

The author wishes to acknowledge the helpful comments of Barbara Torrey and Peter Saunders on an earlier draft.

Data

The demographic and spending accounts data base developed by the Organization for Economic Cooperation and Development (OECD), which has provided much of the material for OECD reports on social expenditure (OECD, 1985, 1988), is the best source of broadly comparable information on patterns of social spending and demographic composition in developed countries. Because OECD is concerned only with data for its member countries, mostly relatively developed in international economic terms, its data are of higher quality and suffer from fewer gaps than data from agencies such as the United Nations or the International Monetary Fund, which seek global coverage. More important for present purposes, the spending data base was conceived with a view to the kinds of social spending institutions and categories that are common in mixed welfare-capitalist economies.

Certain data limitations should be noted, however:

1. There are as yet no good comparative data on the magnitudes of tax expenditures. This limitation can to a large extent be overcome by examining the value of tax and transfer spending on children to an average worker, which is done in table 9.5.

2. Some spending and program detail is sacrificed in fitting data into an international framework.

3. Early analyses using this data base (for example, OECD 1985) did not distinguish family benefits (cash transfers paid specifically and only to families with children) from other benefits included in a residual "other social expenditure" category. Fortunately, separate data are now available for family benefits, and trends in their per capita values and their relationship to per capita benefits for the elderly are the subject of a central section of this chapter. However, the parts of the chapter that build upon the OECD (1985) decomposition analysis are based only on education, health, and pensions data.

4. Although data are available on both the public and the total (public plus private) level of spending on health care, other data on "private social spending" are less adequate, notably with respect to family benefits and pensions. The chapter draws attention to the existence of relevant private provision as far as is possible, so that the understanding of the quantitative data on public spending is embedded in some qualitative awareness of private provision.

Time Period

The data base provides information on spending trends from 1960 onward, and the emphasis in much of the analysis is on two subperiods since then—the optimistic period of relatively sustained economic growth until the oil price shocks of the mid-1970s, and the more recessionary and, in social expenditure terms, more skeptical and cost-conscious period since then. The OECD (1985) analysis does suggest a clear break in social spending trends between these periods, but the issues to be investigated are the extent to which the shift was common (both in magnitude and timing) across countries and programs, and the variation, if any, in the relative role of factors such as demography and generosity in accounting for spending changes in each period.

Countries

The chapter focuses on ten of the countries covered by the OECD data. Inclusion of the seven major OECD countries (Canada, France, Italy, Japan, the United Kingdom, the United States, and West Germany) is presumably self-explanatory. In addition, Australia, the Netherlands, and Sweden are analyzed. Sweden was included because of its presence in other chapters in this volume, its general interest for social policy analysis, and its high social spending and low rates of poverty among the elderly (see, for example, Hedstrom and Ringen 1987). By contrast, Australia, though it has a relatively equal income distribution, has relatively low levels of social spending, an income- and asset-tested pensions system, and a less aged population profile. It is also, more consciously than most countries, using immigration policies to reduce its elderly dependency ratio, a policy it shares with Canada. The Netherlands was included because preliminary data searching and analysis for the remaining OECD countries indicated that particularly detailed information was available for that country on a number of questions to be examined. Another reason for including the Netherlands is that it is also projected to have one of the most rapidly increasing proportions of elderly people in the population and one of the most rapidly falling proportions of children.

Table 9.1 POPULATION CHANGES, SELECTED YEARS, 1960–83

	Total population (1980 = 100)				
	1960	1968	1975	1980	1983
Australia	71.8	83.7	94.5	100	104.7
Canada	74.4	86.1	94.4	100	103.5
France	84.8	92.6	97.8	100	101.6
Germany, F.R.	90.3	96.6	100.4	100	99.8
Italy	89.0	93.9	98.3	100	100.7
Japan	79.8	86.5	95.5	100	102.1
Netherlands	81.2	90.0	96.6	100	101.5
Sweden	90.0	95.2	98.6	100	100.2
United Kingdom	93.0	98.0	99.8	100	100.1
United States	79.3	88.1	94.8	100	103.0

Source: OECD (1986).

TRENDS IN POPULATION SIZE AND COMPOSITION

Table 9.1 shows the relative changes in the total population of the ten countries for the period since 1960; table 9.2 sets out the recent and projected changes in the age composition of their populations.

Recent population growth has been much slower in the six European countries under discussion than in the other four (table 9.1). The populations of each of the others—Australia, Canada, Japan, and the United States—grew by almost a quarter in the 20 years prior to 1980 and have continued to grow relatively rapidly since then. By contrast, only France and the Netherlands had population growth of one-eighth or more between 1960 and 1980; and the populations of West Germany, Sweden, and the United Kingdom now seem to be essentially static.

These trends are partly reflected in the relative "aging" of the population of these countries (table 9.2). Australia, the country with the most rapid population growth, has the largest proportion of children in its current population and is projected to have the lowest proportions of elderly people during the early decades of the next century. West Germany has, and is projected to continue to have, the lowest proportion of children; it is unique in this group of countries in already having as many elderly people as children.

Population growth is not the only factor contributing to this diversity. It is notable, for example, that the five countries where the proportion of children is projected to be highest during the early

Table 9.2   AGE STRUCTURE, SELECTED COUNTRIES, 1950–2020 (percentage of population)

	1950	1980	2000	2020	1950	1980	2000	2020
	Australia				Canada			
0–14	26.6	25.3	21.4	19.2	29.7	23.0	19.5	17.0
15–64	65.2	65.1	66.9	65.4	62.6	67.5	67.6	64.4
65 and over	8.1	9.6	11.7	15.4	7.6	9.5	12.8	18.6
65–69		3.6	3.4	5.0		3.4	3.9	6.0
70–79		4.3	5.6	7.1		4.3	6.1	8.4
80 and over		1.7	2.6	3.3		1.8	2.8	4.2
	France				Germany, F.R.			
0–14	22.7	22.3	19.2	17.0	23.5	18.2	15.5	13.4
15–64	65.9	63.8	65.5	63.6	67.1	66.3	67.4	64.8
65 and over	11.3	14.0	15.3	19.5	9.3	15.5	17.1	21.1
65–69		4.3	4.6	6.0		5.1	5.5	6.5
70–79		6.8	7.3	8.5		7.8	7.9	9.3
80 and over		2.9	3.3	5.0		2.6	3.6	5.3
	Italy				Japan			
0–14	26.4	22.0	17.1	14.6	35.3	23.5	17.5	16.8
15–64	65.5	64.6	67.6	66.0	59.5	67.4	67.3	63.0
65 and over	8.0	13.4	15.3	19.4	5.2	9.1	15.2	20.9
65–69		4.7	5.0	5.9		3.4	5.4	6.0
70–79		6.4	7.6	8.9		4.3	7.3	10.4
80 and over		2.2	2.6	4.6		1.4	2.5	4.5
	Netherlands				Sweden			
0–14	29.3	22.3	18.2	15.8	23.4	19.6	17.4	16.3
15–64	62.9	66.2	68.3	65.3	66.3	64.1	66.0	62.9
65 and over	7.7	11.5	13.5	18.9	10.2	16.3	16.6	20.8
65–69		3.8	4.2	6.2		5.3	4.4	5.9
70–79		5.4	6.3	9.1		7.8	7.7	10.4
80 and over		2.2	3.0	3.6		3.1	4.4	4.5
	United Kingdom				United States			
0–14	22.3	21.1	20.5	19.9	26.9	22.5	21.1	19.2
15–64	66.9	64.0	65.0	63.8	64.9	66.2	66.8	64.7
65 and over	10.7	14.9	14.5	16.3	8.1	11.3	12.1	16.2
65–69		5.1	4.3	5.1		3.9	3.4	5.7
70–79		7.2	6.9	8.0		5.1	5.8	7.3
80 and over		2.7	3.2	3.3		2.3	2.8	3.1

Source: OECD (1988).
Note: The demographic projections are based on a medium fertility variant and baseline mortality assumptions supplied by the countries to the OECD. Up to 1995, fertility is assumed to continue to be low, thereafter converging to replacement levels (a total fertility rate of 2.1) by 2050. The downward trend in mortality rates is assumed gradually to flatten out.

part of the next century—Australia, Canada, France, the United Kingdom, and the United States—are those that have admitted significant numbers of permanent immigrants in the recent past.

Despite this diversity, all ten countries show a similar sharp increase in the ratio of elderly to children. This shift is prospectively greatest in the case of Japan, which moves from having one old person for every seven children in 1950 to a projected ratio of around nine elderly per seven children in 2020. Both Canada and the Netherlands, having had around four children per elderly person in 1950, are projected to have slightly less than one for one in 2020.

Focusing only on the changes that have already taken place (and have therefore already affected the spending trends to be reviewed later) makes it clear that Japan and West Germany have had sharp falls in the proportions of children and very large relative rises in the numbers of elderly people. In Sweden, Italy, the United States, and the Netherlands, the proportion of children has similarly fallen; the rises in the proportion of elderly, though considerable, have not been quite so great. For Canada, the relative change has been mainly a decline in children. For France and the United Kingdom, the proportions of children have changed only marginally; but the relative numbers of elderly have risen. Only in Australia have changes in the proportions of both children and the elderly been fairly slight up to now.

MAGNITUDES AND SHARES OF SPENDING ON SOCIAL PROGRAMS IN 1980

In all the countries, expenditure on social programs dominates the consumption of public resources (table 9.3). Ranging from over one-sixth to one-third of national income, this spending accounts for at least one-half of total government spending in all of the countries and rises toward two-thirds in the larger continental European countries.

How these social expenditures break down into different program shares is examined in table 9.4. Government spending on education accounts for between 5 percent and 6 percent of gross domestic product (GDP) in most countries, with only Sweden and the Netherlands—the two countries where total social expenditure as a proportion of GDP is highest—spending more than this. The two

Table 9.3   GENERAL GOVERNMENT SPENDING BY SELECTED FUNCTIONS AS
A PERCENTAGE OF GROSS DOMESTIC PRODUCT (GDP), 1980

	Total	Public order[a]	Defense	Economic services[b]	Social services[c]
Australia	34.6	4.8	2.5	4.3	18.9
Canada	40.5	4.7	1.6	5.9	21.8
France	43.6	3.1	3.0	3.0	30.6
Germany, F.R.	48.8	3.7	2.7	3.9	32.6
Italy[d]	46.3	4.2	1.9	7.5	28.0
Japan[d]	32.4	3.0	0.8	5.6	21.5
United Kingdom	43.3	4.5	5.2		24.3
United States	33.8	2.9	4.8	2.6	18.3

Sources: Data for Italy and Japan are from United Nations (1983), table 2.3. Data for other countries are from International Monetary Fund (1986).
Note: No adequate comparable data for Sweden and the Netherlands and for economic services in the United Kingdom were available. The data refer to calendar years for European countries, to July 1979–June 1980 for Australia, to April 1980–March 1981 for Canada and Japan and to October 1979–September 1980 for the United States. The British data are for 1979; later data were not available in any of the international sources.
a. Public order includes general public services and public order and safety.
b. Economic services includes fuel and energy, agriculture, forestry, fishing and hunting; nonfuel mining, manufacturing, and construction; and transport and communication, and other economic services.
c. Social services includes education, health care, social security and welfare, and housing and community activities.
d. To make the Italian and Japanese data comparable to those from the other sources, a number of assumptions were required. The most significant of these was that all government spending categorized as "all current transfers and other property income" was taken as social spending.

lowest spenders—Japan and West Germany—had, respectively, the second largest and the smallest proportions of children. The variation across countries in spending on education is much less than the variation in government spending as a whole; thus, even the countries with much lower levels of government spending provide about the same proportion for education as do the other countries. This means that in terms of priorities within public or social spending, greater *shares* of public resources go to education in the four non-European countries.

Government spending on health care on average accounts for a proportion of national income similar to spending on education, but the variation in relative spending is much greater, and follows the broad pattern of differences in the overall importance of total

208   *The Vulnerable*

Table 9.4   SOCIAL PROGRAM EXPENDITURES AS A PERCENTAGE
OF GDP, 1980

	Australia	Canada	France	Germany, F.R.	Italy
Education	5.9	6.0	5.7	5.1	5.6
Health care	4.7	5.4	6.1	6.5	6.0
(Total health care[a])	(7.6)	(7.3)	(8.5)	(7.9)	(6.8)
Family benefits	1.1	0.6	2.7	1.1	1.1
Pensions	5.4	4.5	11.5	12.1	11.8
Unemployment	0.8	2.4	1.6	0.9	0.5
Other social expenditures	1.3	2.1	0.6	5.0	2.0
Total social expenditures[b]	18.8	21.0[c]	28.3	30.8	26.9
Total government expenditures	30.6	39.9	46.0	46.6	42.2

	Japan	Nether-lands	Sweden	United Kingdom	United States
Education	5.0	7.2	6.5	5.6	5.7
Health care	4.6	6.5	8.8	5.2	4.1
Total health care[a]	(6.4)	(8.2)	(9.5)	(5.6)	(9.5)
Family benefits	1.6	2.1	1.6	1.6	0.5
Pensions	4.5	11.0	10.9	6.7	7.2
Unemployment	0.4	1.7	0.4	0.9	0.6
Other social expenditures	0.8	3.5	4.3	2.2	2.7
Total social expenditures[b]	16.9	32.0[c]	32.5	22.0	20.7
Total government expenditures	30.1	56.9	61.0	44.4	35.4

Sources: Data derived from OECD (1985, 1987a, 1988).
Note: For definitions of expenditures included in the various program and total categories, see annex.
a. The total health care figure includes both public and private expenditures on health care. The social expenditures total includes only public spending on health care.
b. The total social expenditure definition used here is more restricted than that in table 9.3 because it does not include spending on housing and community activities.
c. Total social expenditures (including "other social expenditures") data for Australia and the Netherlands differ as between the 1985 and 1988 sources; in each case the later data were used.

spending on social programs. The data also show the different degrees of private health care spending in each country. At one end of the range, government spending accounts for less than half of total health care spending in the United States. At the other extreme, public spending in Sweden and the United Kingdom accounts for the vast majority of health care spending.

The degree of variation in health care spending is not much

reduced if total spending rather than government spending is examined. The majority of the countries retain their approximate position in terms of relative spending, with France, the Netherlands, Sweden, and West Germany being among the five largest spenders on either measure. The greatest change is to the position of the United States, which moves from being the lowest ranked in terms of the magnitude of government health spending to joint highest (with Sweden) when the measure is total spending. Partly because of the effect of private spending, health care accounts for a smaller share of government spending than education in all the non-European countries, and it is also less important in the Netherlands and in the United Kingdom than in the other European countries.

The five continental European countries spend much more on pensions than Japan and the four Anglo-Saxon countries, but Australia, Canada, and Japan were the only countries in which less than 10 percent of the population was aged over 65 in 1980, so their position as the lowest spenders has some demographic justification. With a similar, relatively low proportion of persons over 65 years of age, the United States spends only two-thirds as much on publicly provided pensions, relatively speaking, as the Netherlands. West Germany's high spending is consistent with its position as the country with the second greatest proportion of persons over 65, but Italy joins the Netherlands (and to some extent France) as countries that seem, even allowing for their demographic structures, to be relatively high spenders. British spending, in contrast, seems low, reflecting both the role of private pensions and the low levels of public pensions currently being paid (a consequence of the much later implementation of a structure of earnings-related provision).

If the ten countries' spending on pensions, as on health care, is commensurate with the broad pattern of social spending magnitudes, spending on family benefits seems much more a product of specific national policies and cultures. Australia, Canada, and the United States are again low, but spending is little higher in Italy or West Germany. Japan's spending is exceeded only by France and the Netherlands. Even in the latter two countries, however, spending on family benefits is low compared to spending on health, education, and pensions.

The family benefits data presented in table 9.4 understate the degree of governmental recognition of family needs in some countries because of the absence of cross-national data on the costs of tax expenditures. Both Canada and the United States, for example, rely to some degree on the tax system to substitute for or complement

Table 9.5   TAX AND TRANSFER BENEFITS FOR CHILDREN, 1984

	Percentage distribution by tax transfer states			Total as a percentage of	
	Tax allowance	Tax credit	Cash transfer	Gross earnings	Disposable earnings[a]
Australia	0	0	100	3.5	4.1
Canada	15.3	46.7	38.0	7.0	7.8
France	0	0	100	7.5	8.1
Germany, F.R.	6.6	0	93.4	5.3	6.8
Italy	0	5.7	94.3	10.3	11.9
Japan	100	0	0	2.3	2.6
Netherlands	0	0	100	7.0	9.8
Sweden	0	0	100	6.9	9.4
United Kingdom	0	0	100	8.7	10.6
United States	100	0	0	1.4	1.8

Source: Derived from OECD (1987b).
Note: The calculations are based on the tax-benefit position of a one-earner couple with two children earning an amount equal to the average earnings of a production worker in manufacturing industry. The calculations assume only standard tax relief and credits and transfers, that is, those that would apply to all such households.
   The total is the sum of the following components: the tax saving (calculated at the average rate payable by this type of family) from any tax allowances in respect of children; the value of any tax credits in respect of children; and the net of tax value of any family allowance type of cash transfers (such transfers are taxable in Canada and the Netherlands but nontaxable in the other six countries which have them).
a. Disposable earnings are the calculated take-home pay plus cash transfers for a family of this type.

cash payments for children, so that their total public finance commitment is greater than indicated here.

TAX EXPENDITURES

The different roles played by instruments of the tax system in improving the economic welfare of the family are illustrated in table 9.5. Using OECD calculations of the tax-benefit position of the stereotypical male worker with a nonemployed wife and two children, the table indicates the total net value of tax allowances, tax credits, and cash transfers payable for children, the relative contributions of each of these policy instruments to the total, and the value of the total compared with gross and disposable (posttax-posttransfer) earnings.

Five of these countries—Australia, France, the Netherlands, Sweden, and the United Kingdom—use only direct cash transfers; two others—Italy and West Germany—rely on cash transfers to provide over 90 percent of the total benefit to such a family. Of the remaining three, transfers account for just under two-fifths of the total in Canada, but play no role in Japan or the United States. (The data in the table do not include specific or additional cash assistance to one-parent families or families in poverty.) These two countries relied only on tax allowances for general income support to families; such allowances were also used in Canada and West Germany, although they were of only minor importance in each. Credits against tax liability had a minor role in Italy but were the most important of the three mechanisms in Canada (the only country to use all three), accounting for almost half the total net value of benefits to children.

The table also shows the value of these benefits in relation to gross and disposable earnings, and it modifies the picture (including only transfer spending on family benefits) that emerged from table 9.4. In relation to average earnings, the total family benefit package is shown in table 9.5 to be highest in Italy and the United Kingdom, followed by Canada, France, the Netherlands, and Sweden. (Higher tax rates in the latter pair of countries make the package more valuable in relation to disposable earnings than in the former pair.) The situation in the remaining four countries is quite varied, with the relative value exceeding 5 percent only in West Germany and falling below 2 percent in the United States, which, along with Japan, has the smallest overall package. The relatively limited contribution of the total package even in the more generous countries is clear; it only narrowly exceeds one-tenth of disposable earnings in two of the ten countries.

The comparisons in table 9.5 must be treated with caution. The stereotypical family is not especially representative, the data are derived from an application of formal rules, and the calculations of the ratios in relation to average recorded manufacturing wages may distort comparisons of generosity. Indeed, the data for Italy in this table present the Italian system in a more generous light than other data (such as those in tables 9.4, 9.7, and 9.8) suggest. But the table is undoubtedly valuable in pointing to the extent to which the degree of assistance to families in Canada would be understated if the role of the tax system were ignored. For the other nine countries the role of the tax system is either nonexistent or sufficiently slight not to affect the broad conclusions to be drawn from spending comparisons.

The following sections analyze spending trends over time (to see which population groups appear to have benefited and to compare trends across countries) and trends in per capita spending levels, in order to throw more light on the changing contribution of government spending to the economic welfare of young and old.

SPENDING ON CHILDREN AND THE ELDERLY, 1960–84

From 1960 to 1975 government spending on education, health care, and pensions increased significantly as a proportion of GDP in each of the countries (table 9.6). The proportion of GDP taken by government spending on health care more than doubled in eight of the ten countries. Total health care spending relative to GDP also increased by at least two percentage points in most countries. The range of the share of GDP being spent on publicly financed education across the ten countries shifted from between 2.4 percent and 4.6 percent in 1960 to between 4.9 percent and 7.6 percent in 1975. Similarly, the share of GDP that pensions accounted for rose by around five percentage points in Italy and the Netherlands, compared with around one point (from a much lower base) in Canada and Japan— but the trends were uniformly upward.

By contrast, relative spending on family benefits was generally low in 1960 and it fell in four countries over the 15 years. In four other countries it increased by no more than one-half of a percentage point. Only in Japan (where there had been no spending for family benefits in 1960) and in West Germany (where it had been negligible) did the increase exceed one percentage point, and even then each country was spending only 1.4 percent of GDP on family benefits by 1975. Family benefits were therefore an exception to the general expansion of social programs that accompanied the period of steady economic growth during these 15 years.

From 1975 to 1980 education spending as a proportion of national income declined in seven of the countries, was broadly unchanged in Japan, and increased only in Italy and Sweden. In contrast, the proportion spent on health care increased in five countries and was fairly steady in three, falling only in Australia and Canada. Relative spending on pensions grew sharply in nine of the countries, declining only in West Germany.

Family benefits fared no better in this period than they had previously. Their spending share rose significantly only in Australia and the United Kingdom, and in the latter case this rise reflects the transformation of child tax allowances into cash payments (and thus "spending") during this period, rather than any sharp increase in the overall value of benefits to families. There were slight increases in spending in Japan and the Netherlands, but spending in the other four countries was either broadly constant or fell. By 1980, spending on family benefits had therefore generally declined relative to spending on pensions or health care compared to the situation in 1960.

From 1980 to 1984 the share of expenditures for health care and pensions generally increased, although the sizes of the increases were often fairly small, whereas the share for education and family benefits decreased. The share of spending for health care rose in six countries, was fairly constant in two, and fell slightly in West Germany and Sweden. The share of spending for pensions similarly increased in five countries, was broadly unchanged in three, and fell only in Australia and (by one-fifth of a percentage point) in the Netherlands.

By contrast, the share of spending for education rose clearly only in France and fell in seven countries. The fall usually exceeded half a percentage point (10 percent of its relative share), and it exceeded a full percentage point in the Netherlands. The share of spending for family benefits rose slightly only in Australia and the United Kingdom, falling in five of the remaining eight countries.

At the level of overall spending trends, therefore, the 1980–84 period continued the pattern of the previous five years, with child-oriented spending—education and family benefits—generally declining and health care and pension spending continuing to increase in relative magnitude.

These spending trends tell little about the factors that accounted for them. In particular, the trends are likely to have been affected by the different economic performances and demographic experiences of the various countries. Some reworking of the earlier OECD decomposition analysis of changes in social spending offers further insight into these trends. Unfortunately, family benefits were not included in this analysis, and so data are available only for education, health care, and pensions.

The average annual real change in spending on each of these three

Table 9.6   TRENDS IN MAJOR SOCIAL PROGRAM SPENDING AS PERCENTAGE
OF GDP, 1960–84

	Australia	Canada	France	Germany, F.R.	Italy
Education					
1960	2.8	3.0	—	2.4	3.7
1970	4.2	6.9	—	4.0	4.5
1975	6.1	6.4	5.8	5.4	5.0
1980	5.9	6.0	5.7	5.1	5.6
1984	6.0	6.1	6.0	4.6	5.1
Health care[a] (total)					
1960	2.4 (5.2)	2.4 (5.5)	2.5 (4.3)	3.1 (4.7)	3.2 (3.9)
1970	3.2 (5.7)	5.1 (7.2)	4.3 (6.1)	4.2 (5.5)	4.8 (5.5)
1975	5.6 (7.6)	5.7 (7.4)	5.5 (7.6)	6.6 (7.8)	5.8 (6.7)
1980	4.7 (7.4)	5.4 (7.3)	6.1 (8.5)	6.5 (7.9)	6.0 (6.8)
1984	5.6 (7.8)	6.3 (8.4)	6.4 (9.1)	6.3 (8.1)	5.9 (7.2)
Pensions					
1960	3.4	2.8	5.9	9.8	5.5
1970	3.1	3.2	8.5	10.6	8.2
1975	5.0	3.8	8.4	12.9	10.4
1980	5.4	4.5	11.5	12.1	11.8
1984	5.0	5.3	12.5	12.0	11.7
Family benefits					
1960	1.0	1.4	3.8	0.3	2.6
1970	0.6	0.7	2.7	0.4	1.6
1975	0.6	1.2	2.8	1.4	1.8
1980	1.1	0.6	2.7	1.1	1.1
1984	1.3	0.6	2.8	0.8	0.8

services for the periods before and after 1975 and their relative elasticity over the two periods—that is, the ratio of spending growth to GDP growth in the latter as compared to the earlier period—are shown in table 9.7. A relative elasticity figure of 1.0 indicates that the rate of spending growth declined in the same degree as the rate of economic growth; an elasticity of greater than 1.0 implies a smaller relative decline in spending, while less than 1.0 implies a greater relative decline.

These elasticity data also demonstrate the shift in service priorities between the two periods, with spending on pensions as the gainer. For both health care and education spending, six countries show elasticities of less than 1.0; for pensions, this is the case in only two countries, West Germany and the United States. These data have fiscal rather than policy significance, however, until the various

	Japan	Netherlands	Sweden	United Kingdom	United States
Education					
1960	4.0	4.5	4.6	3.7	3.6
1970	3.6	6.7	6.2	5.3	5.3
1975	4.9	7.6	5.7	6.8	6.3
1980	5.0	7.2	6.5	5.6	5.7
1984	4.3	6.0	5.9	5.3	5.3
Health care[a]					
(total)					
1960	1.3 (3.0)	1.3 (3.9)	3.4 (4.7)	3.4 (3.9)	1.3 (5.3)
1970	3.0 (4.4)	5.1 (6.0)	6.2 (7.2)	3.9 (4.5)	2.8 (7.6)
1975	4.0 (5.5)	5.9 (7.7)	7.2 (8.0)	5.0 (5.6)	3.7 (8.6)
1980	4.6 (6.4)	6.5 (8.2)	8.8 (9.5)	5.2 (5.6)	4.1 (9.5)
1984	4.8 (6.6)	6.7 (8.6)	8.5 (9.4)	5.3 (5.9)	4.3 (10.7)
Pensions					
1960	1.4	5.2	4.4	4.1	4.2
1970	1.2	8.7	6.2	5.2	5.3
1975	2.7	10.7	8.2	6.3	6.9
1980	4.5	11.0	10.9	6.7	7.2
1984	5.1	10.8	11.1	7.0	7.2
Family benefits					
1960	0	1.3	1.3	0.6	0.2
1970	0.8	1.9	1.2	0.9	0.5
1975	1.4	1.8	1.6	0.7	0.6
1980	1.6	2.1	1.6	1.6	0.5
1984	1.4	1.9	1.2	1.9	0.4

Source: Computation by author from the OECD, Social Expenditure Database.
a. Disposable earnings are the calculated take-home pay plus cash transfers for a family of this type.

"passive" and "active" factors in policy choice are distinguished. (Passive factors reflect unchanged policy in the face of a changed policy environment such as demographic or relative cost pressures; active factors involve decisions to change generosity or eligibility.)

Table 9.8 draws on the OECD (1985) decomposition analysis to present the various elements that account for total spending growth for the three services in each of the two periods. Four factors are defined to account for total growth in deflated spending: the relative price effect, shifts in population size and composition, shifts in program coverage, and changes in the generosity of real benefits or service quality (the residual in the calculation).[1]

Table 9.7   ANNUAL GROWTH IN GDP AND IN SOCIAL SPENDING IN 10 OECD COUNTRIES, 1960–75 AND 1975–81

Country	Average annual real change in spending[a]				Relative elasticity of spending[b]		
	GDP	Educa-tion	Health care	Pensions	Educa-tion	Health care	Pensions
Australia							
1960–75	5.2	8.9	9.1	8.5	0.3	–0.1	1.0
1975–81	2.4	1.2	–0.5	4.0			
Canada							
1960–75	5.1	8.4	13.0	8.3	0.2	0.4	1.3
1975–81	3.3	1.0	3.0	6.8			
France							
1960–75	5.0	n.a.	10.9	7.7	—	1.0	2.0
1975–81	2.8	1.0	6.3	8.7			
Germany, F.R.							
1960–75	3.8	7.2	6.6	6.3	0.3	0.4	0.4
1975–81	3.0	1.6	2.1	2.1			
Italy							
1960–75	4.6	4.6	6.7	9.6	1.2	0.0	1.2
1975–81	3.2	3.9	0.1	7.7			

Japan							
1960–75	8.6	5.7	12.2	12.7	1.3	1.0	2.0
1975–81	4.7	4.1	6.6	13.7			
Netherlands							
1960–75	4.5	4.3	11.4	10.3	0.6	0.9	1.1
1975–81	2.0	1.1	4.4	5.2			
Sweden							
1960–75	4.0	3.4	11.3	8.7	2.5	1.2	3.2
1975–81	1.0	2.1	3.4	6.9			
United Kingdom							
1960–75	2.6	5.0	3.4	5.9	−1.0	1.5	2.0
1975–81	1.0	−2.0	2.0	4.5			
United States							
1960–75	3.4	6.1	10.3	7.2	0.1	0.4	0.7
1975–81	3.2	0.4	3.8	4.4			

Source: Klein and O'Higgins (forthcoming), table 1.

a. The real spending data have been deflated both by the GDP deflator and by the service-specific relative price effect.

b. The relative elasticity data are calculated by dividing the ratio of the rate of growth of the particular spending item to the rate of growth of GDP in the 1975–81 period by the corresponding ratio for the 1960–75 period.

Table 9.8 COMPONENTS OF SOCIAL SPENDING GROWTH, 1960–75 AND 1975–81

| | Annual growth rates (percentage) | | | | | | | | | |
| | 1960–75 | | | | | 1975–81 | | | | |
	Real expenditure[a]	Relative price effect[b]	Demographic change	Coverage change	Generosity change	Real expenditure[a]	Relative price effect[b]	Demographic change	Coverage change	Generosity change
Australia										
Education	10.9	1.8	2.1	−0.5	7.2	1.5	0.3	0.2	0.2	0.8
Health	11.1	−1.8	2.0	1.8	5.1	−0.2	0.3	1.2	1.3	−2.9
Pensions	8.1	−0.4	2.2	2.6	3.5	4.3	0.3	3.1	−0.3	1.2
Canada										
Education	10.5	1.9	1.3	0.9	6.1	2.7	1.7	−0.4	1.2	0.2
Health	11.4	−1.4	1.6	2.6	8.4	3.0	0.0	1.2	0.0	1.8
Pensions	7.4	−0.9	2.4	2.8	2.9	6.6	−0.2	3.3	0.4	3.0
France										
Education	—	—	1.2	0.7	—	2.4	1.4	−0.6	−0.1	1.7
Health	10.8	−0.1	1.0	1.0	8.7	5.6	−0.7	0.4	0.3	5.6
Pensions	7.5	−0.2	1.9	1.9	3.7	8.9	0.2	0.8	3.0	4.7
Germany, F.R.										
Education	9.6	2.2	0.6	1.9	4.6	2.2	0.6	−0.9	0.0	2.5
Health	9.0	2.3	1.0	0.5	5.0	2.8	0.7	0.0	0.0	2.1
Pensions	5.7	−0.6	3.1	−0.3	3.4	2.5	0.4	0.9	1.4	−0.2
Italy										
Education	6.6	1.9	0.3	3.0	1.2	7.7	3.7	−0.2	1.3	2.8
Health	8.8	2.0	0.6	0.9	5.1	3.8	3.7	0.4	0.2	−0.5
Pensions	9.2	−0.4	2.6	0.3	6.5	7.4	−0.3	2.5	−2.9	8.2

Japan									
Education	10.1	4.2	-0.2	0.4	5.5	1.0	-0.3	2.4	2.0
Health	16.9	4.2	1.2	0.3	10.5	1.0	0.9	0.0	5.6
Pensions	13.4	0.6	3.4	4.2	4.6	1.6	3.7	4.2	5.2
Netherlands									
Education	8.1	3.6	0.7	1.2	2.3	-0.2	-0.5	0.3	1.3
Health	15.1	3.7	1.2	1.3	8.7	-0.2	0.6	2.5	1.2
Pensions	9.6	-0.6	2.7	-0.2	7.6	0.3	2.0	0.4	2.7
Sweden									
Education	5.4	1.9	0.2	1.0	2.2	1.5	-0.3	1.7	0.7
Health	9.3	-1.8	0.6	0.0	10.6	1.1	0.3	0.0	3.1
Pensions	8.3	-0.4	2.3	0.2	6.0	0.3	1.7	2.7	2.3
United Kingdom									
Education	6.9	1.8	0.6	1.1	3.2	0.3	-0.4	-0.5	-1.1
Health	5.3	1.8	0.4	0.0	3.0	0.2	0.0	0.0	2.0
Pensions	5.6	-0.3	1.6	0.9	3.3	-1.0	1.0	0.8	2.6
United States									
Education	7.4	1.2	1.1	0.9	4.0	0.3	-0.2	-1.3	1.9
Health	10.8	0.4	1.2	4.1	4.7	1.8	1.0	0.0	2.8
Pensions	6.9	-0.3	2.1	2.9	2.0	0.0	2.5	0.7	1.1

Source: OECD (1985), tables A-1, A-4, and A-7.
a. The annual growth rate of nominal expenditure deflated by the GDP deflator.
b. The relative price effects shown for pensions are explained by differences between the GDP deflator and the rate of inflation of consumer prices.

By separating out the various elements that together account for spending growth, the data in table 9.8 allow an examination of the extent to which the shift in priority away from education and toward pensions was simply a consequence of demographic pressures, and the extent to which it may also have reflected active or discretionary policy choices.

Over all these countries, the (unweighted) average annual rise in the generosity of health care spending was 7.0 percent in the period up to 1975, followed by rises of 4.4 percent for pensions and 4.0 percent for education. After 1975, pensions had the greatest generosity growth rate (3.1 percent) followed by health (2.1 percent) and education (1.3 percent). Between the two periods, therefore, the average growth in generosity declined sharply, reflecting the reductions in economic growth; but the decline was smallest in the case of pensions. This shift in priorities is not countered by the pattern of change in coverage growth, but is reinforced. For all three services the coverage growth rate actually increased in the second period, but whereas the pre-1975 annual growth rates had been fairly close (1.1 percent for education, 1.3 percent for health care, and 1.5 percent for pensions), after 1975 the rates rose to 1.3, 2.1, and 3.1 percent, respectively.

Italy and the United Kingdom had the most generous pension growth in both periods; Japan, France, Sweden, and the United States gave priority to health care. Canada and the Netherlands switched priorities from health to pensions. Australia switched from education to pensions. Only West Germany switched to education (from health care). Both the expenditure share and the deflated spending data suggested that a general switch of priorities to pension spending has taken place in recent years. Whatever their limitations, these data suggest that the switch was not simply a consequence of demographic pressures. Both the coverage and the generosity elements of the decomposition also show shifted or strengthened priorities for pensions.

PER CAPITA SPENDING ON CHILDREN AND THE ELDERLY

The data thus far have focused on broad spending aggregates, except for the accounting decomposition of spending trends, which did not deal with family benefits. The data in this section are cast in terms of per capita benefits in order to allow a better examination of the

Table 9.9   RELATIVE PER CAPITA SPENDING ON OLD-AGE AND FAMILY
BENEFITS, SELECTED YEARS, 1960–84

	Per capita family benefits as a percentage of per capita old-age benefits				
	1960	1970	1975	1980	1984
Australia	8.5	5.6	3.7	7.9	10.3
Canada	11.3	6.0	10.1	5.7	5.0
France	28.0	16.2	15.4	14.4	13.5
Germany, F.R.	1.4	2.3	7.4	8.1	6.4
Italy	18.1	9.3	8.7	5.3	4.5
Japan	0	21.6	17.7	13.9	11.9
Netherlands	9.8	10.7	8.7	9.7	10.3
Sweden	15.8	13.4	14.8	12.2	10.1
United Kingdom	7.8	9.8	7.3	18.0	21.1
United States	1.4	3.2	3.6	3.3	3.0

Source: Varley (1986).
Note: Per capita spending on old age is spending on old age, survivors, and
disability transfers per person age 65 and older. Per capita spending on family
benefits is family benefits spending (including both universal and income-tested
programs) per person age 15 or younger. The data from which these ratios are
derived are expressed in U.S. dollars at 1980 prices and purchasing-power parities.

relative effects of social spending on the economic welfare of the
elderly versus the young.

Changes in relative per capita spending on family benefits and
pensions within each country since 1960 present a mixed picture
(table 9.9). In 1960 family benefits as a percentage of pensions were
greatest in France, Italy and Sweden (they were then in the range
one-sixth to one-quarter); all have declined sharply since then. In
France the percentage fell by more than half and in Italy the fall
was even greater; in both cases the greater part of the drop took
place before 1970. The percentage also fell in Canada, but this is
offset by Canada's introduction of tax credits for children.

It rose, either from a low base or only very slightly in Australia,
West Germany, and the United States, while it remained broadly
constant in the Netherlands. The only countries in which it rose
substantially are Japan and the United Kingdom. In Japan, it rose
from zero in 1960 to 22 percent in 1970, but then declined to 12
percent by 1984. The rise in the United Kingdom was substantial
and gave it the biggest percentage, 21 percent, in 1984, although the
relatively low value of pensions in the the United Kingdom (see
table 9.10) is a contributing factor. In addition, as noted earlier,

Table 9.10   TRENDS IN REAL PER CAPITA SPENDING ON OLD-AGE
AND FAMILY BENEFITS, SELECTED YEARS, 1960–84

		Index (1980 = 100)					Value (U.S. dollars)
		1960	1970	1975	1980	1984	1980
Australia	FA	46.8	41.0	47.1	100	130.0	393
	OA	43.5	57.7	100.3	100	99.9	4,982
Canada	FA	71.7	62.6	149.1	100	99.4	318
	OA	36.1	59.5	83.9	100	113.2	5,601
France	FA	57.2	66.9	84.6	100	113.7	1,148
	OA	29.4	58.8	79.2	100	120.9	7,978
Germany, F.R.	FA	9.7	21.9	86.7	100	83.8	631
	OA	55.8	77.3	94.1	100	106.3	7,829
Italy	FA	99.2	112.4	134.1	100	106.8	423
	OA	29.2	64.5	81.6	100	125.0	7,445
Japan	FA	0	41.6	77.1	100	100.4	560
	OA	15.2	26.8	60.8	100	117.9	4,020
Netherlands	FA	23.3	60.7	70.2	100	99.0	923
	OA	23.2	54.8	78.5	100	93.3	9,514
Sweden	FA	41.8	62.6	90.5	100	82.7	977
	OA	32.3	57.2	74.4	100	100.1	8,006
United Kingdom	FA	21.5	38.6	36.4	100	134.2	637
	OA	49.7	71.0	89.8	100	114.8	3,533
United States	FA	18.4	67.2	100.8	100	95.1	244
	OA	44.2	70.6	92.3	100	105.7	7,319

Source: Same as table 9.9.
Note: See explanation of per capita spending on old age and family benefits in note to table 9.9.
FA = family benefits   OA = old-age benefits

much of the British growth between 1975 and 1980 was due to accounting conventions rather than to a real increase in generosity.

Trends in real per capita spending on family benefits and pensions with each country reinforce this conclusion (table 9.10). The real value of family benefits grew more slowly between 1960 and 1980 in Canada, France, Italy, and Sweden, and significantly faster in Japan, the United States, and West Germany (all from very low bases), and the United Kingdom. Since 1980, family benefits per capita have grown faster than pensions per capita only in Australia and the United Kingdom (although they declined less sharply in the Netherlands). Sweden and West Germany have had particularly large drops in the real value of per capita family benefits.

The real values of family benefits and pensions across countries

Table 9.11   RATIO OF AVERAGE PER CAPITA PUBLIC EXPENDITURE ON
HEALTH CARE ON ELDERLY TO NONELDERLY, 1980
(persons age 0.64 = 1)

Country	Expenditure ratio	
	Persons age 65 and over	Persons age 75 and over
Australia	4.9	8.0
Canada	4.5	6.7
France	2.4	2.8
Germany, F.R.	2.6	3.1
Italy	2.2	—
Japan	4.8	5.3
Netherlands	4.5	6.2
Sweden	5.5	9.2
United Kingdom	4.3	6.6
United States	7.4	—

Source: OECD (1988), table 15.

in 1980 using purchasing power parities for conversion are also shown in the table. These data confirm the relative generosity of France, the Netherlands, and Sweden with respect to family benefits, and place Italy in a relatively low position, but still well above the United States.

These ratios should be interpreted cautiously. As noted in previous chapters, elderly people and children are in different situations: we no longer generally expect elderly people to be financially dependent on their adult children in the way that children are dependent on their parents, so the ratios for family benefits and pensions might be expected to differ significantly. Furthermore, private provision of day care and income support and public provision of health services vary between countries and by age group, so these ratios tell only part of the story. They do, however, capture the dimensions of the differences in the per capita public resources flowing to the elderly and the young and the way in which the gap continues to increase.

Spending on pensions, education, and family benefits all have obvious relevance *either* to children *or* to the elderly. This is not the case with health care spending, which provides direct benefits to all segments of the population. Table 9.11 presents estimates for recent years of the ratio of social spending on health care for elderly persons to that for the nonelderly. For persons ages 65 and older,

Table 9.12   RELATIVE PER CAPITA SOCIAL PROGRAM EXPENDITURE BY AGE
GROUP, AUSTRALIA AND THE NETHERLANDS, 1981

Australia	0–15	16–24	25–59	60–64	65–69	70–74	75 and over
Income transfers	100	106	107	489	757	914	977
Health care	100	132	191	399	501	576	1,308
Education	100	76.0	11.5	2.6	2.9	—	—
Total[a]	100	92.3	49.6	143	210	248	342

Netherlands	0–19	20–44	45–64	65–79	80 and over
Income transfers	100	129	348	707	785
Health care	100	81.0	134	343	889
Education	100	14.2	—	—	—
Social services	100	45.5	118	845	4,555
Total	100	52.7	109	240	389

Source: OECD (1988), tables 16 and 17.
Note: Spending on the youngest age group has been indexed equal to 100.
a. Total spending for Australia also includes minor spending on employment and
welfare services.

the ratio ranges from around 2.5 to 1 in France, Italy, and West
Germany to almost 7.5 to 1 in the United States, with most other
countries around 5 to 1. If persons age 75 and older are compared
with the nonelderly population, the ratios remain relatively low in
France and West Germany (perhaps because of more extensive use
of family care or non-health-based social care), but rise to between
6 and 8 to 1 for other countries and to over 9 to 1 in Sweden. Given
the aging of these countries projected in table 9.2, this means that,
even without any quality or generosity changes, the proportion of
social spending on health care devoted to the elderly will rise in
coming decades. For these ten countries the estimated shift is from
an unweighted average of 37 percent in 1980 to 47 percent in 2020
(OECD 1988, table 31).

The most detailed per capita distribution of benefits to different
age groups are available for Australia and the Netherlands (see table
9.12). For both countries these data demonstrate the extent to which
it is spending on education rather than on health care or on family
benefits that direct some public resources to children. For social
spending as a whole, older people receive 2.5 to 3.5 times as much
of the resources as children. For health care the elderly receive

Table 9.13   RELATIVE PER CAPITA SOCIAL SPENDING BY AGE GROUP, 1980

Country	Age group		
	0–14	15–64	65 and over
Canada	100	72.0	265
France	100	51.4	263
Germany, F.R.	100	59.5	316
Italy	100	110.0	380
Japan	100	44.0	235
Sweden	100	43.0	234
United Kingdom	100	53.3	213
United States	100	66.9	381

Source: OECD (1988), table 18.
Note: Spending on the youngest age group has been indexed equal to 100.

about 5 to 7 times as much; for income transfers the elderly receive about 8 times as much per capita as children.

No similar breakdowns are available for the other eight countries examined in this paper, but table 9.13 presents estimates of the per capita values of total social spending by age group. All these produce ratios in the range suggested by the data for Australia and the Netherlands: per capita spending on the elderly is roughly two to four times as great as spending on children. The ratios are greatest in Italy and the United States, a finding that is consistent with the earlier indications in table 9.6 and with the priority given to pension spending in Italy shown in table 9.7.

CONCLUSIONS

Perhaps even more so than is usually the case with international comparative research—because the analysis was multi-program as well as cross-national—the results of the analysis presented here must be regarded as tentative and indicative, rather than definitive.[2] This caution notwithstanding, the conclusions are relatively clear.

First, the trend of public policy in recent years has been to give greater priority to pensions than to other important social programs. This trend is not simply the fiscal consequence of demographic pressures; it also reflects decisions to increase pensions. Similarly, the relatively slowed growth in education reflects a generally lower priority accorded it even apart from demographic changes.

Second, countries vary in the generosity with which they provide family cash benefits. France, the Netherlands, and Sweden spend most in this area; the United States spends least, with Australia also a fairly low spender. Thus, the main direct contribution of public resources to children is through the education system. Spending on education far outweighs that on family benefits and, as far as the limited evidence suggests, is the principal factor preventing the elderly-to-children ratio for public spending from being much greater. This finding suggests that, although the generosity of pensions may indeed be an important factor in explaining differences in the economic welfare of the elderly relative to other population groups in various countries, family benefits are not large enough to play the same role vis-à-vis children.

Nonetheless, the evidence in chapter 5 suggests that the risk of family poverty is greater in countries that are shown here to have less generous family benefits for children, such as Australia and the United States. Although other income sources and income-related factors such as inequalities in labor force participation, wages, and unemployment also are likely to be important in explaining the risk of family poverty, the importance of family benefits in reducing the risk of family poverty may be greater than their overall spending magnitude would suggest. The most obvious explanation is that even if their overall magnitude is slight, their relative value is greatest to those who are most at risk of poverty.

It is fashionable to assume that public policies do not work. The evidence presented here suggests that those policies, particularly in the last decade, have favored programs benefiting the elderly while according a lower priority to programs directed mainly at children. Despite fashion, then, both the relative improvement in the economic position of the elderly and the greater risk of poverty for children in countries with less generous family benefit regimes plausibly depend on the way in which public policy treats the elderly and the young.

Notes

1. The nature and limits of these data and calculations have been extensively discussed; see, for example, the series of papers in the March 1986 issue of the *Journal of Public Policy*.

2. The data and analysis in the chapter do, however, suggest one promising avenue for further research into some of the underlying questions. Three of the countries analyzed here—Australia, Canada, and the United States—have strikingly similar demographic and spending indicators. Each has had and continues to have significant population growth (see table 9.1). Each has a somewhat young population than most other countries, and the recent trends in and current age composition of that opulation are similar (table 9.2). Each spends similarly small amounts on family benefits and similar amounts on education (table 9.4). There are further similarities in other features not examined here—such as immigration and a recent frontier culture. They therefore would provide an intriguing threesome with which to test the propositions underlying the debate on the economic welfare of the elderly and children.

References

Hedstrom, P., and S. Ringen. 1987. "Age and Income in Contemporary Society." *Journal of Social Policy* 16 (April).

International Monetary Fund. 1986. *Government Financial Statistics Yearbook 1986*. Washington, D.C.: International Monetary Fund.

Klein, R., and M. O'Higgins. 1988. "Defusing the Crisis of the Welfare State: A New Interpretation." In *Social Security: A Reassessment*, edited by T. R. Marmor and J. L. Mashaw. Princeton, N.J.: Princeton University Press.

Organization for Economic Cooperation and Development (OECD). 1983. *Tax Expenditures: A Review of the Issues and Country Practices.* Paris: OECD.

———. 1985. *Social Expenditure 1960–1990: Problems of Growth and Control.* Paris: OECD.

———. 1986. *Labor Force Statistics.* Paris: OECD.

———. 1987a. *Financing and Delivering Health Care: A Comparative Analysis of Organization for Economic Cooperation and Development Countries.* Paris: OECD.

———. 1987b. *The Tax Benefit Position of Production Workers 1983–1986.* Paris: OECD.

———. 1988 *Ageing Populations: The Social Policy Implications.* Paris: OECD.

United Nations. 1983. *UN National Accounts Statistics: Government Accounts and Tables 1983.* New York: United Nations.

Varley, R. 1986. "The Government Household Transfer Data Base 1960–1984." Working Paper no. 36. OECD, Department of Economics and Statistics. Paris: OECD.

ANNEX 9.1

■ *COMPONENTS OF SOCIAL EXPENDITURE*

The constituents of the various components of social expenditure set out in table 9.4 and used subsequently in text and tables are as follows:

Education	Expenditure on preprimary, primary, tertiary, education affairs and services, and subsidiary services to education.
Health care	Expenditure on hospitals; clinics; medical, dental, and paramedical practitioners; public health; medical equipment, and appliances or other prescribed health-related products; and applied research and experimental development related to health and medical delivery systems.
Family benefits	Cash benefits such as family allowances and one-parent child benefit supplements payable only to families with dependent children (but not necessarily to all such families).
Pensions	Expenditure on old-age, disability, or survivors' benefits, other than for government employees, and government employee pensions.
Unemployment compensation	Expenditure on social insurance and other government schemes to individuals to compensate for loss of income due to unemployment.
Other social expenditure	Expenditure on sickness, temporary disability benefits, other social assistance and welfare affairs, and services.
Total social expenditure	The total of the six categories just listed.

Source: OECD (1985), 75, adapted for the separate identification of family benefits.

Chapter Ten

BEYOND INCOME AND POVERTY: TRENDS IN SOCIAL WELFARE AMONG CHILDREN AND THE ELDERLY SINCE 1960

Christopher Jencks and Barbara Boyle Torrey

During the 1950s and 1960s the low incomes of the elderly played an important role in persuading American scholars and public officials that the elderly faced serious economic problems requiring governmental solutions. By the early 1980s families with children were considerably more likely than the elderly to report incomes below the poverty line. Today, this change is widely cited as evidence that governmental efforts to help the elderly succeeded and that we should redirect our attention and resources to the young.

Unfortunately, income and poverty statistics have severe limitations as indices of relative well-being, partly because there is no general agreement about how much income people of different ages need in order to be equally well off, and partly because income has relatively little effect on many forms of well-being.

The official U.S. poverty threshold for a married couple with three children, for example, is 2.5 times the threshold for an elderly woman living alone. In theory, this means that a married couple and their three children eat as well on $12,500 a year as an elderly woman eats on $5,000 a year (Orshansky 1965). In practice, no one knows what it means. (See the discussion of equivalence scales in chapter 2.)

The fundamental difficulty posed by all such income comparisons is that people need different market goods and services at different ages. Adults need more food than children, the elderly need more medical care than the middle-aged, and so forth. The price of equivalent levels of material welfare therefore varies with age. This is obvious when we talk about being well-fed or well-doctored, but

We are indebted to the Institute for Advanced Study, Ford Foundation, and Sloan Foundation for financial support, to our fellow contributors and editors for helpful comments on earlier drafts, to Susan Mayer and Larry Radbill for both computational assistance and painstaking substantive criticism, and to Matthew Courchane for making tables.

it applies to nearly every domain of material life. The cost of physical mobility varies with age, for example, because most adults can drive themselves around, whereas children and the frail elderly need chauffeurs. Likewise, an infant can often play happily with a broken frying pan, whereas adults usually need more expensive toys to make their leisure equally enjoyable.

One way to dramatize this difficulty is to ask how people who want to maintain a constant level of happiness should allocate their expenditures over their lifetime. Not only do we not know the answer to this question, we do not even know how to go about answering it. Yet without some answer it is hard to say whether the observed distribution of income across age groups is efficient, much less just.

Furthermore, even if we knew that a couple with three children needed $12,500 a year to enjoy the same level of material welfare as an elderly woman with an income of $5,000, we would have no assurance that equal *material* welfare meant equal *subjective* welfare. Even if the old and the young eat equally well and own similar television sets, the old may be lonelier, less healthy, or more afraid of crime. Conversely, because children depend on adults for so many things, they may be more emotionally vulnerable, more subject to abuse, and more worried about how others see them, even when they have the same material comforts as their grandparents.

This chapter therefore takes a different approach to comparing people of different ages. Instead of looking at income, we look at what we loosely call hardship. We begin by discussing material hardships that seem likely to depend heavily on income, namely: not getting enough food, living in substandard housing, not owning an automobile or home, and not having a telephone. We then look at physical hardships that also depend to some extent on income, but that all affluent nations, including the United States, have tried through public policies to ameliorate even among the poor, namely: premature death, poor health, and inadequate medical care. After that we turn to emotional hardships that often affect income but are emotionally costly even when they do not have significant monetary costs, namely: not living with family members you want to live with, unemployment, and criminal victimization. Finally, we discuss two global measures that should, at least in principle, provide clues about the effect of both monetary and nonmonetary factors on overall well-being, namely: self-reported unhappiness, and suicide.

In some cases we let people define hardship for themselves, using their own subjective standards ("Do you have enough money to buy food?"). In some cases we use social definitions, such as whether people have indoor plumbing. In some cases what we label as a hardship would not strike the alleged victim as one; in other cases what the victim views as a hardship would not strike outsiders as one. Nonetheless, because political judgments about the extent and distribution of hardship form the basis of most policies designed to reduce it, these crude measures seem better than none at all.

In discussing these varieties of hardship, we focus on two questions:

□ How well do age-specific poverty rates predict age differences in hardship in the United States today?
□ How well do changes since 1960 in age-specific poverty rates predict changes in hardship among children and among the elderly?

Wherever the data allow, we ask two additional questions:

□ How does the age distribution of hardship in the United States compare with the age distribution in other affluent nations?
□ How well do income differences between the United States and other affluent nations predict cross-national differences in hardship among children and the elderly?

We show that age-specific poverty rates are a poor guide to different age groups' chances of experiencing most hardships. Changes in age-specific poverty rates predict changes in a few hardships fairly well, but even this is the exception rather than the rule. The redistribution of income from young families with children to the elderly that began around 1970 in the United States has not been associated with a parallel redistribution of most hardships from the elderly to the young.

Data limitations leave many gaps in our findings. With one exception (changes in educational opportunities, which we discuss briefly in the conclusion), we deliberately ignored changes that were relevant only to children or only to the elderly. In addition, no reliable trend data exist in many areas (for example, mental health). Thus, the pictures of both children and the elderly presented here are far from complete.

Although our findings will not allow the reader to draw conclusions about changes in the overall well-being of either children or the elderly, they do have two important uses. First, they dramatize the limitations of using poverty statistics for making inferences about changes in overall well-being. Second, they show that different kinds of well-being have changed in very different ways since 1960 among both children and the elderly. This means that people are unlikely to agree about trends in either group's overall well-being until they agree about what aspects of well-being are important.

FOOD CONSUMPTION

Most Americans feel that something is seriously wrong with a society in which people cannot get enough to eat. That is why the original poverty line tried to measure families' ability to buy a nutritionally adequate diet (Orshansky 1965). That is also why Congress dramatically expanded the food stamp program during the first Nixon administration. Yet despite the existence of food stamps—or perhaps because of it—most Americans still assume that poverty statistics ought to tell them something about people's ability to buy enough food.

We therefore begin by asking whether age-specific poverty statistics provide reliable information about the relative likelihood that children and the elderly are getting enough to eat. Because of data limitations we focus exclusively on the United States. We do not have an ideal time series even for the United States; but in 1974, 1984, and 1987, the Gallup survey asked a sample of American adults: "Have there been times during the last year when you did not have enough money to buy food for your family?" (American Institute for Public Opinion 1974, 1984). Such evidence as we have suggests that most respondents interpreted this as a question about whether they had had enough money to buy all the food they needed, not about whether they had had enough merely to stave off hunger.[1]

The Gallup samples are not representative of the U.S. population: the elderly are overrepresented, and the poor elderly appear to be especially overrepresented. But overrepresentation of the elderly is helpful in understanding the relationship of poverty and food consumption in this critical group. When the Gallup sample is disaggregated by both age and poverty status, some of the sample sizes are too small to give precise estimates. But the trends over age groups and poverty levels show consistent and important patterns.

Table 10.1 shows how responses to this question varied by income and age in 1974 and 1984.[2] The 1974 question refers to the 12 months from September 1973 to September 1974, which was a period of relative prosperity. The 1984 question refers to the 12 months from January 1983 to January 1984, which included the end of the

Table 10.1   PERCENTAGE OF ADULTS REPORTING INSUFFICIENT MONEY TO
BUY FOOD AT SOME TIME DURING THE PREVIOUS YEAR, BY AGE
AND POVERTY LEVEL, UNITED STATES, 1974 AND 1984

Year/age	Percentage of respondents in poverty	Income as a percentage of poverty line					
		All	<50 percent	50–149 percent	150–249 percent	250–349 percent	>350 percent
1974							
Under 65	13.6	14.9	63.9	34.3	13.1	6.5	3.8
		(799)	(44)	(134)	(199)	(108)	(314)
65 and over	27.1	9.8	42.1	14.6	2.1	0	0
		(165)	(19)	(49)	(48)	(16)	(33)
1984							
Under 65	14.4	21.9	51.9	46.0	19.4	12.6	6.5
		(1,242)	(65)	(285)	(262)	(287)	(352)
65 and over	24.9	13.1	39.0	24.0	2.8	2.4	0
		(226)	(15)	(95)	(46)	(24)	(49)
Children in household	17.6	26.6	60.3	48.3	20.8	12.1	4.2
		(612)	(44)	(182)	(125)	(141)	(120)
No children in household	14.9	16.2	36.6	33.3	13.9	11.6	5.7
		(855)	(35)	(197)	(172)	(170)	(281)

Source: Computations by authors from original data tapes supplied by the Roper
Center for Public Opinion Research.
Note: Sample size appears in parentheses.
< less than   > greater than.

worst recession since World War II. Unemployment averaged 5
percent during the first period and 10 percent during the second.
Because Gallup asked about *current* estimated income, not actual
income over the previous 12 months, its income measures probably
underestimate the effects of the difference in unemployment between
the two periods.

Not surprisingly, low-income families were especially likely to
report that there had been a time during the previous year when
they could not afford to buy food.[3] Difficulties buying food also
increased between 1973–74 and 1983–84, even among families with
the same "real" income. This difference presumably reflects the
unmeasured effects of unemployment during 1983.

Poverty statistics for different age groups are not a reliable guide
to their groups' likelihood of saying they did not have enough money
for food. The poverty rate among elderly Gallup respondents was
almost double that among younger adults in 1974 and 1984.[4] Yet in

both years elderly Gallup respondents were considerably *less* likely than younger adults to say that there had been times when they did not have enough money to buy food.

Poverty thresholds for families of different sizes and ages supposedly measure their relative need for income. In theory, therefore, if two families of different sizes or ages are living at the poverty line, they should have equal difficulty buying food. The same should hold for families with incomes twice the poverty line or half the poverty line. Yet table 10.1 shows that even when we compare families at the same "poverty level" (families with incomes between 150 and 249 percent of the poverty line, for example), the elderly are far less likely than younger adults to report not having had enough money for food. Indeed, table 10.1 shows that elderly respondents living at 50 percent to 149 percent of the poverty line are almost as likely to have enough money for food as younger adults with incomes that are 150 percent to 249 percent of the poverty line. This suggests that the official poverty line may represent a higher standard of living for the elderly than for younger adults.

At least in 1984, families with children were also more likely than families without children to report that they did not have enough money for food.[5] This gap persists when we compare families at the same poverty level. The poverty line thus seems to represent a somewhat lower standard of living for families with children than for families without children.

Even if the poverty line represents a lower standard of living for the young than for the old, however, *changes* in age-specific poverty rates should still predict changes in different age groups' ability to buy enough food. Table 10.2, which covers 1974, 1984, and 1987, supports this view, at least as long as we focus on changes in the *official* poverty rate. The picture is less clear when we focus on changes in Gallup respondents' own poverty rates, which are in principle more relevant but are available only for 1974 and 1984.[6]

With respect to trends for the population as a whole, table 10.2 shows that the fraction of all adults who said they were unable to buy food rose from 14 percent in 1973–74 to 21 percent in 1983–84 and then fell to 16 percent in 1986–87. This pattern is consistent with changes in the official poverty rate, which went up from 11 percent to 15 percent, and then down to around 13 percent. It is not consistent with trends in the poverty rate among Gallup respondents, which was 16 percent in both 1974 and 1984.

Table 10.2 also suggests that the elderly's ability to buy enough food improved between 1973–74 and 1986–87 (p = 0.93), whereas

Table 10.2   PERCENTAGE OF GALLUP RESPONDENTS REPORTING
INSUFFICIENT MONEY TO BUY FOOD AT SOME TIME DURING
THE PREVIOUS YEAR, UNITED STATES, 1973–74, 1983–84, AND
1986–87

				1983–84	
Age group	1973–74	1983–84	1986–87	Children in home	No children in home
All ages	14	21	16	27	16
	(999)	(1,547)	(n.a.)	(639)	(907)
18–29	18	30	20	34	25
	(291)	(437)	(n.a.)	(220)	(217)
30–49	15	22	19	24	19
	(333)	(534)	(n.a.)	(354)	(179)
50–64	11	12	10	18	11
	(206)	(314)	(n.a.)	(55)	(258)
65 and over	10	13	6	65	11
	(169)	(263)	(n.a.)	(10)	(253)

Source: See table 10.1 for the source of the 1973–74 and 1983–84 data. The 1986–
87 data are from the *Washington Post*, National Weekly Edition, 6 April 1987, 37.
Note: Sample size appears in parentheses.
n.a. Not available.

the situation of those under the age of 50 deteriorated ($p = 0.94$).
This broad pattern also is consistent with trends in official poverty
rates, which fell among people over the age of 65 and rose among
those between 18 and 64 over this 13-year period.
    The Gallup data lead us to two conclusions:

□ Direct questions about whether people have enough money to
buy food make the elderly look better off relative to the young than
age-specific poverty rates do.
□ Recent changes in different age groups' chances of saying they
had trouble buying food seem to parallel changes in official age-
specific poverty rates.

    To check these conclusions we also looked at the National Food
Consumption Surveys conducted by the U.S. Department of Agriculture (USDA) in 1955, 1965, and 1977.[7] These surveys exclude
households with no female homemaker and households in which
members ate fewer than 10 meals at home during the week prior to
the survey. They are not, therefore, representative of the nation as
a whole, and they are especially unrepresentative of persons living
alone, since they exclude all men living alone. Nonetheless, they

do allow us to explore the connection between poverty rates and food consumption among households with children and among elderly couples. To facilitate interpretation of our findings, we have converted all grocery expenditures to 1985 food prices.

We begin by comparing childless households with female home-makers over and under the age of 60. In both 1955 and 1965 the poverty rate for this group was almost 30 percentage points higher among elderly households surveyed by the USDA than among their nonelderly counterparts. The elderly also spent 21 percent less per person than the nonelderly on groceries in both years.[8] It is tempting to suppose that the expenditure difference was a product of the income difference, but matters are not quite that simple.

When we compare families at the same income level in these years, the elderly still typically spend 12 percent less than the nonelderly. This suggests that more than half the age disparity in grocery spending was attributable to differences in appetite, taste, or the efficiency with which different age groups bought food rather than to income differences.

By 1977 the poverty rates for the elderly and the nonelderly had converged somewhat, and the disparity in grocery spending per person had fallen from 21 percent to 15 percent. With the poverty level held constant, the elderly were spending only 9 percent less than the nonelderly. Thus, although the bulk of the expenditure gap between the elderly and the nonelderly was still independent of income, both the effects of income and the effects of appetite, tastes, and shopping practices appeared to have fallen slightly.[9]

In order to estimate how many households of various ages were spending as much as they "needed" to spend, we need an objective standard for defining "need."[10] One plausible possibility would be to treat expenditures in households with incomes 200 to 300 percent of the poverty line as a benchmark for defining "adequate" spending in a given year. When we do this, we find that the elderly typically spent 89 percent of the middle-income norm in all three years, whereas the childless nonelderly typically spent 99 percent of the middle-income norm, and nonelderly families with children raised their spending from 80 percent to 99 percent of the middle-income norm. We might, therefore, expect the elderly to have been less satisfied than the nonelderly with their grocery spending during these years. Yet the Gallup results for 1974 suggest that the elderly were more likely than the nonelderly to feel that they had enough money for food.

Our primary concern, however, is whether *changes* in age-specific poverty rates are a good guide to changes in different age groups' likelihood of experiencing problems with getting enough to eat. To answer this question, we must first look briefly at the overall trend in grocery spending.

From 1955 to 1965 real grocery expenditures per person rose slightly. This was true for both the elderly and the nonelderly, and for families with and without children. The increase was largely due to rising family incomes.

From 1965 to 1977 grocery spending per person fell slightly. This decline is found at every income level above the poverty line, with the largest decline among the most affluent families. Changes in what people bought suggest that the decline derived largely from increased concern with obesity, increased aversion to cholesterol-rich butter, eggs, and red meats, and perhaps increased use of restaurants for unusually expensive meals. Whatever the reasons, income had less effect on grocery spending in 1977 than in 1965.

Because the link between grocery spending and poverty weakened between 1965 and 1977, changes in age-specific poverty rates are not a reliable guide to age-specific changes in grocery spending. Poverty declined dramatically in childless families during this period, but so did grocery spending. This was true for both the elderly and the nonelderly.

In households with children the divergence between poverty statistics and grocery spending after 1965 is even more striking. The poverty rate for USDA households with children remained essentially constant during this period. Yet grocery spending among poor families with children rose 20 percent, while grocery spending among affluent families with children fell 14 percent. It is hard to avoid the suspicion that increased grocery spending among poor families with children had something to do with the growth of the Food Stamp program in the early 1970s.[11] Whatever the cause, the result is that trends in poverty tell us next to nothing about trends in grocery expenditure.

Taken together, the Gallup and USDA data lead us to two conclusions:

□ At a single point in time, official poverty statistics are not a reliable guide to cross-sectional differences in age groups' chances of reporting that they have enough money for groceries. Fewer elderly than nonelderly say there have been times when they could not buy food. This was true even in 1974, when the poverty rate was higher among the elderly them among the nonelderly. The elderly spend less than the nonelderly with comparable incomes in every year, but they are more likely to judge their expenditures adequate.[12]

□ Changes in age-specific poverty rates do not predict absolute changes in an age group's grocery spending. Although the poverty rate among USDA respondents fell from 1955 to 1977, food expenditures remained remarkably stable. However, changes in age-specific poverty rates from 1973 to 1986 do seem to predict changes in an age group's chances of saying it has enough money for food.

HOUSING CONDITIONS, AUTOMOBILES, AND TELEPHONES

Housing conditions are probably the most visible indicator of a society's material welfare, especially to outsiders. The high rate of homeownership in the United States, the spaciousness of American homes, and the near universality of flush toilets, bathtubs or showers, refrigerators, and gas or electric stoves have traditionally played a major role in convincing both Americans and Europeans that the United States was richer than Europe. The visible decay of housing in this country's urban ghettos has also played a major role in convincing Americans that poverty was a real problem. Partly for this reason, elimination of "substandard" housing has been a major goal of public policy in both the United States and Europe since World War II.

At least in the United States, owning an automobile has ranked second only to owning a home as a symbol of affluence. Universal automobile ownership has never become a goal of public policy, but it has certainly been a major goal of private economic activity.

Telephone service is less important than housing or transportation to most families, but at least in the United States universal telephone service was an important goal of federal regulatory policy until the late 1970s, and it remains important in some states even today.

As we would expect, the richest nations have the best housing, the most automobiles, and the most telephones (OECD 1986a). Around 1980, for example, median family income in the United States was about the same as in Canada, about 20 percent higher than in Sweden, and about 25 percent higher than in the United Kingdom and West Germany. The United States and Canada also had roughly comparable rankings with regard to housing conditions, telephones, and automobiles. (Americans had slightly fewer bathtubs and showers than Canadians, the same number of rooms per person, and more automobiles and telephones.) The United States and Canada, in turn, had more rooms per person, more bathtubs, more automobiles, and more telephones than Sweden, the United Kingdom, or West Germany. The British, Swedes, and West Germans were, in turn, better off on all these measures than the Japanese (for whom we do not have 1980 family income data).

All six nations had more rooms per person, more bathtubs and showers, more automobiles, and more telephones in 1980 than in 1960. This too is expected, since per capita income increased in all these countries between 1960 and 1980. Progress on all these indicators of material welfare was most marked in those countries that were worst off in 1960. This could be because incomes rose more in Europe and Japan than in the United States and Canada. It also could be because the market for extra rooms, bathtubs, automobiles, and telephones was closer to saturation in North America than in Europe or Japan in 1960.

Data on the age distribution of the population in substandard housing, owning automobiles, and having telephones are available only for the United States and the United Kingdom. Table 10.3 shows the data for the United States. By 1980 almost all Americans, regardless of age, lived in households with what the Census Bureau calls "complete" bathrooms (flush toilet, hot and cold running water, and shower or bathtub) and kitchens (refrigerator, stove, and sink). Not everyone owned his or her own home in 1980, but children were no worse off in this respect than the elderly. Air-conditioning also was equally available to all age groups.

The elderly were, however, considerably less likely than children to live in what the Census Bureau defines as "crowded" conditions— namely, more than one person per room. This is an almost inevitable byproduct of the fact that almost all the elderly live in households with only one or two people. Households of one cannot be crowded using the Census Bureau's definition, and households of two almost always have at least two rooms. Very large households, in contrast, often have fewer rooms than people.

The elderly are also somewhat more likely than children to live in a household with telephone service and somewhat less likely to live in a household with an automobile. Both these differences persist even among families at the same poverty level, which suggests that they reflect differences in the relative priority that the young and the old assign to automobiles and telephones. Both children and the elderly improved their position on all these measures of

Table 10.3   PERCENTAGE OF U.S. POPULATION IN HOUSEHOLDS LACKING
SELECTED AMENITIES, BY AGE OF HOUSEHOLD HEAD AND
POVERTY LEVEL, UNITED STATES

Hardship	Year	All respondents			Less than 75 percent of poverty line		
		Less than 19 years	19–65 years	66 years and over	Less than 19 years	19–65 years	66 years and over
Lacks	1960	8.3	6.1	9.6	30.1	26.4	26.6
complete	1970	2.3	2.1	4.6	10.5	11.7	12.8
kitchen	1980	2.1	1.8	2.0	5.3	6.4	5.9
Lacks	1960	16.5	13.0	19.1	51.7	46.7	47.1
complete	1970	5.5	4.9	9.2	21.9	20.5	20.1
bathroom	1980	2.3	2.4	3.9	7.7	8.0	8.5
More than 1	1960	35.3	14.7	3.5	65.7	35.3	5.1
person per	1970	26.3	10.3	2.2	58.0	25.6	2.3
room	1980	15.0	6.5	1.6	29.8	15.5	2.0
Lacks air-	1960	88.0	86.4	91.4	99.0	96.6	95.2
conditioning	1970	65.6	61.1	68.2	84.2	78.1	81.5
	1980	46.0	42.9	46.7	65.1	60.1	62.7
Does not own	1960	37.0	36.2	27.0	60.9	49.8	36.3
home	1970	32.9	34.2	29.1	63.7	57.1	33.8
	1980	28.8	30.5	26.7	59.5	55.8	43.1
No auto	1960	17.9	20.0	41.4	45.1	44.8	64.2
available	1970	9.9	9.6	30.9	39.2	32.5	58.1
	1980	6.9	6.2	24.4	33.1	27.1	48.4
Lacks	1960	26.0	21.0	22.6	60.8	54.3	45.0
telephone	1970	14.2	10.6	11.3	47.6	34.1	18.3
	1980	8.2	5.8	3.2	22.2	18.2	7.8
Number of	1960	6,639	9,315	1,550	1,268	1,073	391
cases	1970	7,128	10,468	1,905	666	581	298
	1980	6,838	13,906	2,307	788	815	153

75–125 percent of poverty line			175–225 percent of poverty line			275–325 percent of poverty line		
Less than 19 years	19–65 years	66 years and over	Less than 19 years	19–65 years	66 years and over	Less than 19 years	19–65 years	66 years and over
9.3	12.0	7.8	0.7	2.4	2.2	0.0	0.9	3.8
5.5	6.7	5.2	0.6	1.6	2.9	0.0	0.4	0.8
3.6	4.3	2.9	2.7	2.4	0.5	0.1	0.5	0.6
20.2	23.0	16.7	4.4	8.2	10.9	0.6	2.7	2.5
12.3	13.4	11.5	2.7	5.2	4.5	1.0	1.7	2.7
4.0	8.4	10.9	1.6	2.4	2.1	0.6	1.0	1.3
54.1	31.6	4.6	18.2	10.7	2.3	11.0	4.4	1.0
43.3	24.1	3.2	28.9	16.7	2.9	12.9	7.5	2.5
29.3	16.1	1.8	16.9	9.0	2.7	10.8	6.8	3.2
88.7	89.4	95.1	86.5	86.7	96.0	82.7	84.8	92.0
77.7	77.3	74.8	67.8	71.1	67.2	54.4	57.6	62.0
59.9	60.0	54.7	46.2	47.7	51.1	42.9	44.0	34.2
49.3	50.6	29.0	28.7	37.2	26.5	18.6	28.7	20.0
53.2	51.7	36.4	29.5	39.3	24.1	22.4	30.3	21.2
50.8	47.6	23.4	35.8	36.9	28.4	20.6	24.4	20.9
22.5	28.7	58.7	4.9	19.2	36.7	4.2	9.5	20.7
19.1	23.6	43.2	7.2	11.0	28.9	3.0	6.7	13.2
14.9	20.2	53.3	3.7	6.3	22.3	1.6	3.7	12.6
40.6	39.9	28.0	10.2	16.3	11.1	4.1	10.1	7.6
34.6	28.1	21.0	8.5	11.0	4.1	4.9	6.3	7.1
21.0	16.2	8.7	8.4	8.6	3.8	3.2	2.6	0.0
1,168	1,080	303	1,022	1,315	132	392	778	105
752	728	315	1,166	1,127	204	792	1,108	121
649	882	381	857	1,240	264	743	1,264	190

Source: 1/10,000 samples of 1960, 1970, and 1980 U.S. Censuses.

material welfare both during the 1960s and 1970s. Despite the fact that poverty declined among the elderly and rose among children during the 1970s, there is no evidence that the elderly gained more ground than children on these measures during the 1970s. Where one group made more progress than the other, the group that gained more was always the one that had been worse off initially, not the one whose poverty rate had fallen the most.[13]

Children were more crowded than the elderly in 1970, for example, and crowding declined more among children than among the elderly over the ensuing ten years. This happened partly because families with children got smaller and partly because they moved to larger homes. There was little crowding among the elderly even in 1970, so it could not decline much.

In addition, children were less likely than the elderly to live in families who owned their homes in 1970. This disparity also declined during the 1970s, despite the dramatic increase in housing prices, the increase in poverty among children, and the decline in poverty among the elderly.

Finally, the elderly were less likely than children to live in families that owned an automobile in 1970, and this difference also narrowed over the next ten years. It also narrowed during the 1960s, when poverty was falling as fast among children as among the elderly.

In summary, table 10.3 does not support the hypothesis that the redistribution of income from young to old that began around 1970 led to parallel changes in the age distribution of housing, automobiles, or telephones. When we look at changes in the position of persons living near the poverty line, the story is much the same. Poor people of all ages improved their housing conditions and access to telephones from 1960 to 1980. This suggests that the poverty line may have represented a higher standard of living in 1980 than in 1960—an inference consistent with the data on grocery spending.[14]

In the United Kingdom, the age distribution of housing conditions, automobiles, and telephones is quite different from that in the United States. Table 10.4 shows that the elderly in the United Kingdom are worse off than the young on every indicator for which we have data. Not only are the elderly less likely to have automobiles, which might simply be a byproduct of the fact that they are less likely to be able to drive, but the elderly are also less likely to have telephones and central heat—amenities that are almost certainly more important to the elderly than to the young. The same pattern holds for refrigerators, washing machines, dishwashers, televisions, and a number of other amenities not shown in table 10.4. Elderly British households are

Table 10.4   PERCENTAGE OF POPULATION IN HOUSEHOLDS WITHOUT
SELECTED AMENITIES, UNITED KINGDOM, 1973 AND 1982.

Amenity	All households	Elderly households	Households with children
Telephone			
1973	33	65	50
1982	24	32	22
Automobile			
1973	46	75	31
1982	41	67	27
Central heating			
1973	48	70	51
1982	40	48	31
Refrigerator			
1973	22	40	14
1982	7	16	4
Homeownership			
1959	62	56	n.a.
1982	41	48	n.a.

Source: United Kingdom Central Statistical Office (1983). United Kingdom Office of
Population Census and Surveys (1984).
n.a. Not available.

worse off than the young even in terms of homeownership, reflecting
the fact that homeownership was very low in the United Kingdom
when today's elderly might have bought homes. These disadvantages
are consistent with the high rate of poverty among the British elderly
(see chapter 5 of this volume).

Table 10.4 also shows that in the United Kingdom, unlike the
United States, households with children have more amenities than
the average household. Again, this holds not only for automobiles,
where households with children have an advantage in the United
States as well, but for telephones, refrigerators, central heating, and
many other amenities not shown. The material advantages enjoyed
by British children are not surprising, because the poverty rate
among British children is slightly lower than that for the population
as a whole (see chapter 5, table 5.2).

Since 1973 the consumption of telephones, automobiles, central
heating, and refrigerators has increased among both the young and
the elderly in the United Kingdom, just as it has in the United
States. And just as in the United States, the elderly, who had fewer
durables in 1973, enjoyed the biggest increases. But the advantage
of the young relative to the elderly in the United Kingdom stands

in contrast to the situation in the United States, where the young are worse off than the elderly.[15]

These figures raise important questions about cross-national comparisons of income and poverty levels. Chapter 5 shows that when U.S. poverty thresholds are converted to British equivalents using purchasing power parities, the 1979 poverty rate among the elderly was almost three times as high in the United Kingdom as in the United States (37 percent versus 13 percent). This finding is consistent with our tables 10.3 and 10.4. But the 1979 poverty rate among children was half again as high in the United States as in the United Kingdom (17 percent versus 11 percent). This is hard to reconcile with tables 10.3 and 10.4, which show that American children live in households with far more amenities than their British counterparts have. If American children's unusually high poverty rate does not imply that their families have fewer automobiles, telephones, and refrigerators, or that their parents are less likely to own their home, we must ask what it does imply. Unfortunately, we have no data suitable for answering this question.

PREMATURE DEATH

Most of us view our life expectancy as the most important single determinant of our well-being. We see death as the ultimate catastrophe and knowledge that death is imminent as the penultimate one. This view of life inevitably implies that children are better off than their elders.

The question that concerns us here, therefore, is not whether the young are better or worse off than the elderly but how their relative positions have changed over time. To answer this question, we look at changes in death rates, first among children and then among the elderly.

Ideally, trends in age-specific death rates should be examined from conception to age 18. We have chosen to focus on perinatal mortality because perinatal death rates are readily available for almost all the nations covered by this volume. (Perinatal mortality is the sum of fetal deaths that occur more than 28 weeks after conception and infant deaths that occur within a week of birth.)

Perinatal mortality has fallen steadily since 1950 in all nine of the countries covered by this volume, but it has fallen less in the United States than in most other countries (table 10.5). In 1950

Table 10.5   PERINATAL MORTALITY RATES, SELECTED COUNTRIES, 1950–80
(per 1,000 births)

Country	1950	1960	1970	1975	1980	Decline during 1950s	1960s	1970s
Australia	36	29	23	20	15	7	6	8
Canada	36	28	20	17	12	8	8	8
France	36	31	23	18	14	5	8	9
Germany, F.R.	50	36	26	19	12	14	10	14
Japan	47	41	22	16	12	6	19	10
Norway	28	24	19	14	11	4	5	8
Sweden	34	27	16	11	9	7	11	7
United Kingdom	39	34	24	20	13	5	10	11
United States	33	29	23	18	13	4	6	10
Mean	38	31	22	17	12	7	9	10

Source: OECD (1986a), 35.
Note: Perinatal mortality covers deaths after 28 weeks' gestation and deaths within one week after delivery.

perinatal mortality ranged from 2.8 percent in Norway to 5.0 percent in West Germany. The United States was near the low end of the distribution with a rate of 3.3 percent. By 1980 perinatal mortality ranged from 0.9 percent in Sweden to 1.5 percent in Australia, and the United States was near the high end of the distribution with a rate of 1.3 percent.

Perinatal mortality rates depend on many factors, including the health status of prospective mothers, the extent to which prospective mothers seek and follow medical advice during pregnancy, cultural norms about how pregnant women should care for themselves, and the state of medical knowledge. The universal decline in perinatal mortality presumably reflects improvements in all these areas, but we have no way of saying what their relative importance has been.

Cross-sectional studies show that perinatal mortality is usually lower in rich countries than in poor countries and that within rich countries it is lower in rich families than in poor families. All else being equal, therefore, one might expect perinatal mortality to have declined more in the United States during the 1950s and 1960s, when poverty among families with young children was declining, than during the 1970s and early 1980s, when poverty among such families was rising. Table 10.5 does not support this expectation, however. Perinatal mortality in the United States fell as much during the 1970s as during the 1950s and 1960s combined.

By putting this story in comparative perspective, table 10.5 shows that the question is not why the United States made so much progress during the 1970s but why it made so little progress during the 1950s and 1960s. The U.S. perinatal mortality rate was 88 percent of the eight-nation average in 1950. It rose to 94 percent in 1960 and 106 percent in 1970. It was still 106 percent in 1980. The progress during the 1970s was thus "normal" for an affluent society. What was "abnormal" was the relatively low rate of progress during the 1950s and 1960s.

The most obvious difference between the United States and other affluent nations during the 1950s and early 1960s was the U.S. commitment to fee-for-service medical care. This commitment almost certainly left poor pregnant mothers and newborns underserved. In the late 1960s the United States began to introduce programs aimed at ensuring that all pregnant women and newborns got appropriate medical care, regardless of their ability to pay. We cannot prove that this change stopped the deterioration in the U.S. position relative to the positions of other advanced nations. Nor can we prove that the spotty coverage of these programs explains why the U.S. perinatal mortality rate was still above the eight-nation average in 1980. But both arguments are plausible.

The most readily available measure of changes in death rates among the elderly is life expectancy at age 60. Life expectancy at age 60 in, say, 1980 is simply the cumulative product of the death rates observed in 1980 at all ages above 60. Life expectancy has risen among the elderly in every advanced society since 1950. The position of the United States relative to other nations has hardly changed, however. Life expectancy at age 60 in the United States was 0.1 year above the average for the eight nations in table 10.5 from 1950 through 1970 and 0.2 year above the average in 1980 (OECD 1986a).

The average retirement age has also been decreasing as life expectancy has lengthened. Therefore, the elderly in industrial countries spend many more years in retirement today than in the past. Because women live longer than men in every industrial country and the retirement age for women is lower than for men in some countries, the increase in life expectancy at retirement is most dramatic for women. On average the retired life expectancy of American women has increased 32 percent since 1961, compared with 26 percent for American men. And the universal decrease in both labor force participation rates and unemployment rates for the elderly, especially men, suggests that the lengthening of retirement is more voluntary than enforced.

Since 1970 the average increase in life expectancy in the United States has been comparable to that in other industrial countries. But the United States had more variance around its mean life expectancy in 1982 than any of the other countries compared in this chapter (LeGrand 1987). As with income, large variances may lead to a substantial reduction in well-being. Most people would surely rather live in a society where almost everyone dies between the ages of 65 and 75, for example, than in a society where many people die before they reach age 30 and many others live to be 100.

POOR HEALTH

There are no generally accepted measures of health. The best U.S. trend data come from the Health Interview Survey (HIS), which has been conducted annually since 1958. From 1962 through 1980 the HIS asked three questions about household members' health, each of which covered the two weeks prior to the survey:

□ The number of days each person had stayed in bed "all or most of the day" because of illness;
□ The number of days of school or work the person had missed because of illness; and
□ The number of days each person had "cut down on things (he/she) usually does" because of illness.

For simplicity, we refer to these questions as measuring "sick days."

Children's sick days fell during the 1960s and rose during the 1970s (table 10.6).[16] So far as we have been able to discover, nobody has a plausible explanation of either the decline during the 1960s or the subsequent rise.[17] The deterioration in children's reported health status during the 1970s appears too large to blame on declining infant mortality. Reductions in infant mortality raised the number of children who survived by about 1.0 percent between 1970 and 1980. Poterba and Summers (1987) have labeled these "extra" children "marginal survivors." Even if we make the implausible assumption that marginal survivors were the sickest 1.0 percent of all children in 1980, eliminating them would not reduce sick days in 1980 to 1970 levels.

Sick days changed in much the same way among the elderly as among children, declining during the 1960s and then rising during the 1970s.[18] The elderly's bed days remained essentially stable

Table 10.6   NUMBER OF SICK DAYS PER PERSON PER YEAR, BY AGE, UNITED STATES, 1962–63, 1970, AND 1980

Age group	Restricted-activity days			Bed-disability days			Work-school loss days[a]		
	1962–63	1970	1980	1962–63	1970	1980	1962–63	1970	1980
All ages	16.2	14.6	19.1	6.6	6.1	7.0	5.9	4.1	4.1
Less than 17	10.9	9.4	11.6	4.9	4.4	5.2	5.6	4.9	5.3
17–24	10.4	9.7	12.5	4.7	4.4	4.7	4.1	2.8	3.3
25–44	13.9	13.4	16.5	5.4	5.2	6.1	5.3	3.8	3.7
45–64	21.9	20.0	26.5	7.9	7.5	8.4	7.6	3.9	3.9
65 years and over	37.1	30.7	39.2	15.9	13.9	13.8	9.3	4.3	2.2

Sources: The 1963 data are from the U.S. Department of Health, Education, and Welfare (1964b). The data for 1970 are computations by authors from tapes supplied by the Interuniversity Consortium for Political and Social Research, Ann Arbor, Michigan. The 1980 data were supplied by the National Center for Health Statistics.
a. Work loss days are days lost from work due to illness or injury; they are computed only for persons 17 years and over who were employed during the two weeks preceding the survey. School loss days are days lost from school due to illness or injury; they are computed only for persons under age 17 who were enrolled in school in the previous year.

during the 1970s, but this apparent stability may be misleading, since the HIS does not cover inmates of institutions. The elderly also lost fewer days of work in 1980 than in 1970, but this is almost surely a byproduct of the fact that improvements in Social Security and private pensions encouraged workers with chronic health problems to withdraw from the labor force.

Most of the foregoing trends in sick days parallel age-specific trends in income and poverty. For children both sick days and poverty rates declined during the 1960s and rose during the 1970s. For the elderly both sick days and poverty declined during the 1960s. For the elderly, however, sick days rose again during the 1970s, despite the fact that their poverty rate declined. This suggests that we need to look more closely at the connection between sick days and income.

When we look at individuals, the association between sick days and income is relatively weak. As a result, all the trends shown in table 10.6 persist even when we compare persons at the same poverty level in 1962, 1970, and 1980. Whatever the factors that produced these changes, changes in income do not appear to be among them.

ACCESS TO MEDICAL CARE

For political purposes, changes in the medical resources society allocates to different age groups may be more important than changes in the health of these age groups. People who are sick usually want medical advice even when it does not make them better, and society as a whole wants medical care distributed equitably even if it does not improve health.

Unfortunately, we have no comparative data on access to physicians in different countries. The HIS does, however, provide data for the United States (table 10.7). During the 1960s physician contacts (including telephone contacts) declined slightly among both children and the elderly. The most obvious explanation is that people were healthier in 1970 than they had been a decade earlier (see table 10.6). We do not know how often people with sick days contacted physicians in 1957 to 1959, but by 1970 such people accounted for about half of all physician contacts. If this was also true around 1960, the 15 percent decline in sick days among children would have reduced physician contacts by about 8 percent. The actual decline was 9 percent. Among the elderly, the expected decline in visits would be 9 percent. The actual decline was 3 percent.

During the 1970s, there was little overall change in the frequency with which Americans saw physicians, but physician contacts were redistributed in two important ways. First, physicians increased their contact with children while decreasing their contact with nonelderly adults. Second, within every age group the poor either gained more or lost less than the affluent. It is tempting to suppose that these changes were attributable largely to the spread of insurance policies that paid for physician visits, but the evidence for this explanation is relatively thin.

The HIS data suggest that health insurance had a very modest effect on people's chances of seeing a physician in either 1970 or 1980. Insurance had no effect whatever on whether parents contacted a physician about children who were put to bed because of illness, for example. Insured families did contact physicians more often about children who were not put to bed because of illness, but the difference is quite modest. Tabulations for children with incomes below the poverty line indicate that both insured and uninsured children had more contact with physicians in 1980 than in 1970. Whether this reflected changes in poor parents' conviction that

Table 10.7   NUMBER OF PHYSICIAN VISITS PER PERSON PER YEAR, BY AGE
AND REAL FAMILY INCOME, UNITED STATES, 1957–59, 1970, AND
1980

Age group and income	1957–59	1970	1980
All ages and incomes	5.0	4.9	4.8
Under age 15			
All incomes	4.6	4.2	4.7
Less than $6,000	3.0	3.6	4.5
$6,000–$10,000	3.7	3.8	3.9
$10,000–$15,000	5.0	3.8	4.9
$15,000+	5.7	4.4	4.8
15–44			
All incomes	4.8	4.7	4.4
Less than $6,000	4.0	5.5	5.2
$6,000–$10,000	4.5	4.7	4.6
$10,000–$15,000	4.9	4.5	4.4
$15,000+	5.5	4.6	4.2
45–64			
All incomes	5.4	5.5	5.2
Less than $6,000	5.1	6.3	8.1
$6,000–$10,000	5.4	5.8	4.8
$10,000–$15,000	5.4	5.1	5.2
$15,000+	5.6	5.3	4.7
65 and over			
All incomes	6.8	6.6	6.5
Less than $6,000	6.5	6.3	6.5
$6,000–$10,000	6.6	6.3	6.2
$10,000–$15,000	6.9	7.0	6.6
$15,000+	8.7	7.1	6.8

Sources: The 1963 data are from the U.S. Department of Health, Education, and Welfare (1964a). The data for 1970 are computations by authors from tapes supplied by the Interuniversity Consortium for Political and Social Research, Ann Arbor, Michigan. The 1980 data were supplied by the National Center for Health Statistics.
Note: Income is reported in 1980 dollars using the family income categories available in the 1980 survey. For 1957 to 1959 the income groups are: (1) less than $2,000; (2) $2,000 to $4,000; (3) $4,000 to $7,000; and (4) $7,000 and over. For 1970, the income groups are: (1) less than $3,000; (2) $3,000 to $6,000; (3) $6,000 to $10,000; and (4) $10,000 and over. These groups are not quite mutually exclusive. We do not know how respondents with incomes of, say, exactly $6,000 classified themselves.

seeing a physician would be helpful or changes in the medical profession's attitudes toward the poor we cannot say.

Given the vast differences between the medical problems of children and the elderly, simple counts of medical visits are never likely to reveal whether different age groups are getting as much care as they need. One possible alternative is to ask people whether they got as much care as they thought they needed. We have not been able to locate such data. The Gallup survey has, however, asked national samples of adults: "Have there been times during the past year when you did not have enough money to pay for medical or health care?" About 15 percent of all adults said they had not been able to pay for medical care at some time during 1973–74. This figure rose to 25 percent in 1983–84 and fell to 21 percent in 1986–87. We do not know what fraction of those who could not pay for care actually went without it, what fraction got care for nothing, and what fraction got care they had to pay for later. Nonetheless, the age distribution of responses to the Gallup question is instructive. Elderly respondents were somewhat less likely than the nonelderly to say that they had been unable to pay for medical care, a pattern that recurs at all income levels. Medicare presumably helps explain this difference, but we cannot be sure whether it is the whole story. There was no statistically reliable difference between families with and without children in 1984, so we infer that on this criterion children were no worse off in 1984 than adults ages 18 to 64, despite their higher poverty rate.[19]

A third measure of access to medical care is hospital insurance coverage. In 1962 the elderly were less likely than the nonelderly to have hospitalization insurance in the United States (table 10.8). By 1970 the advent of Medicare had reversed this pattern, making the elderly the best-covered age group instead of the worst covered. Among the nonelderly, children and young adults were somewhat less likely to be covered than persons between the ages of 25 and 64.

The effects of income on coverage declined substantially between 1970 and 1980. Because of the link between Medicaid and Aid to Families with Dependent Children (AFDC), coverage grew especially rapidly among poor children. However, poor children still had less coverage than almost any other group in 1980.

Overall, our examination of changes in access to medical care, like our examination of changes in morbidity and mortality, suggests that these indicators do not move in tandem with income. Trends in relative income do not, therefore, tell us any more about trends

Table 10.8   PERCENTAGE OF PERSONS WITH HOSPITAL INSURANCE, BY AGE
AND FAMILY INCOME, UNITED STATES, 1962, 1970, AND 1980

Age group and family income	1962	1970[a]	1980
Under 15 years			
All incomes	*68.7*	*75.5*	*83.7*
Less than $6,000	21.9	25.1	65.9
$6,000–$10,000	42.8	42.3	67.2
$10,000–$15,000	78.2	78.0	79.5
$15,000 and over	87.6	90.4	92.7
15–24 years			
All incomes	*66.1*	*74.9*	*78.8*
Less than $6,000	41.6	56.3	68.2
$6,000–$10,000	49.4	53.5	64.3
$10,000–$15,000	73.7	76.6	75.5
$15,000 and over	82.6	86.1	87.8
25–44 years			
All incomes	*76.3*	*83.3*	*86.4*
Less than $6,000	30.9	31.4	55.1
$6,000–$10,000	52.7	55.7	66.0
$10,000–$15,000	81.8	82.8	83.6
$15,000 and over	90.0	92.6	93.8
45–64 years			
All incomes	*75.7*	*82.6*	*88.2*
Less than $6,000	37.9	41.8	63.8
$6,000–$10,000	63.1	67.6	77.2
$10,000–$15,000	83.5	86.9	86.5
$15,000 and over	90.5	93.0	94.5
65 and over			
All incomes	*54.0*	*97.8*	*98.3*
Less than $6,000	39.0	96.9	97.5
$6,000–$10,000	58.4	98.4	99.1
$10,000–$15,000	66.4	98.3	98.7
$15,000 and over	70.3	98.8	98.5

Sources: Same as table 10.7.
Note: See note to table 10.7.
a. Includes Medicare but not necessarily Medicaid.

in access to medical care than about trends in mortality or health status.

CRIMINAL VICTIMIZATION

Most observers agree that crime rose a lot during the late 1960s, leveled off in the early 1970s, and dropped somewhat in the early 1980s. Little is known about the reasons for these changes. Changes in the number of teenagers are only part of the story. It is tempting to suppose that rising family incomes somehow helped loosen the bonds that held American society together and that falling real incomes helped retie these bonds.

In 1984 Americans between the ages of 12 and 24 were more than 10 times as likely as those over age 65 to report that they had been victims of violent crimes (table 10.9). The young were also more than five times as likely to report that they had been victims of property crimes. Nonetheless, victimization appears to worry the young less than it worries the elderly (Cook and Skogan 1984).

Violent crime against different age groups changed relatively little between 1974 and 1984. Insofar as rates did change, the elderly were the biggest gainers and 20- to 24-year-olds the biggest losers. Thefts from all age groups declined considerably between 1974 and 1984, but the young were the biggest gainers. The elderly gained relatively little, and the black elderly were actually victimized more in 1984 than in 1974.

Taken as a whole, by far the biggest change between 1974 and 1984 was the reduction in thefts from whites ages 12 to 35 and from blacks ages 16 to 35. Trends in victimization are thus the mirror image of trends in real family income or poverty.

NOT LIVING WITH PEOPLE YOU WANT TO LIVE WITH

Living arrangements are among the most important determinants of human happiness, but no one arrangement is ideal for everyone. Most adults prefer living with a spouse they love to living alone, for example, but prefer living alone to living with a spouse they loathe. Likewise, most children prefer living with both parents as long as the parents get along reasonably well. If their parents quarrel

Table 10.9   CRIMINAL VICTIMIZATION RATES, BY RACE AND AGE OF
VICTIMS AND TYPE OF CRIME, UNITED STATES, 1974 AND 1984
(per 1,000 population)

	Crimes of violence			Crimes of theft		
Race and age group	1974	1984	Change	1974	1984	Change
Whites						
12–15	52.35	53.80	1.45	176.35	123.70	− 52.65
16–19	68.05	66.30	− 1.75	168.50	127.85	− 40.65
20–24	62.65	65.45	2.80	151.00	117.20	− 33.80
25–34	36.85	35.60	− 1.25	106.70	85.35	− 21.35
35–49	19.95	20.55	0.60	79.55	63.25	− 16.30
50–64	11.10	9.10	− 2.00	50.35	41.60	− 8.75
65 and over	9.15	4.70	− 4.45	22.05	19.95	− 2.10
Blacks						
12–15	53.60	52.40	− 1.20	109.65	105.05	− 4.60
16–19	70.65	76.50	5.85	104.00	82.95	− 21.05
20–24	54.75	62.25	7.50	123.45	99.25	− 24.20
25–34	54.25	51.90	− 2.35	109.60	75.30	− 34.30
35–49	31.10	30.40	− 0.70	79.55	64.35	− 15.20
50–64	18.95	19.60	0.65	42.95	30.10	− 12.85
65 and over	10.60	6.80[a]	− 3.80	23.70	26.85	3.15

Source: U.S. Department of Justice (1977, 1986).
Note: Data shown in this table are arithmetic means of estimates presented separately for male and female victims in the original source.
a. Estimate based on 19 or fewer sample cases.

incessantly, children may be happier when their parents separate. Some elderly widows and widowers prefer living with their children, others prefer living alone.

We begin by looking at children's living arrangements. If we asked children to order such arrangements from best to worst, we would probably find that almost all children thought living with both their natural parents was the best arrangement. Failing that, almost all would prefer living with at least one natural parent. Given a choice between living with only one natural parent and living with both a natural parent and a stepparent, children would probably be divided. Almost all children would surely consider living with neither of their natural parents the least desirable of all options.

Statistics on the frequency of these different arrangements are hard to find, because census data seldom distinguish children who live with both their natural parents from children who live with one natural parent and one stepparent. Data on the percentage of children living in "two-parent" families therefore exaggerate the percentage living with both natural parents. We can, however, use adults' retrospective reports of their living arrangements when they were children to reconstruct the history of children's living arrangements in twentieth century America. Table 10.10 attempts this task. The data are arranged according to the decade in which respondents reached the age of 16.

Readers may be surprised to see that the proportion of teenagers living with both their natural parents hardly changed from 1910 to 1980. Throughout the twentieth century, a quarter of all children have been separated from at least one natural parent before reaching the age of 17. The fate of children separated from their natural parents has changed appreciably over the course of the century, however. Children's chances of staying with their mother have risen, while their chances of staying with their father have fallen. This reflects the fact that fewer mothers are dying young. The proportion of children living with neither parent has also declined, partly because fewer mothers die young and partly because the advent of Aid to Families with Dependent Children (AFDC), improved job opportunities for women, and general affluence have made it easier for single mothers to keep their children with them.

Another important dimension of children's living arrangements is the number of siblings with which a child must compete for parental attention and support. Although parents' notions about optimal family size have fluctuated over time, all available evidence shows that children have always been better off in small families. This holds regardless of whether we look at children's IQ and achievement scores in elementary school, their persistence in school and college, or their economic success as adults. It also holds regardless of what parental characteristics we control (Sewell, Hauser, and Wolf 1980). Table 10.10 shows that by this yardstick the situation of children improved fairly steadily during the twentieth century.

Children's preferences aside, most adults assume that, for both economic and psychological reasons, two-parent families are better for children than one-parent families, even if one of the two parents is a stepparent. The percentage of children living in single-parent families has risen dramatically in the United States since 1970 (figure 10.1). These data at first appear to contradict the retrospective reports in table 10.10, which showed very little change between 1910 and 1980, but the two are not really comparable. To begin with, table 10.10 shows decade-long averages, and its data for 1970–79 come

Table 10.10   PERCENTAGE OF ADULTS REPORTING VARIOUS FAMILY ARRANGEMENTS AT AGE 16 AND MEAN NUMBER OF SIBLINGS BY DECADE THE RESPONDENT REACHED AGE 16, UNITED STATES

Type of family	Decade reached age 16						
	1910–19	1920–29	1930–39	1940–49	1950–59	1960–69	1970–79
Mother-father	74.3	73.1	75.7	75.8	75.9	77.0	74.5
Father-stepmother	2.0	2.9	2.2	1.8	1.8	1.2	1.3
Father only	4.3	4.0	3.0	2.2	1.2	1.8	1.9
Mother-stepfather	1.9	2.9	2.7	2.9	4.4	4.9	5.6
Mother only	9.9	9.0	8.8	10.3	11.1	11.0	12.1
Other relative	5.3	5.9	5.3	4.7	4.0	3.1	2.9
Nonrelative	2.2	2.1	2.4	2.3	1.7	1.0	1.9
Total[a]	100	100	100	100	100	100	100
Mean number of siblings	5.3	5.2	4.7	4.2	3.9	3.7	2.9
Sample size	994	2,032	2,901	2,898	3,300	4,573	2,836

Source: National Opinion Research Center, General Social Surveys, conducted annually (with occasional omissions) from 1972 to 1986. Computations by authors from data tape made available by the Roper Center for Public Opinion Research.

Note: Based on data collected by the National Opinion Research Center's General Social Survey in annual surveys of individuals 18 or over, conducted between 1972 through 1986. Respondents who turned age 16 in the early 1970s were eligible for inclusion in almost all these surveys, whereas respondents who turned age 16 in the late 1970s were only eligible for the later surveys. As a result, table 10.9 oversamples respondents who turned 16 during the earlier part of the decade and somewhat understates the magnitude of the changes between 1960 to 1969 and 1970 to 1979.

a. Detail may not add to 100 because of rounding.

Figure 10.1   PERCENTAGE OF CHILDREN IN SINGLE-PARENT FAMILIES

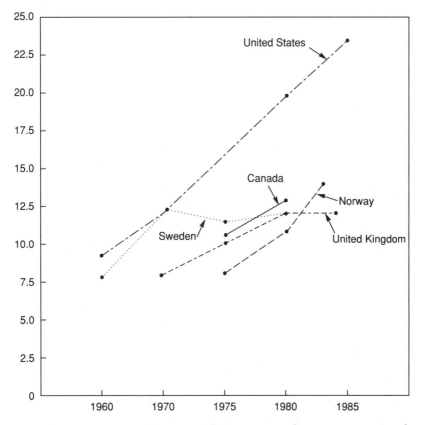

Sources: United Kingdom: Office of Population Census and Surveys (1984). Canada: Statistics Canada (1984). Norway: Statistics Sentralbyra (1983). Sweden: Statistics Sweden (1987). United States: Bureau of the Census (1985).

primarily from the early 1970s, whereas figure 10.1 reports data for specific years. In addition, table 10.10 describes the living arrangements of 16-year-olds, whereas figure 10.1 covers all children under 18. Changes in both illegitimacy and divorce affect young children more quickly than teenagers, so figure 10.1 shows more change.

Figure 10.1 shows that the patterns which prevailed during the first two-thirds of the twentieth century began to break down in the United States during the 1970s. It tells a similar but far less dramatic story for other advanced industrial countries. In every country but Sweden, children's chances of living with a single parent rose

Table 10.11   PERCENTAGE OF ELDERLY LIVING ALONE, BY AGE, SELECTED
COUNTRIES, SELECTED YEARS, 1960–83

Country	Age group	Percentage living alone			
		1960	1970	1980	1983
Canada	65 and over	12.4[a]	18.4[b]	24.0[c]	—
Sweden	65 and over	37.9[d]	41.5	47.1	—
United Kingdom	65–74	—	23.2[b]	25.5	28.0
	75 and over	—	31.5[b]	39.3[c]	47.0
	65 and over	18.6	26.6[b]	30.3	30.2
United States	65–74	17.3	23.3	25.2	24.9
	75 and over	21.4	32.4	39.1	38.9

Sources: Statistics for Canada are from Statistics Canada. Statistics from Sweden
were received in a personal communication, 1987. Statistics for the United Kingdom are from the Central Statistical Office (1983) and the Office of Population
Censuses and Surveys (1984). U.S. statistics were taken from U.S. Bureau of the
Census (1985).
a. Data refer to 1961. b. Data refer to 1971. c. Data refer to 1981. d. Data refer to
1965.

between 1970 and 1980. But nowhere was the change anything as
marked as it was in the United States.

The social and psychological consequences of living in a single-
parent family are hard to assess. For most white children the situation
is only temporary. They live first with both natural parents, then
with their mother alone, then with their mother and a stepfather.
The extent of the scars left by these changes is a matter of continuing
controversy, but such evidence as we have suggests that they are
relatively modest. One way to put the problem in perspective is to
note that, at least in the 1950s, an extra sibling reduced a child's
expected educational attainment and occupational status by as much
as coming from a broken family did (Sewell, Hauser, and Wolf 1980).
Thus, the decline in average family size may be helping children as
much as the decline in family stability is hurting them.

The connection between changes in children's living arrangements
and changes in age-specific poverty rates is both obvious and
problematic. The increase in single-parent families has contributed
directly to the increase in children's poverty. The decline in black
men's ability to support families at a level above the poverty line
may also have contributed significantly to their reluctance to live
with or support their children (Wilson and Neckerman 1986).
Nonetheless, the most striking fact about these changes is that they

Table 10.12   PERCENTAGE OF ELDERLY IN VARIOUS LIVING
ARRANGEMENTS, UNITED STATES, SELECTED YEARS, 1960–85
(noninstitutionalized population)

Age group	Year	Living alone	Married living with spouse	Living with other relatives	Living with nonrelatives only
65–74	1960	17.3	58.2	19.6	4.9
	1970	23.3	58.6	14.7	3.4
	1980	25.2	61.9	10.9	2.0
	1985	24.9	62.2	10.6	2.3
75 and over	1960	21.4	36.1	35.8	6.7
	1970	37.4	38.1	26.2	3.4
	1980	39.1	39.2	19.6	2.2
	1985	38.9	39.2	19.3	2.6

Source: U.S. Bureau of the Census (1986).

seem to have begun in the late 1960s, a period of unprecedented prosperity both in the United States and elsewhere. What we see at work here, therefore, may be a peculiar byproduct of the cultural liberalization induced by rapid economic growth, followed by a period of economic stagnation that makes cultural liberalism a luxury many people can no longer afford.

While the number of children in one-adult families increased in all industrial countries, the number of elderly living in one-adult households also increased in all such countries (see table 10.11). In Sweden and the United Kingdom, almost half of all people who are over the age of 75 are living alone. Until recently, many such people were too poor to maintain their own home, even if they wanted to. Their growing economic ability to exercise this option presumably improves their social welfare. The overall increase in economic autonomy among the elderly may, however, have made it harder for the frail elderly to turn to their children when they need help managing their daily lives.

More detailed information on the living arrangements of the American elderly is shown in table 10.12. The fraction of the elderly between the ages of 65 to 74 living with a spouse rose during the 1970s because people were living longer. The fraction living alone also increased steadily. The fraction living with their children fell. From census data we know that among persons over 75, the fraction living in group quarters—mostly nursing homes—has also risen somewhat. This change is partly a byproduct of Medicaid subsidies for nursing home care. Such changes in the living arrangements of the elderly may also reflect attenuation of family ties, but we have no direct evidence of such attenuation.

Taken as a whole, the data on living arrangements suggest that children's chances of living with two parents declined after 1960. But because the birthrate also began to decline in 1960, the number of children in a family got smaller; and the benefits of this change may well exceed the costs of family break-up. Among the elderly, living with a spouse has become more common, but so has living alone or in a nursing home. We cannot say whether the net result has been to make the elderly more or less satisfied with their living arrangements. The one thing we can say with confidence is that both children and the elderly care more about such changes in living arrangements than about small changes in their relative income.

UNEMPLOYMENT

Employment and unemployment are hard to measure precisely and even harder to compare across countries. The definition of the unemployed in most countries includes people who are looking for a job but have not found one they judge acceptable. It does not include discouraged workers who want a job but are no longer looking.

For people over the age of 65 in affluent countries, unemployment rates were low in the 1960s and 1970s and even lower in 1980. The highest rates were 2.8 percent for Swedish women and 4.2 percent for American women. For the young in every country, however, the rates were much higher. The unemployment rates for youths of both sexes and all ages have increased considerably in every country examined since 1966. These were the years when post-World War II baby boom youths began to enter the labor force and when growth began to slow.

Unemployment rates for 20- to 24-year-olds are lower than the rates for 15- to 19-year-olds in Canada, Japan, Norway, the United Kingdom and the United States but not in Sweden or West Germany (see table 10.13). But unemployment at age 20 to 24 is also more serious than at age 15 to 19. The unemployment rates for 20- to 24-year-old males vary considerably in 1980, from 4 percent in Japan to 22 percent in the United Kingdom, with the United States having the third highest rate. The change since 1966 also varies considerably.

Table 10.13   UNEMPLOYMENT RATES AMONG THE YOUNG, BY SEX,
SELECTED COUNTRIES, 1966, 1976, AND 1980

Country	Sex	Age group	Unemployment rates		
			1966	1976	1980
Canada	Males	15–19	10.0	16.3	20.6
		20–24	5.3	11.1	17.0
	Females	15–19	6.7	15.1	16.7
		20–24	2.7	9.8	13.4
Germany	Males	15–19	0.2	3.3	6.6
		20–24	0.2	4.0	9.1
	Females	15–19	0.2	5.7	9.8
		20–24	0.4	6.2	12.1
Japan	Males	15–19	0.9	5.2	8.9
		20–24	0.8	3.0	3.8
	Females	15–19	1.4	2.7	5.6
		20–24	1.3	3.8	4.5
Norway	Males	16–19	—	6.7	8.1
		20–24	—	4.0	5.3
	Females	16–19	—	9.6	10.5
		20–24	—	4.5	5.7
Sweden	Males	16–19	2.7	4.1	4.7
		20–24	1.7	2.2	6.4
	Females	16–19	5.1	7.0	4.5
		20–24	2.3	3.4	6.3
United Kingdom	Males	16–19	—	17.4	27.7
		20–24	—	8.9	22.2
	Females	16–19	—	14.7	21.5
		20–24	—	5.3	16.2
United States	Males	16–19	10.5	17.9	18.6
		20–24	3.6	11.0	10.4
	Females	16–19	14.0	18.6	17.5
		20–24	6.2	11.8	10.6

Source: OECD (1986b).

Japan and West Germany had almost no unemployment in this age group in 1966, so they had the biggest proportional increases. But if we measure change in absolute terms, the situation of young job seekers deteriorated most in Canada and West Germany, with Japan, Sweden, and the United States showing less deterioration. The United States was the only country where the unemployment rates for both men and women 20 to 24 years old actually decreased slightly from 1976 to 1980.

When American youths looked for a job in 1980, they were at a real disadvantage relative to their predecessors in 1966, but the United States has done no worse in this regard than most other industrial nations.

SUBJECTIVE WELL-BEING

Perhaps the simplest strategy for comparing the relative well-being of children and the elderly is to ask them how they feel about their lives. We have not been able to find surveys that ask children such questions, but researchers routinely ask adults how happy they are. The General Social Survey (GSS), for example, includes the following question: "Taken all together, how would you say things are these days—would you say that you are very happy, pretty happy, or not too happy?"[20] The GSS has asked this question almost every year since 1972—a period during which the incomes of the elderly rose dramatically relative to the incomes of persons under age 65. Although the GSS does not interview respondents under the age of 18, we can make some inferences about likely trends among adolescents from trends among parents with children at home. (The logic of using parental happiness to estimate children's welfare may seem tenuous here, but it is no more tenuous than using parental income to estimate children's welfare.)

Because the GSS surveys only about 1,500 adults annually, year-to-year fluctuations are hard to interpret. We can, however, make reliable comparisons between longer periods, such as the 1970s and the 1980s (table 10.14). Several results deserve comment:

□ There was a statistically reliable but substantively insignificant decline in the percentage of adults who said they were "very happy," but no increase in the percentage who said they were "not too happy."

□ The percentage of respondents who said they were "very happy"

Table 10.14   TRENDS IN ADULT HAPPINESS, BY AGE AND PRESENCE OF CHILDREN, UNITED STATES 1972–1978 AND 1980–86 (percentage)

	Very happy		Pretty happy		Not too happy		Sample sizes	
	1972–78	1980–86	1972–78	1980–86	1972–78	1980–86	1972–78	1980–86
Age group								
18–24	27.9	26.7	56.4	59.7	15.7	13.6	1,425	1,063
25–64	34.8	31.4	53.2	56.4	12.0	12.2	7,445	6,522
65 and over	37.0	38.9	48.6	48.1	14.4	13.0	1,744	1,731
Adults with								
Children at home	33.7	30.0	53.9	58.1	12.5	12.0	5,121	3,734
No children at home	34.8	33.8	51.9	53.4	13.3	12.9	5,464	5,540
Total	34.3	32.3	52.9	55.2	12.9	12.5	10,614	9,316

Source: Same as table 10.10. Pooled annual samples.

increased with age both during the 1970s and during the 1980s. The percentage who said they were "not too happy" did not vary much with age. Age, therefore, increased both the mean and the variance of happiness, but both effects were quite small.

□ There was no statistically reliable pattern of change in the happiness of persons under the age of 25.

□ Respondents over the age of 65 were marginally happier in the 1980s than in the 1970s, but the change was substantively insignificant and statistically unreliable.

□ Respondents who had children at home were about as happy as those without children at home in the 1970s. By the 1980s, respondents with children were marginally less happy than those without children.

The GSS suggests, in short, that the elderly gained a little ground and that the young lost a little ground between 1972 and 1986, but that the changes were very small.

Direct questions about happiness are obviously subject to a wide range of biases. The elderly may, for example, be more reluctant to complain than the young, even when they are equally unhappy. It is therefore important to check judgments based on direct questions against judgments based on people's behavior.

Suicide is one obvious behavioral measure of extreme unhappiness. Suicides are not always reported, however. Underreporting may distort both differences between countries and trends over time within a given country.[21] Nonetheless, we examined both the United States and six other affluent nations (Canada, Japan, Norway, Sweden, the United Kingdom, and West Germany). In all seven nations reported suicides are much more common among the elderly than among the young. There is no consistent difference in suicide rates between the "young-old" (persons 65 to 74 years old) and the "old-old" (persons over 75 years old). The "young-old" are more likely to take their own lives in Japan, the United States, and West Germany; the "old-old" are more likely to do so in Canada, Norway, and Sweden.

The fact that suicide rates are higher among the elderly than among the young tells us more about the way different age groups view the future than about the way they feel at the moment. The young may be as unhappy as the elderly, for example, but may be more inclined to believe that the future will bring an improvement. Since the future is much less predictable for the young than for the elderly, this assumption is probably rational.

Once again trends within age groups are more significant than cross-sectional differences between age groups. In the United States suicide rates among the young increased both during the 1960s and during the 1970s—although the overall increase among 15- to 24-year-olds conceals a modest decline among 15- to 24-year-old women during the 1970s. Among Americans between the ages of 65 and 74, there was no clear trend from 1962 to 1972; and a modest decline from 1972 to 1982. Among Americans over age 75, this pattern was reversed: suicides declined slightly from 1962 to 1972 and rose slightly from 1972 to 1982.

The suicide rate among Americans is neither conspicuously higher nor lower than the rates in other affluent nations. Youth suicides rose from 1962 to 1982 in Canada and Norway as well as in the United States, but they fell in Japan and the United Kingdom and showed no consistent trend in Sweden or West Germany. Suicide among the elderly fell in Japan and the United Kingdom, as well as the United States; rose in Canada, Norway, and West Germany; and showed no consistent trend in Sweden.

We have not tried to link age-specific trends in suicide to age-specific trends in income. The economic status of the elderly improved almost everywhere throughout this period, yet suicide rates moved in completely unpredictable ways. Like questions about happiness, suicide rates suggest that we should be cautious in generalizing from income to other indicators of well-being.

CONCLUSIONS

This volume asks how the situations of the young and elderly in the United States have changed since 1960 both in absolute terms and relative to each other. Previous chapters have discussed the progress of these two groups primarily in terms of income and wealth. This chapter investigated whether trends in nonmonetary measures of hardships or well-being were consistent with economic trends.

We limited ourselves to measurements that existed for both the young and the elderly, but having a common yardstick is deceptive. Children and the elderly have such different lives that even apparently similar measures mean different things to them. Therefore, our first conclusion is that cross-sectional comparisons between the

Figure 10.2   CHANGES IN POVERTY AND HARDSHIP SINCE 1960: SUMMARY

Measure of well-being	Young 1960s	Young 1970s	Elderly 1960s	Elderly 1970s	Source
Income					
Poverty rate	▼	▲	▼	▼	Smolensky, et al.
Material hardships					
Incomplete bathroom	▼	▼	▼	▼	Table 10.3
No automobile	▼	▼	▼	▼	Table 10.3
No telephone	▼	▼	▼	▼	Table 10.3
Crowded	▼	▼	▼	▼	Table 10.3
Does not own home	▼	▼	▲	▼	Table 10.3
Not enough money for food	n.a.	▲	n.a.	▼	Table 10.2
Physical and medical hardships					
Perinatal mortality	▼	▼			Table 10.5
Life expectancy at 60			▼	▼	OECD 1986a
No hospital insurance	▼	▼	▼	▼	Table 10.8
Restricted activity days	▼	▲	▼	▲	Table 10.6
Annual doctor visits	▲	▼	▲	▲	Table 10.7
Emotional hardships					
"Not too happy"	n.a.	n.a.	n.a.	▼	Table 10.14
Suicides	▲	▲	▼	▼	WHO
Living in one-adult household	▲	▲	▲	▲	Figures 10.1 and 10.12
Unemployment	n.a.	▲	n.a.	▼	Table 10.13
Victim of violent crime	n.a.	*	n.a.	▼	Table 10.9
Victim of burglary	n.a.	▼	n.a.	▲	Table 10.9

Note: Decade with the larger change has larger arrow.
* = no change   ▲ = increased hardship   ▼ = decreased hardship   n.a. = not available.

young and elderly are rarely instructive. We need to compare birth cohorts when they are the same age.

Our second general conclusion is that trends in hardship for specific age groups do not parallel trends in their relative income or poverty rates in any consistent way. Figure 10.2 summarizes the hardships we have examined, dividing them into the three broad categories set out at the beginning of the chapter, according to their expected dependence on income. What we call *material hardships* include poor housing, not having a telephone, not owning an automobile or a home, and not having enough money for food. These hardships should, in principle, be fairly closely related to income and poverty. What we call *physical and medical hardships* involve high mortality rates, poor health, and limited access to medical care. These hardships should be less related to income and poverty. What we call *emotional hardships*—unhappiness, suicide, unemployment, living apart from those you want to live with, and criminal victimization—should be least related to income and poverty.

Most material hardships declined for both children and the elderly both during the 1960s and during the 1970s. Thus, the increase in official poverty rates among children during the 1970s does not appear to have been accompanied by any clear-cut decline in material well-being. The Gallup question about having enough money for food does suggest, however, that families of childbearing age were somewhat worse off in the mid-1980s than they had been in the mid-1970s.

When we turn to physical and medical hardships, we find a very mixed story. Mortality declined in all age groups, especially in the 1970s. Health apparently improved in the 1960s and deteriorated during the 1970s. Use of doctors shows no simple trends. There is no evidence that any of these changes are related to changes in income or in poverty rates.

Finally, when we look at emotional hardships, we find no consistent pattern of change for either children or the elderly during the 1970s—despite the fact that the real incomes of the elderly were rising while the real incomes of families with children were falling. The apparently random relationship between trends in these emotional hardships and trends in poverty suggests that we should be especially cautious in generalizing from trends in poverty to trends in overall well-being, because these emotional measures are likely to be more closely related to subjective well-being than income is.

The list is obviously incomplete. As we noted at the outset, it is confined to measures that can, at least in principle, be constructed in more or less parallel form for both children and the elderly. It conspicuously fails to say anything about change in children's access to education or the amount they learn in school. In fact, enrollment trends are broadly consistent with trends in income and poverty among children, but their performance was more mixed.[22]

Our third conclusion is that cross-sectional comparisons of poverty rates for different affluent nations are a poor guide to the relative likelihood that citizens of these countries will experience other hardships. Chapter 5 showed that by 1980 American children were much more likely to live in poor families than children in Canada or affluent European nations. Yet perinatal mortality rates, teenage suicide rates, and teenage unemployment rates in the United States were not conspicuously higher than those in Europe or Canada. And American children seemed to be better off in strictly material terms than their British counterparts, even though far more American children seemed to live in families with incomes below the U.S. poverty threshold.

Our fourth conclusion is that the trends in the United States are broadly similar to trends in other industrial countries where comparable indicators exist. Material hardship has declined everywhere. Life expectancy has improved. Single-adult households have become more common, and so has youth unemployment. Only suicide seems to have changed in different ways in different countries.

Economists will inevitably feel that our ad hoc measures of material welfare and hardship are a poor substitute for statistics on total family income and expenditure, because income statistics do not prejudge what is important to people. There is some truth in this. But income differences are instructive only when we use them to compare people who want roughly the same things and when these people buy the things they want in the same markets.

Most of the social indicators discussed in this chapter involve either things that are not for sale in any well-defined market, or things whose value varies in ways that are, to a significant extent, independent of their price. Americans cannot buy longevity or good health the way they buy coffee or motorcycles. In theory they can buy medical care, but in practice the poor now consult physicians more than the rich do—although they may get worse advice. Americans can buy housing on the open market, but at least among homeowners the quality of housing seems to depend as much on when they bought as on what they paid.

Parents cannot buy domestic harmony for their children, and children cannot mortgage their future incomes in order to prevent their parents from having additional children. The elderly cannot keep their spouses alive by spending more on health care, and they can seldom even make their children love them by promising to leave them money. There is a brisk market in devices that are supposed to reduce people's chances of becoming the victims of crime, but the success of these products is still very limited. Overall, although the rich are undoubtedly happier than the poor, the difference is extremely modest (Bradburn 1969, Easterlin 1974).

In light of all these market imperfections, income statistics tell us far less about the lives of either children or the elderly than we may imagine. Given the trend in U.S. family income over the past 15 years, this is surely an encouraging conclusion.

Notes

1. A recent Chicago survey, described in Cook, Jencks, Mayer, Constantino, and Popkin (1986) asked respondents: "Over the past year was there a time when you needed food but couldn't afford to buy it?" One respondent in six reported that there had been a time when he or she could not afford to buy needed food. Yet only one in sixteen said, in answer to a follow-up question, that he or she had gone hungry as a result.

2. The 1987 data were not yet available for secondary analysis when this book went to press.

3. A surprising number of apparently affluent respondents reported that they did not have enough money for food at some time during the previous year. These responses presumably reflect the effects of changes in family membership, changes in family income, and reporting errors. The poverty ratios in table 10.1 are based on families' *current* size and income. The food question covers the respondent's experience during the previous 12 months. Changes in family membership are common for all groups, but especially for the young. Changes in family income were probably especially common between January 1983 and January 1984, because this was a period of rapid economic recovery. A number of families with relatively high 1984 incomes probably experienced a fairly long spell of unemployment in 1983; and because few families have appreciable savings, protracted unemployment could easily mean that these families felt they did not have enough money for food.

4. Poverty rates for Gallup respondents are approximate, because Gallup respondents report their incomes in categories. We assigned all respondents the estimated mean for their income category in order to determine whether their families were poor. For reasons we cannot explain, the poverty rate among elderly Gallup respondents is roughly twice the official rate for the same year (27 versus 15 percent in 1974 and 25 versus 12 percent in 1984). The poverty rate among Gallup respondents ages 25 to 64 also exceeds the official rate, but by less (14 versus 9 percent in 1974 and 14 versus 12 percent in 1984).

5. Table 10.1 does not include separate data on families with children in 1974, because the 1974 data do not include information on the age of family members other than the respondent.

6. Official poverty statistics for 1986 to 1987 were not available at press time, so we estimated the rate using data on poverty and unemployment from 1980 to 1985 and unemployment in 1986 to 1987. The poverty rate for Gallup respondents in 1987 also was unavailable, but we did not try to estimate it.

7. The U.S. Department of Agriculture (USDA) conducted another Food Consumption Survey in 1987, but no results were available before this book went to press. The Consumer Expenditure Surveys, conducted in 1960 to 1961, 1972 to 1973, and quarterly since 1980 also provide data on grocery spending; but our analyses of these data were just beginning at press time. We are indebted to Reuben Buse and the USDA for supplying the data tapes from the National Food Consumption Surveys and for technical advice on their use. The tabulations discussed in the text are available from Christopher Jencks on request.

8. To adjust for changes in meals eaten away from home, we inflated all households' grocery spending to the amount we would have expected them to spend if all members had eaten all their meals at home during the week prior to the survey. To do this we multiplied weekly grocery expenditures by $21N/(21N - A)$, where N is the number of persons in the household and A is the number of meals eaten away from home.

9. We have not tried to explain year-to-year fluctuations in the pattern of interactions

between poverty level and age, because most such fluctuations are probably due to chance. We have only 100 to 200 elderly respondents at each poverty level in 1955, 200 to 400 in 1965, and 150 to 300 in 1977. The number of childless, nonelderly households at each poverty level is considerably larger in each year.

10. The USDA publishes food budgets that are widely used to determine how much families of various sorts need to spend, including one that is used to set food stamp allotments. On examination, however, these budgets turn out to be based entirely on what families at various income levels actually spend, not on what they "need" to spend in order to achieve some specified level of nutritional adequacy or subjective satisfaction with their diet.

11. Although the 1977 food stamp budget was quite low, a significant number of low-income families reported spending less than this amount on groceries in 1965. Such families could have sold their food stamps and used the money for other purposes in 1977, but the "street value" of food stamps is usually less than two-thirds their grocery store value, so recipients have a strong incentive to use them in grocery stores.

12. For evidence on this point in Chicago, see Cook, Jencks, Mayer, Constantino, and Popkin (1986).

13. In measuring rates of change, we focused exclusively on changes in the absolute percentage difference between two groups. Cutting a group's chances of not having a telephone from 30 to 20 percent thus represents the same amount of progress as cutting the chances from 15 to 5 percent. Our approach reflects the fact that the number of households acquiring a telephone for the first time is the same in both cases.

14. The most important partial exception to the generalizations in the text is the change in homeownership patterns among the poor. Homeownership declined among the poor during the 1960s, perhaps in part because the poor were more urban in 1970 than they had been in 1960. Homeownership trends among the poor during the 1970s are inconsistent, probably because of sampling error.

15. The British data in table 10.4 are not strictly comparable to the U.S. data in table 10.3, largely because the British data weight all households equally, regardless of whether they have one or more members in the relevant age group, whereas the U.S. data weight households according to the number of children or elderly in them. In addition, the age cutoff for the "elderly" is 60 in the United Kingdom, and 66 in the United States. The age cutoff for "children" is 18 in the United Kingdom and 19 in the United States. But when we reweighted the U.S. data to make them comparable to the British data, we still found that Americans of all ages had more automobiles and telephones in 1980 than their British counterparts had in 1982. Americans of all ages were also more likely than their British counterparts to own their homes and to have refrigerators.

16. OECD (1986a) reports that in the late 1970s American children averaged three more sick days per year than Canadian children, the same number as Australian children, and five fewer than British children. Unfortunately, OECD does not report the wording of the questions in different countries, but it seems likely that the wording varies, so we have little confidence in the validity of these cross-national comparisons.

17. These trends are not attributable to flu epidemics or other short-term influences. They recur using three-year averages.

18. OECD (1986a) reports the following figures for sick days per year among the elderly in the late 1970s: Australia, 35; Canada, 35; Norway, 61 Sweden, 27; the United Kingdom, 43; and the United States, 39. For annual bed days among the elderly, OECD reports Australia, 10; Canada, 13; Norway, 18; the United States, 14. Again, we are uncertain how comparable the questions were in different countries.

19. The 1973–74 and 1983–84 data are from data tapes available through the Roper Center for Public Opinion Research, Storrs, Connecticut. The 1986–87 data are from the *Washington Post*, National Weekly Edition, April 6, 1987, p. 37.

20. Bradburn (1969) discusses the meaning and correlates of responses to this question in detail.

21. Our discussion is based on World Health Organization, World Health Statistics, 1965, 1975, 1984, 1985.

22. A complete treatment of changes in educational opportunity is obviously beyond the scope of this chapter, but it is worth noting that the percentage of American fifth graders who completed high school remained essentially constant from 1966 though 1980 (OECD 1984). The percentage of high school graduates attending college rose during the 1960s but leveled off or fell during the 1970s (U.S. Bureau of the Census 1986). These trends are broadly consistent with trends in income and poverty among children. There is little evidence of long-term change in what elementary or secondary students learn. American junior high school students did worse on the international math test in 1980 to 1983 than in 1960 to 1964, but American high school students did slightly better (Robitaille and Taylor 1985). American high school students scored lower than students in most other affluent countries in both 1960–64 and 1980–83.

References

American Institute for Public Opinion. 1974. Survey 1230G. Storrs, Conn.: Roper Center for Public Opinion Research (September).

———. 1984. Survey SPEC 76-GLOBAL. Storrs, Conn.: Roper Center for Public Opinion Research (January).

Bradburn, Norman. 1969. *The Structure of Psychological Well-Being.* Chicago: Aldine.

Cook, Fay Lomax, Christopher Jencks, Susan Mayer, Ernesto Constantino, and Susan Popkin. 1986. "Stability and Change in Economic Hardship: Chicago 1983–1985." Evanston, Ill.: Northwestern University, Center for Urban Affairs and Policy Research.

Cook, Fay Lomax, and Wesley Skogan. 1984. "Evaluating the Changing Definition of a Policy Issue in Congress: Crime Against the Elderly." In *Public Policy and Social Institutions,* edited by Harrell R. Rodgers, Jr. Greenwich, Conn.: JAI Press.

Council of Economic Advisers. 1985. *Economic Report of the President.* Washington, D.C.

Easterlin, Richard A. 1974. "Does Economic Growth Improve the Human Lot? Some Empirical Evidence." In *Nations and Households in Economic Growth: Essays in Honor of Moses Abramovitz,* edited by Paul David and Melvin Reider. New York: Academic Press.

Government of Canada. 1984. *Living Alone.* Ottawa: Minister of Supply and Services.

Government of Norway. 1983. *Survey of Level of Learning*. Oslo: Statistisk Sentralbyra.

Government of the United Kingdom, Central Statistical Office. 1983. *Social Trends*. no. 14, 1984 edition. London: Her Majesty's Stationery Office.

———. Office of Population Censuses and Surveys. 1984. *General Household Survey, 1983*. London: Her Majesty's Stationery Office.

LeGrand, Julian. 1987. "An International Comparison of Inequalities in Health," Discussion Paper No. 16. London: London School of Economics Welfare State Programme, Suntory-Toyota International Center for Economics and Related Disciplines.

National Opinion Research Center. 1972–86. *General Social Survey*, data tape. Storrs, Conn.: Roper Center for Public Opinion Research.

Organization for Economic Cooperation and Development. 1984. *Educational Trends in the 1970's: A Quantitative Analysis*. Paris: OECD.

———. 1986a. *Living Conditions in OECD Countries: A Compendium of Social Indicators*. Paris: OECD.

———. 1986b. *Labor Force Statistics, 1964–1984*. Paris: OECD.

Orshansky, Mollie. 1965. "Counting the Poor: Another Look at the Poverty Profile." *Social Security Bulletin* 28, no. 1 (January):3–29.

Poterba, James, and Lawrence Summers. 1987. "Public Policy Implications of Declining Old Age Mortality." In *Work, Health, and Income Among the Elderly*, edited by Gary Burtless. Washington, D.C.: Brookings Institution.

Robitaille, David, and Alan Taylor. 1985. "A Comparative Review of Students' Achievements in the First and Second IEA Mathematics Studies." IEA Second International Mathematics Study. September. Manuscript.

Sewell, William, Robert Hauser, and Wendy Wolf. 1980. "Sex, Schooling, and Occupational Status." *American Journal of Sociology* 86:551–83.

Statistics Sweden. 1987. Personal communication, Arne Arvidsson.

U.S. Bureau of the Census. 1986. "Marital Status and Living Arrangements: March 1985," *Current Population Reports*, series P-20, no. 410. Washington, D.C.

U.S. Department of Health, Education, and Welfare. 1964a. *Vital and Health Statistics*, series 10, no. 9, "Medical Care, Health Status, and Family Income." (HRA) 76–1304. Washington, D.C.

———. 1964b. *Vital and Health Statistics*, series 20, no. 5, "Current Estimates for the Health Interview Survey, United States, July 1962–June 1963." Washington, D.C.

U.S. Department of Justice, Bureau of Justice Statistics. 1977. *Criminal Victimization in the United States, 1974*. Washington, D.C.

———. 1986. *Criminal Victimization in the United States, 1984*. Washington, D.C.

Washington Post. 1987. National Weekly Edition (6 April), 37.

Wilson, William, and Kathryn Neckerman. 1986. "Poverty and Family Structure." In *Fighting Poverty*, edited by Sheldon Danziger and Daniel Weinberg. Cambridge, Mass.: Harvard University Press.

World Health Organization (WHO). 1965. *World Health Statistics Report, Annual Statistics, 1965*. Geneva: WHO.

———. 1975. *World Health Statistics Report, Annual Statistics, 1975*. Geneva: WHO.

———. 1984. *World Health Statistics Report, Annual Statistics, 1984*. Geneva: WHO.

———. 1985. *World Health Statistics Report, Annual Statistics, 1985*. Geneva: WHO.

Part Three

COUNTRY STUDIES

Chapter Eleven

TRENDS IN WELL-BEING OF CHILDREN AND THE ELDERLY IN JAPAN

Samuel H. Preston and Shigemi Kono

The aims of this chapter are largely descriptive: to document socioeconomic trends in Japan among the two groups outside the ages of normal labor force participation during the past several decades of radical demographic change and explosive economic growth. In view of Japan's very different cultural traditions, family organization, and social programs, we are particularly interested to learn whether trends in Japan are similar to those that occurred during a comparable period in the United States (Preston 1984) and whether the same forces appear to be at work.

In order to understand the origins of the developments that we describe, it is first necessary to outline the demographic and social context within which they have taken place.

DEMOGRAPHY AND FAMILY

Demographically, Japan is unique. Following slow declines in crude birthrates and crude death rates in the first four decades of the twentieth century (Taeuber 1958), Japan experienced a sudden and very sharp decline in fertility. Between 1947 and 1957 the total fertility rate (average number of children born to a woman who survives to age 50) fell from 4.54 (somewhat above pre-World War II levels) to 2.04 (Japan Institute of Population Problems 1985a). This decline occurred at a time when European and North American countries were typically experiencing their highest fertility levels since the 1920s. Since 1957 the level of fertility has remained near the replacement level in Japan; it was 1.76 in 1985 (Japan Institute of Population Problems 1986b). The small birth cohorts produced by plunging fertility in the 1950s are now in the midst of their own childbearing period and are not producing enough children even to replace themselves. The number of children below age 15 in Japan has declined from 30.1 million in 1955 to 26.5 million in 1984 (Japan 1985c) and will continue declining if current fertility levels continue.

The effects of fertility decline on the age structure have been augmented by declines in mortality that are also the most rapid in the developed world. Life expectancy at birth grew from 52.0 years in 1947, to 67.7 years in 1960, to 77.6 in 1985 (Japan Institute of Population Problems 1985c). This remarkable gain of 25.5 years in life expectancy at birth over the course of 38 years was achieved through mortality reductions at all ages. The probability of surviving from birth to age 65 grew from .44 in 1947 to .85 in 1985, while life expectancy at age 65 increased from 11.1 years to 17.2 years. Life expectancy at birth in Japan (along with Iceland) is now the highest in the world.

The sharp falls in fertility and mortality have produced an extremely rapid aging of the Japanese population. The percentage of the population above age 64 more than doubled from 4.8 percent in 1947 to 9.9 in 1984 (Japan Institute of Population Problems 1985c). The percentage of elderly has grown faster in Japan than in any other country over this period. It is still below that in most other countries in Europe and North America; however, a great deal more aging is in prospect if current demographic circumstances continue. In the near term, the percentage of Japanese above age 64 is projected to grow to 11.9 percent in 1990, 16.2 percent in 2000, and 23.5 percent in 2020 (Japan Institute of Population Problems 1986b). The percentage of Japanese below age 15 is projected to decline from 21.6 percent in 1985 to 16.5 percent in 2020. The dependency ratio (the ratio of persons below age 15 and over 64 to persons between the ages of 15 and 64) is projected to grow from 0.47 in 1985 to 0.67 in 2020; the ratio of those over age 64 to those between 15 and 64 is projected to increase from 0.15 in 1985 to 0.39 in 2020. It took more than a century for the population over age 64 to increase from 7 percent to 14 percent in France; it will take about 75 years for the United States to traverse this span; it will require only some 26 years in Japan (Way 1984).

The principal source of the rapid aging of Japan is the abrupt change from moderate to very low fertility levels. It is important to recognize that the low levels of fertility are occurring in a household and family context different from that which prevails in Western Europe or North America. The institution of marriage has retained much more of its traditionally specialized character in Japan than elsewhere (Preston 1987). Out-of-wedlock childbearing is negligible in Japan; less than 1 percent of births since 1967 have occurred to unmarried women, compared with over 20 percent of births in the United States in recent years. Marriage is delayed in Japan; only 22 percent of women ages 20 to 24 were married in 1980, compared with 50 percent in the United States in 1980 and 43 percent in 1984. Once a woman marries in Japan, she typically proceeds immediately to childbearing. The large majority of Japanese women have a child in the first two years of marriage, and less than half practice contraception before having a second birth (Morgan, Rindfuss, and Parnell 1984; Atoh 1985). Marital fertility levels below age 30 scarcely differ from those in 1930. Finally, the divorce rates are low in Japan, less than a third of the rates in the United States since 1960. Approximately 12 percent to 15 percent of Japanese marriages will end in divorce according to recent rates of marital disruption.

The sharp behavioral boundaries surrounding marriage in Japan are undoubtedly related to an unusually high division of labor by sex. Japan has the lowest labor force participation rates outside the home for married women (26 percent in 1980) of any industrial country (Mincer 1984). Japanese men work more hours in the market and fewer in the home than men in any other developed country investigated (Morgan, Rindfuss, and Parnell 1984). Although there are signs that attitudes among women regarding the division of labor are changing, there is little indication of change among men. (For abundant detail, see Japan Economic Planning Agency 1983.)

The inner workings of the Japanese family have been described by a Japanese sociologist, Takeshi Ishida (1971):

When a couple has children, their interest, particularly that of the mother, tends to be concentrated on the children. . . . Even in the case of a family of the new middle class, which represents in many ways the most radical departure from tradition, it is reported that the mother provides her children with continuous attention. For instance, she usually sleeps with the child, and she carries it on her back when she goes out shopping. . . . The intimate relationship continues to exist until the children reach late adolescence, although occasionally they revolt because they feel the close tie with their parents to be a burden. Many students who come to take the university entrance examinations are accompanied by their mothers or even by both parents.

The ordinary middle-class husband has little time to spare for his family. Naturally, he leaves the running of the home to his wife; and while the husband depends on his wife in this way, the wife feels that the harder he works, the better his, and therefore her, future will be. (51–53)

Yamamura (1986) argues that a "sanctification" of the child occurs in Japan and that parents strive to maintain the child's purity through abundant attention and indulgence. The elevated status of children is long-standing. Namaye (1919) notes that Japan was then termed a "paradise for children," citing prevalent images of Gods and Goddesses regarded as protectors of children in all parts of Japan. Befu (1986) cites the coalition of mother and child as the basic union in Japan, in contrast to the American pattern where the husband-wife coalition is more fundamental:

For Japanese women, on the other hand, the rank order of their various commitments—to motherhood, to being a wife, to fulfilling personal goals, and so forth—is clear-cut and absolute: motherhood comes first. Neglect of one's responsibility as a mother is inexcusable under any circumstances. (25)

Evidence of child-centeredness is also available from opinion polls produced for the prime minister's office. In 1979 more adult respondents preferred "a family centered on children" (37 percent) than "a family centered on the couple" (31 percent). However, the gap between the responses was less than in 1972. Ninety-one percent of adults opposing divorce in a poll taken in 1981 cited "the influence of the divorce on the children" as their principal reason (Japan Economic Planning Agency 1983).

LIVING ARRANGEMENTS

The traditional household arrangement in Japan is a stem family household in which the parents, their eldest son, his wife, and their children live in the same dwelling. Such three-generation family households are still common in Japan, although they have been declining. In 1955 over one-third of Japanese households were three-generation households. In 1985 almost 20 percent of Japanese households were three-generation households, compared with 17.5 percent of one-person households and 14.3 percent of husband-wife only households (table 11.1). Surprisingly, the proportion of nuclear family households has increased only modestly since the 1950s, and in the past ten years it has decreased. One of the major causes for such a decrease is the decrease in the number of marriages. Between 1970 and 1974 there were more than a million marriages a year; by 1985 the number had declined to only 735,852.

The distribution of household types containing at least one elderly

Table 11.1 TRENDS IN HOUSEHOLD STRUCTURE, JAPAN, SELECTED YEARS, 1955–85 (percentage)

Year	Total households (thousands)	Nuclear family households				One-person households	Three-generation households	Nonrelative households
		Total	Husband and wife only	Husband wife and children	Single parent and children			
1955	17,383	59.6	6.8	43.1	9.7	3.4	36.5	0.5
1960	19,678	60.2	8.3	43.4	8.6	4.7	34.7	0.4
1965	23,085	62.6	9.9	45.4	7.3	7.8	29.2	0.4
1970	26,856	63.5	11.0	46.1	6.4	10.8	25.4	0.4
1975	31,271	64.0	12.5	45.7	5.7	13.7	22.2	0.2
1980	34,106	63.4	13.1	44.2	6.0	15.8	20.7	0.2
1985	36,452	62.6	14.3	41.7	6.7	17.5	19.7	0.2

Source: Statistical Bureau, Management and Coordination Agency, *Population Censuses*, various years.
Note: Detail may not add to total because of rounding.

person makes the prevalence of three-generation households even clearer (table 11.2). In 1970, for example, 70 percent of households with elderly members were three-generation households; by 1985 the proportion was still over half (56 percent).

The distribution of elderly persons by household type is shown in table 11.3. In 1985 only 9.5 percent of persons ages 65 years and over lived alone, and 23.1 percent were currently married and living only with their spouse. Nearly 65 percent lived with their children, married or unmarried, and nearly 48 percent lived with their married children. Among those ages 75 years and over, 73.4 percent lived with their children. In sharp contrast, 28.7 percent of the Americans ages 65 and over lived alone in 1981 (38.8 percent of women lived alone), and 51.0 percent were married couples with no one else in the household (Siegel and Davidson 1983).

It is a widely accepted view that urbanization and industrialization encourage the formation of isolated nuclear families (Parsons and Bales 1955; Goode 1963). The continued strength of the three-generation family household in Japan calls into question this venerable generalization (Morgan and Hirosima 1983). The persistence of a very high, though declining, proportion of three-generational households among total households—and particularly among the households of the elderly—is noteworthy in view of the fact that Japan is now ranked among the highly industrial nations and by some measures has surpassed the United States in per capita income. Obviously, the extended household remains a workable option, one with strong cultural underpinnings. A 1985 survey conducted by the Japan Institute of Population Problems (1986d) reveals that a much larger number of Japanese considered the three-generational family "a more natural and human" living arrangement than a nuclear family. According to Palmore and Maeda (1987):

The main explanation for relatively high status and integration of older adults in Japan is the tradition of respect for elders that has its roots in the vertical society and in religious doctrines of filial piety. Respect and affection for elders are shown on a daily basis by honorific language; bowing; priority for elders in seating, serving, bathing, and going through doors. It is also reflected in popular sayings, celebrations of special birthdays, the Respect for Elders Day, the National Law for Welfare of the Aged, special programs for elders, and the power of elders in society. (3)

In addition to cultural traditions that support the three-generation household, it is adaptive to the high cost of housing in Japan (Morgan and Hirosima 1983; Hashimoto 1986a). It is often also a simple

Table 11.2   CHANGES IN THE COMPOSITION OF HOUSEHOLDS CONTAINING THE ELDERLY, JAPAN, SELECTED YEARS, 1970–85

Year	Total (thousand)	Nuclear family households					Three-generation households	Nonrelative households	One-person households
		Total	Couple only	Couple and children	Father and children	Mother and children			
1970	5,821	22.4	10.1	7.6	1.1	3.6	70.7	0.2	6.7
1975	6,881	25.8	13.2	7.4	1.0	4.3	65.4	0.2	8.6
1980	8,078	28.9	15.8	7.3	1.0	4.8	60.7	0.1	10.3
1985	9,252	31.4	17.8	7.2	1.0	5.4	56.1	0.1	12.4

Distribution (percentage)

Source: Same as table 11.1.

Table 11.3   ELDERLY PERSONS, BY HOUSEHOLD TYPE, JAPAN, 1985

			Distribution (percentage)				
		Living		Living with child			
Age group	Number of persons (thousands)	Alone	With spouse only	Total	Married child	Unmarried child	Other
Total 60 and over	17,429	8.7	25.8	61.8	42.2	19.7	3.7
60–64	5,318	7.3	31.9	55.7	29.1	26.5	5.1
65–69	4,111	9.1	29.9	57.4	38.0	19.4	3.6
70–74	3,601	10.0	25.3	61.9	46.2	15.7	2.8
75–79	2,370	9.7	19.4	68.2	55.0	13.3	2.7
80–84	1,329	8.6	11.1	77.7	62.2	15.5	2.6
85–89	536	8.0	6.8	82.4	64.4	18.1	2.7
90 and over	164	6.7	5.9	84.6	60.4	24.2	2.8

Source: Same as table 11.1.
Note: Detail may not sum to total because of rounding.

adaptation to the death of an elderly spouse or to the loss of physical or mental vigor. The three-generation family is not without problems, however, which have been frequently noted in Japan. The conflict between the mother and daughter-in-law is a classic one; the generations often have different tastes in food, waking-up and sleeping times, preferences in room temperatures, and, more generally, ways of thinking and behaving. Mounting strains on the daughter-in-law are reported as prolonged illness or disability among the elderly grows (Hashimoto 1986a). And suicide rates of the elderly are reported to be substantially higher among the three-generation families than other families (Ueno 1981).

With respect to children, nearly 70 percent live in nuclear families, up from 64 percent in 1970 (table 11.4). However, almost 30 percent still live in three-generation households (down from 34 percent in 1970).

SOCIAL PROGRAMS

Japan ranks 17th out of 19 Organization for Economic Cooperation and Development (OECD) countries in the percentage of its gross national product (GNP) spent on social programs (Rose 1985). There are very few means-tested welfare benefits in Japan and, until

Table 11.4   CHANGES IN THE HOUSEHOLD CHARACTERISTICS OF JAPANESE
YOUTH UNDER AGE 18, SELECTED YEARS, 1970–85

		Distribution percentage					
		In nuclear households			In other households		
Year	Population under age 18 (thousands)	Total	Both parents	One parent	Total	Three-generational households	Living alone
1970	29,252	64.2	60.5	3.7	35.8	34.2	0.1
1975	31,682	68.5	65.1	3.4	31.5	30.2	0.1
1980	32,339	69.9	66.0	3.9	30.0	28.9	0.1
1985	31,464	69.4	64.7	4.8	30.5	29.3	0.1

Source: Same as table 11.1.
Note: Detail may not add to total because of rounding.

recently, the social security system was immature. But Japan has a large, universal, and relatively generous health insurance system. We discuss the three categories of social expenditure in turn, in descending order of importance: health insurance, pensions, and welfare services.

Health Insurance[1]

The Japanese health insurance system is characterized by universal access, essentially open-ended third-party financing, and very low out-of-pocket costs. Social insurance protection for workers began in 1922, and by 1961 health insurance protection had been extended to the entire population. By 1985 the universal health insurance system accounted for 90 percent of all medical care expenditures. This system is both employment-based and community-based and is financed by individual contributions, employee contributions, and government subsidies. An additional 5 percent of medical expenses represent public funds paid to needy persons through provisions of the Public Assistance Law of 1950. Three percent of expenditures are public funds for care of specific diseases (for example, tuberculosis), and the remaining 2 percent are patients' direct payments for services. (Not included in this 2 percent are cost-sharing payments discussed later.)

The largest subsystem of the health insurance system in Japan is Employee Health and Insurance, covering 60.3 percent of the population in 1985. Under this system, cost-sharing payments are 10 percent for employees and, for dependents, 20 percent for inpatient services and 30 percent for outpatient services. Premiums are paid equally by employers and employees. Government subsidies represent less than 10 percent of expenditures. Payment for services is made according to a fixed schedule depending upon the treatment received.

The other major subsystem is community-based National Health Insurance, which covers those not eligible for Employee Health Insurance—in particular, agricultural workers, self-employed persons, and retirees, as well as their dependents. Subsidies from the national government covered 45 percent of benefits in 1982; individual premiums covered the bulk of the remainder. Cost-sharing payments, at 30 percent, are higher than under Employee Health Insurance. However, for retirees the rate is only 20 percent. In 1984 special financing for retirees was introduced, replacing the national government subsidy with contributions from the Employee Health Insurance Scheme. This reduced to 40 percent the national government's subsidy.

A special Health and Medical Services for the Aged program was implemented in 1983 and covers all persons over age 69 and disabled persons over age 64. This system replaced the system that had been in effect since 1973, which provided essentially free medical services to the elderly. It introduced small copayments and is subsidized by insurers (70 percent), the national government (20 percent), and local governments (10 percent). According to the Ministry of Health and Welfare, the 1983 reform was introduced to correct inequities in the previous system resulting from different proportions of elderly being served by different health systems. In addition, the earlier system had "weakened health-awareness among the aged, who consulted doctors even for trivial problems, encouraged by the easy access to medical services" (Japan Ministry of Health and Welfare 1985a).

Most outpatient and inpatient medical care is delivered through the private sector. However, prices are strictly regulated. Government bodies are responsible for licensing, quality control, and medical education. Public hospitals and clinics are provided. Nursing homes and intermediate care facilities are not well developed.

National medical care expenditure peaked in 1983 at 6.6 percent of national income, having increased from 3.1 percent in 1960. In 1985 it was 6.3 percent. Increased cost-sharing introduced for the elderly in 1983, and for others in a 1984 reform of the Health

Insurance Law, appears to be responsible for the slight expenditure decrease since that time.

Persons over age 65, who constituted 10 percent of the population in 1985, accounted for 35 percent of medical expenditures (Japan Institute of Population Problems 1986c).

Pensions[2]

The Japanese pension system now in place started in the 1950s as an immature but generous system designed to lead ultimately to earnings-related pensions with a replacement rate of 83 percent. Recent reforms have scaled back the replacement rate but have extended coverage so that it is almost universal, in particular, improving women's eligibility in their own right. The system implies not only high average retirement income but probably high protection against poverty in old age.

The first national pension scheme in Japan was Workers Pension Insurance, introduced in 1942 for male employees of factories and mines. In 1944 coverage was extended to office employees and to women and the name was changed to Employee Pension Insurance (EPI). The system underwent a large-scale restructuring in 1954, when certain occupational groups broke away from EPI and formed their own pension associations. In 1962 the National Pension scheme (NP) was established for persons not covered by the employee schemes, including agricultural workers and the self-employed. There is now nationwide pension coverage in Japan: EPI covers general employees; four mutual aid associations (MAAs) cover public service employees; and NP covers the self-employed, farmers, and certain others.

Each of these systems provides insurance coverage for old age, disability, and death. Under EPI and MAA, the insured person pays a predetermined ratio of earnings as a contribution, and pension benefits are based on the period of insurance and wage history. Since October 1985, employers and employees have each contributed 6.2 percent (women, 5.7 percent) of monthly wages (in the range from 68,000 to 470,000 yen—roughly U.S. $380 to $2,625) to EPI. The central government accounts for 20 percent of total payments from the fund. Under NP, individuals contribute 6,740 yen per month, and benefits are proportional to months of contribution. The government pays one-third of the benefit costs. In June 1985 EPI covered 26.3 million of the 58.3 million contributors and had 2.7

million of the 13.0 million beneficiaries; NP covered 25.7 million of the contributors and had 6.3 million beneficiaries.

Eligibility for pensions varies among the systems. A worker becomes eligible at age 60 under EPI, age 65 under NP, and age 56 in the MAAs. Salaried workers typically face a mandatory retirement age of 60 (sometimes younger), but many take another job. If both jobs are under EPI, the employees cannot collect pension benefits while in the second job. However, previous public employees can collect their NP pensions while in an EPI-covered job.

The typical new EPI beneficiary has contributed to the pension fund for 32 years, and has a benefit that is 69 percent of the average wage of those currently employed. Benefits per beneficiary under NP are only approximately one-fifth as high as benefits under EPI.

In addition to pensions paid under these programs, Japanese employers typically provide lump sum retirement allowances. Although not stipulated by law, these payments are standard and are also paid at most other forms of employment termination. In a typical instance, a person who has been in a firm for 35 years will receive a lump sum payment of 35 to 45 times his monthly salary (Murakami 1985). Lump sum payments are taxed preferentially compared with annuities, accounting for much of their popularity. Public pensions themselves are not taxed.

As a percentage of national income, pensions grew from 1.3 percent in 1965 to 5.8 percent in 1981 (Way 1984) and 6.5 percent in 1984 (Japan Institute of Population Problems 1986c). The increasing actuarial maturity of the system, combined with rapid projected aging, produced dramatic projections of pension costs if changes were not made in benefit schedules. In the early part of the twenty-first century, pension costs were projected to amount to 38 percent to 50 percent of earnings (Murakami 1985; Japan Ministry of Health and Welfare 1985b).

These projections led to a major reform in pension regulations, which took effect in 1986 and was designed to reduce benefits per unit of contribution over a 20-year period. This reform did not take the form of delaying the age of retirement or ending indexation of benefits, although such changes were actively discussed. Instead, benefit entitlements under NP will cease accumulating after 25 years and benefits under EPI will be fixed at approximately 69 percent of wages (the current level), rather than allowed to undergo the projected increase (Murakami 1985).

These changes were predicated on, or at least rationalized by, concern for maintaining generational equity as voiced by many

Japanese commentators (see Murakami 1985, Takayama 1982, and the Japan Ministry of Health and Welfare 1985b).

Welfare Services

Japan has a small public assistance program that is "designed to ensure the minimum standards of wholesome and cultural living for those persons who for some reason have fallen into distress and cannot sustain themselves through their own efforts" (Japan Ministry of Health and Welfare 1986). In 1984 just over 1 percent of the population received such assistance, and in no age group was the proportion over 2 percent. Of the households receiving assistance in that year, 33 percent were elderly, 44 percent contained a sick or disabled person, and 14 percent were fatherless households. The proportion that were elderly households has grown over the last 20 years (from 23 percent in 1965), reflecting the increased proportion of elderly in the population as a whole.

Japan instituted a small-scale child allowance scheme in 1972, funded by the national and local governments and by employers. Persons eligible are those who are caring for two or more children, at least one of whom is below school age, and whose household income (based on a six-person household) was less than 4.09 million yen (U.S.$22,850) in 1985. The large majority of households have incomes below this figure. The allowance is 2,500 yen (U.S.$14) per month for the second child and 5,000 yen (U.S.$28) per month for the third child and beyond. Because the mean monthly household expenditure in 1985 for households with children under age 5 was approximately 165,000 yen (U.S.$922), the allowance is obviously a minor component of income for most households.

In addition to the national programs described in this section are a variety of local programs. In a comparison of communities in the United States and Japan, Hashimoto (1986b) found that local services for the elderly in Japan are predominantly needs-based, whereas in the United States they are predominantly age-based.

TRENDS IN INCOME BY AGE

Economic growth in Japan has been extremely rapid during the post-World War II period. According to income estimates prepared by Summers and Heston (1984), real per capita income in Japan increased by a factor of 7.4 between 1950 and 1980.

Table 11.5   MEAN MONTHLY HOUSEHOLD EXPENDITURE IN JAPAN, BY AGE, 1975, 1980, AND 1985 (thousand yen, 179 yen = U.S.$1)

Age at last birthday	1975	1980	1985	Percentage change 1975–85
0–1	125.5	154.9	166.4	32.6
2–4	121.4	153.7	164.4	35.5
5–9	121.4	159.7	170.7	40.6
10–14	124.4	170.8	188.4	51.4
15–19	125.7	177.7	204.1	62.3
20–39	134.9	174.7	193.5	43.4
40–59	137.8	194.4	222.5	61.5
60–64	124.8	174.3	209.7	68.0
65–74	114.6	161.4	189.3	65.2
75–84	111.8	157.7	186.5	66.8
85 and over	110.8	157.0	183.5	65.6
All ages	129.9	175.6	198.6	52.9

Source: Unpublished tabulations prepared at the Institute of Population Problems from Social Surveys conducted for the Japan Ministry of Health and Welfare.
Note: Adjusted to 1985 price levels. Also adjusted to express expenditures in terms of their equivalent in a three-person household.

It would be surprising if any sectors or age groups in Japanese society had not benefited from this growth. Unfortunately, Japanese data on income do not permit examination of income trends by age. To fill this gap in part, we have tabulated data from the Social Survey conducted for the Health and Welfare Administration, using data for 1975 (the earliest year for which data tapes exist), 1980, and 1985. Because household income is not available on these tapes, we have used data on monthly household expenditure as a proxy for income.[3] We have adjusted the expenditure data so that they are expressed in 1985 prices. We have also adjusted for household size, using equivalence scales developed for defining the poverty population in the United States.[4]

There is very little variation by age in mean monthly household expenditure, although the variation has increased somewhat over time (see table 11.5). The range divided by the overall mean was only 0.20 in 1975, 0.23 in 1980, and 0.29 in 1985. The similarity of mean expenditures across the age scale undoubtedly reflects, at least in part, the high degree of integration among different generations in the Japanese household. As we have seen, the vast majority of children live in two-parent households, and most elderly people

Table 11.6   PERCENTAGE OF JAPANESE LIVING IN HOUSEHOLDS WITH
MONTHLY EXPENDITURE LESS THAN 100,000 YEN (U.S. $559), BY
AGE, 1975, 1980, AND 1985

Age at last birthday	1975	1980	1985
0–1	25.1	14.1	12.7
2–4	26.1	14.8	13.3
5–9	25.5	12.3	11.5
10–14	24.9	10.4	8.1
15–19	25.7	12.6	8.9
20–39	21.1	10.4	8.8
40–59	22.4	9.1	6.9
60–64	34.8	16.6	11.7
65–74	41.4	20.1	14.4
75–84	42.3	22.3	15.5
85 and over	45.9	22.5	16.2
All ages	25.0	12.0	9.5

Source: Same as table 11.5
Notes: Adjusted to 1985 price levels. Also adjusted to express expenditures in
terms of their equivalent in a three-person household. Households with unknown
income are included in the base. These were 0 percent of all households in 1975,
2.1 percent in 1980, and 4.5 percent in 1985. There was very little age variation in
these percentages.

live with their own children. The stability of Japanese marriages,
the minute fraction of out-of-wedlock births, and the tendency of
elderly people to live with their children clearly knit the generations
together in terms of household economic circumstances.

Nevertheless, there are clear differences in the expenditure trends
by age, especially among the low-income populations (table 11.6).
The low-income cutoff used here is roughly equivalent to two-thirds
of the U.S. poverty line, correcting for differences in saving in the
two countries.[5] Between 1975 and 1980 the proportion of persons
in low-income households dropped sharply and to a similar degree
for all age groups. Since 1980, however, declines have been highly
concentrated in the groups age 60 and above. The low-income
proportion of every age group above 60 dropped at least 4.9 percentage points over this period; no age group below 60 (except those
ages 15 to 19) had a drop as large as 2.5 percentage points. The
prevalence of low income among children and the elderly was
brought into rough equivalence by 1985, when the overall age pattern
became saucer-shaped. These patterns are shown graphically in

Figure 11.1   PERCENTAGE LIVING IN HOUSEHOLDS WITH MONTHLY
EXPENDITURE LESS THAN 100,000 YEN

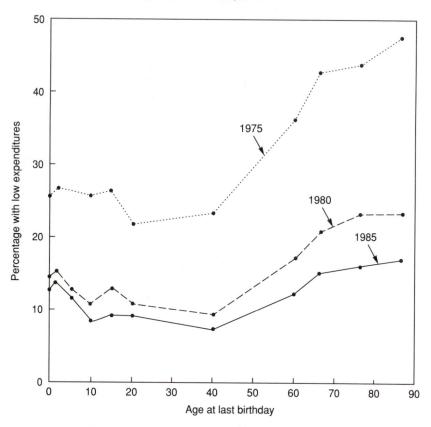

Source: Same as table 11.5

figure 11.1. The relative improvement in the position of the elderly is also in the data on mean expenditure. Table 11.5 shows that, in terms of mean household expenditure, children exceeded the elderly in 1975 and had fallen short of them by 1985.

The exceptional reductions in the proportion of the elderly with low incomes between 1980 and 1985 are likely to be related to the expansion of pension benefits noted earlier. Total benefit expenditures in EPI and NP grew from 2.4 trillion yen (in 1986 prices) in 1975 to 9.9 trillion in 1986 (Japan Ministry of Health and Welfare 1986c). Averaged over persons age 60 or more, pension expenditures in real terms increased by a factor of 2.89 between these years. By

1982 annuities and pensions made up 43.3 percent of income in "households of the old," which are those containing no adults over age 17 except men older than 65 or women over 60 (Japan Economic Planning Agency 1983). Earned income made up an almost equal share (43.6 percent). It is unlikely that the relative improvement in the economic status of the elderly reflects upward trends in earnings, however, because older Japanese are retiring from the labor force at younger ages.[6]

Income gains tended to be somewhat smaller for children than for other groups over the period, especially since 1980. Percentage increases in mean household expenditure for children under age 2 were only half as large as increases for people over age 60. Part of the explanation is that people between the ages of 20 and 39, who were most likely to have a young child, also had below-average gains. Older children did better than younger children, in part because adults ages 40 to 59 did better than younger adults. Still, children under age 10 had slower gains than any other group.

This trend is puzzling. It could reflect widening social-class differences in fertility, so that children in 1985 were drawn in greater proportion from poorer classes. But this explanation seems implausible because social-class variation in fertility in Japan appears to have been all but eliminated (Atoh 1985; Population Problems Research Council 1984). Although a minority of married women in Japan are employed outside the home, the percentage has increased; if the families of working women have fewer children and higher incomes, the economic circumstances of the generations could have diverged. But differences in fertility related to women's work status are also quite small, although the available evidence relates to cohorts and could obscure recent period-specific trends (Population Problems Research Council 1984). In any case, offsetting any such trend would be the increased tendency for mothers of young children to work and to earn; labor force participation rates for mothers whose youngest child was under age 6 rose from 26.6 percent to 36.2 percent between 1974 and 1979 alone (Japan Bureau of Statistics).

Rising levels of divorce may have contributed to the below-average income gains for young children, because women experience sharply diminished incomes after divorce when they take custody of the child, as they did in 69 percent of divorce cases in 1982 (Japan Economic Planning Agency 1983). The rapid increase in the proportion of public assistance going to "fatherless households" between 1975 and 1984 (from 9.5 percent to 14.0 percent) provides some support for the importance of this phenomenon. The percentage of all children living only with their mother grew from 2.9 to 4.1 percent over the same period. Small as this change is, it can account for about one-third to one-half of the divergence between trends in child poverty and poverty trends for all ages shown in table 11.6, on the assumption that each child affected was moved into poverty as a result.

Intriguing as the *relative* deterioration in children's economic circumstances may be, it should be emphasized that it is not an *absolute* deterioration like the one that has occurred in the United States (Preston 1984). Obviously, children have shared in Japan's rising prosperity. Furthermore, the age differences in economic well-being in Japan are much smaller than those in the United States, where 22.2 percent of children under age 15 lived in poverty in 1984, compared with only 11.3 percent of persons above age 21 (U.S. Bureau of the Census 1986). It should also be noted that the age patterns of economic well-being in Japan relative to the United States underestimate the relative well-being of children in Japan, because we did not apply an adult-equivalent scale to adjust for their below-average needs.

TRENDS IN PHYSICAL AND MENTAL HEALTH

As already noted, improvements in mortality have been spectacularly rapid in Japan, to the point that Japanese life expectancy at birth is (with Iceland's) the highest in the world. Relative to other countries, Japan's advantage is particularly evident for males and for cardio-vascular diseases. The cardiovascular advantage is long-standing and is probably associated with a diet high in fish and rice. The rapid postwar gains, conversely, are principally a result of progress against infectious diseases. All ages have participated in the mortality improvements (table 11.7). Proportionate gains have been largest for persons under 15; absolute gains have been largest for the very high ages. Above age 75, at least three lives are saved for every 100 persons each year under 1983 to 1984 conditions relative to 1963 conditions. This general age pattern of change is typical when mortality improves (see Coale and Demeny 1966). However, Japan's mortality change has been so rapid that it is well beyond the range where changes can be compared to empirically based model life

Table 11.7   AGE-SPECIFIC DEATH RATES, JAPAN, SELECTED YEARS, 1963,
1971, AND 1983–84 (per 1,000 population)

Age group	Males			Females		
	1963	1971	1983–84	1963	1971	1983–84
0–4	6.82	3.88	1.81	5.46	3.00	1.49
5–9	0.79	0.55	0.29	0.51	0.35	0.19
10–14	0.51	0.36	0.21	0.31	0.24	0.13
15–19	0.97	1.13	0.70	0.52	0.41	0.24
20–24	1.63	1.23	0.91	0.95	0.64	0.36
25–29	1.89	1.35	0.90	1.18	0.80	0.45
30–34	2.14	1.63	1.03	1.40	0.97	0.58
35–39	2.74	2.38	1.48	1.85	1.32	0.83
40–44	3.82	3.41	2.39	2.55	1.93	1.26
45–49	5.99	4.69	4.03	3.89	2.85	1.92
50–54	9.19	7.51	6.39	5.82	4.48	2.92
55–59	15.30	12.29	9.47	8.96	6.87	4.46
60–64	24.60	20.27	14.04	13.93	11.21	7.06
65–69	39.51	34.55	22.67	23.98	19.79	12.01
70–74	64.64	55.57	40.94	42.16	33.81	22.95
75–79	103.93	89.63	70.46	74.89	60.86	43.34
80+	182.19	164.05	139.40	150.46	137.84	108.40

Sources: Japan Institute of Population Problems (1985); United Nations (1984), 50.

tables to gauge the age-specificity of changes relative to normal patterns, as was done in the United States (Preston 1984).

One of the important trends in physical well-being is the recent considerable increase in height and weight among youth. The physical condition of youth has improved tremendously, particularly among those in junior high school (table 11.8). The average 14-year-old boy is 18 centimeters taller in 1986 than in 1948 (12.3 percent) and 14.4 kilograms heavier (37.0 percent). Gains for females are somewhat smaller but still conspicuous. The gains have slowed since 1970 but continue to occur at all ages. Factors associated with these dramatic improvements undoubtedly include improved nutritional intake, reduced incidence of childhood infectious diseases, and better medical treatment. These, in turn, reflect improvements in incomes and superior knowledge about medical and nutritional practices.

Table 11.9 presents patient rates by age since 1955 (numbers of patients per 1,000,000 population who visit or are hospitalized in medical institutions on the survey date. Figures include in-patients

Table 11.8   AVERAGE HEIGHT AND WEIGHT, JAPANESE STUDENTS, SELECTED AGES, 1948–86

	Males (years)				Females (years)			
	5	10	14	17	5	10	14	17
Height (cm)								
1948	103.7	126.1	146.0	160.6	102.5	125.7	145.6	152.1
1960	107.4	131.6	155.1	165.0	106.2	132.0	150.7	153.7
1970	109.6	135.3	160.5	167.8	108.5	136.2	154.2	155.6
1980	110.3	137.3	163.6	169.7	109.4	138.3	156.0	157.0
1986	110.8	137.9	163.9	170.3	109.9	138.9	156.3	157.7
Weight (kg)								
1948	17.5	26.0	38.9	51.7	16.8	25.6	40.1	49.1
1960	17.7	28.0	45.3	56.1	17.2	28.2	45.3	50.4
1970	18.5	30.5	49.6	58.7	18.0	31.0	48.3	52.1
1980	19.0	32.4	52.4	60.6	18.5	32.6	49.6	52.1
1986	19.2	33.1	53.3	61.8	18.8	33.3	50.0	52.8

Source: Japan Ministry of Education (1986).

Table 11.9   PATIENT RATE, BY AGE AND SEX, SELECTED YEARS, 1955–84 (per 100,000 of population)

	1955	1960	1965	1970	1975	1980	1983	1984
Sex								
Males	3,542	5,076	5,991	6,808	6,586	6,555	6,955	5,902
Females	3,142	4,550	5,831	7,160	7,498	7,130	7,884	6,888
Total	3,301	4,805	5,910	6,987	7,049	6,847	7,427	6,403
Age								
0	3,631	5,189	7,361	9,104	7,735	6,915	7,416	7,281
1–4	2,559	4,974	5,740	8,136	7,222	6,788	7,098	5,495
5–9	—	—	—	6,458	6,944	6,423	7,026	4,404
10–14	1,888	3,136	4,728	3,577	3,865	3,891	4,064	2,614
15–19	—	—	—	3,607	2,993	2,725	3,026	2,598
20–24	3,590	4,902	4,826	5,476	4,428	3,960	4,110	3,660
25–34	4,823	5,619	6,082	6,256	5.187	4,526	4,834	4,204
35–44	4,129	5,377	6,504	7,155	6,334	5,454	5,363	4,705
45–54	3,773	6,121	7,010	8,506	8,142	7,836	8,014	7,010
55–64	3,502	5,163	7,942	10,403	10,335	10,222	11,012	9,824
65–69	3,250	4,317	8,310	11,595	13,383	13,383	15,064	13,455
70–74				11,694	18,861	18,465	19,844	18,343
75–79	2,418	4,168	6,572	10,757	19,995	19,384	22,707	21,108
80+				8,824	16,812	19,174	23,041	21,275

Source: Japan Ministry of Health and Welfare, Patient Survey, various years.

and out-patients). Trends in these series reflect both demand and supply factors and are not unambiguous indicators either of health needs or of the adequacy of health services. For example, a large decline in rates between 1983 and 1984 (not shown) probably reflects the increase in copayment charges between these years. Among persons over 65, at least, the trend had been strongly upwards before 1983. Declines in patient rates for children below 10 between 1975 and 1983, conversely, almost certainly reflect improvements in health that reduced the need for hospitalization.

The frequency of patients with mental disorders has been increasing in recent years, especially for persons older than 35. In 1975 and before the rate peaked around age 35 to 44. But in 1982, 1983, and 1984, the most recent years for which the patient survey is available, there are two peaks. One occurs for the group ages 45 to 54, reflecting a peak in schizophrenic psychoses and neurotic disorders, after which the rate declines appreciably. It then begins rising again after ages 65 to 70. This rise at older ages may reflect either rising rates of senile or presenile dementia or older people's improved access to mental health care.

Mortality caused by mental disorders has been declining since 1950, when the vital statistics data became available. The overall trend masks divergent trends for different diseases. Since 1950, mortality caused by senile and presenile dementia for women, alcoholic psychosis for men, and alcoholism for both sexes have been increasing, whereas the mortality rates from schizophrenia, affective psychoses, and mental retardation have been decreasing.

Since Durkheim (1912) wrote his classic work on suicide, many analysts have used the death rate from suicide as an indicator of mental health. Figure 11.2 shows the death rates from suicide in Japan for 1959 to 1961 and 1979 to 1981. Suicide rates dropped among both the young and the old between the two periods; the decline is particularly large for persons in their late teens and early twenties. But suicide rates for the middle-aged increased between the two dates. It is important to note that suicide rates in Japan for persons age 65 and over are more than double those in the United States. Although rates declined sharply among the elderly in the United States between 1960 and 1980, producing a pronounced leveling off of the age pattern of suicide (Preston 1984), proportionate declines have been much more modest in Japan; and the sharp upward slope of the age pattern has been retained.

Although suicide rates among youth have decreased in recent years, violence and abuse in junior and senior high schools (but not

Figure 11.2   DEATH RATES FROM SUICIDE IN JAPAN, 1959–61 AND 1979–81
(per 100,000)

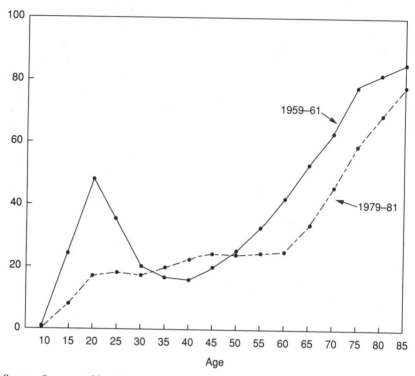

Source: Same as table 11.5.

in universities) have apparently increased. The severe competition to enter ranking universities is believed to give rise to much anxiety and frustration among students who do not succeed in getting into ranking junior or senior high schools or who rank poorly in their school. It has been argued that their pent-up aggressiveness, once directed inwardly, is now expressed in violence toward other classmates and abuses of mentally and physically weaker students (Fuse 1985). Although much attention has been focused on this issue in Japan, international comparisons suggest that Japanese youth are unusually mild mannered. The 1978 rate of arrest for juveniles ages 10 to 18 for murder in Japan is only 7 percent of the rate in the United States, for example. Arrest rates for rape are 23 percent of the rates in the United States, and for assault and battery 26 percent. Japanese rates are also far below those of West Germany (Japan Economic Planning Agency 1983).

EDUCATION

The heavy emphasis on education in Japan that impresses even the casual observer and has been mentioned several times in this chapter suggests that the subject deserves more detailed treatment in our assessment of social trends among children. The level of schooling in Japan is among the highest in the world and is matched only in North America. At present, approximately 40 percent of persons ages 20 to 24 enter colleges and universities. An average student in a Japanese elementary school spends 20 to 30 percent more hours in school and learning hours at home than a British student (Dore 1986).

Even in the Tokugawa era of the sixteenth to eighteenth centuries, Japan had a private schooling system in the temple and private homes; and in the eighteenth century the national literacy rate was reportedly somewhere close to 40 percent—probably among the highest in the world. This fact is often not recognized outside Japan; many people believe that the Japanese educational system burgeoned in 1868 when the new Meiji government ended national seclusion and elements of a Western educational system were introduced. But the indigenous development of mathematics including calculus was already advanced in the eighteenth and nineteenth century. Japan is in the perimeter of Confucian culture of East Asia, where education, hard work, and discipline have been emphasized. The importation of the Western education system in 1868, however, certainly promoted the spread of elementary education.

The emphasis on education is most naturally considered the Confucian recipe for Japan's industrial success. But there is a highly pragmatic element as well; schooling is important because a degree from a ranking university virtually guarantees entree to government service or a ranking firm or corporation and to rapid promotion (Tominaga et al. 1979). Within the government there are two classes of public servants—the career officers who passed the highest civil service examination and the noncareer officers who passed middle-level or junior-level civil service examinations. The person in the noncareer service never reaches the rank of vice minister or director general. Although any person can attempt to pass the highest civil service examination, graduates from nonranking universities have rarely achieved the necessary scores because in the quality of teaching staff, facilities, classmates, and learning environment are much lower than those at the ranking universities (Dore 1976).

The severe competition to enter ranking universities has created a feeling of crisis among parents and politicians alike. The typical teenager takes 6 hours of regular class work in school, then rushes to evening cram school for 3 to 4 hours, and returns home to study 4 to 5 more hours, totaling 13 to 15 hours of study a day. This regime has been compared with child labor in the Victorian England (Morishima 1984). In most homes where there are teenagers striving to enter ranking universities, Saturdays, Sundays, and holidays do not exist for them or their parents. "Examination war" or "examination hell" in Japan is a social malaise that deeply affects the personality and behavior of youth.

Perhaps not surprisingly, given this pressure, the level of educational attainment of the Japanese population has been steadily increasing. According to census figures, 75.0 percent of the Japanese born between 1946 and 1950 completed high school, compared with only 30.4 percent of the 1916–20 cohort. More than 14 percent of the 1946–50 group completed college, compared with 2.5 percent of the earlier cohort. College enrollment trends, on the other hand, have declined slightly since 1975, especially for males (figure 11.3). Senior high school enrollment rates for 15- to 17-year-olds have held steady since 1978 at about 92.5 percent, and are about two percentage points higher for females than for males (Japan Ministry of Education 1985).

Government spending on education, as a percentage of GNP, was nearly identical in Japan and the United States in 1982 (5.7 versus 5.8 percent). Average class sizes, at 32.0 in primary school and 38.2 in junior high school, are much larger in Japan than in other industrial countries. As already mentioned, however, most Japanese students receive substantial private tutoring in addition to their public schooling, especially in long-term preparation for university entrance exams. According to a recent survey of Tokyo residents, the average monthly expenditure for education among households having senior high school students is 72,000 yen (U.S.$402), more than 20 percent of total household expenditures (Tokyo Metropolitan Government 1986).

Japanese students perform very well in international comparisons. Stevenson et al. (1986a) have reviewed the superior performance of Japanese students in math and science (exceeding those of American students by more than two standard deviations at ages 16 to 18). They trace performance differences back to the first grade, with differences widening by the fifth grade. The differences are attributed to the fact that Japanese elementary school children spend about

Figure 11.3   TRENDS IN COLLEGE ENROLLMENT RATIO IN JAPAN, 1955–85

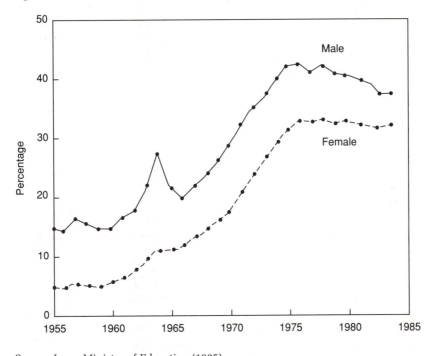

Source: Japan Ministry of Education (1985).
Note: The college enrollment ratio is calculated by dividing the number of college freshmen in a year by the number of students who graduated from junior high school three years before that year.

twice as much classroom time learning math as American children do, as well as longer hours doing homework. They are also more attentive in class. However, differences in reading ability in the first and fifth grade were small and inconsistent in direction (Stevenson et al. 1986b).

As in the United States, the relative salaries of Japanese school-teachers have slipped in recent years. In real terms, monthly salaries for primary school teachers declined from 235,600 yen (U.S.$1,316) in 1974 to 233,800 yen (U.S.$1,306) in 1983, whereas junior high school teachers' salaries rose slowly from 235,100 to 237,800 yen (U.S.$1,313 to $1,328) (Japan Ministry of Education 1974, 1983). Salaries in other occupations in Japan were rising rapidly over the same period, as indicated by the overall increase in household expenditures between 1975 and 1985 of over 50 percent (see table

11.5 presented earlier). It is possible that declining demand for teachers because of shrinking school age populations is reflected in these figures, as was suggested for the United States (Preston 1984). However, the declining economic status of teachers in Japan, and any deterioration in teacher quality that may have been associated with it, does not appear to be reflected in trends in student standardized test scores in Japan.

SUMMARY AND DISCUSSION

Two features of Japan distinguish it sharply from the United States in ways that are pertinent to understanding comparative trends in the well-being of dependent groups: (1) the much faster rate of economic growth in Japan and (2) the much greater integrity of Japanese families. Nearly all Japanese children live with both parents, and two-thirds of elderly people live with their children.

In these circumstances it is clear that, to borrow a Chinese phrase, the rising tide has lifted all boats. Gains in household income and reductions in poverty were very rapid for all age groups between 1975 and 1985. Health and mortality conditions have improved dramatically throughout the postwar period across the age span. Children's physiques have become far more robust. Suicide rates have declined both for youth and the elderly. These gains were achieved in the face of a means-tested public assistance program that reaches only a tiny fraction of the population.

The same two features may also be responsible for the apparent absence of any age-based political conflict in Japan, although we are not qualified to make judgments in this area. Competition for resources seems likely to be greater when the resources available are stagnant or declining than when they are expanding rapidly. And the close identification of Japanese with their family unit seems likely to have impeded the development of strong age-based constituencies (Davis and van den Oever 1981). Surely the frank statements by the Japanese Ministry of Health and Welfare justifying recent cutbacks in pensions and health subsidies on grounds of generational equity and misuse of services would provoke heated debate and organized reaction in the United States. They appear to have been accepted without protest in Japan.

In other respects, however, recent Japanese developments echo trends in the United States. An enormous expansion of public pension benefits occurred between 1965 and 1985, and these are likely to be the main reason why elderly Japanese have enjoyed the fastest income gains of any age group over the past decade. As in the United States, the age profile of poverty has changed from a pattern of much higher rates among the elderly to one that, for adults, changes little with age. The fact that this expansion occurred in Japan without a visible "gray power" movement calls into question age-bloc politics as the political explanation of a similar trend in the United States. In any event, such explanations are not persuasive in the United States because public pension programs have been extremely popular across the age spectrum (Preston 1984; see also chapter 14 of this volume). The rapid expansion of pension benefits in Japan occurred in a demographically pliant environment, in which the proportion of elderly persons was unusually low for an industrial country. That period has ended, and so too has the rapid increase in benefits.

A hint of relative deterioration in the economic position of children, similar to what has occurred in the United States, is also present in Japan. Between 1980 and 1985 income gains among children under age 10 were slower than for any other age group. It is probable that a small rise in the fraction of Japanese children living in female-headed families is responsible for some of this relative deterioration. But out-of-wedlock childbearing is extremely low in Japan, divorce relatively infrequent, and social-class differences in fertility very small. These demographic conditions tie the economic circumstances of children closely to those of the parental generation—and to grandparents as well. These ties have weakened somewhat in the course of modern economic growth, but not nearly so much as most social scientists would have predicted two or three decades ago.

The Japanese "solution" to the care of dependents in an aging population is not without its own drawbacks. Although most Japanese consider a three-generation household to be the natural social arrangement, it is clear that residence with children can present special psychological strains for the elderly. And the child-centeredness of the Japanese family, combined with a deeply rooted cultural emphasis on education, has created intense pressures on Japanese youth for success in school. Some Japanese envy the more carefree childhood of American youth and the greater options available to American elderly. It is easy to take for granted the virtues of one's own culture and society and focus on the problems. These problems are more likely to be solved in another society precisely because some other social goal, less salient in that society, has been sacrificed. Comparative analysis can clarify the terms of the trade-offs that are available, but the choice among them obviously must occur at a deeper level.

Notes

1. Unless otherwise noted, this section is based on Japan Ministry of Health and Welfare (1985a).

2. Unless otherwise noted, this section is based on Japan Ministry of Health and Welfare (1985b).

3. The Social Survey is self-weighted. The surveys gathered information on 331,303 persons in 1975, 295,469 persons in 1980, and 283,854 persons in 1985.

4. Our scale, used by the U.S. Census Bureau in 1985, is identical through household size five to the poverty line equivalence scale discussed in chapter 2, and they differ by only 0.01 at family size six, a range that covers most Japanese households. At seven and above, our equivalence values are higher.

5. The low-income category in table 11.6 is arbitrarily defined to include households with monthly expenditures of U.S.$559. According to U.S. poverty definitions, the monthly income poverty line for a family of three in 1984 was $690. Japanese households save, on average, 20 percent of their income. This saving rate would make $559 in expenditures equivalent to $699 in income. (Throughout this chapter we are using the exchange rate of June 1986 of 179 yen per dollar.) Poor households are unlikely to save as much as their richer counterparts, making this an upper bound. Differences in costs of food and exchange rate fluctuations add further uncertainty.

6. According to the Japanese population censuses of 1975 and 1985, labor force participation rates for men age 65 and older declined from 49.7 percent in 1975 to 41.5 percent in 1985; comparable rates for women declined from 15.8 percent to 15.1 percent.

References

Atoh, Makato. 1985. "Changes in Fertility and Fertility Control Behavior in Japan." In *Basic Readings on Population and Family Planning in Japan*, edited by Minoru Muramatsu and Tameyoshi Katagiri. Tokyo: Japanese Organization for International Cooperation in Family Planning, Inc. (JOICFP).

Befu, Harumi. 1986. "The Social and Cultural Background of Child Devel-
    opment in Japan and the United States." In *Child Development
    and Education in Japan*, edited by Harold Stevenson, Hiroshi
    Azuma, and Kenji Hakuta. New York: W. H. Freeman.
Coale, Ansley J., and Paul Demeny. 1966. *Regional Model Life Tables and
    Stable Populations*. Princeton, N.J.: Princeton University Press.
Davis, Kingsley, and Pietronella van den Oever. 1981. "Age Relations and
    Public Policy in Advanced Societies." *Population and Development
    Review* 7, no. 1:1–18.
Dore, Ronald P. 1986. *The Diploma Disease: Education, Qualification and
    Development*. London: George Allen and Unwin Ltd.
Durkheim, Emile. 1912. *Le Suicide*. Paris: Librairie Felix Alcan.
Fuse, Toyomasa. 1985. *Jisatsu to Bunka* (Suicide and Culture). Tokyo:
    Shichosha.
Goode, William J. 1963. *World Revolution and Family Patterns*. New York:
    Free Press.
Hashimoto, Akiko. 1986a. "Determinants of Change in the Structure of
    Familial Support in Japan." Paper presented at the 39th Annual
    Scientific Meeting of the Gerontological Society of America. Chi-
    cago.
———. 1986b. "Formal and Informal Support Systems in Comparative
    Perspective: Japan and U.S.A." Paper presented to XIth World
    Congress of the International Sociological Association, New Delhi.
Ishida, Takeshi. 1971. *Japanese Society*. New York: Random House. (Re-
    printed by University Press of America, Washington, D.C.)
Japan Bureau of Statistics. *Employment Status Reports*. Various issues.
    Tokyo.
Japan Bureau of Statistics. Management and Coordination Agency. Popu-
    lation Censuses. Various years. Tokyo.
Japan Economic Planning Agency. 1983. *In Search of Greater Latitude in
    the Household Economy and a New Image of the Family*. Annual
    Report on the National Life for Fiscal 1983. Tokyo.
Japan Institute of Population Problems. 1985a. "Population Reproduction
    Rates for all Japan: 1983." *Journal of Population Problems* 173
    (January):74–81.
———. 1985b. "The 37th Abridged Life Tables: 1983–84." *Journal of
    Population Studies* 173:82–94.
———. 1985c. *Selected Demographic Indicators of Japan*. Tokyo.
———. 1986a. "Abridged Life Tables for Japan, 1985." Manuscript. Tokyo.
———. 1986b. "1985 Population Projections for Japan." Manuscript. Tokyo.
———. 1986c. *Social and Economic Implications of the Aging Popu-
    lation*. United Nations International Symposium on Population
    Structure and Development, Tokyo. September 10–12. IESA/P/A-
    C. 20/4.
———. 1986d. *Report on the Field Survey of the Family Life Course and
    Change in the Household Structure*. Tokyo.

Japan Ministry of Education. 1974. *Report on the Statistical Survey of School Teachers.* Tokyo.

——. 1983. *Report on the Statistical Survey of School Teachers.* Tokyo.

——. 1985. *Summary of Education Statistics.* Tokyo.

——. 1986. *Health Statistics Relating to Education.* Tokyo.

Japan Ministry of Health and Welfare. 1985a. "Outline of Recent Japanese Policy on Health. The Background and Measures for Reform." Presented to Joint Japanese–OECD Conference of High-Level Experts on Health and Pension Policies in the Context of Demographic Evolution and Economic Constraint. Tokyo. November 25–28.

——. 1985b. "Outline of Recent Japanese Policy of Pensions: The Background and Measures for Reform." Presented to Joint Japanese–OECD Conference of High-Level Experts on Health and Pension Policies in the Context of Demographic Evolution and Economic Constraint. Tokyo. November 25–28.

——. 1986. *Health and Welfare Services in Japan.* Tokyo.

——. *Patient Surveys.* Various years. Tokyo.

Mincer, Jacob. 1984. "Inter-Country Comparisons of Labor Force Trends and of Related Developments: An Overview." NBER Working Paper Series. Working Paper No. 1438. Cambridge, Mass.: National Bureau of Economic Research.

Morgan, S. Philip, Ronald R. Rindfuss, and Allan Parnell. 1984. "Modern Fertility Patterns: Contrasts Between the U.S. and Japan." *Population and Development Review* 10, no. 1:19–40.

Morgan, S. Philip, and Kiyoshi Hirosima. 1983. "The Persistence of Extended Family Residence in Japan: Anachronism or Alternative Strategy?" *American Sociological Review* 48, no. 2:269–81.

Morishima, Michio. 1984. *Why Has Japan Succeeded?* Tokyo: TBS Britannica.

Murakami, Kiyoshi. 1985. "Pension Schemes in Japan. Appraisal of Pension Reform and Future Prospects." Presented to Joint Japanese–OECD Conference of High-Level Experts on Health and Pension Policies in the Context of Demographic Evolution and Economic Constraint. Tokyo. November 25–28.

Namaye, Takayuki. 1919. "Child Welfare Work in Japan." In U.S. Department of Labor, Children's Bureau. *Standards of Child Welfare.* Washington, D.C.: U.S. Department of Labor. (Reprinted by Arno Press, New York.)

Palmore, Erdwan B., and Daisaku Maeda. 1987. "The Honorable Elders Revisited: Growing Old in Japan." Duke Center for the Study of Aging and Human Development. *Advances in Research* 10, no. 3:1–5.

Parsons, Talcott, and Robert F. Bales. 1955. *Family, Socialization and Interaction Process.* Glencoe, Ill.: Free Press.

Population Problems Research Council. 1984. *Summary of Seventeenth National Survey on Family Planning.* Tokyo: Mainichi Newspapers.

Preston, Samuel H. 1984. "Children and the Elderly: Divergent Paths for America's Dependents." Demography 21, no. 4:435–57.

———. 1987. "The Decline of Fertility in Non-European Industrialized Countries." In Causes and Consequences of Non-Replacement Fertility. Supplement to Vol. 12 of Population and Development Review, edited by Kingsley Davis, Mikhail Bernstam, and Rita Ricardo-Campbell. New York: The Population Council.

Rose, Richard. 1985. "Welfare: The Lessons from Japan." New Society 28 (June):473–75.

Siegel, Jacob S., and Maria Davidson. 1983. "Demographic and Socioeconomic Aspects of Aging in the U.S." Current Population Reports, Special Studies, series P-23. Washington, D.C.

Stevenson, Harold, Shin-ying Lee, James Stigler, Seiro Kitamura, Susumu Kimura, and Tadahisa Koto, 1986a. "Achievements in Mathematics." In Child Development and Education in Japan, edited by H. Stevenson, H. Azuma, and K. Hakuta. New York: W.H. Freeman.

———.1986b. "Learning to Read Japanese." In Child Development and Education in Japan, edited by H. Stevenson, H. Azuma, and K. Hakuta. New York: W.H. Freeman.

Summers, Robert, and Alan Heston. 1984. "Improved International Comparisons of Real Product and Its Composition: 1950–1980." Philadelphia, Pa.: Department of Economics, University of Pennsylvania.

Takayama, Noriyuki. 1982. "Japan." In The World Crisis in Social Security, edited by Jean-Jacques Rosa. San Francisco: Institute for Contemporary Studies.

Taeuber, Irene B. 1958. The Population of Japan. Princeton, N.J.: Princeton University Press.

Tokyo Metropolitan Government. 1986. Educational Survey in 1986. Tokyo.

Tominaga, Kenichi, et al. 1979. The Structure of the Japanese Social Stratification. Tokyo: University of Tokyo Press.

U.S. Bureau of the Census. 1986. Current Population Reports, series P-60, no. 152. Washington, D.C.

Ueno, Masahiko. 1981. "Suicide of the Elderly." Medical Journal of Nihon University 40, no. 10 (in Japanese).

Way, Peter O. 1984. Issues and Implications of the Aging Japanese Population. Center for International Research. CIR Staff Paper. Washington, D.C.: U.S. Bureau of the Census. December.

Yamamura, Toshiaki. 1986. "The Child in Japanese Society." In Child Development and Education in Japan, edited by Harold Stevenson, Hiroshi Azuma, and Kenji Hakuta. New York: W. H. Freeman.

Chapter Twelve

THE EFFECTS OF THE SOCIAL WELFARE SYSTEM IN SWEDEN ON THE WELL-BEING OF CHILDREN AND THE ELDERLY

Robert Erikson and Johan Fritzell

The care of children and the elderly is one of the universal problems in human society, but the character of this problem has changed in the industrial nations during the last century. There are relatively fewer children but they are dependent for a longer period; there are more elderly and they are living longer. In the United States the number of children under 15 years of age decreased by 7 percent from 1960 to 1980 while the number of persons 65 years old and older increased by about 54 percent (Preston 1984). The corresponding figures for Sweden (for the 1960–81 period) are 4 percent and 56 percent. But the birth and death rates are lower in Sweden than in the United States. Thus, the Swedish population has a more extreme age distribution, nearly exactly the one predicted by the Organization for Economic Cooperation and Development (OECD) for the United States in 2020 (see chapter 9 in this volume for further discussion).

The Swedish picture may therefore be of interest to Americans both as an indication of their own possible future and as a check on how specific to the United States the American picture is. Preston (1984) concludes that the demographic changes in the United States have dramatically altered the age profile of well-being to the benefit of elderly people. Is this development paralleled in Sweden? This is the first question we address in the chapter.

In contrast to demographic trends, the social policies of the two countries are almost polar opposites, and there is little evidence to suggest that they are moving closer together. Because the well-being of children and the elderly depends substantially on the social policy followed, we can ask whether Swedish social policy leads to

We would like to thank Walter Korpi, Jack Meyer, Joakim Palme, John Palmer, David Popenoe, and Eugene Smolensky for helpful criticism and comments on earlier drafts.

other outcomes and problems of well-being than those observed in the United States. This is the second question we address.

We review the trends in well-being for children and the elderly in Sweden in terms of both income and nonmonetary indicators.[1] Because a large part of the income of dependent persons is paid through transfers from the employed population, we report on the importance of such transfers for the two groups. Inasmuch as material well-being depends not only on the size of disposable incomes but also on the amount and character of services rendered outside the market, we also estimate the costs of the social welfare programs benefiting the two dependent groups. To provide the context for our discussion, we begin with a short account of Swedish social policy.

THE SWEDISH MODEL OF WELFARE POLICY

As is also noted in other chapters, social policy in the United States is in important respects targeted to groups judged in the greatest need, through income- and asset-tested programs, sometimes with additional eligibility restrictions. Swedish social policy, in contrast, consists mainly of universal programs that may be earnings-related but are normally not means-tested.

Full employment has for 50 years been one of two principal elements of social policy in Sweden. Considerable efforts have been made to make room in the labor market for everyone who wants a job. Even during and after the recession in the 1970s, when unemployment reached levels like 9 percent in the United States and 11 percent in the Common Market countries, it never exceeded 3.5 percent in Sweden (Layard 1986). Thus, priority is given to programs to help the unemployed by creating jobs, moving jobs or the unemployed to each other, or reeducating the unemployed to equip them for available jobs.

The other basic element of Swedish social policy is a series of large-scale social insurance programs. Child allowances, pensions for the elderly, parent allowances, supplementary pensions, sickness insurance, unemployment insurance (a contributory program, in contrast to the other ones administered by the unions), and housing allowances are among the more important. Child allowances and old-age pension benefits are given to all parents with children under age 16 and to all persons age 65 or older, respectively, with the benefits independent of income. The size of the parent benefits, sickness benefits, supplementary pensions, and unemployment benefits are positively related to income forgone. Housing allowances, on the other hand, are negatively related to income and thus constitute an important supplement for families with children and low incomes. Means-tested welfare payments constitute a residual program, quite small compared with the others mentioned.

In addition to full employment and universal social insurance, health care, education, and many other services are available free or at very low cost to the user.

The costs of all these programs are covered by taxes and by employers' contributions. About 38 percent of the gross national product (GNP) in Sweden is used for consumption and investment in the public sector, mainly social welfare spending; in addition, large sums are transferred among different population groups via the public sector. The sectors on which most money is spent for public consumption, and for which the greatest increases in spending have appeared in recent years, are health care and education— programs directed mainly toward the two dependent groups, the elderly and the young. The tax systems in Sweden and the United States probably differ more in average tax rate than in progressiveness. Aguilar and Gustafsson (1987) estimate the average tax rate, calculated as the ratio between total income taxes and total gross income, in Sweden to be 30 percent in 1981 as compared with 21 percent in the United States. On progressiveness, O'Higgins, Schmaus, and Stephenson (1985, tables 12 and 15) found that the ratio of the share of income taxes paid to the share of market income for those with gross incomes in the highest quintile was higher in the United States than in Sweden.[2]

SOCIAL EXPENDITURE ON THE YOUNG AND THE ELDERLY

As documented in previous chapters, in the past two decades, U.S. support for the elderly has increased compared with the support for children. To identify whether a similar development has occurred in Sweden, we compared the trends in social expenditures per capita for the two groups and then trends in disposable income at different stages in the life cycle.

Per capita social expenditures for children and the elderly are shown in table 12.1, with cash benefits (mainly social insurance)

Table 12.1   SOCIAL EXPENDITURES ON CHILDREN AND THE ELDERLY,
SWEDEN, SELECTED YEARS, 1961–84 (1980 prices, 1,000 Swedish
crowns)

	Young (per capita)			Elderly (per capita)			Relative expenditures young/elderly	GNP per capita
Year	Cash programs	In-kind service	Ratio	Cash programs	In-kind services	Ratio		
1961	1.60	4.13	0.39	9.91	5.39	1.84	0.37	34.85
1971	4.36	10.94	0.40	18.35	14.42	1.27	0.47	50.75
1981	5.64	19.18	0.29	32.35	21.76	1.49	0.46	62.90
1984	5.71	20.61	0.28	32.48	21.37	1.52	0.49	67.02

Sources: Statistics are from *Statistical Abstracts of Sweden* (1962, 1965, 1974,
1982a, 1986, 1987); SPRI (1983); Olsson (1987).
Note: The per capita calculations are in terms of the appropriate groups.
Exchange rates vary for a lot of reasons, some of which are unrelated to purchasing
power. The figures below show the amount in U.S. dollars equivalent to 100
Swedish crowns in selected years: 1967, 19.2; 1973, 22.7; 1980, 23.8; 1985, 11.6.

shown separately from in-kind services (such as health care, education, home services).[3]

Because children and the elderly have very different needs, it is not particularly illuminating to compare the expenditures within years. Rather, it is the relative trends that are of interest. The 1961–84 period saw substantial increases in cash and in-kind expenditures on children and the elderly. Over the period as a whole, expenditures on services have increased at about the same rate for the two groups, with the largest increase for the elderly appearing in the 1960s (related to the development of the health care system) and the largest increase for children appearing during the 1970s (related to the development of day care centers). Cash benefits increased more than three times for both children and the elderly; but because the elderly were receiving more transfers in 1961, they received a much greater increase in absolute terms.

Since 1971 an increasing part of the expenditure for children has been in the form of service benefits. In fact, almost the entire increase in real per capita expenditures for children during this period was for services. An increasing share of the cash benefits to both children and the elderly were income-related social insurance payments (not shown). For instance, the general child allowance (not based on income), although keeping up with inflation, constituted a smaller part not only of the total expenditure for children but also of the cash benefits. In the early 1980s the total costs for parent allowances (an earnings-related benefit) were approximately the same as the costs for the general child allowances, compared with a ratio of around 1 to 5 in 1971.[4] The increases in cash benefits and services to children and the elderly have been much greater than the increase in the GNP.

The trend in the relationship of cash transfers to services for the elderly has been the reverse. A growing share of the costs for the elderly is for cash benefits, despite the rapid growth in the costs for the health system. This development stems mainly from the implementation of general supplementary pensions according to a superannuation scheme. The law regulating this pension system was passed in 1959 but has not yet come into full effect. As it matures, transfers for supplementary pensions will increase relatively rapidly up to 1990, rather slowly after that until around 2005, and sharply again as the big cohorts born in the 1940s reach retirement age (Stahlberg 1985).

There is, of course, no straightforward relationship between welfare expenditures to various sociodemographic groups and the average well-being of these groups, as the needs of different groups vary considerably. The correspondence between expenditure and well-being might be especially problematic in the case of services to children, because the children themselves have practically no influence on whether the services are used. Day care centers, for which the costs have grown tremendously over the last 15 years, seem to be appreciated by parents and thus have presumably raised the well-being of parents. Whether the centers have also had a positive effect on the well-being of preschool children involved cannot, a priori, be taken for granted.

RELATIVE POVERTY AMONG CHILDREN AND THE ELDERLY

Real average disposable income in Sweden increased until the middle of the 1970s and then stayed more or less constant during the rest of the decade (Statistics Sweden 1982b). Average real earnings, however, actually fell from around 1975 to the early 1980s (Statistics Sweden 1984). Because the incomes of families with children consist of earnings to a much larger extent than is the case for elderly people, we can expect to find the elderly gaining relative to children over the period. The incidence of poverty is very low in Sweden absolutely and relative to other countries (see chapter 3 of this volume). Table 12.2 shows figures for average adjusted disposable income and the incidence of relative poverty in 1967 and 1980. The

Table 12.2 AVERAGE ANNUAL INCOME AND RELATIVE POVERTY AMONG
CHILDREN AND THE ELDERLY, SWEDEN, 1967 AND 1980 (1980
prices, 1,000 Swedish crowns)

	Adjusted disposable average income[a]			Relative poverty[b]		
Year	Children	Elderly	Ratio	Children	Elderly	Ratio
1967	55.7	50.2	1.11	7.5	8.9	0.84
1980	70.4	73.4	0.96	6.8	1.5	4.53

Source: Swedish Level of Living Surveys, 1968 and 1981.
a. The income concept, adjusted disposable income, is calculated by dividing the disposable income of the household with a factor that depends on the number of family members as follows:

Number of family members   1   2   3   4   5   6
Equivalence scale   0.5   0.75   1.0   1.25   1.5   1.75, etc.

Average income among children refers to income of the adults in families with children.
b. Relative poverty refers to the number of persons living in families where the adjusted disposable income is below half the median of adjusted disposable income.

estimates are based on the Swedish Level of Living Survey[5] and the equivalence scale of the Luxembourg Income Study (LIS).[6]

There was great improvement among the elderly, in terms of both average income and relative poverty between 1967 and 1980. This is probably mainly a consequence of the implementation of the supplementary pensions scheme. The average income of households with children also increased considerably over the period but, as expected, lost ground in comparison with the elderly.

The most dramatic change is in relative poverty among the elderly. The percentage of the elderly living in relative poverty exceeded that among children in 1967. By 1980 relative position was reversed, with very few elderly people falling under the poverty line.[7] The average income in households with children has been raised considerably, but the figures on relative poverty are rather stable. The trends in income and poverty for our two target groups thus resemble the corresponding trends in the United States, although with a much lower poverty level.

INCOME AND POVERTY BY LIFE-CYCLE STAGES

As early as 1901, Rowntree suggested the existence of a life-cycle of poverty among the British working class, summarized in what

Figure 12.1   ROWNTREE'S LIFE CYCLE OF POVERTY

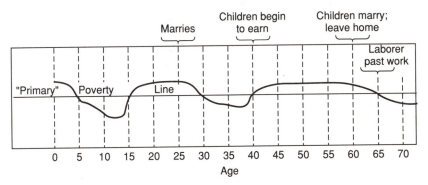

Source: Rowntree (1901), 137.

became a famous diagram (see figure 12.1). Poverty, according to Rowntree, appeared at three stages of the life cycle: early childhood, the childbearing years, and old age—the first two because one worker's wage was insufficient to provide decent support for a whole family with dependent children, the third when no one in the family was any longer working. Returning in the late 1970s to descendants of the group that Rowntree interviewed, Atkinson, Maynard, and Trinder (1983) found a similar income pattern over the life cycle, with the lowest average income among the elderly and a clear dip between ages 25 and 45. The results just reviewed suggest that Rowntree's pattern perhaps does not hold for the elderly in Sweden but might still be valid for Swedish families with children.

Income for people at different stages of the life cycle is shown in table 12.3. The life-cycle scheme is based on age, marital status, age of children, and number of economically active earners in the family. All groups are categorized according to the number of adults active in the labor market. The dividing line between the adult life-cycle stages is drawn at age 45. For couples, the wife's age is the divider, because we define older couples as those who can be expected to be beyond the child-bearing age.

The overall income increase observed for the population as a whole was shared by each stage of the life cycle, with the greatest increase for older people without children. As mentioned before, supplementary pensions became more widespread during this period and probably account for a large part of the increase. Supplementary pensions cannot be the whole explanation, however, because the elderly groups have experienced marked increases in average in-

Table 12.3   ADJUSTED DISPOSABLE INCOME BY NUMBER OF ECONOMICALLY
ACTIVE EARNERS IN THE FAMILY AND DIFFERENT STAGES IN
LIFE CYCLE, SWEDEN, 1967 AND 1980 (1980 prices, 1,000 Swedish
crowns)

Life cycle stage	Income	
	1967	1980
Single, under age 45, no children, not employed	44	54
Single, under age 45, no children, employed	73	84
Married, under age 45, no children, 1 employed	78	91
Married, under age 45, no children, 2 employed	107	114
Single, with children, not employed	37	52
Single, with children, employed	63	72
Married, with children, 0 employed	36	53
Married, small (0–6) children, 1 employed	51	64
Married, small (0–6) children, 2 employed	71	80
Married, only big (7–18) children, 1 employed	58	67
Married, only big (7–18) children, 2 employed	68	84
Married, age 45 and older, no children, 1 employed	77	93
Married, age 45 and older, no children, 2 employed	92	118
Single, age 45 and older, no children, employed	70	92
Married, age 45 and older, no children, 0 employed	46	78
Single, age 45 and older, no children, not employed	41	65
Total	65	82
Variance accounted for by life cycle (eta^2)	25	28

Source: Same as table 12.2.
Note: Persons are defined as employed if they work 1,000 hours per year or more.
The few young married couples with no economically active earner are included in
the first category. If the family consists of husband and wife, the age of the wife is
used for the classification.

comes, regardless of their activities in the labor market. Families
with children in which no family member is active in the labor
market experienced relatively large increases as well.

If we disregard the group of nonemployed young single persons
without children, which probably consists largely of students, we
find that the groups with the lowest adjusted disposable income in
1967—those with no labor market activity—received the greatest
increases. Thus, differences in income between life-cycle stages have
decreased substantially from 1967 to 1980, mainly as a result of a
general decrease in income differences from 1967 to 1980.[8]

To some extent, income inequality has fallen because of changes
in labor force participation during the period. The substantial
increase in labor force activity among married women has raised

the proportion of employed persons. Even so, total hours worked have decreased for several reasons. Large numbers of women work part time, and regular working hours per week in full-time employment was reduced in 1973 from just over 42 hours to 40. The Law on Vacations was amended in 1978 to increase the normal length of vacations from four to five weeks. Parent allowances—offering any of the parents of newborn children the option of taking leave for nine months with nearly full income compensation—were introduced in 1974. Part-time early retirement was introduced in 1976, making it possible for persons between the ages of 60 and 65 to combine part-time work with a partial pension. A considerable part of the productivity increase, thus, was taken in the form of a decrease in working hours, while the number of persons active on the labor market increased. Along with the decrease in inequality in hourly pay and an increase in transfers to persons outside the labor market, these changes in labor force participation probably explain most of the decrease in income inequality.

Both in 1967 and in 1980, life-cycle income as reflected in table 12.3 follows a Rowntree-like curve. Rowntree, however, discussed poverty rather than average income. Relative poverty rates for the life-cycle categories are very uneven among our categories (table 12.4). In 1967, relative poverty seems largely explicable by labor market participation; families with no economically active earners showed especially high poverty rates. In 1980 we find a similar pattern, but it is less systematic; and the differences generally are much smaller. The decline in poverty rates within several categories is quite dramatic, however, particularly for elderly people outside the labor market and for single-parent families, which is consistent with a previous study using another concept of poverty (Fritzell 1985). The latter effect probably results from changes in the eligibility rules for housing allowances, which greatly benefited single parents. In contrast to the general pattern of poverty reduction, poverty increased among two-parent, one-earner families with children from 6 percent to just over 10 percent. This result is consistent with the widespread perception in Sweden that it has become more difficult to support a family on just one income. Not surprisingly, this traditional family constellation is much less common now than in the 1960s because of the growing labor market participation of married women with children. The increase in poverty among these families, despite the decrease in their number, may explain why the proportion of children living below the poverty line decreased relatively little.

The poverty rates therefore indicate that there still seems to be

Table 12.4   RELATIVE POVERTY BY NUMBER OF ECONOMICALLY ACTIVE
EARNERS IN THE FAMILY BY STAGE IN LIFE CYCLE, SWEDEN,
1967 AND 1980

Life-cycle stage	Percentage in relative poverty	
	1967	1980
Single, under age 45, no children, not employed	32	25
Single, under age 45, no children, employed	3	5
Married, under age 45, no children, 1 employed	5	2
Married, under age 45, no children, 2 employed	1	1
Single, with children, not employed	53	15
Single, with children, employed	3	1
Married, with children, 0 employed	49	22
Married, small children, 1 employed	6	10
Married, small children, 2 employed	5	3
Married, only older children, 1 employed	6	11
Married, only older children, 2 employed	2	3
Married, age 45 and older, no children, 1 employed	3	2
Married, age 45 and older, no children, 2 employed	2	2
Single, age 45 and older, no children, employed	7	3
Married, age 45 and older, 0 employed	11	0
Single, age 45 and older, no children, not employed	17	5
Total	6.5	4.7

Source: Same as table 12.2.
Note: Relative poverty includes all persons with adjusted disposable income less
than half the median of the adjusted disposable income of the whole population.

some truth for Sweden in Rowntree's thesis, but only some. That is,
in 1967 we found relatively high poverty rates for some types of
families with children as well as for pensioners. In 1980, however,
this pattern reappears only for families with children. Rowntree
found that low wages were the most common cause to poverty in
York, England, around the turn of the century. For Sweden in the
1980s a corresponding pattern appears only among the diminishing
group of one-earner families. Our observations thus suggest that
poverty in Sweden results mainly from not having a stable position
on the labor market, a finding supported by other research (Gustafsson
1986).

The changes in the income distribution since the 1960s seem
mostly to have favored the elderly. That variation in poverty rates
among different life-cycle groups has diminished suggests that
people's dependence solely on employment for their economic

situation has decreased, even if being out of a job remains the most important determinant of poverty.

SOCIAL INDICATORS OF WELL-BEING

As is true of almost every other society, we have little systematic information on children's well-being in Sweden. Thus, we have to be content mainly with measuring children's well-being indirectly through data on their parents' living conditions. However, for some classic measures of well-being (or lack of it)—namely, suicide and infant mortality rates—we do have direct data. Preston (1984) found that when comparing persons age 65 and over with persons between the ages of 15 and 24 in the United States the ratio of suicide among the elderly to suicide among youth changed from 5 to 1 in 1969 to about 1.5 to 1 in 1981. In figure 12.2 the corresponding figures for Sweden are shown for the 1961–84 period. The change is much less dramatic than in the United States, although the trend during the 1960s went in the same direction. The changing relationship stems mostly from a slightly increased rate for young persons in the 1960s. During the 1970s the mortality rates from suicide changed little for any of the groups, and for the past seven years the trend seems to have reversed. Hence, in Sweden in the middle of the 1980s, the relative suicide rate for the two groups was nearly the same as it was at the beginning of the 1960s.

The suicide rate is, however, a problematic indicator of general well-being (see further discussion in chapter 10). Suicide is, fortunately, a rare phenomenon. It is questionable whether changes in such a phenomenon say very much about changes in well-being for the majority of the population.

Infant mortality rates for Sweden have been decreasing for a very long period and are now among the lowest in the world. The infant (under 1 year of age) mortality rate per 1,000 live births was 15.4 in 1962 and has remained stable at just below 7 during the 1980s. The corresponding figures for the United States are around 25 for 1962 and 12 for the early 1980s.

In the Swedish Level of Living Surveys mentioned earlier, respondents were asked about conditions in their parental family. In figure 12.3 the answers to some of these questions are shown by year of birth for the respondent. The curves, of course, have to be interpreted cautiously, but the general trends are indicative. The downward

Figure 12.2   SUICIDE RATES, UNITED STATES AND SWEDEN, SELECTED AGE
GROUPS, 1961–84

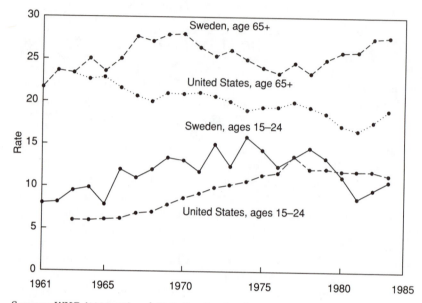

Sources: WHO (1983–86) and Statistics Sweden (1961–1984), "Causes of Death."

sloping curve on economic difficulties shows that people do measure
their material conditions to some extent in relation to past conditions,
rather than comparing themselves only with other people in the
same age group.

Of special interest here is the small increase in the proportion of
persons who reported dissent in their families during their child-
hoods and the absence of change in the proportion of Swedes who
grow up in a two-parent family. Many researchers of the family have
claimed that children's conditions have become worse, as indicated
by the upward trend in divorce rates. Popenoe (1987) even suggests
that the increasing divorce rates and the increasing proportion of
couples that live together without being legally married may, if
continued, lead to the end of the nuclear family as an institution.
The proportion of Swedish children who grew up in a two-parent
family has, however, changed remarkably little since 1890. The
explanation of this rather unexpected result lies in the fact that
death of a parent was more common at the beginning of the period,
and the number of children born out of wedlock was greatest in the

Figure 12.3 CONDITIONS IN RESPONDENTS' FAMILIES DURING THEIR
UPBRINGING, BY YEAR OF BIRTH, 1892–1966

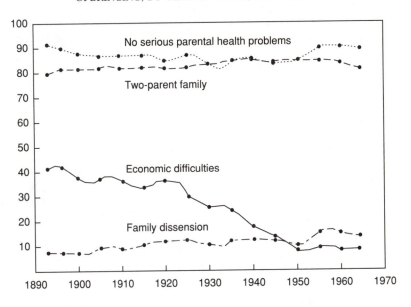

Source: Erikson (1984).

1920s. These trends counteract the upward trend in divorce during
the more recent period.

FURTHER INDICATORS OF WELL-BEING

In this section we look at some further indicators of the well-being
of children and the elderly[9] based, for the children, on the level of
living of the parents. Some indicators of consumption patterns for
the two groups are shown in table 12.5. As discussed in more detail
in chapter 10, for these indicators—even more so than for income—
it is important to look at changes over time within the groups rather
than to compare the young and the elderly at a given point, because
the needs and habits of the two groups can be so different. For
instance, going on vacation is likely to be related to health and
activity, as well as to income, and owning a car is more of a necessity
for families with children than for the elderly.

Table 12.5 PROPORTION OF CHILDREN AND THE ELDERLY WITH VARIOUS
ECONOMIC ASSETS, SWEDEN, 1968 AND 1981

Economic assets	Percentage of children		Percentage of elderly	
	1968	1981	1968	1981
Owns car	82	86	20	48
Owns boat	16	23	10	14
Owns summerhouse	21	27	12	22
Took a vacation last year	54	71	34	44
Owns dwelling	51	71	51	56
Has cash margin	82	86	76	88
Has no asset or only one	13	7	34	20

Source: Same as table 12.2.
Note: If the household in which the person is living owns or has any of the assets
in the table, he or she is counted as owner. For further detail, see Erikson and
Aberg (1987).

The general trend for these consumption indicators is consistent
with the rising income trends for the two groups discussed earlier
and shown in table 12.2. The proportion with access to the different
economic resources is higher in 1981 than in 1968 for every indicator.
But the consumption trends do not support the more favorable trend
for the elderly relative to children that is suggested by the income
data. Only for one indicator, cash margin, did the elderly do better
than the young. Of the six indicators in table 12.5, this one is
probably most highly correlated with income. For some of the other
indicators, like "took a vacation trip last year," the change seems to
be more in the favor of the young. The changes in the proportions
of persons with no asset or only one—another measure of relative
poverty—can scarcely be said to be more favorable for the elderly.

Housing conditions, in terms of amenities and space, also indicate
a remarkable improvement for both groups (not shown). The proportion of the elderly living in fully equipped dwellings increased
from 60 percent in 1968 to around 90 percent in 1981, and families
with children showed an increase from 87 to 98 percent.

Indicators on leisure activity, political resources, and health status
show improved conditions for the elderly. (In these areas it is less
relevant to compare elderly with families with children, because

our data refer to the situation for the parents and not for the children.) The improved health status among the elderly is largely in the reduced frequency of some common forms of illness, such as aches and circulatory problems. The elderly's political resources have improved in terms of the proportion voting in the general election (around 95 percent for persons between 65 and 75 years of age voted in 1985, compared with around 90 percent of the population at large), writing articles, and attending political meetings. For one important indicator, social relations—measured as frequency of contacts with friends and relatives—we found no change over time. The proportion of the elderly who live alone with very little or no social contact seems fairly constant at about 14 percent.

With regard to children we have fewer direct indicators of well-being. As already mentioned, housing conditions have improved. The housing of families with children differs from that of families without children in three respects: (1) better amenities, (2) smaller space per family member, and (3) higher incidence of homeownership.

One of the most dramatic changes in Swedish society over the past 20 years—the increased participation of married women on the labor market—can be expected to have affected the situation of children in several respects. The level of employment among married or cohabiting women with small children (age 0–6) has risen dramatically, from 34 percent in 1968 to 78 percent in 1981. The corresponding figure for all married or cohabiting women rose during the same period from 50 percent to 77 percent. This pattern is somewhat similar to the increase in the United States, where around 40 percent of married women with children were employed in 1970 and around 53 percent in 1978 (Hill 1983). An important concomitant of the increase in female labor force participation in Sweden was the growth in the number of municipal day care centers. Parents in all social classes have placed their children in such centers, although the proportion of children from the working class is actually less than the proportion from other social classes. One area in which the change in the number of employed mothers could influence the conditions of smaller children is the time they spend with their parents. An indirect measure of available leisure time after work (including domestic work) of parents with small children shows a minor decrease over time (between 1974 and 1981) for the mothers and no change at all for the fathers.

Before summing up we look at one condition that is seen as a major explanation of the increasing poverty rates for children in the United States—the economic situation of children after a divorce or other separation between the parents.

INCOME TRENDS AND FAMILY COMPOSITION CHANGE

In the United States changes in individual income can to a considerable degree be explained by family composition changes (see Duncan 1984). The life event that perhaps influences economic conditions most in the United States is divorce or separation (Hoffman and Holmes 1976, Duncan and Morgan 1981). Are the results similar for Sweden? Using panel data from the Swedish Level of Living survey, table 12.6 compares the level and change of adjusted disposable income for persons married or cohabiting in 1973 and living with or without a spouse in 1980, with those married or cohabiting in both years.[10] Only households which in both years contained at least one child are included in the analysis.

In Sweden, the incomes of those who remained married increased only slightly more than the incomes of those who became single.[11] The proportion of those who experienced a decrease in real income is also similar for the two groups. This is in sharp contrast to the patterns in the United States as described in other chapters in this volume. The differences in the social welfare system may explain this difference. In Sweden, the proportion of income via public transfers for persons leaving marriages rose from 12 percent to 33 percent; the corresponding rate for those who remained married did not change.

CONCLUSIONS

Material well-being increased among both children and the elderly in Sweden between 1967 and 1980. Both transfers to and services for the two groups have increased substantially. The increases are, to the extent that they differ, to the advantage of children in relative terms but to the advantage of the elderly in absolute terms. Incomes have on average risen in both groups, but more so among the elderly. In particular, very few of the elderly fell below a relative poverty line in 1980. Low incomes and poverty seem to depend mainly on

Table 12.6 ADJUSTED DISPOSABLE INCOME AND TRANSFERS FOR FAMILIES WITH CHILDREN, BY MARITAL STATUS, SWEDEN, 1973 AND 1980 (1980 prices, 1,000 Swedish crowns)

Marital status	1983		1980		
	Income	Percentage accounted for by transfers	Income	Percentage accounted for by transfers	Percentage with negative change
Married in 1973 and 1980	63	13	76	14	24
Married in 1973, single in 1980	65	12	72	33	28

Source: Swedish Level of Living Surveys (1974, 1981).
Note: Total number of families in the subsample is 1,162, reflecting only families with children in both 1973 and 1980. Number of divorced, separated, or widowed in 1980 is 65.

activity in the labor market, but differences in income between people in the labor market and those outside it have diminished over time. Families with only one breadwinner on average have fairly low incomes. Differences in disposable incomes among demographic groups fell from 1967 to 1980 both overall and at different stages in the life cycle. Nonmonetary social indicators do not reflect the divergent trends in well-being for the two groups that are reflected in the income figures. Divorce or separation does not seem to have serious economic consequences for families with children in Sweden.

With respect to average income and poverty rates, we find a parallel in Sweden to Preston's (1984) finding of a relative improvement in the position of the elderly, compared with the position of children in the United States. The difference in the rate of change in average income for the two groups is slight, however, and there is no evidence of improved conditions for the elderly, compared with children, in other indicators of well-being. We therefore suggest that Preston's implication that this development is a consequence of demographic changes is not generally true, because Sweden's age profile is changing in the same direction and more rapidly than that of the United States.

The second question we raised in the introduction concerns the implications for the well-being of children and the elderly of the particular social welfare system that operates in Sweden. Of course, we are not in a position to answer this question, as we have not systematically compared the levels and trends in well-being in nations with different social policies. But we hope that this chapter on conditions and trends in Sweden in a book mainly concerned with the well-being of dependent groups in the United States will enable the reader to make some comparative judgments on the effects of different types of social policies. In comparing income levels and trends for different groups in different countries, for example, it is necessary also to look at what must be bought with these incomes in order to get a full picture. From this perspective it is crucial to note the expenditures on public services for young and elderly. In Sweden, education, medical treatment, and medications, to mention only the most important items, are provided at practically no charge. The cost of day care for children is also heavily subsidized, although not available to all families. The total effect of low unemployment rates, transfers and taxes, and in-kind services together lead to a comparatively low degree of inequality in Sweden.

Notes

1. We do not discuss subjective elements of well-being.

2. When decomposing Gini coefficients of income redistribution for ten countries into estimated values depending on tax progressivity and average tax rate, Tachibanaki (1981) found that more of the difference between Sweden and the United States is accounted for by the average tax rate than by the progressivity in the tax system.

3. The expenditures included are health care costs, income maintenance (basically, pensions, child allowance, parent allowances, housing allowances, and student support), child care costs, assistance to the elderly, and costs for education. Not included in the figures are unemployment and sickness benefits. We were able to locate most of the costs directed to children or to the elderly. For some costs, approximations were necessary. First, the proportion of health costs directed to the elderly is based on figures for 1981. The estimated percentage from that year is used for all other years. This might seem inappropriate because the number of old people grew considerably over the period. Several studies (including Jonsson 1980) show, however, that only a small part of the growth of health expenditure in Sweden is explained by the number of old people at different points in time. This is consistent with the OECD figures, where annual growth in health costs is decomposed into different components. Only a small part of the Swedish annual growth rates in health costs is due to shifts in the overall size and demographic composition of the population (see chapter 9 of this volume). Second, the proportion of costs for education directed to young people is based on figures for 1981; the same percentage is used in all years.

4. The ratio in 1971 is based on costs for maternity benefits, because parent allowances were not introduced until 1974.

5. Approximately 6,000 persons between 15 and 75 years of age were interviewed in 1968, 1974, and 1981. For further detail see Erikson and Aberg (1987).

6. The number of children and elderly who lived in relative poverty in 1980, according to the Swedish Level of Living Survey, slightly exceeds the number in 1981 according to LIS. There are several likely reasons for this difference. Part of the variation obviously stems from the different years studied and part may reflect slightly different ways of defining families and children. In the Swedish data set within LIS, persons over 18 years of age are defined as families of their own even if they in fact belong to another family (Ringen 1986). Because these persons are likely to have relatively low incomes, this will not only exaggerate the figure of relative poverty for 15- to 24-year-olds, but also will somewhat underestimate of the poverty line. This, in turn, will probably lead to a lower percentage living in relative poverty in other groups, including the elderly. In the data set used in this chapter, young people living with their parents are included in the parents' family.

7. The low proportion of elderly under the poverty line in 1980 is not an effect of the restricted age limits in the sample. Even if people over the age of 75, who often have no supplementary pension, had been included in the sample, the poverty rates would have been extremely low, as the general pension itself places pensioners over the poverty line. It is possible that a higher poverty line would result in a much higher rate of poverty among the elderly, as a large proportion of them may have incomes just above the poverty line used here. If, however, we compare the proportions of children and elderly who have incomes in the lowest sextile—that is, who are among the 16.7 percent with the lowest incomes—(see Rainwater, Rein and Schwartz 1986), we get in essence the same results as in table 12.2. Thus, the proportion among children in the lowest sextile increased from 19 percent in 1967 to 24 percent in

1980, whereas the proportion among the elderly in the lowest sextile decreased from 37 percent to 14 percent. With this more generous poverty line, however, the figures for the elderly probably to some extent are influenced by the upper age limit in our sample.

8. However, the categorization into life-cycle groups accounts for slightly more of the variation in 1980 than in 1967. The considerable decrease in income differences between these groups then is mainly the result of a general decrease in income differences from 1967 to 1980, together with some systematic changes in income distribution among life-cycle groups. The coefficient of variation among groups decreased substantially (from 52 in 1967 to 38 in 1980), mirroring the reduction in income inequality over the period. According to a recent study, the income equalization in Sweden has not continued into the 1980s (Gustafsson 1987). In fact it seems as if the income distribution reached its highest level of equality in 1980, and since then incomes have become slightly more unequal. In an international perspective the recent change is minor. Sweden still probably has one of the most equal income distributions in the Western world.

9. More information about the well-being of the elderly and children in Sweden is given in Jonsson and Lundberg (1984) and Fritzell (1985), respectively.

10. This analysis may seen inconclusive in that we do not control for selection bias. Persons divorced or otherwise separated in 1980 constitute a selected group, which has passed two processes: selection into the divorced status and nonselection out of that status (Glass, McLanahan, and Sørensen 1985). Our major concern here is how the welfare state reacts to different conditions for children regardless of the causes of changes in these conditions.

11. Means-tested social assistance is not included in family income. Had it been, the differences between the two groups would, presumably, have been even smaller.

References

Aguilar, Renato, and Bjorn Gustafsson. 1987. "The Role of Public Sector Transfers and Income Taxes." Department of Economics, University of Gothenburg (Sweden). Photocopy.

Atkinson, A. B., A. K. Maynard, and C. G. Trinder. 1983. *Parents and Children: Income in Two Generations.* London: Heineman.

Duncan, Greg J. 1984. *Years of Poverty, Years of Plenty.* Ann Arbor: Institute for Social Research, University of Michigan.

Duncan, Greg J., and James N. Morgan. 1981. "Persistence and Change in Economic Status and the Role of Changing Family Circumstances." In *Five Thousand American Families: Patterns of Economic Progress* 9, edited by Martha Hill, Daniel Hill, and James Morgan. Ann Arbor: Institute for Social Research, University of Michigan.

Erikson, Robert. 1984. "Uppvaxtvillkor under 1900-talet" in *Valfard i Forandring*, edited by Robert Erikson and Rune Aberg. Stockholm: Prisma.

Erikson, Robert, and Rune Aberg, eds. 1987. *Welfare in Transition: A Survey of Living Conditions in Sweden 1968–1981*, Oxford, U.K.: Clarendon Press.

Fritzell, Johan. 1985. *Barnfamiljernas Levnadsniva*. Stockholm: Swedish Institute for Social Research.

Glass, Jennifer, Sara McLanahan, and Aage B. Sørensen. 1985. "The Consequences of Divorce: Effects of Sample Selection Bias." In *Life Course Dynamics*, edited by Glen H. Elder, Jr. Ithaca, N.Y. and London: Cornell University Press.

Gustafsson, Bjorn. 1986. "Bidragsmottagarna: antal och in komster." In *Socialbidrag*. Finansdepartementet Ds Fi 1986:16. Stockholm: Liber.

———. 1987. *Ett decennium av stagnerande realinkomster*. Stockholm: Statistics Sweden.

Hill, Martha S. 1983. "Female Household Headship and the Poverty of Children." In *Five Thousand American Families: Patterns of Economic Progress 10*, edited by Greg J. Duncan and James Morgan. Ann Arbor: Institute for Social Research, University of Michigan.

Hoffman, Saul, and John Holmes. 1976. "Husbands, Wives and Divorce." In *Five Thousand American Families: Patterns of Economic Progress 4*, edited by Greg J. Duncan and James Morgan. Ann Arbor: Institute for Social Research, University of Michigan.

Jonsson, Bengt. 1980. *Den Andrade Aldersfordelningens Effekter pa Sjukvardskostnadernas Utveckling*. Lund: Swedish Institute for Health Economics.

Jonsson, Janne, and Olle Lundberg. 1984. *De Aldre i Valfarden*. Stockholm: Swedish Institute for Social Research.

Layard, Richard. 1986. *How to Beat Unemployment*. Oxford, U.K.: Oxford University Press.

O'Higgins, Michael, Gunther Schmaus, and Geoffrey Stephenson. 1985. "Income Distribution and Redistribution: A Microdata Analysis for Seven Countries." LIS–CEPS Working Paper No. 3, July.

Olsson, Sven E., 1987. "Welfare Programs in Sweden." In *Growths to Limits—The West European Welfare States Since World War II 4*, edited by Peter Flora. Berlin, West Germany; Aldine, New York; and Mouton, The Hague: De Gryter.

Popenoe, David. 1987. "Beyond the Nuclear Family: A Statistical Portrait of the Changing Family in Sweden." *Journal of Marriage and the Family* 49 (February):173–83.

Preston, Samuel. 1984. "Children and the Elderly: Divergent Paths for America's Dependents," *Demography* 21, no. 4:435–57.

Rainwater, Lee, Martin Rein, and Joseph E. Schwartz. 1986. *Income Packaging in the Welfare State*. Oxford, U.K.: Clarendon Press.

Ringen, Stein. 1986. *Difference and Similarity. Two Studies in Comparative Income Distribution*. Stockholm: Swedish Institute for Social Research.

Rowntree, B. Seebohm. 1901. *Poverty: A Study of Town Life*, London: Macmillan.

Smeeding, Timothy, Gunther Schmaus, and Sandro Allegreza. 1985. "An Introduction to LIS." Luxembourg Income Study—CEPS Working Paper No. 1, presented at the LIS Conference, July.

SPRI. 1983. *Aldreomsorg och ekonomi*. Stockholm: SPRI.

Statistics Sweden. 1962, 1965, 1974, 1982a, and 1987. *Statistical Abstract of Sweden*. Stockholm: Statistics Sweden.

———. 1982b. *Perspektiv pa Valfarden*. Stockholm: Statistics Sweden.

———. 1984. *Yearbook of Labour Statistics*. Stockholm: Statistics Sweden.

———. 1986. *National Insurance*. Stockholm: Statistics Sweden.

———. 1961–1984. *Causes of Death*. Stockholm: Statistics Sweden.

Stahlberg, Ann-Charlotte. 1985. *Transfereringar mellan den Forvarvsarbetande och den Aldre Generationen*. Finansdepartementet Ds Fi 1985:5. Stockholm: Liber.

Tachibanaki, Toshiako. 1981. "A Note on the Impact of Tax on Income Redistribution." *The Review of Income and Wealth* 3, (September).

World Health Organization. (WHO) 1963–1986. *World Health Statistics*, Annual. Geneva: World Health Organization.

Part Four

INSTITUTIONAL, SOCIAL, AND POLITICAL PERSPECTIVES

Chapter Thirteen

INSTITUTIONAL AND POLITICAL FACTORS AFFECTING THE WELL-BEING OF THE ELDERLY

Gosta Esping-Andersen, Lee Rainwater, and Martin Rein

In contemporary societies, the well-being of the elderly is closely connected with social transfers. The findings presented in chapter 5 show that transfer income provides the main source of income for the elderly in such diverse countries as Sweden, West Germany, and the United States. Among the elderly—persons 65 years and older—continued employment has clearly become a very small source of income; therefore, the issue of poverty in old age must be analyzed primarily in terms of retirement income.

This is a historically recent phenomenon. Retirement in old age was not the norm until after World War II (Graebner 1980, Myles 1984). Life expectancy was substantially lower during the early phases of industrialization. And were a worker to survive to old age, there was no expectation of retirement. Around the turn of the century, 70 percent of American and European men over age 65 continued to work (Ball 1978, Guillemard 1980). Well-being in old age was a function of earning capacity. Early social policy for the elderly was not intended to supplant work, only to compensate for loss of a livelihood through work. Until World War I, the dominant mechanism was the poor law; thereafter old-age assistance and social insurance emerged. In neither case was there a public policy commitment to adequacy. For example, the average pension of an insured German worker in the 1920s was hardly better than prevailing poor relief rates (Myles 1984). Given the widespread incapacity of older people to work, poverty among the elderly was rampant. In the nineteenth century the aged and infirm crowded the alms houses. A 1929 New York survey showed that more than 50 percent of elderly persons depended on support from family or friends (Weaver 1982, 42).

There is no doubt that poverty in old age has been reduced dramatically over the past decades. This reduction has coincided with the institutionalization of a retirement age which, in turn, was made possible by political decisions to extend and upgrade social security. Yet, as chapter 5 demonstrates, poverty rates among the elderly still vary widely across nations (see chapter 5 for more detail). In this chapter we compare the United States with West Germany and Sweden. The proportion of elderly families who are poor after taxes and transfers (using the LIS equivalence scale) ranges from 2.6 percent in Sweden to 17.1 percent in West Germany and 18.7 percent in the United States. Among persons over 75 years of age, poverty rates reach 25 percent in the United States. Why do such sharp differences exist among similarly rich and advanced nations? Answering this question requires analysis of the ways in which the elderly derive their incomes.

The direct effects of market-derived income on the elderly are small for a number of reasons. First, as already noted, transfer incomes provide the main source of income among the elderly in the nations under study. Second, cross-national differences in the role of employment income do not seem to be closely related to poverty rates. The percentage of elderly households with any wage or salary income ranges from 13.7 percent in West Germany to about 24 percent in Sweden and 33 percent in the United States. Third, data on asset and investment income suggest that such income plays some role in the United States but almost none in West Germany and Sweden (Esping-Andersen 1986). Investment income, together with private pensions, is normally a significant source only for the population above the median income. It thus affects the income distribution among the elderly but has little direct influence on their poverty rates.

Although the direct effects of the market are marginal for an understanding of cross-national poverty rates among the elderly, the indirect effects are likely to be significant. In countries with earnings-related social insurance, prevailing wage differences influence retirement benefits. Where social security is designed also to stimulate development of private insurance, the scope and distribution of the latter will affect the income packaging as a whole. Where pension entitlements are linked to employment record, persons who lack significant work experience will be disadvantaged. It is crucial to take these kinds of indirect effects into account when exploring the effects of different social security systems on poverty rates among the elderly.

Each country's overall system of income provision for the elderly is constructed on the basis of social policy rules governing who is entitled to benefits and how much they are entitled to. Thus, a person's well-being will be affected by the number of contribution years required for full benefits, legal or mandatory retirement age, stringency of the income or means test in public programs, rules governing earnings for pension recipients, treatment of spouses, tax rules, and the presence of a guaranteed minimum or a stipulated maximum pension.

The institutionalized rules have direct consequences for individual well-being and for income distribution among the elderly; and the importance of the rules is closely linked to the system characteristics of old-age protection, which we call *pension regimes*. The distributional characteristics of the pension regimes surveyed in this chapter can be traced to the ways in which different regimes have attempted to respond to the issues of social equity among groups (called solidarity in West European countries) and income adequacy.

Our analysis of cross-national differences in poverty among the elderly focuses on three countries that reflect three major types of pension regimes.

CONDITIONS FOR RETIREMENT INCOME TRANSFERS IN SWEDEN, WEST GERMANY, AND THE UNITED STATES

Each of the three countries we have chosen—West Germany, Sweden, and the United States—has a basic minimum pension, an income-tested program designed to increase the adequacy of retirement income for persons with low income, and a system of earnings-related superannuation benefits. In addition, each country has a system of private pensions. Despite these similarities, the relative importance of the different parts of the systems produce remarkably different levels of poverty among the elderly. To understand why, we must examine how pension entitlements and benefit levels became established. We begin by reviewing the eligibility and benefit rules that governed the pension systems of the three countries in the year of the LIS survey—1981 for Sweden and West Germany and 1979 for the United States.

Sweden

The first tier of the Swedish system is a basic universal pension. All citizens and aliens with at least 10 years' residence are automatically entitled at age 65 to a basic flat-rate benefit. The second tier of the system is an earnings-graduated labor market pension (the ATP pension) which, legislated in 1959, provides mandatory coverage for all employed persons (with voluntary buy-in membership for the self-employed and the nonemployed). Eligibility for the mandatory coverage requires 20 years' covered employment. To be covered, a worker needs an annual income of no more than about a third of the average worker's income. Thus, even most part-time and low-wage workers will be insured. In addition to its universal pension and the ATP pension, Sweden has introduced a system of income-tested transfers. All persons who qualify for the universal pension are entitled to a supplement if they are not eligible for the earnings-related pension. Pensioners below a liberally defined income threshold are also eligible for housing allowances, be they renters or homeowners.

This entitlement structure means that pensioners receive not only the guaranteed basic pension, but also either an income-tested supplement or an earnings-related pension (or both if the latter is low). In addition, almost half of Swedish pensioner households receive a housing allowance.

The universal pension benefit, which everyone receives at age 65, is defined as 95 percent of the "base amount" for a single person and 155 percent for couples. This benefit alone would not enable recipients to escape poverty. For a single pensioner, the benefit was 16,103 Kronor in 1981, whereas the corresponding poverty line stood at 21,667 Kronor. However, for persons with no entitlement to earnings-related ATP pensions, the automatic income-tested supplement means that a single person would receive an additional 45 percent of the base amount (giving a total of 140 percent of the base amount, or 23,730 Kronor—U.S. $4,668—which is above the poverty line). The corresponding effective minimum guarantee for a couple in 1981 was 32,500 Kronor (U.S. $6,394)—at least 40 percent above the poverty line.

The Swedish pension regime clearly guarantees against poverty. It also produces relatively narrow income differentials among the elderly. The difference between the guaranteed minimum and the average pension, for example, is in the ratio of 3 to 4; the Gini coefficient for the elderly in Sweden is less than 0.15, indicating a very low degree of income inequality.

The Swedish system also leaves little additional need for private sector plans. Through collective bargaining, occupational pensions in Sweden have spread to almost all groups in the labor market. Yet they are a small part of the pension system, accounting for a mere 4.5 percent of total old-age benefits (O'Higgins 1986).

West Germany

The West German pension system contrasts in many ways with the system prevailing in Sweden. Its core comprises a number of administratively distinct social insurance schemes, organized on the basis of economic and occupational status, with separate funds for manual workers, white-collar salaried employees, civil servants, miners, and farmers. The basic principle is that entitlements should be tailored to occupation and economic performance, as reflected in work history and earnings. The traditional segregation has been substantially diminished over the past decades as legislated reforms have succeeded in homogenizing most of the provisions applying to the two largest schemes, the blue-collar and the white-collar plans. However, civil servants continue to enjoy particular pension privileges. The fund for farmers is peculiar in the sense that the essentially flat-rate benefit is contingent on the recipient's surrendering the farm.

As a result of the legislation of a flexible retirement provision in 1972, the entitlement structure has become quite complex. A person who has a minimum of 35 years of contributions can retire any time between ages 62 and 67. To qualify for a pension at age 65, a minimum of 15 contribution years is required. In calculating years for contribution purposes, the system is quite liberal in that a person can be credited for periods of sickness, unemployment, military service, and even schooling after the age of 16.

Instead of a basic universal pension, the West German system has special provisions for high-risk groups. Low-wage workers are credited with 75 percent of the average benefit provided they have been covered for at least 25 years; thus such persons are assured pensions at about half the rate of a full-career worker who earned average wages. (The program is no longer in effect for new workers.) Widows and widowers are entitled to a pension equal to 60 percent of the pension for which their spouse would have been eligible. The system does not provide special spouse supplements. For persons who fall outside the special provisions just mentioned, the only recourse is a means-tested social assistance program. About 3 percent of the elderly in West Germany make use of social assistance.

Poverty in old age is not precluded in the West German system. Benefits are a function of years of contribution and past earnings. For each year of coverage, workers receive an entitlement equal to 1.5 percent of their relative wages. This means that a wage earner with average wages and 35 years' contributions can expect a pension replacement rate roughly equal to 50 to 55 percent of prior wages.

Because there are no spouse supplements, a one-earner couple would receive the same. The couple is just above the poverty line (which is equal to about half of average wages).

The risk of poverty increases for a worker whose earnings have been lower or whose contribution record is shorter. The minimum pension for insured workers assures that a single person remains above the poverty line, but it places a couple below it. The provision for widows also entails some risk of poverty. If the spouse's expected pension would have been just above the poverty line, the survivor's pension will fall below.

The United States

The basis for the U.S. pension system is the Social Security program. Social Security is an earnings-related social insurance program based on compulsory membership for all wage and salary earners (except federal employees, some local government employees, and railroad employees). A large share of local government workers have joined the system, and federal employees have been covered by it since 1986. The eligibility conditions for Social Security are relatively liberal. For a person retiring at age 65 in 1980, the full pension required a total of 27 years' coverage. A minimum of 7.5 years suffices to qualify. Unlike West Germany, however, the system allows no credits for non-work-related activities.

Like West Germany, the United States has no universal pension; instead, it provides means-tested old-age assistance benefits under the Supplemental Security Income program (SSI) to elderly persons with inadequate Social Security income. Roughly 7 percent of Social Security recipients also receive SSI payments; the majority of SSI recipients (70 percent) receive some Social Security.

Social Security benefit amounts are based on the five-year period of highest earnings in a person's work and earnings history. In comparison with West Germany, the U.S. Social Security system is more redistributive toward low-wage workers. Benefits are calculated on the basis of average indexed earnings on a sliding scale that provides for 90 percent of the first $180 a month and a declining percentage of higher earnings. An alternative computation method, which is based solely on years covered, can be applied to workers with particularly low-income earning histories. The maximum benefit in this case is $230 per month. Also, unlike West Germany's system, the U.S. Social Security system provides for a supplement of 50 percent for spouses who are age 65 or older.

The Social Security benefit system does not guarantee against poverty among the elderly. The 1979 minimum monthly benefit under Social Security was $122, the maximum was $503. The 50 percent spouse supplement is exactly equal to the adjustment amount in the LIS equivalence scale. This means that single elderly persons who are not poor will not be poor if they are married. But single elderly persons who are poor will also be poor if married.

The alternative computation method based on years of covered employment is no guarantee against poverty either, because the $230 per month maximum falls well below the poverty line. A full-career worker needs to have earned at least three-quarters of the average monthly wage of covered workers in order to escape poverty through the Social Security benefit alone.

For persons who do not escape poverty through their Social Security benefit alone, the SSI program provides some help but does not ensure escape from poverty either. The maximum monthly SSI benefit for couples is $300. Persons who combine the minimum Social Security benefit ($122) with $300 from SSI will not be able to escape poverty.

THE THREE PENSION REGIMES COMPARED

The classical liberal dogma that the state intervenes only when self-reliance in the market is rendered impossible no longer holds anywhere in the West for the elderly. As Perrin (1969) observes, the issue of social protection has passed through several stages.

The Common Ground

By World War I, the industrial countries generally were moving toward state-sponsored guaranteed minimum pensions in old age. This approach sought two goals: (1) basic benefits designed to assure against starvation, and (2) targeting of protection toward the most vulnerable groups in the economy. This era gave birth to two types of pension systems. One was social insurance, as in Bismarck's pioneering legislation, a program designed specifically for blue-collar workers and defined as a disability (not old-age retirement) pension. Benefits were to be actuarial, computed on the basis of contributions, not earnings. The other pension system, adopted in Scandinavia and many Anglo-Saxon nations, was means-tested, old-age assistance—a development out of the poor law tradition.

The second stage in pension evolution, after World War II, was the inauguration of full retirement from active employment in old age. Most Western democracies signed the International Labour Office (ILO) Convention, which stipulated a commitment to the principles that underpin most pension systems today: retirement at age 65, pension coverage for all employed persons and their dependents, and income adequacy (defined as a pension equal to at least 50 percent of "normal" wages). The differences among contemporary pension systems reflect the different ways in which nations made the trade-off between universal entitlement and income adequacy for the most vulnerable people in society.

Three Solutions

Three institutional responses to the ILO goals can be distinguished. One response emphasized universal entitlement, as exemplified by Sweden. Pension policy was to aim toward equal and uniform protection of the entire population, regardless of prior social status or labor market performance.

A second response emphasized rewards based on past occupational performance. This model dominates continental European approaches to social security. In the earliest periods, separate insurance schemes were constructed for occupational status groups. Thus, nations such as France, Italy, and Germany evolved separate schemes for civil servants, manual workers, salaried employees, miners, seamen, craftsmen, and farmers. In some cases (Italy, for example) this resulted in a labyrinth of more than 100 special occupational funds, all with different eligibility and benefit regulations and separate financing and administration.

The third regime emphasized provision of a social safety net for the most vulnerable group. The relatively low benefit levels of Social Security in the United States, for example, combined with SSI for the poor elderly, leave ample incentives for the private pension market. Higher-income earners are encouraged to find private pensions or to make investments for retirement income. Favorable tax provisions constitute a second incentive for the development of private pension plans. Under such a system, a large share of government transfers are targeted explicitly to the poor on the basis of a means test.

These differences in the systems do not influence how much money is spent on the elderly, but rather how it is spent. The combined expenditure (as a percentage of gross domestic product

[GDP] in 1980) on social security, public employee, private occupational, and individual pension annuity plans amounted to 11.8 percent in West Germany, 11.4 percent in Sweden, and 8.2 percent in the United States. When we adjust for national differences in the proportion of elderly (persons 65 years and older) in the three countries, the per capita expenditure level is essentially identical for Germany, Sweden, and the United States (Esping-Andersen 1986, Rein 1982). In other words, total resource use is a poor predictor of old-age poverty and income distribution. How have these regime differences evolved?

THE DEVELOPMENT OF DIFFERENT PENSION POLICY REGIMES

A country's original pension legislation is a poor predictor of current outcomes. As the world's pioneer, Germany introduced the social insurance model for workers in the late nineteenth century, followed by a salaried pension fund in 1911. Sweden legislated a more universal type of social insurance pension in 1913. The United States introduced a purely social insurance plan in the 1935 Social Security Act. All were designed to provide an income floor.

The decisive political changes that differentiate the three pension policy regimes we are concerned with here are to be found after World War II, when nations institutionalized the principle of full retirement. None of the three nations' original pension systems was equipped to handle the new demands for a comfortable retirement, and the political responses to new demands in the three countries varied.

West Germany

The origins of the German system lie in the wish of a strong political leader (Bismarck) to use the power of an authoritarian state as a tool for repressing the emerging political mobilization of the working classes and for gaining the allegiance of workers by offering progressive legislation to improve the position of workers in retirement. Bismarck wanted a unitary system that paid flat-rate pensions and was financed by the state from general taxation. He did not get his way. The legislation that passed in 1889 was an outgrowth of the existing system that was based on relief, insurance, and employers' liability. The miners' scheme served as a prototype; it provided for employer contributions, compulsory insurance, and self-administration. The result was a fragmented scheme organized by industry, social position, and region.

In 1911, when white-collar workers demanded a social insurance somewhat more generous than the scheme that industrial workers had obtained under Bismarck, the Germans took a decisive step. By creating a separate insurance scheme for salaried workers, they hoped that a middle class would emerge separate from the working-class movement. From this point of view, the legislation was effective; but it also established the white-collar insurance as a "pace setter" for future legislative reforms.

Originally the system covered only 40 percent of the employed and 10 percent of the total population; today the scheme is virtually universal, covering all employed persons and 90 percent of the total population. In 1972 the government offered housewives the opportunity to buy into the scheme on a voluntary basis, thus opening the pension to all citizens and departing from the principle that entitlement depends on paid work. Not only was the system made virtually universal, but benefit differentials between white- and blue-collar workers were gradually reduced. Half of all funds spent on occupational pensions go to white-collar workers in the public sector. These additional pensions are designed to equalize the benefits of public sector white-collar workers and civil servants. The principles of strict actuarial accounting of benefits and contributions (equivalence) and of full funding were changed, and elements of universality were introduced. In the 1940s the value of pensions amounted to only 28 percent of earned income. By 1985 the value was 65 percent for workers who had achieved the standard benefit based on a working life of 40 years, and an average of 50 percent for all persons who retired.

How did this transformation occur? Both economic and political forces contributed. West Germany experienced a 20 percent economic growth rate in 1948–49 and about a 10 percent rate from then until the mid-1950s. The so-called economic miracle provided the resources, and with it came the political desire to let the elderly participate in the fruits of this growth. The first pension reform in 1957 can be interpreted as an obligation to repay the workers for their loss of assets and for their wage constraint, which helped bring about the rapid economic recovery of West Germany after World War II.

The basic idea underlying the reform was to transform the old-age pension from a subsistence level to a level that would enable workers to maintain their previous standard of living. The key to adequacy was the automatic adjustment of pensions to wage levels by a system of indexing. Pensions, therefore, were no longer calculated on the nominal value of their contributions.

The pension reform of 1957 also established another principle that was to be very important in the later development of the pension scheme—the introduction of a retirement age of 60 after one year of unemployment. This meant that at 59 years of age workers could regard themselves as virtually retired.

The pension reform of 1957 was followed by more pension reform in 1972, introducing two principles that had a decisive effect on the adequacy of benefits and went a long way toward universality. Pensions were to be calculated on the basis of a minimum income so that the ratio of a worker's earnings to the average was assumed to be at least 75 percent, regardless of the actual average. The purpose was to balance out low wages in the past, thus, in effect, moving one step further toward the idea of a minimum pension. The second principle was to entitle workers to disability pensions after 5 years of work history, instead of 15 years. This change of access rules was designed to make it easier for women to get pensions. This law was later extended to old-age pensions, so that today workers can get pensions after making contributions for only 60 months.

In the economic recessions that have developed since 1975, economic stringency was introduced. Between 1975 and 1985 the aggregate value of pensions as a percentage of gross national product (GNP) fell by 1 percent, but these cutbacks were realized within the basic structure of the system that had been created in the two great postwar reforms (1957 and 1972). Reductions were achieved by tinkering with the rules of indexing, tightening disability rules, integrating separate pension fund financing, and the like.

There is some evidence that the cutbacks have ended; indeed, a debate has now begun about the new poverty among the elderly, particularly among long-term unemployed persons and persons who were never employed. Central to this debate is concern about the position of women among the aged poor. This has led to a renewed debate about the feasibility of introducing a new basic flat-rate pension. The debate appears likely to stimulate the introduction of social equity into the existing equivalence system and further steps to reduce poverty levels.

Sweden

Sweden's pension system began with old-age insurance legislation in 1913. The system covered virtually all men and women between the ages of 16 and 66. It was a strictly actuarial system, however, implying that few would ever receive adequate benefits under the 1913 plan. Indeed, until after World War II, most elderly households in Sweden were heavily dependent on social assistance or employment income.

The major change came when legislation was passed instituting a universal flat-rate pension to replace the old 1913 contributory plan. Financed entirely from general revenues, the scheme abolished the link between past labor market performance and benefits. Its relatively high benefits also reduced by three-fourths the number of pensioners receiving means-tested assistance.

The flat-rate pension yielded substantial benefits (in comparison to earnings) for low- and middle-income earners but was naturally considered inadequate by higher-income groups. Private sector pensions grew substantially among the richer groups, stimulating the trade unions to press for similar advantages for their members.

During the late 1950s supplementary earnings-related pensions became the single most controversial issue in Sweden. Several parliamentary commissions failed to reach agreement on pension reform. An earnings-related pension scheme was finally passed (the ATP pension), guaranteeing a net pension replacement rate of 75 percent of past earnings and assuming a minimum of 20 years' contribution. During the phase-in period, a large number of elderly persons did not have the required number of contribution years and were excluded from coverage. This gap was filled with the introduction of a supplementary pension attached to the existing universal pension scheme. Retirees who did not qualify for ATP, or whose ATP pension entitlement was low, automatically qualified for the supplement. As the ATP scheme reached full maturity, covering the entire labor force, supplementary pension expenditures declined rapidly.

The pension system has experienced only marginal changes in recent years. The major changes relate to finances. Originally, the ATP scheme was based on a split employer-employee contributory financing. As part of an incomes policy agreement in 1973, the trade unions traded potential wage gains for a refinancing of pensions. Since then, employers have paid all ATP contributions. This unusual arrangement evolved because of the difficulty of bargaining for real wage increases in an inflationary environment with high marginal tax rates and the constraints of international cost-competitiveness.

In 1976 the pension age was reduced from age 67 to 65, and a flexible retirement age arrangement like the one in West Germany, was introduced, permitting persons between the ages of 60 and 70 to retire at any time, assuming at least 30 years' coverage under ATP.

Even the small private sector occupational pension system covers all workers equally. About 75 percent of male and 45 percent of female pensioners (ages 66 to 69) receive a private benefit. The amount is invariably small in comparison with social benefits, however.

The United States

The issue of a public commitment to old-age pensions was successfully kept off the national policy agenda in the United States until the 1930s. There were two reasons: (1) the extraordinarily liberal distribution of pensions for veterans which, at the beginning of this century, covered a large share of (white) men; and (2) the relatively generous benefits that the more privileged trade unions were able to negotiate for their members.

By the 1930s, however, the efficacy of both had been exhausted. A number of states (notably Wisconsin) had led the way toward a public pension system, and in 1935 the Social Security Act was passed. The fundamental part of the economic security system this act put in place for the elderly was the Social Security system, embodying a contractual right to retirement benefits based on prior labor market performance. In addition, an Old Age Assistance component was passed; it was expected to "wither away" as the Social Security system matured. The original act limited coverage to workers in commerce and industry (about 60 percent of the labor force). It was to be financed by a payroll tax of 2 percent of covered wages, shared equally by employer and employee. To assure that no government subsidies would be needed, the tax rate was to be gradually raised to 6 percent. The insistence on actuarialism meant that the system was to be fully funded by accumulated reserves. The individual beneficiary's entitlement would be a function of accrued interest.

A host of factors conspired to erode the strict actuarial approach. The system would not be able to distribute adequate benefits for decades, leading to severe pressures on the old-age assistance plan. Moreover, the insurance and business community was uneasy about the system's accumulation of enormous reserves ($50 billion), fearing they would crowd out capital markets and create irresistible political pressures to expand the program.

In 1939 the system was transformed into a pay-as-you-go program.

The reform also recast the benefit structure so that the recipient unit would be the family (covering spouses, widows, and dependents), rather than the individual worker. To accelerate benefit adequacy, recipients would be eligible for full benefits as early as 1940. Finally, benefits were to be calculated on average rather than covered earnings (Stein 1981). The system thus became redistributive through the severing of the direct correspondence between contributions and benefits.

Social Security was intentionally designed so as not to threaten the vitality of private pension markets (Derthick 1979). Indeed, it was designed specifically to coexist with, and rely on, a separate tier of occupational plans and individual savings. The alignment with a private market was not undertaken via decisions to exclude groups from coverage. The people initially excluded were predominantly seasonal and low-wage workers. Rather, the system was designed through the benefit structure (the low replacement rate for middle- to high-income earners) to assure that those earners would have the incentive to seek private sources to supplement retirement incomes.

It is often held that public pension growth crowds out the private sector. This is an untenable argument, for the U.S. Social Security program did not replace private plans; there was little to replace. On the eve of the Great Depression, total coverage (including the railroads) was only 7.5 percent of the labor force (Weaver 1982, 49); less than 10 percent of the covered workers actually ever came to enjoy a pension (Latimer 1932) and, if they did, they were hardly assured against poverty. The average pension in 1919 was $45 per month, equivalent in 1980 prices to $300 per month (Esping-Andersen 1986. The story is one of concomitant growth. Over most of the postwar era, private pension growth has been about as rapid as has Social Security (Munnell 1982).

Despite the inherently redistributive impact of the 1939 amendments, however, Social Security alone was not generous enough to prevent widespread poverty in old age. To compensate for insufficient Social Security benefits and lack of private pension coverage, low-wage workers were still heavily dependent on the means-tested Old Age Assistance program, a state-administered system.

Incremental improvements over the next 20 years certainly helped strengthen Social Security's ability to satisfy goals of adequacy. But policymakers refused to permit the system to become a program designed primarily to aid the poor; its long-term survival was held to be contingent on the principle of earned benefits (Derthick 1979).

A gradual improvement of benefits over the 1950s and 1960s served primarily to solidify the system's attraction among middle-income earners.

It was not until the early 1970s that the relationship between Social Security, private pensions, and means-tested assistance was recast. The Social Security Amendments of 1972 provided a one-shot, 20 percent increase in benefits and introduced the automatic indexing of benefits to keep pace with inflation. The Supplemental Security Income (SSI) Act of 1973 established what was essentially a uniform basic minimum pension. The Employee Retirement Income Security Act (ERISA) of 1974 introduced public regulation of private pensions. With the virtually simultaneous enactment of these three pieces of legislation, the United States took a major step in the direction of guaranteeing adequacy for both the low-income and middle-income groups.

From the point of view of eradicating poverty and assuring adequacy, the 1972–74 reforms were quite effective; and there are indications that Social Security's redistributive effect has been strengthened. In 1950 23 percent of the elderly were recipients of old-age assistance; by 1975 the SSI program assisted 10 percent. As noted earlier, about 7 percent of Social Security recipients now receive SSI as well. For couples with the lowest income, Social Security represented in 1984 82 percent of aggregate income, up from 79 percent in 1980 (U.S. GAO 1986).

However, another consequence of the 1972 reforms was to jeopardize the financial stability of the system. A series of measures were introduced in different years to cope with the mounting deficits. Contributions were increased, and the wage base for contributions was raised. The system of indexing was altered to adjust solely for wage increases, thus stabilizing wage replacement rates but not purchasing power. More significant changes were introduced in the 1983 amendments to the Social Security Act, making the system somewhat more redistributive and including all public employees in it. (They had previously been covered by a separate system.) Social Security benefits beyond the base amount became taxable, and the retirement age was extended to age 67.

IMPLICATIONS FOR THE UNITED STATES

Sweden, the United States and West Germany have all developed systems of old-age protection that present a mix of income-tested

Table 13.1   REPLACEMENT RATES OF SOCIAL SECURITY OLD-AGE PENSIONS
FOR WORKERS WITH AVERAGE WAGES IN MANUFACTURING,
GERMANY (F.R.), SWEDEN, UNITED STATES, 1980

	Single worker	Couple
Germany, F.R.	49	49
Sweden	68	83
United States	40	66

Source: Torrey (undated).

assistance, insurance-based, legislatively mandated pensions, and private pensions. Adjusted for the size of the elderly population, all three spend about the same proportion of their GDP on protecting the elderly. Insurance-based pensions (social security) provide the majority of income for retirees in all three countries, with varying wage replacement rates (table 13.1). Sweden has the highest replacement rates for both single workers and couples. West Germany has a higher replacement rate for single workers than the rate in the United States but a lower one for couples.

The pension systems in three countries reached their current status through very different routes. The German system grew through establishing earnings-related pension schemes that were different for different occupations. Although this is still the case in principle, the system has in fact become virtually universal, at least for persons with work histories, as the components have become increasingly uniform in their provisions. The Swedish system began with a flat-rate pension combined with an earnings-related component; it has now evolved into a universal pension, largely independent of earnings history. The U.S. system began as an earnings-related actuarial system with the benefits based on contributions. Then it evolved into a system in which the replacement rate varied inversely with earnings history, providing some income redistribution among beneficiaries. The system is now reverting somewhat toward the insurance principle.

The major difference between the U.S. system and the systems of the other two countries examined here is that the U.S. public and private systems have coverage and benefit levels that are largely independent of one another. This leaves the income-tested SSI program bearing substantially more of the burden of income security to the elderly than is true in the other two countries.

The reason for the difference is relatively clear: it is the U.S.

tradition to minimize the role of government, in contrast to the long social planning histories in the other countries. This comparative perspective makes it clear that the substantial dependence of the elderly on means-tested assistance is due not to the inadequacies of the Social Security system, which is extremely successful in achieving its stated goals, but to the lack of employment-related private pension coverage for a significant number of American workers.

References

Ball, R. 1978. *Social Security*. New York: Columbia University Press.
Derthick, M. 1979. *Policy Making for Social Security*. Washington, D.C.: Brookings Institution.
Esping-Andersen, G. 1986. "State and Market in the Development of Social Security Regimes." Working paper series. Florence, Italy: European University Institute.
Graebner, W. 1980. *A History of Retirement*. New Haven, Conn.: Yale University Press.
Guillemard, A. 1980. *La Vieillesse et l'Etat*. Paris: Presses Universitaires.
Latimer, M. 1932. *Industrial Pensions Systems in the United States and Canada*. New York: Industrial Relations Counselors.
Munnell, A. 1982. *The Economics of Private Pensions*. Washington, D.C.: Brookings Institution.
Myles, J. 1984. *Old Age in the Welfare State*. Boston, Mass.: Little, Brown.
O'Higgins, M. 1986. "The Public-Private Interaction in Social Policy." In *The Public-Private Interplay in Social Welfare*, edited by M. Rein and L. Rainwater. New York: M. E. Sharpe.
Perrin, G. 1969. "Reflections on Fifty Years of Social Security," *International Labour Review* 99:249–92.
Rein M. 1982. "A Comparative Study of Pension Policies in Europe and the United States." A paper prepared for the Berkeley Conference on Social Welfare and the Delivery of Services in the U.S. and the U.S.S.R., November 12–14.
Stein, B. 1981. "Funding Social Security on a Current Basis: The Policy Change in the United States." Ithaca: N.Y.: Cornell University. Photocopy.
Torrey, Barbara Boyle. Undated. "International Comparison of Retirement Income Systems." Washington, D.C.: U.S. Bureau of the Census. Photocopy.

U.S. General Accounting Office (GAO). 1986. *An Aging Society: Meeting the Needs of the Elderly while Responding to Rising Federal Costs.* Washington, D.C.

Weaver, C. 1982. *The Crisis in Social Security.* Durham, N.C.: Duke University Press.

Chapter Fourteen

SOCIAL POLICY AND CHILDREN IN THE UNITED STATES AND EUROPE

Sheila B. Kamerman and Alfred J. Kahn

Why does the economic situation of children in the United States seem to be so much worse, relative to other population groups, than the situation of children in other industrial countries? The focus in this chapter is on the policies that lead to the outcomes for children presented earlier, particularly in chapters 3 and 5. To provide a context for the discussion, we use illustrations principally from Northern and Western Europe.

In the United States, as in the other countries discussed, the economic well-being of children is closely tied to the income and wealth of their parents and to the earnings, labor force status, and number of earners in their families. When parents' earnings are nonexistent, irregular, or inadequate, children's well-being depends on public transfers. Earlier chapters have shown that certain children in the United States—those in single-parent families and in minority families—are the worst off, by far.

In accounting for the better economic situation of children in several other countries, we conclude that the European countries, in varying degrees, provide income transfers to all children or at least to all poor children, whereas the United States provides benefits only to some poor children (and at nonuniform levels); that social insurance benefits for children in Europe are more generous and more extensive than in the United States; and that the European countries have stressed the use of income transfers to supplement earnings and family income, especially for families with children, whereas the United States has largely maintained a separation between earned income and transfer income.

In accounting for why the United States has not pursued alternative child policy strategies, we conclude that the United States began the development of its national income transfer programs much later than the other European countries; that the country's complex pluralism constrained development of national child or family policies; and that policy development was inhibited by the need to deal first with race and unequal access to social benefits by blacks. Unlike the situation in several other countries, children's economic well-being has never been high on the agenda of either political party in the United States, nor has any one party been known as a special champion of children.

Our final conclusion is that the United States cannot make much progress in dealing with the economic situation of poor children without a larger public investment in income transfer programs.

WHY FOCUS ON FAMILY BENEFITS?

As indicated, for the United States as well as other industrial countries, the economic well-being of children is closely tied to the income of their parents and thus to the earnings, labor force status, and number of earners in their families. Demographic factors also are important, but it seems clear that as important as these factors may be, the United States is not unique with regard to them.

Unemployment varies widely across countries, with the United States (at 7 percent in 1985) between the low end of the range (just over 2 percent in Norway and Sweden) and the high end (over 10 percent in 1985 for Canada, France, and the United Kingdom) (table 14.1). Labor force participation rates for women vary across countries but have risen dramatically in all industrial countries over the past 25 years. Among the Western countries, female labor force participation rates are highest in Sweden, where about 85 percent of the women with children and more than 80 percent of women with preschool-age children are in the labor force, largely part-time. Female labor force participation rates are medium to high in Canada, Norway, and the United States where about 65 percent of the women with children and 55 percent of women with preschool-age children are in the work force, most of them full-time in the United States and Canada. The rates are low for many other countries such as France, the United Kingdom, and West Germany (about 50 percent or lower for women with young children). They are lower still in Japan, but increasing. Labor force participation rates for women with very young children are among the lowest in the United Kingdom (about 27 percent), where most such mothers who are in the labor force work only part-time. The participation rates for single mothers

Table 14.1   SOME BASIC SOCIAL INDICATORS ACROSS COUNTRIES, 1985

	Population (thousands)	Crude birth rate	Total fertility	Infant mortality	Unemployment as percentage of labor force	Female labor force participation (percentage)	Per capita GNP at market prices (US$)[a]	Government disbursements as percentage of GDP	Government revenue as percentage of GDP	Single-parent families as percentage of all families with children
Canada	25,379	14.9	1.7	9	10.4	62.4	14,959	43.7	38.9	n.a.
France	55,162	14.1	1.9	8	10.1	55.0	11,333	49.4	48.5	10
Germany, F.R.	61,015	9.6	1.4	10	7.8	50.4	12,158	43.4	45.4	13
Japan	120,754	12.5	1.8	6	2.6	57.1	11,666	27.1 (1984)	30.3 (1984)	14
Norway	4,148	12.4	1.6	8	2.5	68.3	14,098	44.0	56.1	19
Sweden	8,350	11.8	1.6	6	2.8	78.0	12,586	59.6 (1984)	59.8 (1984)	32[b]
United Kingdom	56,618	13.3	1.8	10	11.5	59.8	10,882	44.8 (1984)	42.8 (1984)	14
United States	239,283	15.7	1.9	11	7.1	64.0	16,494	35.3	31.1	26

Sources: OECD (1987); UNICEF (1987), tables 1 and 5; Kamerman and Kahn (1987b).

n.a. Not available.

a. Uses purchasing power parities.

b. Includes 18 percent of families with children in which the parent lives alone with children and 14 percent in which the parent cohabits with another adult.

are higher than for married mothers in most countries, but not in Norway, the Netherlands, and the United Kingdom.

The United States is not unique with regard to its birthrate nor in the numbers of children per family. Nor is the U.S. proportion of single-parent families (26 percent) unique. Several other countries have high rates, for example, Sweden (32 percent) and Denmark (26 percent).

In short, there is nothing unique in any of these statistics or in the family situation of children in the United States—the number of earners in families, the level of employment, the level of earnings, or even the family structure—that *by itself* would explain fully the distinctly poorer U.S. economic situation for children, even though we do not rule out several elements as part of the picture. (This point was developed in more detail in chapter 5 of this volume.) The key difference, we find, is in the readiness or reluctance to create, through government, a foundation of income or to supplement earned income or other benefits on behalf of children.

As one observer notes, "The provision of welfare[1] differs in societies that are similar in their high standard of material wealth" (Rose forthcoming). They rely variously on household, market, and state, and the nature of the "welfare mix" depends on culture, family traditions, economy, the country's political alignments, and other factors. The United States, although below the mean for the Organization for Economic Cooperation and Development (OECD) in total public expenditure and in public expenditure for social programs as a percentage of gross national product (GNP), does not spend absolutely less in some fields (because of its higher GNP). Moreover, in some areas, U.S. public expenditures are relatively high, whereas in others (such as medical care) tax expenditures, employee benefits, and consumer expenditures compensate for the smaller direct role of the state. Where the United States lags is in the domain focused on here—family benefits or public transfers for families with children.

All the industrial countries provide free compulsory education (primary and secondary) from age 5, 6, or 7 until age 15 or 16. Almost all the continental European countries—including Belgium, Denmark, France, Italy, and West Germany—provide free (or low-fee) and optional, public or publicly financed preschool or child care programs for children from about age 3 (or younger) to school age. The United Kingdom does not have such a system; Canada is currently debating substantial expansion. All the countries mentioned thus far, and many others including Japan, but not the United

States, provide universal health insurance or health services for children and their families. All have somewhat comparable social insurance systems covering the elderly, survivors, the disabled, and the unemployed. Pension wage replacement rates vary, as do disability benefit levels. The U.S. unemployment insurance system compares unfavorably in both replacement rates and duration, thus adding to the poverty and low-income problems affecting families with children.

All the countries, again including Japan but not the United States, also provide statutory short-term disability or sickness benefits through their social insurance system and provide paid maternity or parental benefits for employed parents on leave from their jobs for some time following childbirth. Almost all provide some more or less important means-tested social or public assistance, sometimes standardized for the country as a whole and sometimes discretionary and linked to service provision at the local level.

Finally, in contrast to the situation for pensions, health care, disability, and sickness—where the private sector may be said to be particularly important in the United States to compensate for certain government inaction—there is no private (fringe benefit) provision of family benefits in the United States. Moreover, except in minuscule amounts, U.S. employers provide no support services such as child care for families with children (Kamerman and Kahn 1987, Kahn and Kamerman 1987).

Public family benefits (public income transfers for children and their families) for various countries are compared in table 14.2. We define these benefits to include cash benefits that are universal and non-income-tested, such as child or family allowances provided in many countries to families with children in accordance with the number of children in the family; cash benefits that are income-tested, such as some family allowances and supplementary family allowances, but reach a significant portion of all families with children; cash benefits that are means-tested and subject to rigorous income and asset tests and are usually limited to the very poor; cash equivalents or near-cash benefits, such as housing allowances or food stamps; and tax benefits (credits or allowances) for children or their families. Dependents' benefits added onto individual recipients' social insurance benefits, such as additions to unemployment benefits, and maternity or parental insurance benefits, also are included.

When parents' earnings are absent, irregular, or inadequate, children's economic well-being depends on public income transfers. For children in low-income families, these public income transfers

Table 14.2   CORE PUBLIC INCOME TRANSFER PROGRAMS, SELECTED COUNTRIES, 1983

Country	Family (child) allowance	Housing allowance	Social assistance "welfare"	Child support (government)	Unemployment insurance	Other unemployment benefits	Child allowance supplement	Food stamps	Refundable tax credits	Maternity benefits
Australia[a]	X	—	X	—	—	X[b]	—	—	—	—
Canada	X	—	X	—	X	—	—	—	X	X
France	X	X	X	X	X	—	X	—	—	X
Germany, F.R.	X	X	X	X	X	X[b]	—	—	—	X
Israel	X	—	X	X	X	—	—	—	—	X
Sweden	X	X	X	X	X	X[c]	—	—	—	X
United Kingdom	X	X	X	—	X	—	—	—	—	X
United States										
New York[d]	—	—	X	—	X	—	—	X	X	X[e]
Pennsylvania[d]	—	—	X	—	X	—	—	X	X	—

Source: Kahn and Kamerman (1983), 8.

Note: Generic names for programs are used; within these broad categories, programs differ substantially. For example, the British child benefit is not the same as the child allowance in Germany.

a. Australia is classified under unemployment assistance and social assistance even though it is debatable how these income-tested benefits should be regarded.

b. Unemployment assistance.

c. Labor market assistance.

d. New York is a high-benefit state. Pennsylvania is often used as the average state. See note (a), table 14.3.

e. Temporary Disability Insurance (TDI), covering pregnancy and childbirth.

play a critical role. Although public family benefits across countries may account for a small portion of family income except in the case of low-income families, these benefits can make a significant difference for these low-income, single-parent, and large families—the families in which children are most likely to be at economic risk.

The difference that public transfers make to the income of an employed single mother of two earning half the relevant average wage is compared for programs and countries in table 14.3. In Sweden, for example, income for such a family almost doubled in 1979 as a consequence of family benefits; in France it was raised by 60 percent. We have found similar impacts elsewhere. Table 14.4 referring only to universal programs shows family or child benefits as a percentage of take-home pay for one-earner families with two children in various countries. For example, family benefits raised take-home pay in 1985 for such a family by 10 percent to 12 percent of gross earnings in Norway, Sweden, and the United Kingdom, and 12 percent to 20 percent in Austria, Belgium, Greece, the Netherlands, and New Zealand. For below-average earners these universal (non-means-tested) benefits are even more significant; they are likely to be most significant of all for single-mother families and for large families. As a final illustration of the point, we note that potential poverty rates in France in 1984 were reduced by family benefits from 18 percent to 5 percent in two-parent families, and from 37 percent to 14 percent in single-parent, mother-only families (CNAF 1987).

It is in this context that we turn now to the U.S. family benefit programs. After reviewing these benefits, we describe the strategies other countries use that improve the economic well-being of children and how these strategies differ from those employed in the United States.

FAMILY BENEFITS IN THE UNITED STATES

The United States has no universal cash child benefit (see tables 14.2 and 14.4 presented earlier). What it does have is a family tax allowance, but this helps only families with incomes above the tax threshold. Moreover, this help increases as incomes increase. Children who are dependents of recipients of social insurance benefits or their survivors are eligible for benefits, as they are in other

Table 14.3   PUBLIC INCOME TRANSFERS AS A PERCENTAGE OF NET YEARLY FAMILY INCOME FOR AN EMPLOYED SINGLE MOTHER EARNING HALF THE AVERAGE WAGE (FAMILY WITH TWO CHILDREN AGES 2 AND 7)

Countries	Percentage of income by program										Net income as a percentage of average production worker's wage
	Family allowance	Family allowance supplement	Housing allowance	Social/ public assistance	Refundable tax credit	Advance maintenance	Food stamps	Subtotal—public income transfers	Earned income minus deductions and taxes	Total	
Canada	5.4	—	—	4.1	8.4	—	—	17.9	82.1	100.0	75.9c
France	8.4	15.3	13.9	—	—	b	—	37.6	62.4	100.0	87.8
Germany, F.R.	13.1	—	8.2	—	—	b	—	21.3	78.7c	100.0	70.9c
Sweden	10.1	—	16.7	—	—	21.8	—	48.6	51.3	99.9	123.1
United Kingdom	16.9	—	7.9	—	—	—	—	24.8	75.2	100.0	83.0
United States											
Pennsylvania	—	—	—	6.9	5.2	—	4.7	16.8	83.2	100.0	69.2

Source: Kahn and Kamerman (1983), table AB-2.

Note: These are the benefits that were legally available in 1979 to families of the type specified. It is not claimed that all such families collected the benefits.

a. In 1979 Pennsylvania had slightly above the U.S. average production worker's wage (APWW), ranked 22 among the 50 states in highest permissible AFDC payments for a family of 4, and had an average AFDC grant of $292.37 (U.S. average was $256.96). The total food-stamp and AFDC grant for the Pennsylvania family of four was 87 percent of the poverty line in 1979; New York City grants were 101 percent of the poverty level. All U.S. benefits were subsequently eroded by inflation. In 1979 high-benefit AFDC states like New York and California (which constituted a small minority of states) compared very favorably with the Europeans in overall income as a percentage of APWW, because the benefit level and work incentive amendments of OBRA 1981 had not yet taken effect.

b. Germany and France inaugurated varied versions of the child support guarantee after these calculations.

c. An anomaly in the German tax code created this relatively unfavorable result. It was subsequently corrected, and this family's net income now would be significantly higher. The Canadian system is much like the U.S. system despite the small child allowance. The Australian "insurance-assistance" system is not contributory and is mostly means-tested.

Table 14.4   UNIVERSAL FAMILY OR CHILD BENEFITS AS A PERCENTAGE OF
TAKE-HOME PAY,[a] ONE-EARNER FAMILIES WITH TWO CHILDREN,
AVERAGE EARNINGS IN MANUFACTURING, SELECTED
COUNTRIES, 1985

	Exclusive of family benefits	Including family benefits	Increment via family benefits (percentage)
Austria	76.0	91.4	20.3
Belgium	70.2	82.1	17.0
Canada	85.8	89.0	3.7
France	84.8	92.3	8.8
Germany, F.R.	72.1	76.9	6.7
Greece	86.8	101.5	16.9
Japan	90.2	90.2	—
Netherlands	65.4	73.5	12.4
New Zealand	75.2	84.5	12.4
Norway	75.3	83.3	10.6
Sweden	66.1	73.8	11.7
United Kingdom	73.1	81.5	11.5
United States	77.7	77.7	—

Source: OECD (1987).
a. After taxes and social security contributions.

countries. (Some states in the United States also have dependents' benefits under unemployment insurance.)

The United States has no income-tested or means-tested cash benefit program for *all* poor children. It does provide a guaranteed minimum income for food for all poor people, however, including children and their families.

The major cash benefit program for poor children in the United States, Aid to Families with Dependent Children (AFDC), provides significantly different benefits in different states because of state variations in eligibility criteria and benefit levels, as well as in policy regarding coverage of poor children in two-parent families. In effect, there is no safety net program for all poor children in the United States, as there is in the United Kingdom, for example.

Overall, for a typical mother-only family with two children—the family most at risk of poverty—44 percent of an average wage, 74 percent of the poverty threshold, and 92 percent of a minimum wage could be provided through transfer payments (AFDC and food stamps) in the median AFDC state in 1987, if the mother had no other income. What such a family could receive in transfer payments if the mother were working and earning half the average wage would vary by the state but would not include any cash benefit; indeed, in all but three states, anyone earning the minimum wage would not be eligible to receive a cash benefit.

Aid to Dependent Children (the forerunner of AFDC) was established by the 1935 Social Security Act and now provides means-tested cash payments for caretakers (mothers, fathers, and other relatives) and needy children if children have been deprived of parental support. Except for the 1.5 percent of cases in which the parent not present is the mother, it is a program for children living without their fathers in the home or, in a small percentage of cases, with unemployed fathers. (A small number also live with other relatives.)

In 1986 almost 3.7 million families received AFDC benefits, about 12 percent of all families with children and half of all poor families; only 253,000 were in the unemployed-father category (U.S. Congress 1987). The 11 million recipients included more than 7 million children (about 55 percent of all poor children). In 1984 blacks constituted about 42 percent of recipient families; non-Hispanic whites, 41 percent; Hispanics, 13 percent; and Asians, 2.3 percent. (Another assistance program, Supplemental Security Income [SSI], aided about 238,000 blind and disabled children.) Of the children receiving AFDC benefits in 1984, 2 percent had fathers who had died, 3.6 percent had fathers who were disabled, and almost 9 percent had fathers who were unemployed. By contrast, 36 percent of families had fathers missing from the home because of divorce and separation; and more than 46 percent were fatherless because the child was born out of wedlock.

Aid for Families with Dependent Children (AFDC) is a federal and state program. Each state establishes its own needs standards on which it bases payment. (Payment standards are invariably below the need standards.) The federal share of these payments ranges between 50 percent and 78 percent, plus half of administrative costs.

The AFDC program is also a passport benefit to Medicaid, food stamps, and school meals. A small number of the families also have access to public housing programs as well.

In May 1986 the average per-family monthly AFDC payment was $349 ($119 per recipient). Family benefits in high-benefit states (Alaska, California, and Minnesota) range from $500 to $600 and in low-benefit states (Alabama, Mississippi, and Tennessee) range from $110 to $140. Clearly, an average has little meaning here; we record, nonetheless, that the average 1986 benefit was equal to about 25

Table 14.5   AFDC BENEFIT, MEDIAN AND MAXIMUM FOR A FAMILY OF
FOUR, SELECTED YEARS (1986 dollars)

Year	Median benefit	Maximum benefit
1970	621	1,054
1975	534	1,004
1980	463	745
1983	403	685
1984	396	695
1985	405	813
1986	415	823

Source: U.S. Congress, House Committee on Ways and Means (1987), 416.

percent of the wage for a full-time production worker in the private sector and about 60 percent of the minimum wage for a full-time worker.

Benefits from AFDC are not indexed for inflation. This failure to correct for price increases and an increasingly insensitive public response to recipients have led to considerable erosion in AFDC benefits since 1970. The median and maximum monthly benefit for a family of four in constant 1986 dollars for the 1970–86 period is shown in table 14.5.

Food stamps are received by 83 percent of AFDC families, but the latter constituted less than half of the 21 million average monthly caseload in fiscal 1985. About 69 percent of all poor children received food stamps in 1982, including those receiving AFDC; the proportion is known to have declined since then. The fiscal 1985 average monthly food-stamp benefit per person was $45, and the maximum allotment to a four-person family was $264.

In theory, food stamps are designed to compensate for the difference between 30 percent of a family's countable cash income (20 percent to 25 percent of gross) and the U.S. Department of Agriculture's "Thrifty Food Plan;" hence the allotment varies by family size and cash income. (There are some employment-related requirements here, too, as in AFDC.) The means test for eligibility is far less onerous than that for AFDC, and the benefit is available to qualified persons regardless of marital status or presence of a child. In many parts of the country, food stamps are the only financial aid available to two-parent poor families and their children. Nonetheless, Ruggles (1985) reported for 1983 that 70 percent of recipient units were families headed by a woman and almost 20 percent were elderly. The comparable figures for 1975 were 59 percent and 24 percent. Clearly, few two-parent families with young children are among current recipients.

Federal spending for food stamps amounted to $11 billion in fiscal 1987, compared with less than $9.3 billion for the federal share of AFDC in 1986. Total state expenditures for AFDC were $8.2 billion. Both these totals are small compared with social insurance expenditures ($256.3 billion in fiscal 1987) described below.

The Earned Income Tax Credit (EITC), established in 1975, was essentially a corrective enactment in a negotiated tax legislation package. Escalating Social Security payroll taxes and concern with the effects of inflation on the income tax loads of the poor led to this relief. Almost 6 million low-income families with children received EITC in 1984, a decline from 7 million in 1979 and 6.4 million in 1982. Some $1.7 billion was paid in 1984 ($2.1 billion in 1979). The per-family credit, which was about $285 in 1986, has changed little since the late 1970s. As of 1988 the EITC has been indexed, with $6,214 as the income level for the maximum credit ($870) and a "phase-out" range between $9,840 and $18,540 (Steuerle and Wilson 1987). The credit has the advantage of being refundable to persons whose tax liabilities are lower than their entitlements. Although there are many proposals for increased use of this income supplementation device, it remains a very limited benefit for families with children.

Social insurance benefits for families with children in the United States are limited to dependents' benefits for children of retirees, survivors' benefits, benefits for the disabled, and unemployment insurance benefits (UI), all of which exist in all the major industrial countries. Unemployment insurance benefits are much less generous in the United States than in the other major Western countries, and there is no unemployment assistance program available to low-income workers when UI benefits end, such as the programs in Austria and West Germany. The earlier AFDC and food stamp data may be compared with the following social insurance benefits in current status in December 1986 (U.S. Congress 1987):

□ 450,000 children of retired workers (average monthly benefit per child, $204);
□ 1 million children of disabled workers (average monthly benefit per child, $141);
□ 1.9 million children as survivors of insured workers (average monthly benefit per child, $337).

Not surprisingly, the combination of modest food stamp benefits and eroded AFDC benefits leaves most recipient families getting the maximum AFDC grant below the poverty threshold. The mythical "median" state in 1986 granted benefits to a single-mother family of three persons at the level of 74 percent of poverty; only one state, Alaska, provided benefits above the poverty line (and only just). Eight states raised the benefits of persons receiving the potential maximum AFDC grants plus food stamps to within 10 percent of the poverty level; more than half of the states had maximum benefits that raised families to between 65 percent to 90 percent of the poverty line; four states had combined benefits equal to 55 percent or less of the poverty line.

Nonetheless, between 1969 and 1983, from 4 percent to 11 percent of poor families and 3.5 percent to 10 percent of poor children were lifted from poverty each year by cash welfare payments, the lowest percentages in most recent years and the highest in the 1970s. The late 1970s were also the time of the highest AFDC "take-up" rates—benefit recipients as a percentage of all potentially eligible single-parent families. Take-up rates have since declined (U.S. Congress 1985).

Finally, of particular importance, the United States has stressed a sharp distinction between work and receipt of benefits. Except with regard to food stamps and a modest earned income tax credit for families, there are no benefits designed to supplement low wages. From the late 1960s public assistance policy sought to create incentives for work by encouraging the use of AFDC as an earnings supplement (with only limited success), but the policy since 1981 largely discourages such use of AFDC. Only 4.6 percent of AFDC recipients had earned income in 1986, and of these most worked part time. And except for a very small amount of public housing and a modest program of housing assistance to some poor households, there is no national program of housing allowances available to subsidize the costs of rental housing for low-income families with children.

COMPARISON WITH OTHER COUNTRIES

In contrast to the United States, almost all industrial countries provide a public, universal, child benefit—a child or family allowance—either as a direct cash benefit or a refundable tax credit, based on the presence and number of children in a family. Typically, such allowances are equal to about 5 percent to 10 percent of average gross wages for each child, although the benefits are more generous in several countries (see table 14.4 presented earlier). Clearly, this is a modest amount; but it is worth relatively more to single-mother families and to large families than to the typical two-parent family with children. These benefits are usually provided on a per-child basis, but they sometimes vary in value by the birth order and age of the child. Income-tested supplements may raise the value of these benefits still more.

Some countries (such as Israel, the Netherlands, Sweden, and the United Kingdom) have eliminated their tax allowances for children, replacing them either with a direct cash benefit, as in the United Kingdom, or with a refundable tax credit, as in Israel.

A growing trend among the European countries is provision of a guaranteed minimum child support payment (Kahn and Kamerman 1988). This benefit is advanced to the custodial or caretaking parent by a government agency when child support payments owed by the absent parent are not paid, paid irregularly, or are too low (because what the parent can afford, or pays, is below what is viewed as the minimum income needed to maintain a child). In the countries that provide such a benefit, the same or another public agency assumes responsibility for the collection of child support from the absent parent, crediting what is collected against the payments advanced. Austria, Denmark, Finland, France, Israel, the Netherlands, Norway, Sweden, and West Germany are among the countries with such a policy.

Because mother-only families with children constitute an increasingly large proportion of families with children in all the industrial countries, and because these families are at high risk of poverty everywhere, these benefits constitute an important form of social protection and can provide a significant component of family income. Even though the benefits are insufficient by themselves to support the whole family, they do offer an important supplement to earned income. Where provided on a universal basis (as in most countries) they create a strong work incentive as well. In Sweden, for example, 14 percent of all children benefited from the advance maintenance payment in 1981. Seventy-five percent of the court-ordered support payments were collected from the absent parent by the social security agency, constituting 35 percent of what was advanced by the agency. About 85 percent of single mothers work outside the home in Sweden, including those with very young children.

One- and two-parent, low- or modest-income families with children, in addition to benefiting from the child or family allowances mentioned above (and the advance maintenance payments just described), may be entitled to income-tested housing allowances as well. Housing allowances constitute an entitlement in several countries, including France, West Germany, and all the Scandinavian countries. Combined with family allowances, these income transfers were worth about one-third of the average wage to a working single-mother family with two children in France and Sweden in 1979, and only a little less to a similar two-parent family, with one wage earner earning an average wage. These benefits, too, constitute a significant supplement to family income and are especially important in countries where access to housing presents a financial obstacle to many families.

Finally, all the European countries, as well as Canada and many others, provide special cash benefits to replace income forgone at the time of childbirth and provide job-protected leaves as well (maternity or parental benefits and leaves). The cash benefits tend to replace between 80 percent and 100 percent of wages (up to the maximum covered under the country's social security system); and the benefit lasts from a minimum of three months to a maximum of about one year, with five to six months the typical pattern in Europe.

Most important, in sharp contrast to the United States, much of what the European countries provide in family income benefits—through universal entitlement, or an income test high enough to cover all or part of low wages, or benefits contingent on work—is designed to supplement earned income and link earnings more closely to family need. Thus, for example, in Sweden a single working mother with two children ages 5 and 9 would receive a family allowance for each of her children, a guaranteed minimum child support benefit for each child (to be collected to the extent possible from the noncustodial father), and a housing allowance, as well as heavily subsidized child care (Kahn and Kamerman 1983). In France, a two-parent family with two children ages 2 and 4 in which only the father works and earns the average wage would receive several types of family allowances, plus a housing allowance and free preschool.

The differences between the United States and these European countries, as delineated here, go beyond totals and amounts. They reflect very different commitments, as we now discuss.

HISTORICAL PERSPECTIVES: THE UNITED STATES

It is useful to begin by reviewing the background of AFDC (ADC until 1962) as the primary U.S. cash child benefit. From colonial times, indenture, large-scale institutionalization, and foster home care were virtually the only provisions for children in poor households. In the context of an important wave of "child saving," which moved on many fronts during the Progressive Era, reformers called for what were to become widows' or mothers' pensions as a humane alternative (Katz 1986, Leiby 1978). The first White House Conference on Children (1909) had recommended that homes "should not be broken up for reasons of poverty," although it seemed to condone child removal "for considerations of inefficiency or immorality" (Bremner 1970–71). Missouri was the first state to pass a widows' pension law in 1911; 40 states followed within ten years. These pre-Social Security laws were permissive; many of them depended on local initiative and allowed much discretion. Put simply, a state would provide funds to a widow who made an implicit contract to maintain a suitable home. The administrators chose only the "worthy." A 1931 caseload survey (Bell 1965, Burns 1949) showed 82 percent to be "gilt-edged widows"—that is, there were very few unwed mothers and disproportionately few blacks.

Nor was the Social Security Act to change this situation much. The main business of the 1935 legislation was unemployment insurance and old-age pensions. Modest child health and child welfare measures and Aid to Dependent Children (ADC) were added. But ADC offered support only to children (not their caretakers), and the matching grant levels for ADC were extremely low, far below the levels of old age assistance. The 1939 amendments to the Social Security Act added social insurance benefits for widows and dependent child survivors, leading to the expectation that one group of single parents (widows) would be removed from ADC after sufficient build-up of eligibility expansion.

The 1950 amendments saw the addition of the caretaker grant, and the new program name, Aid to Families with Dependent Children (AFDC), was adopted in 1962. But AFDC continued to permit assessment of homes as unsuitable and thus continued some of the opportunities for racial and moral exclusions of the mothers' pension era. Although the law permitted states to include all the categories of single mothers, state discretion was long unchallenged and federal administrative capacity to do so built up slowly. Bell (1965) has documented the many campaigns against allegedly unsuitable homes through the 1950s. Blacks, unwed mothers, and women considered "immoral" because they were involved with men all found it hard to get aid and could be easily dropped from the rolls.

Administrative reform, both federal and state, increased equity concerns, and the civil rights movement generated progress. The fights over suitable homes and man-in-the-house rules continued; but caseloads did grow and became more representative over the 1960s, especially outside the South. Eventually the principle was enunciated and buttressed: a home could not be called unsuitable if children were left in it; if assistance was denied for unsuitability, the denial had to be accompanied by removal of the child for neglect. For the states the sharing of a low-level, means-tested benefit with the federal government was obviously a more attractive prospect than full state assumption of the costs of a much expanded system of foster homes and institutions.

By the 1960s, then, AFDC had the makings of a child allowance for poor children plus a caretaker grant, and it seemed as though it could become available to children in all kinds of single-parent homes. In the context of economic growth, higher eligibility ceilings, the civil rights movement, and other developments, the welfare rolls exploded. Just as the battle for equity seemed to be making progress, however, concern at the very high and rapidly growing caseloads, especially black caseloads, and fear that out-of-wedlock childbirth was being encouraged created renewed hesitation and negative reactions. Opponents also found fraud and inefficiency to attack. People who had always believed that work should prevail over "outdoor relief" (cash relief in one's own home) joined others who observed that labor force dynamics in fact had brought large numbers of married mothers from all groups into the labor force. The AFDC program was given work incentive and work program add-ons, even as it won more objective administration, improved benefits, and wider coverage.

Thus, by the end of the 1960s, a program that had begun on the assumption that some single mothers might be supported without work had become one for which the whole gamut of poor single mothers might qualify but which now compelled some recipients to register for work and to be required to work if jobs were found.

But the forces on the side of greater equity within AFDC and protection of AFDC rights—the very forces that had worked to increase budgets and to simplify eligibility procedures—had also generated enthusiasm for larger reforms. Out of this came the negative income tax and child allowance campaigns, both addressed to the family and child poverty that the 1964 War on Poverty had yet to tackle effectively. Increasingly visible forces in this ambivalent society discussed expanding and improving welfare; opponents pushed caveats, requirements, and restrictions.

The lack of family allowances or other types of family benefits in the United States cannot be attributed to failure of invention or information. Americans have been reporting rather fully on such developments since late in the last century (Henderson 1904), and family allowances have been both proposed and rejected since then.

Paul Douglas, for example, economist and senator, published *Wages and Family* in 1923 in the context of a general discussion of the living wage. He estimated the consequences of such a "living wage" for the economy and for workers and found the proposal too costly for industry and too inefficient as a transfer scheme. Instead, he proposed something like what then existed in France and Belgium, payment of allowances to married workers on behalf of their dependents. Much later, a resolution at the 1950 White House Conference on Children and Youth urged "exploration of improving the economic situations of children and families with inadequate incomes, with particular attention to family allowances, tax exemptions for children, and expenses for working mothers" (Vadakin 1968, 33).

In 1955, Senator Richard Neuberger introduced a resolution (backed by Senators Paul Douglas, Estes Kefauver, Hubert Humphrey, John F. Kennedy, Herbert Lehman, and Wayne Morse) calling for a study of the Canadian family allowance system. None of these initiatives made much progress.

In 1966 Daniel P. Moynihan advocated a family allowance, drawing on a 1963 position paper by Patricia McGuire of the Department of Labor. Steiner (1971) cites a full account prepared by Judith H. Parris at the Brookings Institution in 1967. In the United States, in this period, family allowances were first attacked as a measure favored by Catholics, in the context of their opposition to birth control. Subsequently, they were opposed as possibly increasing birthrates among poor blacks. Child allowances were also attacked as economically inefficient, because most would go to people above the poverty line. In response to this argument, Moynihan spoke of the urgency, in the wake of the urban riots and the assassination of Martin Luther King, Jr., of stressing unifying, universal measures, not divisive income-tested ones. By then Representative John Conyers and others had included a provision for a family allowance in a comprehensive Full Opportunity Bill in 1967. The Citizens' Committee for Children of New York had run a major conference on the subject, and a coalition was attempting to persuade the 1969 President's Commission on Income Maintenance (the Heineman Commission) that this was the way to go (Burns 1968, Shlakman 1970). Brazer (1968) suggested how the target inefficiency question could be solved through a tax recoupment scheme.

It was not a close fight. The Heineman Commission chose the new negative income tax strategy, which had attracted both free-market economists like Milton Friedman and the reformers identified with the Office of Economic Opportunity and the Department of the Treasury. The latter were followed by a large, progressive constituency attracted to the guaranteed minimum income concept. Moynihan, based in the White House, designed what became President Richard Nixon's Family Assistance Plan (FAP) proposal. Earlier Moynihan had described AFDC as "in effect a family allowance for broken families," perhaps contributing to the alarming increase in family breakup (Vadakin 1968). He would now try to cover all poor working and nonworking families, including two-parent families.

The story of the proposals, variations, efforts, and failures during the Nixon, Ford, and Carter years is known (Patterson 1985). The case for universalism via family allowances lost in open combat against the champions of economic efficiency, target efficiency, and a guaranteed income, although it is not clear in retrospect that this was why family allowances were not adopted; there was to be no negative income tax either. Food stamps, backed by a strong coalition of farm interests and urban antipoverty advocates, became the American guaranteed income and soon had a larger budget than was estimated for Nixon's entire FAP. The ambivalence and unresolved issues remained in the public debate and the mixed signal incrementalism continued.

HISTORICAL PERSPECTIVES: EUROPEAN CONTRASTS[2]

How do developments in other countries compare with this U.S. history?[3] The first major difference is that the social insurance (social security) systems in several European countries are far older than the U.S. system. The foundation of the social protection system in several countries was firmly in place in the late nineteenth and early twentieth centuries, well before we in the United States were considering such programs. And European family benefit systems were elaborated, solidified, and became the norm, largely in the immediate post-World War II period, while the United States was still struggling to implement the most basic social programs: old-age retirement benefits, dependent and survivors' benefits, and, later, disability benefits. Wilensky (1975) and others have found the older systems to be more comprehensive and generous.

The second striking difference is that, while Europe was expanding the social role of government immediately after World War II, the United States was expanding the social role of employers, by encouraging the growth of private fringe benefits (Kamerman and Kahn 1987a). Wage controls imposed in World War II, and later in the Korean War, permitted increases in fringe benefits while ruling out pay increases. Soon after the war, fringe benefits were permitted to be included as a collective bargaining issue; and unions began to focus more on expanding these benefits for their members than on improving social policy for everyone. Despite the significance of these benefits for some workers, only a small proportion of the work force benefited, and many still do not.

Three goals drove the early European family benefit developments: pronatalism, wage supplementation, and social equity. (The European term for the latter as noted in chapter 13 is solidarity. It refers to a commitment to both horizontal and vertical equity and includes the concept of equalization of financial burdens for families with and without children.) Some countries, such as France and Sweden, continued to be concerned about the low birthrates of the Depression years and saw family allowances as a device that would provide modest financial aid to families that had children. Other countries, such as the United Kingdom, saw family allowances as a device that would permit selective supplementation of wages as well as un-employment benefits for workers with children, without stimulating inflation or creating work disincentives.

The search for social solidarity motivated many countries, as they strove to do better by children after a devastating war that revealed widespread deprivation and killed many children and young people. In some eyes, the war demonstrated the need for all members of society to strive together rather than maintain earlier divisions. The solidarity theme was struck repeatedly in the early discussions of family benefits in Europe, even in a country like Sweden that had not been directly involved in the war. Heclo and Madsen (1987, 158) stress that more than in any other country, "social policy in Sweden acquired a tone of solidaristic equality: everyone should participate in the common enterprise of social distribution, and no one should be allowed to push ahead and take precedence over others."

Solidarity never became either a term in the lexicon or a guiding principle in the United States. The war touched only a relatively small proportion of the population. To the extent that considerations of social equity had an impact on reducing cleavages within the United States, it was the issue of race that demanded, and received, attention first—not class, income, or the presence of children.

In contrast to the situation after World War II, when the United States and Europe adopted very different social goals, in the 1960s all the industrial countries tackled the low-income/poverty problem (Abel-Smith and Townsend 1965, Questiaux and Fournier 1978, Lebel 1964, Liljestrom 1978). Where reducing poverty generally was the goal, as in the United States, less seems to have been done for children. Where child poverty became the issue, as in the United Kingdom, more was accomplished for children. Where child poverty was linked with the goal of "equalizing family burdens" by compensating parents for some of the economic costs of rearing children, as in France and Sweden, the most was accomplished for children.

While the Europeans were generally improving and upgrading family allowances and other family benefits in the 1960s and at the beginning of the 1970s, the United States tackled the unfinished business of its welfare state and moved on many fronts: Medicare and Medicaid; the Elementary and Secondary Education Act; indexation of Old Age Survivors' Insurance (OASI); federalized assistance for the aged, blind, and disabled through Supplemental Security Income (SSI)—to name the major ones.

Since the mid-1970s economic constraint has become an important issue in all the industrial countries. Yet none of the European countries has significantly reduced its support of family benefits, although some have stressed income testing and categorization as alternatives to large increases in universal benefits (and some have managed both). Even those countries that assigned more attention to families and children with special needs (including single-parent families) and targeted their strategies more sharply did so in the context of an existing base of universal family benefit coverage. In the United States, in contrast, tax policies in the 1970s and early 1980s increased the incentives for firms, especially large and medium-size firms, to offer more benefits to their employees by exempting such benefits from tax liability. Workers seeking to protect their income in a period of high inflation also were willing to take more of their compensation in fringe benefits, which often were not subject to the taxes on wages.

Perhaps most important, the greatest progress in achieving family benefits in other countries has been achieved when strong political support came from *both* Left and Right or when the party in support had a long history of entrenched power. In France and Sweden, for example, parties across the political spectrum have almost always favored doing more for children, even if they disagreed on the specifics. In France the Right may have stressed pronatalism while the Left pressed for vertical redistribution, but both agreed on the importance of horizontal redistribution as an essential component. In Sweden the political debate was not over whether to support family benefits, but over which of the parties was most generous. Even in West Germany, where there was a debate about child allowances and maternity legislation in the 1950s, basic support came from a combination of the Left, wanting to do more for low-income and single-parent families, and the Right (including strong support from the Catholic church), wanting to do more for traditional families. In the United States, in contrast, children have not been high on the public agenda of either major party since the beginning of this century.

CONCLUSIONS AND IMPLICATIONS

Family benefits are not uniform across countries, nor has their history since World War II been uniform. Americans who note with envy the readiness of some European countries to develop major societal supports for the cost of child rearing must observe, as well, that these benefits vary in number, type, and value. Moreover, in no country do they represent a gradual unfolding of a coherent design. Progress has been made in fits and starts, and there have been periods of neglect. The total construction may be elaborate and obviously significant, as in France and Sweden; or it may be more jerrybuilt, as in the United Kingdom, which also relies on an important national uniform means-tested program; or it may experience shifts in emphasis with changes in party control, as in post-War Germany.

Only in Sweden do family benefits appear to have maintained the same relative value as a percentage of family income (although not as a percentage of social expenditure) as when first established.

Nonetheless in France, as in Sweden, family benefits still constitute a significant child-related income supplement, especially for low- and middle-income families. Even in the United Kingdom, where the benefit has far less value, it still constitutes a nonstigmatized, modest supplement; and the income-tested benefit is valuable for many single mothers.

Over time, family benefits are indexed only in France, to prices. Some Swedish family benefits are indexed to prices; the basic universal benefit has not been indexed at all; the parent insurance is linked to wages. In West Germany the parties have shifted between use of the tax system as the major vehicle for the family benefit (to the advantage of traditional families and the middle class) and stress on family allowances (of value to less-advantaged groups). The British child allowance has not been indexed at all, nor have the other components of the British family benefit package. Taxes and transfers for children have been integrated in Sweden and the United Kingdom, but not in France.

Nonetheless, all the industrial countries have family allowance programs, and some have much more. These and other universal programs clearly reflect assessments and commitments that are very different from the major U.S. public assistance programs to which Americans must compare them. The contrasts justify the question, Why?

One explanation, offered in a voluminous literature, is that U.S. social policy dynamics are shaped by historical voluntarism. We referred earlier to the larger role of the market in the U.S. welfare mix.

Another explanation is U.S. federalism. Most of the European countries discussed here have unitary governments (and are smaller). But federalism cannot be an adequate explanation for our policy toward children. Austria, Australia, Canada, and West Germany are federal systems, and they have family allowances. Moreover, our own social insurance system is national and uniform, as is our "welfare" system for the aged, blind, and disabled (SSI) and food stamps. The U.S. readiness to federalize major programs for the elderly but not for children is part of the question, not the answer.

Modern industrial societies must get things done if the economy is to function and the polity to survive; whatever its traditions, the United States did transform itself in modern times to develop most of the institutions and programs that characterize all welfare states. Explanations other than the ones listed above are probably more potent in this particular domain and should focus specifically on variables central to the debates about family-related matters: church-state separation, ethnic and cultural diversity, and the importance of race in American society.

Objectives vary among European countries and within some countries over time, but all have stressed equalization of family burdens as an important goal—a goal that is seldom even discussed in the United States. In some of those countries, for example France, family benefits have been viewed as a device to compensate for the failure of wages to reflect family needs rather than as a form of social assistance. In other countries, such as Belgium and Italy, family benefits are still regarded as wage supplements. Parents become eligible for family allowances only if they are in the labor force or actively registered as unemployed; parents who are not in the labor force and do not have an employment record cannot receive family allowances for their children. France had a similar policy but changed it in 1978.

The requirement that there be at least one parent in the labor force for the family to qualify for family benefits characterized most of the European countries that established family allowances after World War II. Only since the 1960s in some of the northern countries, and since the 1970s in the others, has labor force attachment been eliminated as an eligibility criterion. The fact that this criterion still remains in effect in Belgium and Italy, however, is important for understanding the role of these benefits as a wage subsidy or wage supplement. Wage supplementation through family benefits has not been part of the U.S. discussion.

Pronatalism, another goal the United States has rejected, also played a role, especially in the early development of family benefits in France and Sweden and in France once again today. It is perhaps latent elsewhere as well. More recently, family policy has been shaped in Sweden and other countries by virtue of its role in implementing gender equity by providing social support (child care) and the benefits (parent insurance, advanced maintenance, child allowances, housing allowances, and training stipends) that facilitate women's participation in the work force, ease their childrearing responsibilities, and compensate through income supplementation for wage losses that occur when parenting responsibilities are primary (Myrdal 1971, Liljestrom 1978).

Unlike the Europeans, the United States has avoided family support activities that some groups in the pluralistic U.S. population would define as infringing on privacy or religious choice, others as favoring religious groups not their own, others as producing children to be supported by citizens who believe in having fewer children, still others as favoring the minority groups who have the highest birthrates.

American society has found symbols and values different from social solidarity and family policy around which to construct its unity. As others have noted, this country has chosen individualism as a central value. It has sustained its complex multicultural and multireligious diversity, and avoided value confrontations by separating church from state and keeping national government out of the family, unless it can define a particular family as dangerous or endangered. This is the land of incrementalism; we enact programs and policies without voting on or explicating values, and we try to avoid actions that create major value confrontations.

There are exceptions, of course, and some value topics are unavoidable. A modern society needs family law to deal with divorce, separation, support, foster care, adoption, guardianship, and inheritance. The United States leaves this important branch of family policy to the states, permitting maximum diversity. States, in turn, relegate much of it to local courts and administrative agencies, which are allowed considerable discretion. Much the same has been the case in the past with regard to family planning and abortion. More recent federal incursion into some of these fields through court and congressional action has generated tension and conflict—and has shown how difficult some of these topics can become.

Traditions notwithstanding, the United States may be approaching a time when some effort to improve the economic situation of children through public policies will seem desirable to a dominant majority. The work ethic has always been a central value in the United States. In contrast to many European countries, the United States continues to create jobs and to expect work and jobs to be available. Ambivalence about having large numbers of women, even mothers of young children, in the labor force seems to be rapidly diminishing. The United States may be ready to shift its family benefit paradigm and organize it around work, labor market policies, attention to the support systems women need to enable them to work outside the home, and to the gap between market wages and family needs, as well as enforcement of individual responsibility in the form of parental support obligations.

The sense of major transitions in the national economy has also resulted in new concern for "human capital." The demographic issues related to smaller youth cohorts entering the labor force, and the disproportionately large groups of minority youth in those cohorts, may also stimulate more widespread concern regarding the society's investment in children.

Americans may even become concerned, as Europeans are, with the general decline in family stability and childbearing (Wattenberg 1987, Moynihan 1986, Carlson 1986) and ask whether society has a stake in future generations and their well-being, whatever their race. But even if this is the case, the United States is unlikely to achieve great progress in the area unless it recognizes that the potential of both family and market source of income are limited with regard to the economic well-being of low-income families with children. A larger measure of direct or indirect public income transfers will be necessary, whether along the lines of some of the European programs or in unique American adaptations. Such a realization could place family benefit proposals once again on the U.S. agenda—perhaps with another rationale and a different name.

Notes

1. As used here, Rose means health care, education, income security, and housing, as well as nonmonetized personal services and food.

2. We have not cited in the text the specific documentation for the family benefit histories as reviewed for France, Sweden, the United Kingdom, and West Germany. Readers will have no difficulty identifying these items, if they wish to, among the references.

3. We acknowledge the help of Lynn Jacobsson, doctoral candidate at Columbia University School of Social Work, in the preparation of this section. She helped us immeasurably by obtaining Swedish material when she was in Sweden in the fall of 1986, and by reading, translating, and interpreting material to which we would not otherwise have had access.

References

Abel-Smith, Brian, and Peter Townsend. 1965. *The Poor and the Poorest.* London: G. Bell and Sons.

Allardt, Erik. 1986. "The Civic Conceptions of the Welfare State in Scan-

dinavia." In *The Welfare State East and West*, edited by Richard
Rose and Rei Sharitori. New York: Oxford University Press.

Ancelin, Jacqueline. 1985. "Family Policy and Social Change in France."
Social Change and Family Policies. Melbourne: Australian Institute
of Family Studies and International Union of Family Organizations.

Bell, Winifred. 1965. *Aid to Families with Dependent Children*. New York:
Columbia University Press.

Bradshaw, Jonathan, and David Piachaud. 1980. *Child Support in the
European Community*. London: Bedford Square Press.

Brazer, Harvey. 1968. "Tax Policy and Children's Allowances." In *Children's
Allowances and the Economic Welfare of Children*, edited by
Eveline M. Burns. New York: Citizen's Committee for Children of
New York, Inc.

Bremner, Robert H. 1970–71. *Children and Youth in America: A Documentary
History*. Vols. I and II. Cambridge, Mass.: Harvard University
Press.

Brown, Joan C. 1984. *Children in Social Security*. London: Policy Studies
Institute.

Burns, Eveline M. 1949. *The American Social Security System*. Boston:
Houghton Mifflin.

Burns, Eveline M., ed. 1968. *Children's Allowances and the Economic
Welfare of Children*. New York: Citizens' Committee for Children
of New York, Inc.

Carlson, Allan C. 1986. "What Happened to the Family Wage?" *Public
Interest* 83:3–17.

Caisse Nationale d'Allocation Familiale (CNAF). 1987. "Prestations Familiales
et Pauvreté." Paris: CNAF. Photocopy.

Ellingson, Lynn M. 1980. "Children's Allowances in the United Kingdom."
Social Security Bulletin 42, no. 12 (December):14–19.

Elmer, Ake. 1983. *Svensk Socialpolitik*. Lund, Sweden: Liberforlag.

Fournière, Jacques, and Nicole Questiaux. 1984. *Traité du Sociale*. 4th
edition. Paris: Dalloz.

Fragonard, Bertrand. 1985. "Le Système Français des Prestations Familiales"
and "L'Evolution du Système des Prestations Familiales." *Droit
Social. Regards sur les Prestations Familiales*. Numéro spécial 5
(May). Paris: CNAF.

Hartmann, Jurgen. 1985. "Social Policy in Sweden (1950–1980)." In *Social
Policy in Western Europe and the USA, 1950–1980*, edited by Roger
Girod, Patrick de Laubier, and Alan Gladstone. London: Macmillan.

Hatland, Aksel. 1986. *The Future of Norwegian Social Insurance*. Translated
for English edition by Sandra Hamilton et al. Oslo: Institute of
Applied Social Research.

Heclo, Hugh, and Henrik Madsen. 1987. *Policy and Politics in Sweden:
Principled Pragmatism*, chapter 4. Philadelphia: Temple University
Press.

Henderson, Charles R. 1904. *Modern Methods of Charity*. New York:
Macmillan.

Kahn, Alfred J., and Sheila B. Kamerman. 1983. *Income Transfers for Families with Children: An Eight-Country Study.* Philadelphia: Temple University Press.

———. 1987. *Child Care: Facing the Hard Choices.* Dover, Mass.: Auburn House.

———. 1988. *Child Support: From Debt Collectors to Social Policy.* Newbury Park, Calif.: Sage.

Kamerman, Sheila B., and Alfred J. Kahn. 1981. *Child Care, Family Benefits and Working Parents.* New York: Columbia University Press.

———. 1987a. *The Responsive Workplace; Employers and a Changing Labor Force.* New York: Columbia University Press.

Katz, Michael B. 1986. *In the Shadow of the Poorhouse.* New York: Basic Books.

Katzenstein, Peter J. 1987. *Policy and Politics in West Germany.* Philadelphia: Temple University Press.

Land, Hillary. 1975. "The Introduction of Family Allowances: An Act of Historic Justice." In *Change, Choice, and Conflict in Social Policy,* edited by Phoebe Hall, Hillary Land, Roy Parker, and Adrian Webb. London: Heinemann.

Langer-El Sempel, Ingrid. 1980. *Familienpolitik: Tendenzen, Chancen Notwendigkeiten.* Frankfurt am Main: Fischer Taschenbuch Verlag.

Laroque, Pierre. 1985. *La Politique Familiale en France Depuis 1945.* Commissariat Général au Plan. Paris: La Documentation Française.

Lebel, Roland. 1964. *Family Allowances: Developments in Family Allowances Legislation since 1953.* Geneva: International Social Security Association.

Leiby, James. 1978. *A History of Social Welfare and Social Work.* New York: Columbia University Press.

Liljestrom, Rita. 1978. "Sweden." In *Family Policy: Government and Families in Fourteen Countries,* edited by Sheila B. Kamerman and Alfred J. Kahn. New York: Columbia University Press.

Lindberg, Ingmar, and Soren Kindlund. 1983. "Sweden." In *Essays on Income Transfers in Eight Countries,* edited by Sheila B. Kamerman and Alfred J. Kahn. New York: Columbia University School of Social Work.

Lindblom, Paul. 1982. *Socialpolitiken Och Den Problematiska Valfarden.* Stockholm: Almquist and Wiksell.

Macnicol, John. 1980. *The Movement for Family Allowances, 1941–45: A Study in Social Policy Development.* London: Heinemann.

Michalsky, Helga. 1985. "The Politics of Social Policy." In *Policy and Politics in the Federal Republic of Germany,* edited by Klaus von Beyme and Manfield G. Schmidt. 58–81. New York: St. Martin's Press.

Moeller, Robert. 1986. "Women and the State in *Wirtschaftswunder:* Protecting Mothers and the Family in Post-World War II West Germany." Paper presented at Rutgers University. Photocopy.

Moynihan, Daniel Patrick. 1968. "Foreword to the Paperback Edition." In Alva Myrdal, *Nation and Family*. Cambridge, Mass.: Massachusetts Institute of Technology Press.

———. 1986. *Family and Nation*. Cambridge, Mass.: Harvard University Press.

Myrdal, Alva. 1941. *Nation and Family*. New York: Harper and Brothers.

———. 1971. *Towards Equality*. Report to the Swedish Social Democratic Party. Stockholm: Bokforlaget Prisma.

Organization for Economic Cooperation and Development (OECD). 1987. "The OECD Member Countries, 1987 edition." *OECD Observer*, no. 145 (April/May).

Patterson, James T. 1985. *America's Struggle Against Poverty*. Cambridge, Mass.: Harvard University Press.

President's Commission on Income Maintenance Programs, Ben W. Heineman, Chairman. 1969. *Poverty Amid Plenty*. Washington, D.C.

Questiaux, Nicole and Jacques Fournier. 1978. "France." In *Family Policy: Government and Families in Fourteen Countries*, edited by Sheila B. Kamerman and Alfred J. Kahn. New York: Columbia University Press.

Rose, Richard, and Rei Shiratori, eds. 1986. *The Welfare State East and West*. New York: Oxford University Press.

Rose, Richard. (forthcoming). "Welfare: The Public-Private Mix." In *Privatization and the Welfare State*, edited by Sheila B. Kamerman and Alfred J. Kahn. Princeton, N.J.: Princeton University Press.

Ruggles, Patricia. 1985. "Changes in Assistance Programs over Time: Are Income Support Programs Losing Their Sensitivity to Changes in Economic Circumstances?" Paper presented at Annual Research Conference, Association for Public Policy Analysis and Management. Washington, D.C. October 24, 1985.

Shlakman, Vera. 1970. *Children's Allowances*. New York: Citizens' Committee for Children of New York, Inc.

Steck, Philippe. 1985. "Les Prestations Familiales de 1946 à 1985: Ruptures ou Constance?" *Revue Française des Affaires Sociales*. Numéro spécial. Paris (July-September):63–99.

Steiner, Gilbert V. 1971. *The State of Welfare*. Washington, D.C.: Brookings Institution.

Steuerle, Eugene, and Paul Wilson. 1987. "The Earned Income Tax Credit." *Focus* (Institute for Research on Poverty, University of Wisconsin) 10 (Spring).

Teitelbaum, Michael S., and Jay M. Winter. 1985. *The Fear of Population Decline*. Orlando, Fla.: Academic Press.

United Nations Children's Emergency Fund. 1987. *The State of the World's Children*. New York: Oxford University Press.

U.S. Congress, House Committee on Ways and Means. 1985. *Children in Poverty*. Washington, D.C.

———. 1987. *Background Material and Data on Programs within the*

Jurisdiction of the Committee on Ways and Means. Washington, D.C.

Vadakin, James C. 1968. *Children, Poverty, and Family Allowances.* New York: Basic Books.

Wattenberg, Ben. 1987. The *Birth-Dearth.* New York: Pharos Books.

Wilensky, Harold L. 1975. *The Welfare State and Equality.* Berkeley, Calif.: University of California Press.

————. 1981. "Leftism, Catholicism, and Democratic Corporatism: The Role of Political Parties in Recent Welfare State Development." In *The Development of Welfare States in Europe and America,* edited by Peter Flora and Arnold J. Heidenheimer. New Brunswick, N.J.: Transaction Books.

Wilensky, Harold L., Gregory M. Luebbert, Susan R. Hahn, and Adrienne M. Jamieson. 1985. *Comparative Social Policy: Theories, Methods, Findings.* Berkeley, Cal.: Institute of International Studies.

Wilson, Dorothy. 1979. *The Welfare State in Sweden.* London: Heinemann.

Chapter Fifteen

GENERATIONAL POLITICS

Hugh Heclo

There has been a recent tendency to frame social welfare issues in terms of a growing political conflict between children and the elderly in a struggle for scarce resources. Although the United States may be particularly susceptible to this trend, there are important political reasons why policy choices probably will not, and most certainly should not, be framed in terms of young versus old. At least that is the thrust of the argument in the first section of this chapter.

The second section of the chapter focuses on a more profound, if slow-moving challenge to political management. Rather than a politics of trade-offs between dependent groups of young and old, the essential political problem in the years ahead will be to sustain a public understanding of the interdependence between generations of the working and of the nonworking. For a number of reasons, this emerging test of our social unity can be expected to grow between us—the working-age baby boomers—and our aging parents and, later, between us as the elderly and our grown children. Policy choices that will avert these dangers and reflect intergenerational bonds of mutual dependence and obligation are possible. Making such choices will, however, require greater feats of political leadership than have recently been the norm in the United States.

THE "NONPOLITICS" OF YOUNG VERSUS OLD

In a novel written recently by an American governor, the president of the United States is warned by his advisers in the year 2000:

Simply put, America's elderly have become an intolerable burden on the economic system and the younger generation's future. In the name of compassion for the elderly, we have handcuffed the young, mortgaged their future, and drastically limited their hopes and aspirations. . . . The biblical story of the prodigal son has been turned on its head: we now have the sad but true story of the "prodigal father." (Lamm 1985, 52–53)

Recent media headlines convey the basic rhetorical mood: "Young, Old Clash over Pace of Life in the Sun Belt" (*Pittsburgh Press*, May 15, 1984); "The Coming Conflict as We Soak the Young to Enrich the Old" (*Washington Post*, January 5, 1986); "Next: Young vs. Old?" *U.S. News and World Report*, November 5, 1984); "Justice Between Generations" (*Atlantic Monthly*, June 1985); and "Children and the Elderly in the U.S." (*Scientific American* 251, no. 6 [n.d.]). The orienting format of this book—a comparison of states of welfare between children and the elderly—is itself testimony to a felt need among at least some American policy experts to respond to charges of intergenerational inequity between the old and the young. Why else wear out the computer disks to make all these comparisons?

This volume is a vast compendium and comparison of material outcomes. Because certain outcomes exist, it is tempting to think that someone must have planned that they should be so. Politicians and other policymakers have an especially strong interest in portraying themselves as knowledgeable and in command of events—rather than, as is more often true, puzzled and wondering what will happen next. If we could examine all the complex history behind the outcomes described in the foregoing chapters of this book, we would probably find few that have been the result of broadly based, self-conscious political choices. Perhaps the most prominent example of such "big choices" about welfare outcomes occurs in the Scandinavian nations. A bundle of studies now exist suggesting that the political dominance of social democratic movements in these countries has played a large part in producing the more uniform distributions of material welfare described in earlier chapters, and deliberately so (Marklund 1982, Shalev 1983, Esping-Andersen 1985, Skocpol and Amenta 1986).

And yet the much more common situation in the United States and elsewhere is for these and other outcomes to have been produced by an unforeseen accumulation of programs and policy initiatives, as well as dimly perceived economic and social changes operating concurrently. Even in Sweden—that Scandinavian country where an egalitarian thrust has been most deliberate and unsparing—a close examination of policy developments reveals Social Democratic policymakers frequently engaged in a retrospective discovery of their intentions (Heclo and Madsen 1987). The general tendency seems clear. In the post-World War II period, there is almost no evidence that any country has framed its social policy choices in terms of the comparative well-being of children and the elderly, much less choices about children versus the elderly. The statistical outcomes discussed at length in this book have been more byproducts than designs. One searches the record in vain for an overall "politics" of youth/age dependency. Why should this be so?

The general answer is that such a politics is likely to be a losing proposition for anyone who would attempt to engage in it, whatever the country. A fuller account would have to recognize at least four pervasive factors. First, elected politicians under any circumstances have a strong incentive to promise benefits and to avoid discussion of unpleasant trade-offs. This is doubly true in the case of children and the elderly, for both these groups arouse immense public sympathy everywhere. Even expert policy analysts have great difficulty (as earlier chapters demonstrate) in drawing conclusions about states of well-being, much less deciding that the unmet needs of one group are greater or lesser than those of another group. In the end these experts must retreat to semiarbitrary rules of comparison—equivalence scales to standardize needs of different-sized families, income statistics as a measure of well-being, poverty lines, and so on. It is not surprising that politicians, who cannot hide their judgments behind such technicalities, shun any opportunity to make comparisons among these dependent groups.

Second, competition among client groups does not encourage policymakers to pursue such trade-offs. One noteworthy effect of creating modern social welfare programs has been the mobilization of beneficiary groups and (especially in the case of children) advocacy organizations devoted to their separate interests. Each benefits from a doctrine of mutual deterrence in the political arena—you don't attack the worthiness of my cause, and I won't attack yours. The same calculation is made by spending agencies within government, agencies that are themselves usually divided by client categories. Budget ministers in Organization for Economic Cooperation and Development (OECD) nations typically face a united front of silence as offices for children's affairs, elderly services, pensions, and all the rest make common cause in not attacking the merits of one another's programs.

A third reason there is no overarching politics of dependency is that so many different political issues are embedded in the seemingly simple demographic categories of young and old. Policies for the elderly or children are, in fact, bundles of different programs, each with its own subsystem politics. Two health care programs, one of which is for children and the other for elderly persons, probably have more in common than two children's programs, one of which is an income transfer and the other a health care program. The point can be expressed a little more systematically, and it seems to be applicable in a number of countries (Flora 1986). Whether for children or the elderly, *income transfer programs* appear especially prone to electoral counterbidding by party politicians (perhaps because such cash benefits can be widely distributed among voters, are easily understood, and are readily compared). By contrast, *social service programs* (health care delivery, early childhood development, and so on) fall more within a political logic that is played out among the bureaucratic and professional purveyors of these services and certifiers of the erstwhile needs. Those policies more closely associated with *labor market relationships* (unemployment and training programs, disability and accident insurance, vocational education, and so on) typically fall within the orbit of so-called corporatist policy making, where choices devolve to representatives of business, labor, and government.

These general tendencies, and they are surely crude ones, are crosscut by variations in government structure so as to produce still more complex political architectures in different countries. In the United States, for example, policies for the elderly are lodged more or less at the national level, whereas policies for children are lodged mainly in state and local government offices. Moreover, these localities, for various reasons of history, economics, and politics, tend to demonstrate diverse operative philosophies when it comes to social welfare programs (Smeeding 1984). Again, the point to be made is that since resources are not in the same pot, the politics of children and the elderly tend to be disconnected. To attempt to impose trade-offs would be a supremely daring political act.

There are, of course, certain overarching political frameworks affecting national social policies in different countries. These frameworks, however, are anchored in quite concrete, historically derived structures of social power, not in age groups. This is a final factor accounting for the nonpolitics of old versus young in most countries. In Western Europe such structures are essentially class-based political configurations. Strong unions, well-entrenched labor parties, enduring occupational demarcations, self-confident business and professional elites—these are the kinds of political forces that continually play across the landscape of European social politics and easily overshadow age-defined cleavages. On this last point the United States, with its more fluid and pluralistic framework is different. Lacking an overarching, class-based framework to inhibit it, might America be more prone to a demographically driven politics of age-group conflict?

THE AMERICAN WAY

One might imagine a continuum along which different nations could be arrayed, from the fairly pure, class-based motif of Scandinavian social democratic regimes, to the more complex mix of class- and occupation-based social programs (say, French social insurance or German health care), and further along the continuum to a country like Japan, where occupational rather than broad class divisions play the major role (Maruo 1986). It is possible to work one's way along this scale without ever encountering the United States. Of course, U.S. social welfare has an occupational component in the form of tax-subsidized employer benefits. Such occupationally based welfare has, however, been largely a policy afterthought, and it is only one of many disconnected features of whatever might be termed the American approach.

A well-worn but still serviceable way to characterize the American approach is to note that it is group-based, fragmented, and pragmatic. The groups in question have frequently been a crazy-quilt design of interests organized along all sorts of different dimensions. Obviously, race has been especially important in the United States. So, too, have ethnic and religious communities, which have, in turn, helped spawn an extensive nonprofit sector of voluntary social service agencies. Fragmented political jurisdictions have reinforced geographic divisions. The business and labor structures of American capitalism have usually served as headings for complex patterns of separate groups, as have the two major political parties and government itself.

This long-standing system of particularistic association has set its stamp on thinking and action regarding social welfare issues. Whereas Europeans are likely to talk about inequalities across the life cycle, especially with regard to class, Americans fall naturally into thinking about the elderly and children as more or less static, separate groups—and in fact almost immediately turn to dividing these into yet other groups of the "frisky elderly," the "old-old," and so on. It is probably no accident that the inspiration for this book comparing the well-being of age groups came from the American side of the ocean. We have a deeply ingrained tendency to define all welfare issues as a distributional problem among groups at a slice in time. Thinking about age cohorts as a distributional problem through stages of one life that we all share seems distinctly foreign.

Amid this pulling and hauling among mobilized groups in quite fragmented public and private structures, Americans remain skeptical of any grand ideological constructions applied to the constellation of social welfare programs that has grown over the years. Particular policies are put into place in order to "fix" (a singularly American expression) the pressing problems of the moment. And the meaning of fixing things that are somehow wrong in American society remains resolutely, not to say monotonously, the same over the years: to strike bargains among groups that enhance individual opportunity and self-sufficiency. This widespread sentiment translates into political routines for sorting through the multitude of potential welfare claims by different groups. Special favor is reserved for those who can claim benefits earned through contributions and other personal efforts. There is a long tradition in the United States—especially regarding "veterans' benefits" for noncombatants and their dependents—of stretching the notion of benefit entitlements based on past contributions.

In the post-World War II era, contributory social insurance and the massive redistribution buried in its esoteric formulas have enjoyed the same kind of protective coloration. Benefits are said, and popularly believed, to have been earned through individual payroll contributions. The popularity of this approach predates any major increase in the number of elderly, their voting power, or their lobbies.

The sorting through of group claims yields a second tier of social programs, programs for persons who must qualify for benefits by proving need without any presumptive linkage to the benefits they have "earned." It follows that these welfare programs, as they are labeled in the United States, are quite easily perceived as publicly supported indulgences for some groups of people who are getting something for nothing. That this yields second-class benefits and political vulnerability in these programs should come as no surprise.

These observations suggest that the United States is probably more prone than other nations to cast social issues in terms of competing group claims between children and the elderly. So far at least, the four general barriers identified earlier have been sufficient to prevent such a development from going beyond the rhetorical level. That is to say, politicians remain loath to make trade-offs between such dependent groups; the groups themselves have every incentive to avoid framing the issue in such a way; program politics cut across age distinctions; and the larger political framework—in the U.S. case, the dynamics of group politics itself—readily engulfs the two age cohorts. Thus in the mid-1980s a new group, Americans for Generational Equity, was founded to suggest ever so gently that perhaps some of the large volume of tax revenues flowing to the elderly could be better used elsewhere. Within two years, it was being countered by another new group, Generations United. This coalition of 70 national nonprofit organizations[1] seeks renewed government funding for programs of mutual interest to children and elderly persons, for example, Social Service Block Grants, access to health care for the uninsured, prevention of child and elderly abuse, and so on.

Of course, it is possible that Americans may yet talk themselves into thinking about social issues in terms of young versus old. In an already fragmented society such a framework would be especially unconstructive. It would divert political attention from disparities and unmet needs within age groups. It would help divide constituencies that often have a common stake. Above all, a politics of young versus old would reinforce an already strong tendency in America to define social welfare solely in terms of a competitive struggle for scarce resources and to ignore shared needs occurring in everyone's life cycle.

As earlier chapters suggest, the prevailing American approach yields important consequences for the well-being of children and the elderly, even though such results are only very indirectly related to deliberate political choices. The elderly as a whole enjoy, as children do not, a significant advantage by virtue of depending on a contributory social insurance program for pensions and health care. Although it is often overlooked that numbers of American children do benefit directly and indirectly from the Social Security program,[2] the general tendency is for education rather than income transfers to be the instrument of choice for dealing with children's needs. The consequence of having to rely mainly on the second-tier and much despised Aid for Families with Dependent Children (AFDC) system to cope with children's other, noneducational welfare needs shows up rather clearly in the statistics on child poverty in the United States.

Direct government programs are only one facet of a complex interrelationship with employment-based and interfamily provisions affecting individual well-being. The American emphasis on earned entitlements and self-sufficient individualism carries with it an abiding suspicion of public support for those who are presumably capable of working. While AFDC epitomizes that danger and preoccupies public and policymakers' attention, support for working but financially hard-pressed persons is a comparative afterthought.[3] Unlike the case in a number of other countries, American government generally avoids intervening to shape market outcomes in some socially preferred direction, such as in matters of job security, wage differentials, and broadly available labor market programs. Workers' material resources reflect quite variable market outcomes, including employer-based welfare provisions that leave large differentials and gaps in pension and health insurance coverage among members of the labor force.

These variations in occupational welfare provisions for working persons are, in turn, reflected in the comparatively large degree of inequality that earlier chapters discover among children and the elderly in the United States. Children's well-being rests heavily on being fortunate enough to be dependent on a parent with steady employment, good private health insurance coverage, access to adequate unemployment benefits, private retraining opportunities, and so on. Likewise, much of the variation in economic well-being among America's elderly today reflects their diverse access to occupational benefits and varying security of employment as working-age persons. Similar tendencies can certainly be found in other nations, but the American approach stands out for its limited attempt to influence the distribution of welfare in the market for labor. It is in the generational interdependencies tied to the labor market—and not some media-hyped competition between young and old—that the real challenge to American politics lies.

WHAT DO THE GENERATIONS OWE TO EACH OTHER?

Many political societies face problems associated with aging populations (although aging also represents a considerable improvement over the alternative). The United States may well have special difficulty coping with the problem, but it will not be because our demographic future is so much more troublesome than that of other nations. The age structure of the Swedish population today is about the same as the one U.S. policymakers will face 30 years from now.

And as earlier chapters show, both young and old Swedes experience little poverty.

My conclusion in this section is not that we should try to imitate a so-called advanced welfare state like Sweden; instead we will have to adapt our own traditions to meet the challenge. What we are facing is not a sudden problem to be quickly fixed but a slow motion crisis that will test our political skill and forbearance. America's difficulty in coping will arise because the demographic facts of life are overlaid by a political proclivity for short-term fixes, by internal social divisions, and by a growing willingness to live beyond our means in an already weak economy.

A Welfare State Laggard?

Liberal academics have a tradition of criticizing the United States as an incomplete, lagging, less-developed welfare state, compared with the nations of Western Europe; conservatives sometimes praise the United States on similar grounds. Much, of course, depends on how we choose to define terms. If being a "true" welfare state means having the kind of big-spending, egalitarian, universal, and comprehensive programs that prevail in Scandinavia, then without question the United States fails to measure up. Yet however congenial it might be to one's political preferences, it probably adds nothing to our understanding to expect a country such as the United States to behave like a continental enlargement of little Sweden. In a longer historical view, the term welfare state would seem most usefully applied to a quite varied—but widely shared—tendency occurring over the last one hundred years or so of political development. That tendency consists of a growing willingness to use government intervention to counter what are deemed to be "diswelfares" in people's lives associated with market economies or, more broadly, to put the imprint of human intention on social forces that were once unconsciously accepted as the natural order of things (Polanyi 1944, Hayek 1976).

Seen in this way, the welfare state becomes not some final destination against which the progress of U.S. social policy is to be measured, but a broad terrain with different pathways or political strategies. To simplify things, we might imagine three basic approaches:

□ Opportunity—a politics claiming to enhance individuals' chances to make their own way in the world;

□ Security—a political orientation to preserve living standards that have been attained and to cushion the collateral risks of individual failure; and

□ Solidarity—a political agenda to strengthen the mutual empathy and shared bonds of community among all citizens.

Of course, these positions are really shadings on a continuum that can apply at different times and in different policy areas within, as well as between, nations. In general terms, however, certain historical experiences and enduring configurations of power have surely inclined nations in particular directions. Scandinavian leaders, for example, can be found worrying that if their social programs lose their universal, "solidaristic" qualities, public tolerance for high taxation levels may be eroded; their American counterparts can just as frequently be heard arguing that more comprehensive, universal programs (health insurance, day care, job training—take your pick) are impossible because of the higher taxes that would be required. This is not the place to try to unravel the knotty question of why national approaches differ. They do. American social policy approaches can be found at the opportunity end of the spectrum, with forays into the more security-based pattern prevailing in much of Europe (when norms of individually earned entitlements and norms of deservedness are met). There is little inclination at all in the United States to strive toward the egalitarian solidarity espoused in northern Europe. Contrary to a famous formulation (Marshall 1965), there is scant evidence that different welfare states will follow some single route of progress from the antipoverty agenda of level 1 above, to the security-as-welfare position advanced at level 2, and on to the communitarian entitlements of social citizenship at level 3.

The American pattern is no less welfare state-ish than other paths. Its commitment to assuring opportunity can leverage large amounts of government intervention, often well beyond what can be found in Western Europe. One thinks of the pervasive role of American courts in social policy. (Where else has judicial interpretation been used to establish rights to community services and education for children of illegal aliens?) In addition, the emphasis on education in general and remedial interventions in particular to improve the functioning of the poor is particularly American (hence the steady stream of foreign visitors to study the work of Head Start, the Manpower Development and Research Corporation, and so on). Perhaps most important of all, Americans now seem to embrace the basic welfare-state premise that political means can and should be used to shape the distribution of well-being in society. When and how that should be done is, of course, a matter of some discussion. Still, the attention being given to the economic status of children and the elderly is itself testimony to the fact that in the United States, as elsewhere, the long-term trend has been to politicize the means of consumption in a manner that would have been unimaginable at the beginning of this century.

Sharing Burdens

Politicizing the means of consumption entails extending into the public household from the private household a potentially troublesome cleavage between persons who can earn the economic resources they need and persons who are dependent on them. Both the young and the elderly fall into the latter category; their well-being depends to a considerable extent on the understanding and forbearance of the working-age segment of the population. Such a relationship is of course expressed first within the particular family setting, but also increasingly nowadays in the public political arena as well— that is to say, in the politics of social policy.

What we are really talking about are the political prospects for sharing burdens across age groups and generations—what I will call generational politics.[4] Policymakers and others are surely correct in pointing out, as they conventionally do, that demographic changes such as an aging population throw down a gauntlet requiring choices. There are, after all, only so many resources to spread around among the different age groups at any one time. However, the generational political perspective asks us to think in terms broader than conventional, budget-like decisions of more for this group and less for that group at one moment in time. It invites us to think less about a time-slice distribution problem and more about time-flow distributions—choices for channeling resources among age groups that themselves age and that are in turn replaced. Unlike the politics of race or gender, generational politics covers a realm in which "we" eventually becomes "they"—the elderly—and in which "they"— our children and the yet unborn—become the "we" on which we will depend in our declining years.

As was noted at the outset, it is unlikely that the relevant political choices will take the form of an explicit trade-off between children and the elderly; rarely, in fact, will final distributions of well-being be attached directly to deliberate political choices. The more realistic question is this: What are the politically plausible choices that the United States—with its complex mix of group politics, pragmatic individualism, and deeply ingrained suspicion of universal welfare entitlements—is likely to back into during the years ahead? The mounting numbers of elderly Americans and of children in one-parent families suggest *what* general topics will be on the public mind, but they tell us little about *how* political agendas will react to the numbers. Unlike the rest of the animal kingdom, in self-conscious human political societies, demography is not destiny.

Contemporary political research suggests that the traditional political attachments that might once have helped to anchor relationships across the generations have been loosening. In the past two decades, most of the 15 demographically defined groups in party coalitions have become more detached in their party allegiances. At the same time voters' preferences have been increasingly more influenced by constantly changing issues than by party identification (Nie, Verba, and Petrocik 1979, Jennings and Niemi 1981, Petrocik 1981). In this more volatile context, two types of intergenerational burden sharing are worth further consideration—once we have recognized the "nonpolitics" likely to apply in the case of the elderly versus children.

■ *OUR PARENTS, OURSELVES*

The first dimension is burden sharing between today's elderly and the working-age population, between our parents and ourselves. The growing number of elderly in the United States constitute an important political force, and they make a large claim on public resources. Some have argued that their demand for government benefits is augmented by the support of middle-age workers, partly because such working-age persons prefer shifting the costs of supporting their parents to the public budget and partly because they anticipate sharing in the same higher pensions and other public benefits in the not-too-distant future.

The elegance of this political model is, however, marred by serious practical difficulties. Studies have shown that the power of the elderly as a voting bloc can easily be overestimated. In fact, the political participation of older persons does not appear to differ greatly from that of other age groups; and their voting behavior does not seem to be easily swayed by age-based appeals (Hudson and Strate 1985). Surveys also show that support for transfers to families with children and transfers to the elderly varies mainly with the income rather than the age of persons being interviewed. Indeed, low-income elderly Americans are more supportive of transfers to low-income families with children than are persons in almost any other age group, and the elderly as a whole do not demonstrate any uniquely strong tendency to favor increased social spending on older persons (Corcoran, Duncan, Ponza, and Groskind 1987). Similarly, the lobbying influence of senior citizen groups seems important mainly in terms of vetoing major cutbacks rather than actively shaping old age policies (Binstock 1985).

Apart from certain bread-and-butter issues—where, for example, elderly agree with nonelderly Americans that Social Security should not be scrapped nor promised cost-of-living increases denied—the elderly and their advocacy organizations are far from a self-conscious, monolithic force in pursuit of self-interested claims on the public budget. Nor should this fact be surprising, once we realize that "the elderly" is really a category created by policy analysts, pension officials, and mechanical models of interest group politics. It is not a category that many persons in late life seem to use to give meaning to their ageless and truer selves (Kaufman 1986).

The idea of middle-aged complicity with voracious senior power to expand benefits also suffers under closer examination. For one thing, such a prospective approach simply does not square with what we know about the retrospective quality of political decision making at the mass level (Fiorina 1981). Voters approaching retirement age, like the rest of voters, look backward rather than forward in their decisions to reward or to punish politicians. Moreover, the confidence with which working-age persons feel they can anticipate future Social Security benefits has apparently been decreasing (Harris 1981). If anything, such a situation should have the effect of undermining rather than enhancing their role as potential allies with today's elderly. On top of all this is a "supply effect" that necessarily runs counter to the potential power of a growing elderly population. Any increase in demands for benefits brought about by the mere numerical voting advantage of more old persons must reckon with the greater intensity with which a relatively smaller working-age population objects to paying the mounting costs of benefits to many persons who do not clearly need them (and perhaps some of the elderly agreeing).

Although more plausible than a joint generational raid on the Treasury, this notion of a turn toward worker-elderly conflict is not an imminent prospect. A number of factors are working against it. In the first place, the immediate future poses no demographic crunch for Social Security. (As we shall see later, the combination of an aging population and soaring health care costs does foreshadow a rapidly approaching crunch in Medicare.) The basic point here is that because of low fertility rates during the late 1920s and 1930s, the ratio of elderly persons to workers, which has risen continually since 1940, will actually remain stable for the next two decades or so, at a level of approximately one Social Security beneficiary to three working-age persons; it is after 2010 that the aged-to-worker ratio increases significantly.

Second, general political support for the concept of earned social insurance benefits clearly buffers the system from sudden reactions that might be predicted on the basis of strictly economic calculations. Between 1970 and 1986 Social Security benefits rose 46 percent in real terms, while wages and salaries for the working-age population fell 7 percent. And yet this situation did not produce a political backlash of any major dimensions. By the same token, Social Security taxes have risen sporadically from 2 percent on the first $3,000 of wages in 1937, to 11.4 percent of wages up to $39,500 by 1985, without apparently producing widespread resentment. Surveys in that latter year showed that two-thirds of young adults thought Social Security taxes were fair and that their level was about right or too low—even though most of these respondents lacked confidence in the future of the system when they might be retiring (Yankelovich, Skelly, and White 1985). Because the actuarial projection shows that these taxes will increase over the next 25 years to 12.4 percent of wages (up to $56,000) in 1985 dollars, the immediate political dangers to be navigated do not loom terribly large when compared with those of the recent past.

■ THE TROUBLE TO COME

The facts we have been talking about, overlaid by politicians' aversion to saying anything remotely controversial in this area, should not lull us into a false complacency about the political security of Social Security. To be sure, no immediate major conflict between working-age persons and the elderly seems to be at hand. But forces are at work that may well eventually produce a more slow motion version of the same intergenerational tension.

First is the problem of the disappearing windfall. It is a common observation—common among policy analysts, but not recipients—that past and current retirees have been receiving Social Security benefits far in excess of what they have ever contributed. This has been an enviable and inevitable result of being in on the early stages of a pay-as-you-go system, when more workers were being brought into the system and were paying payroll taxes to finance benefits for a relatively small number of beneficiaries. For example, persons retiring in the 1960s with average lifetime earnings had paid employee Social Security contributions (for old-age and survivor benefits) amounting to 5 percent to 10 percent of the value of the Social Security benefits they would receive. The remaining 95 percent to 90 percent of the public pension they received was a windfall. That windfall has been declining gradually for some time, and we are just now at the beginning of a period when the pace of its disappearance is going to accelerate. If this is true for average income earners, it is doubly true for higher-income groups. Figure 15.1 shows the situation for men and women with average and high incomes who retire at age 65 between 1960 and 2020. Clearly, we are entering a time when the return for higher-income earners will worsen significantly compared with the return for the typical worker. This is not to say that Social Security (given its inflation-proofed benefits, portability, support for surviving dependents, and so on) is necessarily a "bad deal" even for more affluent citizens. It is to suggest that the benefit bonanza that surely has helped make compulsory social insurance popular is now a steadily diminishing asset, especially for well-heeled Americans whose voices count for much in our political system.

At the same time a growing number of financial alternatives to Social Security are becoming available to more Americans, especially the affluent. Within the past 15 years the creation of Individual Retirement Accounts (IRAs), Keogh plans, and 401(k)/403(b) salary reduction schemes have vastly expanded the options of persons planning for retirement. Although the recent tax reform has imposed some modest income ceilings, the fact remains that these arrangements will continue to benefit mainly higher-income groups. Tax-subsidized employer pensions also have grown in importance and seem poised to further divide the constituencies concerned with old-age security. Thanks to employment shifts away from high- to low-coverage industries and declines in unionization, the expansion in private pension coverage has ceased—down from 56 percent of the work force in 1979 to 52 percent in 1983 (Andrews 1985). New retirees in upper-income groups now receive only a relatively small proportion of their total income from Social Security (as opposed to employer pensions and returns on assets), and this share can be expected to fall in the years ahead, given the 1983 introduction of income tax liability for those with more than $25,000 income a year. In the future, in firms where management has a large investment in

Figure 15.1   PROPORTION OF SOCIAL SECURITY BENEFITS PURCHASED BY
EMPLOYEE OASI TAXES

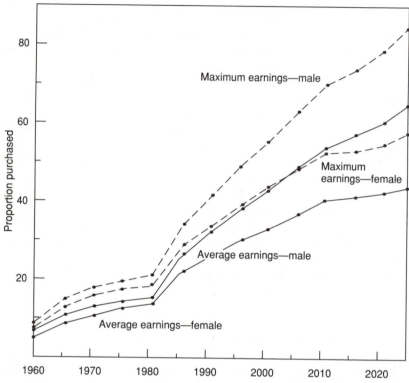

Source: Myers 1985.

Note: Taxes considered here are only those paid by the employee (because these represent direct, out-of-pocket costs to the worker for old-age and survivor benefits). In 1985, 5.2 percent of the total 7.05 percent employee tax rate was for such benefits, with 1.35 percent for hospital benefits and 0.5 percent for disability benefits. These taxes are valued by assuming to be accumulated up to age 65 at an interest rate equal to the average interest return on the Social Security trust fund (a low of 2¼ percent up to 1955 and a high of 13 percent in 1981–82) in the past and a future rate assumed in the annual Trustees Report (slightly over 6 percent after a transition period). Value of benefits after retirement is based on life expectancies and discounting at interest of 2 percent, given the benefit formulas of the law and maximum taxable earnings bases. Future earnings are assumed to rise in accordance with the assumptions in the Trustees Report. Figures shown are for "single" men and women because increasing numbers of spouses are drawers and will draw benefits on their own earnings record. For married couples where only one spouse has an earnings record, the figures for an average-earner couple range from 3.8 percent in 1960 to 31.3 percent in 2025; for maximum-earner couples, the figures are 4.8 percent in 1960 and 46.1 percent in 2025.

its employees and wants to reduce turnover, workers can expect to be enticed by generous employer benefit plans. Other Americans cannot expect that.

The result of all this is a not-unfamiliar paradox: government merrily advances policies with its right hand that tend to undermine the efforts of its left hand. In this case, the array of private provisions publicly encouraged through U.S. tax subsidies poses a double-edged threat to the political base of Social Security. As private options increasingly register among the elderly's resources, it becomes increasingly evident that a significant number of Social Security beneficiaries do not really need all of their public pension support. (The senior citizens' movement itself will undoubtedly and unwittingly further that tendency by stressing that age stereotypes conceal how many retirees are healthy, active, and productive.) For many working-age people as well as for some older persons themselves, the question will increasingly become: Why are our mounting payroll taxes being used to pay benefits to many persons who are very well-off indeed? The 1983 legislation to tax one-half of the Social Security benefits for recipients with more than $25,000 income was a first step in that direction, a provision now applicable to about 15 percent of the elderly population. Some believe that this was also a step away from the concept of an earned entitlement toward nondiscretionary, non-means-tested benefits.

Why they are paying higher payroll taxes to support well-off retirees is a question that working-age people can be expected to ask in the years ahead. Yet doing so adds the second edge to the threat. The more that privately organized resources encourage scaling back benefits to the better-off, the greater the incentive for more affluent persons to try to opt out of the less advantageous parts of the social insurance system. Every cost-conscious yuppie urging restraint in public benefits to Florida's RV set is also helping to diminish the eventual rate of return on his or her own payroll contributions. For the social insurance system, it is a form of cost consciousness that eats away at its own constituency.

At this point it is worth pausing to recognize the intergenerational bargain that has been struck with minimal public awareness in recent years. The 1983 Social Security reform represented an attempt not only to correct a short-term financial problem in the system, but also to prepare for the long-term shortfall that will occur as the baby boom generation reaches retirement age in the next century. The result is an implicit sort of social contract. The 1983 reform and related legislation protect all recent and current retirees from any major cutbacks and only gradually, as illustrated in figure 15.1, squeezed the windfall to soon-to-be-retirees. This hold-harmless condition[5] was no doubt politically essential to enacting any Social Security reform package.

In addition to obviously expressing the latent political power of today's elderly (advocates such as Florida Representative Claude Pepper made sure that the law of anticipated reactions was at work in Washington in 1983), this part of the contract had strong reasons of equity behind it. Reformers doubted that it would be fair to deal with the fiscal burdens looming when today's baby boomers retire by cutting benefits to older Americans, who in good faith have counted on a particular level of income support and who have few options to work or acquire private insurance coverage. However, it must also be said that the effect is a bargain protecting those who have already done quite well out of the system and expecting more from those—the younger segment of today's working-age population—who will necessarily do less well out of the fully matured program. In more technical terms, younger workers will (assuming continued economic growth) have higher real benefit levels than their parents or grandparents, but they will have lower relative wage-replacement rates.

Other parts of the implicit intergenerational bargain will be unfolding from now into the next century. From the year 2000 onward, the age for acquiring full Social Security benefits will gradually rise from the current 65 to 67 years. We have agreed, in effect, that the younger portions of today's working-age population should work longer than the generation now nearing retirement (another contribution to the disappearing windfall).

At the same time we have agreed not to ask our children to pay the much greater payroll tax that would be required to support the pensions going to our swollen ranks of baby boomers (the 75 million persons born between 1946 and 1964 and retiring after 2010). To implement this bargain, we have accelerated payroll tax increases (that would otherwise have occurred later) to 1988 and 1990. Social Security taxes will be rising from 5.7 percent to 6.2 percent of payroll for both workers' and employers' contributions. These increased taxes, when combined with the relatively small number of new retirees in the 1990s who were born in the Depression era, should generate enough revenues not only to pay for current benefits in those years, but also to build up a reserve fund totaling $7 trillion by 2015 (or $2.1 trillion at 1985 prices). Thereafter the fund will be drawn down to help pay for the retiring baby boomers' Social

Security bills. And yet, while the prospect of relief is offered to our youngest children and those yet unborn (those entering the work force after 2010), the situation is similar to the case of the higher retirement age. We have implicitly agreed that their older sisters and brothers who are now entering the labor force will pay higher payroll taxes all their lives than we, the work force's maturing generation, will have paid for most of ours.

The surplus fund is itself a politically problematic bargain. The combination of higher taxes, a smaller retirement cohort, and the last of the baby boom bulge entering the work force ensures that a sizable Social Security surplus will be accumulating over the next several decades. In more ways than one, it will be a fragile, paper surplus. To be of any real benefit to future taxpayers, such a fund would have to be used to increase the eventual size of the economic pie, thereby making it easier to raise any given amount of revenue than it otherwise would have been. This can happen only if the Social Security surplus (a type of forced public saving) results in higher overall domestic savings and productivity-enhancing investment than would otherwise occur. It cannot have this effect if the surplus is used simply to offset deficits in other federal accounts, whether explicitly or implicitly.

This offsetting—in earlier times it was known as eating the seedcorn—has already begun. Today's congressional budget projections show the federal deficit declining from $174 billion in 1987 to $169 billion in 1988 and down further to $162 billion in 1989. Good news? Only on the surface. The entire reduction in the deficit during these years is accounted for by applying the young and growing Social Security surplus to help balance general government finances. *Excluding* Social Security spending and taxes changes the federal deficit projections to $193 billion in 1987, $205 billion in 1988 and $208 billion in 1989 (U.S. Congress, CBO 1987, table II-2). The political beauty of offsetting the deficit with Social Security surpluses is that it leaves no fingerprints. As the surplus grows, it will be raided automatically through existing accounting procedures. No politician needs to step forward and make the case for doing so. To resist this temptation will, by contrast, take substantial political courage. It will require reasserting the original intentions behind the Social Security surplus and its bargain with the future against a host of forces that are mainly interested in consuming in the here and now.

If general deficit reduction does not supply sufficient temptation, there is a more specific problem on the horizon to threaten the

Social Security surplus. Medicare, one of Social Security's sister trust accounts, faces an inexorable and rapidly growing gap between revenues and expenditures beginning sometime in the 1990s. Under assumptions that are far from pessimistic, restoring financial equilibrium to the Medicare program will eventually require at least a doubling of taxes as currently projected or at least a halving of projected expenditures, or some combination of the two options (Holahan and Palmer 1987). This fiscal problem is actually larger then the disequilibrium in Social Security finances that prompted the 1983 pension reform. However, unlike the situation in 1983 there is a politically easy answer for Medicare: transferring surpluses from the Social Security fund. Working-age persons no doubt will be reluctant to see another boost in payroll taxes that will have already been taking more of their income. Reallocating the Social Security surplus will allow them to avoid higher taxes, or perhaps even allow a slight reduction, without cutting back on benefits to current retirees or Medicare claimants.

Of course, much depends on future projections of birthrates, economic growth, and so on. Precise results can be altered by varying technical assumptions. The main political points still stand. In the years ahead, we are going to be asking of our prime-age working population not inhuman sacrifices but a nontrivial degree of political understanding and discipline. In a context of growing opportunities for organizing private security packages, we are asking, especially of the large and politically powerful segment of affluent Americans, a good deal of forbearance when it comes to the "unearned" benefits of recent retirees and the dubious need of at least some elderly. We are asking for forbearance when it comes to a simultaneously growing reserve fund in a program that offers a poorer deal still for younger cohorts of the working population than we older working-age persons have allowed ourselves. And as the stories of a Social Security surplus grow in the 1990s, so, too, will resistance to ever higher payroll taxes in the Medicare account. The plain historical fact is that Americans have never been able to accrue a substantial surplus in Social Security without spending it in some combination of higher pensions, new types of benefits, and/or lower taxes.

Only if the economy grows exceptionally smoothly and fast enough for people to feel generous—that is to say, much faster than the stagnation besetting most workers' real earnings over the past 15 years, faster than the 2 percent real growth of the 1980s, and indeed as fast as the boom years of the 1960s—only then will we be likely to sidestep some politically difficult questions in the years ahead, questions such as these: Why are we transferring resources from young workers, regardless of ability to pay, to elderly persons, regardless of need? Why are we paying for the high, mainly unearned benefits to current retirees, raising our own taxes, and producing a surplus so that a more affluent future generation will not have to raise its taxes?

Of course, no one except economists sits down to calculate returns on payroll taxes, alternative investments, or real versus paper values of surplus reserves. Everything depends on underlying political perceptions and valuations. Similarly, whether the Social Security surplus functions as an intended reserve depends on the political meaning that is given to it and sustained. Forbearance is not an impossible outcome given serious efforts at building public understanding and political support for certain bargains. This is not what has happened. The record shows that serious public discussion about the generational deals being implicitly struck was the last thing that managers of the 1980s reforms to "save Social Security" wanted (Light 1985). Reform passed with the narrowest possible base of informed consent as to what the working-age population had decided to do to itself and others. As on many other occasions, U.S. policymakers had fixed a problem without creating a nationally understood policy. In short: smart politics, bad statecraft.

My conclusion is that we may be on our way toward a less constructive and more conflictual politics of burden sharing between the elderly and the working aged than the current wisdom about Social Security's popularity allows. It will not be a big-bang convulsion but an evolving crisis, as we move out of the 1980s and trends such as the disappearing windfall, private pension provision, distinctions among the elderly, higher payroll taxes, worsening Medicare finances, and a poorly understood surplus accumulate. We do not need to invoke the Scandinavian model. A certain degree of solidarity across the generations *is* what our existing policies now implicitly stipulate. The intergenerational bargain speaks to relations between today's retired elderly and the working elderly, between different groups of working-age persons, between today's working baby boomers and tomorrow's taxpayers. This *is* what is entailed in nationalizing the means of consumption in the public household when it comes to older Americans. And yet as noted earlier, the policy criteria of solidarity have never been a strong suit in the U.S. political system. Whatever policy might stipulate, the generations will owe something to each other only if they believe they do. Through the teaching function that politics can perform, there may be time to forestall the gathering pressures. I find it difficult, however, to see how any politician—given our free-wheeling, nonprogrammatic, nonparty allegiances—has a real incentive to try.

■ OUR CHILDREN, OURSELVES

In looking at things in this way, we are also foreseeing a gradual transformation by which "we" of working-age and "they" the elderly gradually become "we" the elderly and "they" our working-age children. This relationship with our children is the second dimension of generational burden sharing worth considering in greater detail.

As in the theory of voracious senior power, it is possible to imagine simple demographic arguments as to why the United States might be systematically disposed to underinvest in its children. They are a relatively smaller demographic group and a nonvoting constituency. A growing number of adults are childless, thus further shrinking the potential prochild constituency. And whereas everyone hopes to get older and is therefore a potential part of the seniors' constituency, no one expects to have to go through childhood again.

Arguments can, however, also be mustered on the other side. As the relative share of children in the population declines, the more scarce and precious those who are born may become. Changes in birth control technology and abortion laws during the past 20 years also suggest that a growing proportion of children appearing on the scene are truly wanted and therefore more valued; according to one analysis, 42 percent of the overall decline in fertility between 1973 and 1982 is due to the decline in unwanted children. Moreover, it is simply unrealistic to overlook the strong theme in American political culture that places special emphasis on investing in children in order to promote greater opportunity and the future well-being of the country. Without that subtext, much of the extraordinary history of American public education makes little sense (Katznelson and Wier 1985).

In practice, fundamental differences persist between the dependence of childhood and the dependence of old age, when it comes to prevailing conceptions of burden sharing across generations. During the course of this century, Americans have come to accept a substantial government takeover of what were formerly viewed as family responsibilities of grown children for their elderly parents. The proportion of adults saying that children should be financially responsible for their parents dropped from 50 percent in the mid-1950s to 10 percent by the mid-1970s. A similar change is probably under way with regard to services and home help for the elderly, as more working-age women undertake paid employment outside the home (Crystal 1982).

Nothing like that transformation has occurred concerning parental responsibility for children (Steiner 1976, Fischer 1977). The care and support of children remains first and foremost a private, family responsibility; thus there is strong public willingness to enforce the collection of child support from absent parents. By contrast, the few faint attempts to impose obligations on grown children for support of their parents in nursing homes and so on have been political nonstarters. Similarly, there is a marked preference for leaving state and local authorities closer to the people to deal with "family issues" (read children), whereas almost no one nowadays objects to the federal government's involvement in issues relating to the elderly.

These predispositions of a political and cultural nature, when combined with structural changes in the economy and society, help account for the widely documented disadvantages children face. Rather than a question of differences in numerical strength among groups of self-interested voters, the problem is one of political economy in the fullest sense of that term. What political custom expects, what economic relations encourage, and what children require are growing out of line with one another.

The contrasting expectations are clear enough. Elderly persons are expected, and they themselves expect, to live more or less independent lives (notwithstanding a heavy dependence on government programs). Children, of course, are not; they are expected to look to their parents for support. Economic relations also offer a contrasting pattern. Activity in the economic sphere takes at least some account of the costs associated with old age—for example, incentives for personal savings and asset formation, marketing of pension plans, deferred-wage employer benefits, and so on. However the economy takes no account of the costs of children in wage determination, and persons in their child-bearing years (necessarily the earlier, lower phase of their earning careers) are usually in a poor position to save for those costs. Poor mothers and children in one-parent families face the tension between demands of the economic market and of child rearing in especially stark form. For children in families of average economic circumstances, 15 years of stagnation in the growth of primary breadwinners' real after-tax earnings have made an employed wife's second income a greater necessity. Thus while children's expected contributions to elderly parents in later life have fallen, the immediate costs of child rearing (especially in terms of women's forgone earnings) have become substantial.[6] A traditional political rhetoric that insists that families must bear the entire financial burden of support for their children in this country is increasingly out of touch with reality.

And yet that tradition is itself part of the relevant reality. It must be accommodated. Any direct frontal assault in the form of universal children's cash allowances is unlikely. The question is: What more indirect approach to sharing the financial burdens of families with children seems politically workable? Just as the elderly and those of working age are not monolithic groups, neither are children and the policies relevant to their varying circumstances.

Social Security made political sense to many Americans, not because it directly challenged existing family relations, but because it could plausibly be portrayed as reinforcing established expectations—namely, helping people make provision for themselves so as not to become burdens on others. The current political and social setting offers some prospect for a similar strategy to emerge with regard to children's policy. If nationalizing income support to children is too threatening, we may alternatively be inching our way toward greater collective responsibility for the costs of various services associated with children. In an American setting this will certainly be a messier, more haphazard process than admirers of nationally uniform children's programs in Western Europe might care to see. The politically consequential groups are not children but women (on whom most children in or near poverty depend), education professionals, school bureaucracies, day care providers, and state and local politicians. The emerging theme is not that family responsibilities should be altered, but that certain collective provisions need to be improved to help family units continue to function.

Concrete expressions of this development are a political pastiche of differing program initiatives that cannot be covered in any depth here. The recently expanding role of government authorities to collect child support from absent parents is one example; a scant 20 years ago this "service" depended almost solely on the individual mother's resources to hire a lawyer, obtain a court order, and chase down the father. Another indicator at both federal and state levels is the greater ease with which it has been possible to acquire funding for child-oriented services (Head Start; supplemental food for Women, Infants, and Children; health care coverage for low-income mothers and children) than for more direct income transfer programs such as AFDC and food stamps. In almost all states laws on child abuse and neglect have been strengthened in recent years, and 38 states have established children's trust funds designed to finance services for preventing child abuse and neglect (Schwienhart and Koshel 1986). Similarly, through various state-level efforts at "welfare reform," we appear to be backing into developing a patchwork design of employment services, job training, and public day care for welfare recipients; so far, at least, the political approach has been not so much punitive as aimed at making the growing number of female-headed families economically viable (Gueron 1987).

As always, education remains the preferred American policy tool. Even during the much publicized budget austerity of the Reagan years, total national spending on education has gone up 15 percent, thanks mainly to state and local efforts. There are strong signs of a new political coalition emerging from the primal ooze of groups interested in programs for preschool children. Employed women searching for children's day care form one part of the coalition. So, too, do early childhood development advocates who can now lay before politicians at least some good evidence of the long-term cost effectiveness of investing in early education (Schwienhart and Koshel 1986). Long-standing hostility between child development/day care groups on the one hand, and school bureaucracies/teachers' groups on the other, may be diminishing as local settings find child care specialists working in the schools and schools sponsoring early child development and day care programs. The "excellence in schools" reform movement, which has concentrated on high schools, has had the spillover effect of sensitizing not only educators, but also a number of people in business and political circles, to the difficulty of helping older students who have fallen behind for want of investment in their early childhood education. Adding to the constituency is the growing number of parents with broken marriages who worry about their children's readiness for school and adjustment in school. Programs for "children at risk of school failure" will undoubtedly have a broader political appeal than earlier policies for "children below the poverty line." One sign of this emerging coalition is the fact that, whereas 8 states had early childhood education and day care programs costing approximately $150 million in 1984, 22 states had such programs costing double that and more on the drawing boards by 1986.

To repeat, we should not expect these trends to cumulate into a single, European-style system of children's programs. There are simply too many jurisdictions and too many groups and delivery systems serving particular clienteles (mothers' co-ops, for-profit day care businesses, churches, special education advocates, Head Start, Montessori practitioners, and on and on) to allow this to happen. What is more, this inching toward a children's policy is only a small, short-term contribution to the much larger issue of generational burden sharing.[7] In the longer term we will be dependent on our children for our well-being. Because we will depend heavily on what they can produce, ours or other people's children are far from a consumer luxury item. For what sort of politics have we been sowing the seeds when the time comes for our generation to turn to our children in their working years? How will they feel about us? Although highly speculative, it is an issue worth pondering. Here are my speculations toward a conclusion.

There is a good chance that we will be dependent on persons who have had little contact or understanding between their generation and the elderly. Of course, grandparents continue to play a role in children's lives, and programs deliberately designed to improve intergenerational contact do exist (Mothner 1985). And yet these efforts may be overwhelmed by larger social trends toward geographic dispersion given our huge continental scale, toward an increasingly self-contained youth culture, and toward more age-exclusive senior communities. Moreover, the growing instability in family structure works against long-term continuity in intergenerational ties, as our children see their parents and other relatives combining and then recombining into a series of different living arrangements.

At the same time we will probably depend on a more socially divided work force, a large portion of which will have quite limited capacities to produce economic surpluses to support our dependency. Debate still rages among experts on the issue of whether there is a trend under way to substitute low-paid service jobs for high-wage manufacturing employment. Both the number of jobs and real wages within the manufacturing sector have increased, at least since 1982; however, it is also true that low-paid jobs have accounted for an increasing portion of the new jobs being created in the 1980s. What does seem clear is that because of relatively lower birthrates among whites and because of the nature of immigration into the United States, nonwhite children will constitute a significantly greater proportion of tomorrow's potential labor force (Fullerton 1985). And these are precisely the same groups that figure so prominently in the current child poverty statistics recounted in this book. Even if no one can measure the precise long-term effects, it seems clear that today's child poverty is severely constricting the productive potential and future economic contributions of tomorrow's workers. How will they feel—how would we feel if we were they—about supporting the white elderly of tomorrow?

The same tendency toward a more sharply divided workforce will be reinforced as the more affluent segment of today's elderly bequeath their historically high levels of wealth to their children. There is growing evidence that persons entering the labor market are being more clearly divided between those with parents who have kept getting richer in old age (those, who have profited greatly from the past 20 years of appreciating housing values, have enjoyed generous private pension plans, have had surplus income to acquire tax-deferred savings, and so on) and those younger persons without such parents (those who are mainly dependent on Social Security) (Kuttner 1987). Without parental financial backing, this latter and larger segment of young adults finds it much more difficult to carry the student debt that has become increasingly important in acquiring higher education and the ticket to well-paying jobs with good employer benefits. They may also find it next to impossible to take the first step on the escalator of homeownership and the long-term equity this represents without parents who can help with the down payment.[8]

At the same time as we are countenancing the development of a work force with certain diminished capacities, we are piling on the debt our children will have to repay. The ballooning of the federal government's debt in the last seven years is only one instance of a more general phenomenon. During the 1980s the overall ratio of total debt to gross national product (GNP) in the United States has climbed to about one-quarter above its normal historical level. Essentially, we have been borrowing not to invest for the future but to live for the moment, with the inevitable result that workers of the future—our children—will have to use part of their resources to pay for our consumption. Between 1979 and 1986 the share of GNP going to personal consumption increased from 62.6 percent to 65.8 percent (U.S. Congress, CBO 1987). The share of GNP going to government at all levels also increased, from 19.1 percent to 20.4 percent. The share of our GNP going to private domestic investment remained unchanged. How could we spend more than 100 percent of GNP? Put another way, by 1986 we were spending domestically about 4 percent more than the value of what we produced. Becoming a net debtor nation to foreigners allowed us to make up that difference.

These debts are another part of our legacy to the future work force. Technical arguments about these numbers do not alter the message contained in their central tendency. Before in American history, adult generations have imposed major debts on their children as a consequence of fighting wars—their wartime sacrifices in return for the debt was another form of intergenerational burden sharing. We are the first generation of Americans to have imposed such debts on our children's future in order to enhance our own peacetime consumption.

It is, of course, only a personal speculation, sparked by a sense that we first-wave baby boomers cannot seem to stop gorging ourselves. Still, I contend that there has been a lingering sympathy in the body politic for today's elderly, those in our midst who sacrificed and prevailed through Depression and World War II. I doubt that the history our children write about us, and the political impulses they bring to our problems of dependency, will be quite so kind.

Notes

1. To give some flavor of the luxuriant organizational life in American social policy, one might note that this coalition's policy development work is cochaired by the Junior Leagues of America and the American Association of Retired Persons; its public relations is supervised by the National Education Association and the U.S. Center for Understanding Aging; and its state-level lobbying activities are organized by the United Way and the National Association of State Units on Aging.

2. Currently about 3.3 million children under age 18 receive Social Security benefits each month, generally as dependents of deceased or disabled workers. According to the Census Bureau, in 1982, 4.9 million children were living in a home where someone received Social Security (or railroad retirement) benefits. Children can also be said to benefit indirectly by virtue of their parents' social insurance protection against sudden income loss and in terms of the greater availability of family resources when grandparents can live more independently on Social Security benefits. The difficulty of calculating a value for these benefits is another indication of the superficiality involved in drawing conclusions about "generational inequity" from data on public expenditures on children and the elderly (Kingson, Hirshorn, and Cornman 1986).

3. Indicative of this tendency are the almost surreptitious development of low-income tax credits, the long-standing neglect of health insurance gaps in workers' coverage, the dismal record of government employment services, and the relative indifference of public policies to the day care needs of employed mothers who are not AFDC (that is, "welfare") recipients.

4. Given space limitations, I am lumping together several theoretically distinguishable concepts into the one term of "generational politics." Strictly speaking, a distributional

problem among age groups is not the same thing as the issue of what one generation might owe to future generations (Daniels 1983). Just like different age cohorts, present and future generations can be imagined to be in competition with each other for scarce resources. And yet there is a critical difference. Young age cohorts are eventually transformed into elderly age cohorts, but a current generation never becomes a future generation. The former perspective leads one into a life-cycle perspective of prudential self-interest; the latter perspective leads one into questions such as a just savings principle between present and future generations, questions that have recently attracted the increasing attention of political philosophers (Rawls 1971). I use the lumpy term *generational politics* because these two refinements have more in common than either has with the conventional vision of a static age group competition at some fixed moment in time.

5. To be more precise, a modest sacrifice was imposed by virtue of a one-time delay in a scheduled cost-of-living increase for current beneficiaries.

6. One estimate places the cost of caring for a child up to the age of 18 (in a middle-income family of four with the wife working part-time) at $82,000 in 1981 dollars (Espenshade 1984).

7. Despite expansions in funding, Head Start now reaches only 24 percent of the three- and four-year-olds living in poverty. In nursery schools the enrollment rate for three- and four-year-olds has been found to be 29 percent for families with annual incomes below $10,000 and 52 percent for families with annual incomes above $20,000. Similarly, despite their expansion, state programs for early childhood served only some 150,000 children in fiscal 1986; by comparison, the number of three- and four-year- olds living below the poverty line in 1983 was 1.7 million (Schwienhart and Koshel 1986).

8. According to Kuttner (1987), homeownership in the 1980s has increased slightly for persons over age 65, declined for 30- to 35-year-olds (from 59 percent in 1981 to 55 percent in 1985), and fallen most sharply among young families in their 20s with children (from 38 percent in 1980 to 30 percent in 1985).

References

Andrews, Emily. 1985. *The Changing Profile of Pensions in America.* Washington, D.C.: Employee Benefit Research Institute.

Binstock, Robert H. 1985. "The Oldest Old." *Milbank Memorial Fund Quarterly* 63, no. 2.

Corcoran, Mary, Greg J. Duncan, Michael Ponza, and Fred Groskind. 1987. "The Guns of Autumn: Age Differences in Support for Income Transfers to the Young and Old." Ann Arbor, Mich.: University of Michigan, Survey Research Center. Photocopy.

Crystal, Stephen. 1982. *America's Old Age Crisis.* New York: Basic Books.

Daniels, Norman. 1983. "Justice Between Age Groups," *Milbank Memorial Fund Quarterly* 61, no. 3.

Espenshade, Thomas J. 1984. *Investing in Children.* Washington, D.C.: The Urban Institute.

Esping-Andersen, Gosta. 1985. *Politics Against Markets*. Princeton, N.J.: Princeton University Press.

Fiorina, Morris. 1981. *Retrospective Voting in American National Elections*. New Haven Conn.: Yale University Press.

Fischer, David. 1977. *Growing Old in America*. New York: Oxford University Press.

Flora, Peter, ed. 1986. *Growth to Limits*. Berlin, West Germany: Walter de Gruyter and Co.

Fullerton, Howard N. Jr. 1985. "The 1995 Labor Force: BLS' Latest Projections." *Monthly Labor Review* (November).

Gueron, Judith. 1987. "Reforming Welfare with Work." Occasional Paper no. 2. Ford Foundation Project on Social Welfare and the American Future., New York: The Ford Foundation.

Harris, Louis, and Associates, Inc. 1981. *Aging in the Eighties*. Washington, D.C.: National Council on Aging.

Hayek, Friedrich A. 1976. *Law, Legislation and Liberty: The Mirage of Social Justice*. Chicago: University of Chicago Press.

Heclo, Hugh, and Henrick Madsen. 1987. *Policy and Politics in Sweden*. Philadelphia, Pa.: Temple University Press.

Holahan, John, and John L. Palmer. 1987. "Medicare's Fiscal Problems." Washington, D.C.: The Urban Institute. Photocopy.

Hudson, Robert B., and John Strate. 1985. "Aging and Political Systems." In *Handbook of Aging and the Social Sciences*, edited by Robert H. Binstock and Ethel Shanas. 2nd edition. New York: Van Nostrand Reinhold.

Jennings, M. Kent, and Richard G. Niemi. 1981. *Generations and Politics*. Princeton, N.J.: Princeton University Press.

Katznelson, Ira, and Margaret Wier. 1985. *Schooling for All*. New York: Basic Books.

Kaufman, Sharon R. 1986. *The Ageless Self*. Madison, Wis.: University of Wisconsin Press.

Kingson, Eric R., Barbara A. Hirshorn, and John M. Cornman. 1986. *Ties that Bind*. Cabin John, Md.: Seven Locks Press.

Kuttner, Robert. 1987. "The Patrimony Society." *New Republic* (May 11).

Lamm, Richard D. 1985. *Megatraumas: America in the Year 2000*. Boston, Mass.: Houghton Mifflin.

Light, Paul. 1985. *Artful Work*. New York: Random House.

Marklund, Staffan. 1982. *Capitalisms and Collective Income Protection*. Research Report No. 68. Umea, Sweden: University of Umea, Department of Sociology.

Marshall, T.H. 1965. *Class, Citizenship and Social Development*. New York: Anchor Books.

Maruo, Naomi. 1986. "The Development of the Welfare Mix in Japan." In *The Welfare State East and West*, edited by Richard Rose and Rei Shiratori. Oxford, U.K.: Oxford University Press.

Maxfield, Linda M., and Virginia P. Reno. 1985. "The Distribution of Income Sources of Recent Retirees." *Social Security Bulletin* 48 (January).

Mothner, Ira. 1985. *Children and Elders.* New York: Carnegie Corporation of New York.

Myers, Robert J. 1985. "Do Young People Get Their Money's Worth from Social Security?" New York: Study Group on Social Security. Photocopy.

Nie, Norman H., Sidney Verba, and John R. Petrocik. 1979. *The Changing American Voter.* Cambridge, Mass.: Harvard University Press.

Petrocik, John R.E. 1981. *Party Coalitions, Realignments and the Decline of the New Deal Party System.* Chicago: University of Chicago Press.

Polanyi, Karl. 1944. *The Great Transformation.* New York: Rinehart and Co.

Rawls, John. 1971. *A Theory of Justice.* Cambridge, Mass.: Harvard University Press.

Schwienhart, Lawrence J., and Jeffrey J. Koshel. 1986. "Policy Options for Preschool Programs." In *High/Scope Early Childhood Policy Papers.* Ypsilanti, Mich.: High Scope Educational Research Foundation.

Shalev, Michael. 1983. "The Social Democratic Model and Beyond." *Comparative Social Research* 6.

Skocpol, Theda, and Edwin Amenta. 1986. "States and Social Policies," *Annual Review of Sociology* 12.

Smeeding, Timothy. 1984. "Is the Safety Net Still Intact?" In *The Social Contract Revisited,* edited by D. Lee Bawden. Washington, D.C.: The Urban Institute.

Starr, Paul. 1988. "Social Security and the American Public Household." In *Social Security in Contemporary American Politics,* edited by Theodore R. Marmor and Jerry L. Mashaw. Princeton N.J.: Princeton University Press.

Steiner, Gilbert. 1976. *The Childrens' Cause.* Washington, D.C.: Brookings Institution.

U.S. Congress, Congressional Budget Office (CBO). 1987. *Economic and Budget Outlook.* Washington, D.C.

Yankelovich, Skelly, and White, Inc. 1985. A *Fifty-Year Report Card on the Social Security System: The Attitudes of the American Public.* Washington, D.C.: American Association of Retired Persons.

Chapter Sixteen

OUTCOMES, INTERPRETATIONS, AND POLICY IMPLICATIONS

Stephanie G. Gould and John L. Palmer

As Hugh Heclo observed in the preceding chapter, "the statistical outcomes discussed at length in this book have been more byproducts than designs." Certainly the single most startling outcome—the extent of poverty among American children, in comparison with the children of other highly developed societies—would confound the designers of our original social welfare policies. "Preserving the family life" was a major aim of the 1935 Social Security legislation; and knowledge of the prospect that, half a century later, an economically rational baby (as in the Rawlsian paradigm) would choose to be born into a Western European or Japanese family, rather than an American one, would probably have sent the drafters of that legislation back to the drawing board.

Indeed, we think the contents of this volume suggest a strong case for "back to the drawing board," although we do not propose to argue that case here. Nor does the volume provide the kind of policy analysis that would permit close evaluation of alternative policies. What it does provide is solid documentation of the outcomes that existing policies have, to a significant degree, served to shape. In this concluding chapter, we want to lodge those outcomes in a framework that will be conducive to constructive debate over policy alternatives. We should note at the outset that we do not believe the current framing of the debate in the popular press—in terms of "intergenerational equity"—serves a constructive purpose. To the contrary, as we discuss later.

In the first section of the chapter, we use the findings of the volume and other relevant studies to address in summary fashion two general questions: (1) how have children and the elderly been

We wish to thank the participants of the June 1987 conference in Luxembourg based on drafts of the chapters in this volume for helpful suggestions and discussion of what should be emphasized in this concluding chapter and especially Peter Gottschalk, Hugh Heclo, Timothy Smeeding, and Barbara B. Torrey for their detailed comments.

faring in the United States in material terms, and in comparison with the experience of children and elderly in other countries; and (2) of what importance have the economy, demographic changes, and public policies been in producing observed trends in well-being?[1] In the second section, we are concerned with assessing the social, economic, and political context in which American public policies toward children and the elderly are formulated. We attempt to explicate the intergenerational equity debate, because this is an important part of the context at the moment, and we identify those factors underlying the debate that are likely to constrain social policy making in the future. In the final section, we sketch out what, in light of the preceding, we see as the most fruitful directions for future policy.

SUMMARY OF SOCIAL OUTCOMES

When one distills the recent information in this volume and elsewhere on the changing material well-being of children and the aged in the United States and other industrial democracies, three big truths emerge: the economic experience of the two groups in the United States has diverged widely over the past fifteen years; children in the United States have much higher poverty rates than their counterparts in other countries with more or less equivalent overall standards of living; and both population groups in the United States are extremely heterogeneous in economic status.

The first two observations, which are borne out repeatedly in the aggregate data presented in this volume, call into serious question one of the basic tenets of New Deal–post-New Deal social policy making: namely, that poverty and relative economic disadvantage are primarily associated with aging. For much of the last fifty years, elderly people were viewed as—and in fact were—far more likely than other people to be poor; in addition to their higher poverty rates, their mean-income was significantly lower and income inequality among them, significantly greater. Although living standards for all age groups rose rapidly in the prosperous postwar years, age remained, until recently, correlated with relative economic deprivation.

But beginning in the early 1970s, a dramatic shift occurred in economic trends for the young and the old. The economic status of the aged continued to improve (albeit at a somewhat slower pace than over the previous twenty-five years), despite a more rapid reduction in their labor force participation. (The median real per capita income of the aged, for example, has risen—and their poverty rate declined—by well over 50 percent in the last twenty years.) In contrast, the status of children generally deteriorated, despite major increases in the labor force participation of women with children and a sharp decline in average family size. (Between 1973 and 1985, for example, the adjusted real income of all families with children declined by nearly 7 percent, while the poverty rate among children rose by 50 percent.) As a result of this recent wide divergence in the experience of the two populations, average income (adjusted for family size) and income inequality for families with children are now more or less on a par with those of the aged, and the poverty rate among children is now well above that of the aged. (By 1986 the poverty rate for children was 19.8 percent and for the aged 12.4 percent.)

The contrast in economic experience between the two groups does not appear to soften when we integrate, into the income picture sketched above, the other economic factors (wealth, tax burdens, and in-kind transfers) examined in this volume. In contrast to the aged and families without children, families with children realized little average gain in their financial wealth in the decade preceding 1984 and thus experienced a large loss in their relative share of overall wealth, with absolute losses incurring in the lower end of the distribution. Moreover, the total tax burden on families with children is both higher and, if anything, less progressive now than it was at the beginning of the 1970s, notwithstanding the federal income tax cut of 1981 and tax reform of 1986. Although both the elderly and children benefited from the substantial growth in in-kind transfers (especially health insurance) in the late 1960s and early 1970s, the growth was far greater for the elderly—and the cutbacks, in the early 1980s, far less severe. Tax burdens for the aged were generally lower than for families with children over this period, and this disparity has increased in recent years, since social insurance benefits (which are largely untaxed) became far more important to the economic status of the aged and payroll taxes (which the aged generally do not pay) accounted for the vast bulk of the general increase in overall tax burdens.

The net result of all these factors is that the aged made even greater gains in their economic status relative to children in many respects over the past fifteen to twenty years than is reflected in money income measures alone. In fact, one study found that in 1979 aged households were on average about 10 percent to 15 percent better off than all nonaged households (including those without children) on the basis of a "full income" estimate that adjusted for family size and composition and took considerable account of taxes, in-kind benefits, and certain aspects of wealth (Smeeding 1988). A similar estimate for the mid-1980s presumably would show an even greater difference, since nonaged households with children both have a lower average adjusted income than those without children and have lost considerable ground relative to the aged since 1979.

Such comparable data as are available for other industrial democracies underscore both the contrast in economic experience between elderly and children in the United States and the high level of income inequality prevailing within each age group. (We should recall, however, the cautions contained in chapters 2 and 10 concerning how much stock to put in adjusted income measures as indicators of the actual comparative well-being of disparate age groups both within and across various countries.) Whereas the mean income of the aged at the beginning of the 1980s was somewhat higher relative to the national mean in the United States than in the other countries considered in this volume, income equality among the aged was also higher, resulting in a poverty rate for the United States aged (of about 16 percent) that fell in the middle of the range of the other countries' aged poverty rates. Income inequality was similarly higher among families with children in the United States; but because the average income for these families was lower relative to the national mean in the United States than in the other countries, the poverty rate among children in the United States was much higher. At 17 percent in 1979, it was more than twice the average of the all other countries' and nearly double that of the highest European country (the United Kingdom).

When we look more closely at income inequality in the United States, it becomes clear that the economic status of American children and aged depends much less on age per se than it does on other demographic characteristics such as race and family composition, and exposure to certain events such as unemployment of a parent, divorce, illness, and death in the family. Poverty rates for various subgroups illustrate this truth most dramatically.

Although, for example, economic gains over the past forty years have been widespread among the aged, the economic status of white men has advanced more rapidly than that of minority men and of all women. As a result, poverty rates among all aged demographic subgroups are now far lower than they were several decades ago, but range even more widely—from a low of under 5 percent for white, married men to over 60 percent for older black women living alone. In general, the poverty rate for aged women is about three times that for aged men, that of blacks about three times that of whites (Hispanics are about double), and that of single aged persons about three times that of married aged persons. These different statistical outcomes reflect different vulnerabilities to life events. Women, for example, are likely to live longer than men and thus to exhaust their savings, experience the death of a spouse, or incur substantial medical or long-term care expenses, or all of these events. Minorities are more susceptible than whites to unemployment during their working years and consequently have less private means to cushion their retirement. And so on.

As among the aged, variations in economic well-being among children in the United States are considerable. Average adjusted income, net wealth and poverty rates range widely and systematically among children depending on whether or not there is an adult male in the household, the educational level achieved by the head of the household, and the number of siblings. Race and age of the head of household are also significant, though less important, independent factors in determining the economic well-being of children.[2] Poverty rates in 1986 ranged from a low of 9.8 percent for white children in two-parent families to 67.1 percent for black children in single-parent, female-headed families. In general, the poverty rate for children in female-headed families is roughly five times that of children in two-parent families, that of children living in a household where the head of household has no high school degree roughly four times that where the head has a postgraduate level of education, and that for children with four or more siblings roughly four times that for children who have only one or no siblings (Fuchs 1986).

Since wealth is distributed much more unequally than incomes, those families with children at the lower end of the income distribution, in general, and female-headed families with children, in particular, tend to have very little of it. Despite the modest overall gain in wealth among all families with children over the past several decades, the great and growing inequality in the distribution of this wealth led to a modest absolute decline in the value of wealth holdings of white female-headed families and a large absolute decline in those of all black families. By 1983 over half of all such families had virtually no net financial wealth.

Children also face very differing degrees of volatility in their economic status as they grow up—although they are much more likely than the aged to experience increases rather than declines, because their parents are generally passing through a stage of the life cycle during which their earnings and income typically rise. But numerous events can precipitate major declines in the economic status of children, the two most serious ones being long-term spells of unemployment for the family head (which are concentrated among families with initially low economic status) and separation of parents that is not soon followed by remarriage of the wife (since the majority of single women with children receive no support or alimony from the fathers). Both of these factors have contributed to what has to be one of the most distressing facets of the extreme heterogeneity of economic well-being among children: the extraordinarily high percentage of black children who not only experience poverty at some time during childhood, but for whom it becomes a way of life. For example, a full three-quarters of all black children who were under 5 years of age at the beginning of the 1970s were poor in at least one year of the decade, and for nearly half of these children poverty was a long-term condition. In contrast, white children in the same age cohort were only one-third as likely to experience poverty at all and only one-tenth as likely to experience long-term poverty. There is no reason to believe the situation for black children has improved in the 1980s; in fact, it has probably worsened.

What accounts for the deterioration in the economic status of American children in recent years? The evidence offered in this volume indicates that changes in demography, the economy, and public policies have all played a role; but the latter two have been far more important than demographic shifts, per se, in shaping the outcomes summarized above. In essence, both the economy and public policies have treated the aged far more generously than they have children over this time period.

For children, the critical factor has been the meager and unequal growth in earnings that has characterized the economy since the early 1970s. Earnings growth, or lack thereof, accounts for virtually all of the overall stagnation in the real incomes of families with children over the past fifteen years and much of the increase in inequality and poverty among this group. The remainder of the increase in poverty and inequality among children can be attributed to reductions in the antipoverty and equalizing effects of public policies since the mid-1970s, as the real value of per capita cash and in-kind transfers to the poor has declined and the overall tax system has become less progressive (Palmer 1987).

Contrary to popular belief, demographic change—in particular, the increasing number of female-headed families—does not appear to be a direct factor in the recent deterioration of the economic position of children (although it may have an indirect effect on earnings, as we note below). The rate of increase of female-headed families in fact slowed in the 1970s and 1980s relative to the 1960s, when children's economic well-being was rapidly advancing. Furthermore, what additional negative effects there were from this continuing change in family structure for adjusted family incomes were more than offset by positive effects of the sharp decline in family size since the 1960s.

While it is clear that changes in the pattern of earnings have been the critical factor in explaining trends in children's well-being since the early 1970s, the cause of these changes is a more speculative matter. Several explanations have been advanced. The generally slack labor markets and high unemployment rates experienced over most of this period have undoubtedly contributed substantially to both the overall stagnation and growing inequality. Two further reasons for the lack of overall growth in earnings are the slowdown in productivity growth since 1973 (itself not well understood) and the surge of new entrants (baby boomers and older married women) in the labor market. But, although it is easy to see how both the productivity slowdown and baby boom phenomenon could slow overall earnings' growth, these factors are not very helpful in explaining the increasing earnings inequality, which is occurring within as well as across all age cohorts.

Many people have speculated about the linkages between increased earnings inequality and various structural changes occurring in our economy; but for our purposes here it should suffice to note that in contrast to children, the aged have been largely insulated from the negative effects of the economy over the past fifteen years. They depended very little on current earnings at the beginning of this period and even less so more recently, and they have also benefited much more widely from public policies that became increasingly generous over the same time period. Also, the high real interest rates and appreciation in housing values that have been characteristic of the economy in recent years have been largely a boon to the aged, who were much more likely to own their own homes and to benefit from property income than younger adults.

But there can be no doubt that the Social Security program is the major reason for the continued advances in economic well-being made by the aged over the past several decades. The program has grown enormously in importance over the past three decades as a source of income to the aged, due to both the natural maturation of the program—as a rapidly increasing share of workers retired with extensive Social Security coverage—and to legislated benefit increases. This growth was particularly strong in the early 1970s as a result of several large across-the-board increases in benefits, coupled with the institution of an automatic cost-of-living adjustment mechanism that over-compensated new retirees for inflation (until it was adjusted at the end of the decade). And because of the tilt toward lower wage workers in Social Security's benefit formula, the program's great growth fueled not only the increases in average incomes for the aged but also the major reduction in overall inequality and poverty among the aged noted earlier. Of course, Social Security was given a sizable assist in these regards by other public programs, most notably Medicare and Medicaid, which also greatly expanded their assistance for the aged.

The prominent role of public policies in shaping the divergent trends in well-being among children and elderly is underscored by the comparisons of the U.S. data with data from the other countries documented in earlier chapters. The higher degree of overall pretax and pretransfer income inequality in the United States would lead to our poverty rates being higher among both children and the aged in comparison to those of other countries, everything else being equal. But our greater inequality is partially offset by our relatively high overall mean income level and, in any event, cannot explain the very substantial difference in the relative outcomes between the two groups. Neither can our relatively high percentage of female-headed families explain this difference. We share this demographic trait with several other countries that are among those with the lowest child poverty rates. Rather, it is clear our public policies have been far more successful in shielding the aged from poverty than they have children relative to other countries. In particular, the antipoverty effectiveness of our income-transfer system for children is low relative to that of other countries because of its highly categorical nature and general low levels of support. Why the aged should have fared on average so much better than children in our public hands and why this subject is only now coming to the fore as an "intergenerational equity" debate are the next topics of this chapter.

INTERPRETATIONS

The opening and closing lines of a 1986 U.S. News and World Report cover story, entitled "Those 24-Karat Golden Years—Can

They Last?" do a good job of capturing the amalgam of public concerns marshalled together in the service of "intergenerational equity:"

If the 1960s were dominated by youth, the 1980s belong to the older generation. Never before have America's elderly lived so long or been so prosperous. A massive government commitment over the past 20 years to ease the burden of aging has allowed the elderly to achieve a level of health and financial independence scarcely imaginable a generation ago. . . . But the very success of the nation's campaign to better the status of the elderly has a downside that may one day tarnish the golden agers' golden era. . . . Poverty among children has risen and many young men and women find it difficult to match the living standards of their parents. . . . As a result, tax revenues may not be enough to support the current level of benefits for a swelling elderly population. America's backbone of the middle class—and the middle aged—will be hard pressed to pass on a better life to their children. And the current generation of senior citizens may well be the last to know the golden age of growing old.

Two things are curious about this presentation of the issues. First, the opening lines would seem to be reporting on a public policy success—a government social policy that actually worked—which is surely no little cause to rejoice in this era of throw-up-your-hands social policy making. Yet by the end of the article, this very success is made to seem invidious, as if the necessary price of success in one area were failure in another. The second notable thing is the absence of any "gold standard" for the "golden age." The currency of well-being for today's elderly is all relative—to yesterday's or tomorrow's elderly, to today's and tomorrow's children and middle-aged. The article makes no effort to evaluate the well-being of American elderly against some absolute standard such as the poverty standard, or against some relatively absolute standard such as an accepted goal of federal policy, or even against some relatively less relative standard such as their peers in other countries.

We should note that we have not distorted the contents of the article by excerpting only from its beginning and end, nor have we selected an unrepresentative example of popular discussion of this issue. Most such discussions, we have found, imply acceptance of the same assumptions: that there is some kind of cause-effect relationship between federal policies toward one group (the aged) and the well-being of another (children); and that the two groups are sufficiently homogeneous in themselves, and similar in their requirements for well-being, that their claims on the public purse can be straightforwardly compared.

The latter assumption, at least, should have been effectively refuted by the contents of this volume. As we noted in the summary that precedes this discussion, both child and elderly populations in the United States are extremely heterogeneous—income inequality for both groups is in general much greater than prevails in other developed countries—and their particular needs for public support (education vs. nursing home care) are not easily compared. Although it is clear that the elderly benefit more than do children from our federal social policies, it is not at all clear that children's doing worse has enabled the elderly to do better: our poverty rates for the elderly remain on the high side among industrial nations. All we can conclude from this kind of data is that, for a variety of reasons (some of which are touched on below), the United States has been willing to tolerate a much higher degree of economic inequality among its population than have other developed countries and that that tolerance has come to encompass such a large amount of poverty among the American child population as to trigger a number of alarm bells—now ringing in the intergenerational equity debate. Comparative data of the sort examined in this volume have really nothing to say about whether we should be more concerned for a poor young person than for a poor old one; it only documents that we have more of the former than the latter.

For purposes of the policy concerns of this chapter, it is the assumption about tradeoffs in federal policies for children and the elderly that needs to be addressed. Heclo's chapter has already given us ample reason to doubt that the intergenerational equity framework will become the basis for future political decision making in the social policy arena; but the chapter has also given us ample cause for concern that the policy-making process will be fraught with much more intergenerational tension than was true in the past. We suggest here that one important source of tension is a lack of clarity, in both the policy-making process itself and in public understanding of the process, about the multiple concerns to which social policies respond. That is, we view the intergenerational equity framework as lumping together and obscuring many different strands of policy concerns in such a way as to encourage "us-vs.-them" thinking, and we conclude that, if these strands could be untwined in public discussion, some of the tension could be diffused.

While it is obviously beyond the scope of this chapter (or our abilities) to explicate all the factors at play in social policy making, we think the following simple questions do a fair job of reflecting the range of concerns that social policy should address:

□ What do we, as a public, need to do for dependent populations? (What are the particular needs of all of us at different stages of life for extra-familial support and to what extent does our public philosophy or sense of collective purpose imply an obligation to meet these particular needs through public means?)

□ What can we afford to spend on social policies? (What will the effect of different levels and kinds of spending be on public budgets and our economy?)

□ What are we willing to spend? (To what extent are we willing to forgo our own current consumption to serve the interests of dependent populations?)

Obviously, answers to these questions are not independent of one another: our willingness to tax ourselves to support dependent populations will reflect our sense of both obligation and affordability; judgments about what we can economically afford to do will condition our sense of obligation, and so on. Also, judgments about these matters will vary from time to time and place to place. Access to a minister, for example, was regarded as a taxworthy social necessity in Puritan New England, but not so, then, in Virginia and not so, in general, today.

Finally, we must note that, although the questions may seem commonplace and logically linked, they are rarely concurrently addressed in the American political process. Policy analysts and interest group advocates diagnose social needs; economists evaluate the costs and benefits of programs; and opinion pollsters assess public receptivity to taxation. Politicians are left to put all these inputs together, willy nilly, into social policy. Although this is certainly a slapdash characterization of American political decision making, we think the essential point is unexceptionable. As Harold Willensky has observed, in the United States there is little integration of social and economic policy: their interdependence is obscured not only among policymakers but among policy analysts who shape academic and public discussion of failures and successes (Wilensky amd Turner 1987).

Nevertheless, judgments about all three questions are embedded in the actual allocation of public resources that occurs under the rubric of "social policy." As long as that allocation takes place in some kind of political harmony (as it has through much of our postwar history), disaggregating the questions and answers can remain an activity of largely academic interest. But when, as now, the allocation of resources becomes a subject of serious public dispute, failure to articulate the issues clearly can further the fragmentation of political interests.

Just such a fragmentation appears to have developed in the current public debate over intergenerational equity. In this debate the always precarious balance between principled concerns for private and collective good has tilted in an ominously personal direction. Legitimate concerns about the responsiveness of existing policies to actual need—both of dependent groups and of society as a whole— have translated into personal fears of a breakdown in the social compact: "Will tomorrow's working generation feel the same obligation to support me as a dependent as I feel to support dependents today?" Legitimate concerns about the prospects for economic growth have raised personal doubts about the availability of resources in the future to meet obligations incurred under current policies: "Will the economy be strong enough in the future to permit levels of public support for me and my children's children comparable to the levels enjoyed by dependent groups today?" And, finally, the willingness of current and future workers to pay the cost of existing social policies has been called into question by the breakdown of the insurance "fiction" upon which political support for social programs has been premised: "Will I get a fair return on what I have contributed to the system?"

The bulk of this volume has been devoted to shedding light on the first topic: the actual differences in dependency between the young and the old in the United States and the differential responsiveness of public policies toward these populations in the United States and other industrial countries. In the remainder of this section, we first speculate briefly about reasons for the differences—that is, about why the United states might have a distinctive policy orientation toward children and the elderly. We then briefly examine current wisdom about the other two dimensions of social policy concern noted above: the affordability of social programs and the willingness of the American public to tax themselves for social purposes. In covering these last two subjects, we do not pretend to do justice to the range of professional and academic thinking in these areas, but only to identify those strands of thought that seem likely to contribute to a resolution of the intergenerational equity debate.

American Orientation Toward Social Welfare Policy

Numerous writers have speculated about why the United States, relative to other wealthy industrial countries, accepts such a limited public obligation to meet the needs of dependent populations—that is, why we spend so relatively little of our GNP on social welfare policies. Various explanations have been adduced for this American "exceptionalism," including:

□ decentralization of governmental functions, which means (among other things) that the taxing power of the federal government will be limited; the accumulation of administrative and substantive expertise in the social program arena will be inhibited; and uniformity of social policy treatment of different populations will not be highly valued
□ relative weakness of labor movements and fragmentation of working class interests, which means that no strong and coherent political force has coalesced around a social welfare agenda
□ high levels of economic growth compared to the rest of the developed world, which meant that through much of this century, high absolute levels of social welfare could be provided with relatively low tax effort
□ relative lateness of our entry into the ranks of the welfare state
□ perceived need for a high level of military expenditures
□ strong tradition of voluntaristic provision of public support
□ well-developed private marketplace for satisfaction of individual needs
□ heterogeneity of population, which (among other things) inhibits consensus on priorities in social welfare needs
□ a public philosophy that weights "opportunity" and individual "self-sufficiency" much more heavily than "equality" and "collective good"

We cannot here attempt to evaluate the contributions of these various facets of American public life to the current well-being of different segments of the American population. All we can do is note that, among all the peculiarities of American society noted above, only the last two—heterogeneity of population and distinctiveness of public philosophy—seem to have explanatory power for the results noted in this volume. We can find neither intuitive nor empirical reasons for supposing that any of the other phenomena operate selectively on American perceptions of the need for social spending. That is, all together these phenomena may add up to restraint on American susceptibility to a sense of public obligation, but they do not explain why public obligation might be more accepted in one area—for the elderly—and less in another—for children.

With regard to population heterogeneity, we can find both empirical and intuitive reasons for supposing that this factor exerts a strong influence on American support for child-oriented welfare policies.[3] Empirically, we note that, although child poverty (posttax and posttransfer) is much higher in the United States than in any of the other countries (except Australia) examined in this volume, the U.S. poverty figures are closest to those of the more heterogeneous countries—Canada, the United Kingdom, and Australia.[4] As regards the share of resources (GNP) devoted to social welfare purposes in general, only Japan spends substantially less, relatively speaking, than the United States. But the low level of Japanese public support for social welfare is more than offset by higher economic growth and by the much greater—indeed, extraordinary, even by the standards of the most homogeneous European societies—social coherence of the Japanese population. Japanese society has virtually none of the racial, ethnic, and religious diversity so characteristic of the United States in particular and Western society more generally. It also has much less of the cultural diversity: that is, income differentials are smaller, historical antagonisms among groups less widespread, and family integrity broadly shared. Thus, as Kono and Preston note in this volume, Japanese children have shared quite equally in the growth of the Japanese economy, and poverty among Japanese children is negligible.

The point we are making here is that pluralism of population is conducive to neither pretax nor posttax equality of economic circumstance, and that, in a pluralistic society, income inequality is going to be reflected more strongly among children than among the aged. To argue this point more conclusively and empirically, we would like to have a wealth of comparable data not available in this volume (or, as far as we know, anywhere): that is, we would like to know how the United States compares with other countries in terms of racial, ethnic, and religious mix, percentage of foreign-born, and annual immigration as a percentage of current population. Without such data, we can only assert the accord of intuition with the empirical observations noted above. We can only note that the more heterogeneous societies seem to experience more income inequality, and we can observe the logic of this: a heterogeneous population is likely to experience extreme variations in earning capacities, not just for social reasons (discrimination, differences in educational background, linguistic problems and the like, for example) but also because of a constant influx of new poor populations. At the same time, such a society is likely to encounter great difficulty in reaching consensus on public policies to address the problems caused by income inequality. Historic racial and ethnic antagonisms, differing values, lifestyles, and political traditions—in short, all the factors that add up to the notion of heterogeneity—will serve to impede consensus.

It is not intuitively surprising, then, that in a heterogeneous society like ours the claims of children on the public purse would be weighed less heavily than those of the elderly. The elderly, after all, have presumably lived among us for some time, paid their dues to our social insurance system, and become Americanized in some way. Also, they are certainly not going to further the heterogeneity problem by making more people like themselves. But children will be viewed through the lens of their parents, with whom the typical American taxpayer may find little ground for identification. With the major exception of public education, most public benefits for children (income, housing, food stamps) must pass through parents, who are, presumably, able-bodied adults (the ability to beget children creating a fair presumption of an able body). For a number of reasons in addition to the heterogeneity argument advanced here, Americans have historically been wary of transferring public resources to able-bodied adults. This wariness was reflected in the categories of beneficiaries identified as deserving of public assistance in the original Social Security legislation: the aged, blind, disabled, widowed, orphaned, and involuntarily unemployed. All of these are categories which any American might see him or herself falling into by accident of circumstances. But the parents of today's impoverished children do not generally fit into categories with which an average taxpayer might identify his or her own fate: these parents are drawn disproportionately from minority groups, unmarried teenagers, and chronically unemployed adults.

None of these observations should encourage conclusions about an anti-child bias or indifference to child interests among the American populace. To the contrary, in the one public policy arena devoted predominantly to child interests—education—Americans have historically shown themselves far more generous than either Europeans or Japanese in the allocation of public resources. In the context of this discussion of American heterogeneity, the reasons for American enthusiasm for public education seems logical: it is the one public arena in which the issue of the heterogeneity of parents can be bypassed on a local level in some significant way and it is the one "child policy" holding a promise of promoting homogeneity. That American leadership in, and support for, public education should appear to have broken down in recent years also seems logical; as American schools have been compelled to assume more and more general functions of social assimilation (sex and drug education, racial integration, basic social discipline), the confidence in education as a homogenizing force has been eroded.

The American preference for funneling public resources to children through school systems rather than through parents reflects as much the distinctiveness of our public philosophy as it does the heterogeneity of our population. From de Tocqueville through the present, observers of our national life (including Heclo in this volume) have remarked on the peculiarities of the American outlook on public affairs: our extreme emphasis on individualism, our mistrust of central authority, our strong preference for public policies that promote equality of opportunity over those that promote equality of outcome, and our taste for pragmatism and distaste for ideology in political decision making. Without elaborating on all the ramifications of this public philosophy for our social policy making, we would just like to note the complementarity of philosophy and demography in shaping our policies toward children and elderly. Americans observe themselves to be, in fact, very different from their neighbors, and their public philosophy encourages them to remain so. For all the old talk about an "American melting pot" (or the new talk about a "community of hearts" or a "family of Americans"), the reality of the American political tradition celebrates diversity. It is inconceivable, for example, that Americans would embrace the social solidarity and intergenerational equity logic of the Japanese rationale for social insurance reform (as explicated in chapter 11).

Finally, we want to note that the pragmatic strain in American thought and actual American experience in social policy making seem to have been mutually reinforcing in many areas of concern about children and the elderly. We—that is, Americans—do not seem to know what to do, publicly, to arrest the disintegration of our very heterogeneous family population, and what we do do for families—for example, the Aid to Families with Dependent Children (AFDC) program—is seen by many as aggravating the problem. On the other hand, we do seem to understand the problems of our (presumably, as discussed above, more socially assimilated) elderly population—that is, reduced income potential and increased health care needs—and what we do for them seems to work.

In sum, social solidarity as a rationale for policy making has simply gained no purchase on American philosophical soil. If we may be forgiven an overextended metapahor: the American melting pot has produced a stew, not a puree, both because stew ingredients were the ones on hand and because a stew was what the recipe called for. The differential social welfare outcomes for children and the elderly documented in this volume may not be the products of design, but neither can they be regarded as accidental.

Social Policy and Economic Concerns

The issue of the affordability of public spending for social purposes has two distinct but related dimensions. The first, more abstract, involves the concern that excessive social spending will be harmful to our economic health—in particular to long-run economic growth. The second dimension, quite concrete, involves the specifics of our current and prospective budgetary health and commitments: What are the implications for other public spending and tax burdens of sustaining or altering our current social policies? As we discuss below, the budgetary picture depends very much on the future course of the economy, in general, and health care cost inflation, in particular, whereas there is no necessary linkage between the amount of public spending for social purposes (within the range likely for the United States) and future economic growth.

   In thinking about these two issues, we need to keep in mind some basic facts about public spending for social welfare purposes in the United States. Total public social spending currently runs about 20 percent of our Gross National Product (GNP), and about 60 percent of total public spending. Both of these percentages have more than doubled over the past thirty years. (Most of this change took place in the first two decades, as both of these measures have been relatively stable since 1976.) Even so, the United States ranks quite low on both of these measures relative to other Western industrial democracies, as we have a rather distinctive notion of what is publicly affordable in general, and attach a lower priority to social welfare spending within our relatively smaller public sector.

   This public social spending in the United States is distributed by program areas (as a percentage of GNP) roughly 7 percent cash assistance, 5 percent each for education and health, and 3 percent for the remainder (essentially food, housing and social services). The vast bulk of the total goes to the aged (through such programs as Social Security, Medicare, Supplemental Security Income [SSI], and nursing home care under Medicaid) and to children (predominantly elementary and secondary education) or families with chil-

dren (through AFDC, food stamps, acute care under Medicaid)—
with the aged receiving about twice as much in the aggregate and
four times as much per capita as children. Due to the dominant size
of Social Security and Medicare, over three-fifths of total spending
for social welfare purposes—and an even larger share of that for the
aged—is carried out by the federal government. The major program
area at the state and local levels is education.

Just what impact on the economy has this social spending had or
would a further expansion of it have? There seems to be a widespread
perception, at least among many policy makers and business leaders,
that increased social spending and the taxes to pay for it must
necessarily mean a large net loss of economic efficiency. The opinions
of economists are divided on this issue, as on many others. However,
the most recent comprehensive study of the subject, based on a
survey of much of the recent relevant economic literature, concluded
that "the majority view [of economists] is sharply at variance with
the conventional wisdom . . ." (Lampman 1985).[5]

Both current theory and evidence suggest that the effects on
economic growth of social spending and the taxes to support it
can be either positive or negative, but, in any event, are likely to
be modest. Moreover, the impact on such things as work effort,
savings rates and (therefore) the size of the physical capital stock,
and the quality of the labor force—the three major avenues of
impact on economic growth—depend much more on the specifics
of what the money is spent on and on the design of particular
spending and taxing programs than on their aggregate level.
For this reason cross-national studies of various industrial democracies (whose social spending ranged from as little as 13 percent
to as much as 38 percent of their respective GNPs in the early
1980s) consistently fail to show any relationship between levels or
rates of increase in social spending and rates of economic growth
among countries. (For example, in comparison to the United States,
most Western European countries both started out at higher level of
social spending in the early 1960s, increased this spending at a
faster rate over the next fifteen years, and experienced a faster rate
of economic growth over this period.) The best empirical estimate
of the effects of the post-World War II doubling in public spending
for social purposes in the United States shows a negligible overall
impact on the rate of economic growth (Lampman 1985). The specific
changes in social spending and taxes had no measurable impact on
the savings rate, and the modest negative effects on work effort of
the higher taxes and transfer payments were more or less offset by

the positive effects of the increased spending for education on labor productivity.

All this suggests that there is no necessary linkage between future changes in the amount of public social spending, within any politically feasible range, and the future rate of growth of the American economy—although changes in the composition of social spending and the taxes that support it may make a modest difference. In particular, the more concentrated is the spending on capital investments—human and other—and on research and development, the more likely the spending is to have a positive effect. Moreover, how we choose to finance (deficits or taxation) whatever totals we agree upon as a level of public spending is a far more appropriate concern for those worried about the effect of public policies on economic growth than level of social spending. We will not argue the point here but just assert it: deficit financing of the magnitude we have carried out in recent years has clearly depressed our domestic savings and investment rates and otherwise jeopardized our future economic health.

While there may be no effective economic limits on the future level of social spending in the United States, there clearly have been strong political constraints on this level and are likely to be even stronger ones in the future, given the nature of total commitments on the public purse. We discuss the issues of the willingness of the public to spend more for social purposes below, but here we first examine the likely budgetary pressures facing the country under the policies currently in effect.

This can best be understood by focusing first on projected Medicare and Social Security outlays—an obvious primary source of upward pressure on future public budgets because, at 6.6 percent of GNP, they are already the largest component of both social spending and total public spending and are quite sensitive to general economic conditions, population aging, and the continued escalation of health care costs. Estimating the future path of these social insurance outlays under current policies is a complex proposition that requires making assumptions about numerous "iffy" matters such as economic growth, fertility, mortality, and immigration rates, and various factors specific to the behavior of the health care sector. However, it is clear that these outlays will eventually have to increase considerably relative to GNP under the policies now in place. The only questions are just how soon and how sharply.

The key determinants of this future increase about which there is considerable uncertainty are the future rates of increase of both real earnings and of health care costs. On the one hand, under the Social Security actuaries' "intermediate" (but we think relatively optimistic) assumptions—that real earnings grow appreciably faster than their average for the past thirty years and that health care cost inflation gradually slows to the general rate of inflation—combined Medicare–Social Security outlays under current policies would rise little as a percentage of GNP over the next ten to twenty years and then substantially (on the order of 4 percent to a total of 10–11 percent) with the retirement years of the baby boomers. On the other hand, under the actuaries' (relatively) "pessimistic" assumptions—that real earnings grow at about the same rate as the average of the past thirty years and that health care cost inflation subsides less dramatically—combined Medicare–Social Security outlays under current policies would rise modestly as a percentage of GNP over the next ten to twenty years (on the order of 1–2 percent), and then double during the retirement years of the baby boom to more than 16 percent of GNP.[6] In either event, the predominant share of the upward pressure would come from Medicare, not Social Security. Whereas Medicare outlays are projected to rise steadily as a percentage of GNP over the next fifty years, expected spending on Social Security first falls and then rises with the retirement of the baby boom—resulting in the projected build-up of large surpluses in the Social Security trust funds over the next thirty years (estimated to reach a maximum in excess of $2 trillion in today's dollars under the intermediate assumptions), which will then gradually dissipate.

What of other budgetary commitments and pressures? Might they not ease enough, at least under the relatively optimistic scenario, to accommodate the degree of increase in spending levels implicit in current policies toward the aged without requiring an increase in the overall tax burden? We can only speculate, but this appears an unlikely outcome to us. The pressures on other social spending under current policies might ease somewhat due to general growth in incomes (which, for example, could reduce spending in means-tested programs, other things being equal) and a decline in the relative size of the child population attendant to population aging. However, as we noted earlier, the per capita public spending on children is currently far less than that on the aged, and there is ample documentation in this volume that an increasing, rather than decreasing, share of children may not be benefiting from general economic growth. Furthermore, other federal domestic program spending has already declined in the 1980s to a level not seen since the 1950s and is scheduled to decline further as part of congressional efforts to reduce the deficit. In a similar vein, defense spending as a share of GNP now appears to be heading back down towards the level that prevailed when President Reagan assumed office. And even so, the elimination of the projected federal deficit remaining in the early 1990s will still require an increase in the federal tax burden of 2 percent of GNP if social spending is not cut much further. Finally, states and localities are having to raise taxes just to maintain their current service levels in the face of the large reductions in federal assistance that they have been experiencing.

All this suggests that, unless the United States radically reduces its historical commitment to defense spending, simply meeting current public social commitments will require at least a modest increase in tax burdens in the near future and a substantial one eventually, under the best of circumstances. Thus, if there is to be any expansion of public resources for some social purposes, budgetary concerns will compel politicians to couch the expansion in terms of both a tax increase and a reduction of the scope of some existing social spending commitments.

Social Policy and Tax Concerns

The various social and economic concerns discussed above will, as we have already noted, condition significantly the willingness of the American public to foot the higher tax bill that will accompany existing (or expanded) social policy commitments in the future. But there is another dimension to this question of willingness to accept taxation that is more purely political than philosophical or practical. Public reactions to tax and spending proposals are as much a matter of ill-assorted "attitudes"—the pollster's domain—as of well-understood concerns; and social policy outcomes are thus as much a matter of the timing and packaging of initiatives—the politician's domain—as of a rational process of public choice. Indeed, the current debate over intergenerational equity attests to the importance of timing and packaging to the evolution of American social welfare policies. Had the Social Security legislation not been so successfully packaged as an insurance system responding to the exigencies of the depression, its welfare dimensions might be more widely appreciated today, and public understanding of generational interdependence might be further advanced. (Roosevelt, of course, would not agree.)

In what remains of this chapter, we cannot begin to sift and sort the murkiness of public sentiments on such subjects as the overall "fairness" of the tax system, the efficiency of social program administration, and the moral "worthiness" of program beneficiaries—in short, the multiplicity of intangibles that bear on public receptivity to taxation for social purposes. All we can do—and do below—is summarize the main points of agreement among politicians and pollsters about the implications of public sentiments for future support for social policies.

First, we must note the substantial difference between American notions of what is a fair tax share of the private dollar, and European notions on the same subject. Conventional wisdom in this area has long held that the American taxpaying public has a fairly rigid notion of the proper ratio of federal taxes to GNP. Currently, that figure is widely accepted to be about 19 percent, although some years back the magic number was 14 percent and no one—to our knowledge—has convincingly explained the public's change of heart (although obviously economic prosperity had a lot to do with it). During the 1970s, the actual ratio gradually crept up, to about 21 percent, and this fact was often cited as an "explanation" for the Proposition 13 fever that swept the country in the late 1970s. Thus was conventional wisdom hallowed, and the Reagan administration has hued to it: the ratio has dropped back to 19 percent. But the ratio is rising again and, with no change in current policies, it will top 20 percent in the next decade. Furthermore, as we noted earlier, it may have to rise an additional 1 percent or 2 percent in order to eliminate the federal deficit.

Should we assume another and more vehement tax revolt in the making? Probably not. The public has already demonstrated considerable resistance to further social program cutbacks. Also, a strong argument can be made that an aging society *ought* to expect its relative tax burden to rise, and that once the phenomenon of population aging is absorbed in the public consciousness, resistance to a rising tax burden will moderate somewhat. Finally, if we can assume economic growth rates over the next fifty years anywhere near those of the past forty (during which period real per capita income more than doubled), the rising tax burden will fall on a substantially richer population. That is, with economic growth, tax increases of any reasonable magnitude will certainly precipitate no real decline in the standard of living for future generations. Rather, the increases would simply mean that the purchasing power of average taxpayers after-tax income would rise less rapidly than they would otherwise.

Against these pro-tax considerations must be balanced the public's profound and well-documented ambivalence about current federal taxing and spending. Numerous surveys have indicated a widening gap between what the public believes the government *ought* to do and what they are willing to pay for. As Ladd and Lipsit (1980) observed in the wake of the 1970s tax "revolt":

Even as they endorse measures to restrict the growth of government spending and taxation, Americans remain extraordinarily supportive of a high level of government services in virtually all sectors. There are no longer significant class differences in this commitment. Thus, almost identical proportions of business managers and unskilled workers, of high-income people and those in the lowest income brackets, want to maintain or increase current spending for environmental problems, health, urban needs, education, improving the position of blacks, and so on.

Other surveys have linked these ambivalent views to American attitudes toward the federal government, which—never very positive—have taken a decided turn toward the negative over the past few decades. Poll after poll records the public's poor opinion of the federal government's performance in designing and administering social programs. In the public mind, the contradiction between cutting spending and maintaining services can be resolved by simply eliminating waste. Yet the much ballyhooed efforts of both Carter and Reagan administrations at improving program efficiency and eliminating "fraud, waste, and abuse" have produced no lasting gain in public confidence (nor, it should be noted, much in the way of savings).

This stalemate between American public opinion and the reality of American government—firmly rooted though it may be in our history—no longer seems indefinitely sustainable. At some point in the budget crunch ahead, the public is going to have to strike a balance between jettisoning some expectations of government and swallowing some more or less substantial tax increase. Our purpose here is not to try to divine the particular form the balance will take, but to assess the implications of the balancing act for the interests of children and the elderly.

POLICY IMPLICATIONS

As we noted in the introduction to this chapter, we think the findings reported in this volume are sufficiently disturbing to prompt a serious rethinking of some of the fundamentals of American social policy making. Mapping out what such a rethinking would entail is an undertaking far beyond the scope of our present efforts; but from the preceding observations, we can draw three broad conclusions that we think should inform any effort at evaluating policy alternatives.

First, we conclude that economic policy will play, de facto, a much more critical role in shaping future social policies than it has in shaping past ones; and that, therefore, these two spheres of policy making should be approached in a more integrated fashion de jure. It is unlikely that any economic scenario in the foreseeable future will produce the strong overall economic growth that characterized the 1960s and early 1970s (when annual increases in real GNP averaged in excess of 4 percent) and allowed for concomittent highly expansionary social policies and rapidly rising after-tax incomes. Under assumptions of the more likely modest economic growth (say, 2.5 percent to 3.0 percent), existing social policy commitments will place upward pressure on public budgets relative to GNP. Just how much upward pressure, however, will depend crucially on the precise rate of increase of labor productivity and real GNP. And a quarter to half a percentage point in the growth rate one way or the other will make a huge difference over the longer run.[7] Thus, economic policy choices, particularly in regard to overall deficit reduction, investments for human capital programs, and the handling of the Social Security trust funds surpluses should be of primary concern to social policymakers; not only because these choices will have a direct and immediate effect on the shape of social policies, but also because they will have an important indirect and longer term effect on overall resource constraints.

The second conclusion follows from the first. Given constrained budgetary resources for the foreseeable future, some degree of political tension and competition over spending for social purposes are inevitable. This will place a premium on political leadership; that is, on the capacity of the political process to educate the public away from overpersonalized interpretations of social policy issues and toward some better comprehension of common purposes. We do not find as much cause for optimism here as we would hope. As we have argued, appeals to social solidarity are highly unlikely to strike a responsive chord in the American public. The applicability of European-style solutions, depending upon a high degree of cultural homogeneity and civic obligation, to American problems appears quite limited. More consistent with the American public philosophy are the promotion of equality of opportunity (as opposed to outcome) for all and a reasonable degree of economic security for those (and their dependents) who have used this opportunity to earn their way. The latter theme has motivated public policies that have served the elderly quite well over the past fifty years and, if intelligently refined, are likely to continue to do so in the future. However, while equality of opportunity has been the primary motivation for much of the public activity undertaken over this same period for children, most notably under the War on Poverty and Great Society, the reality obviously has fallen far short of the rhetoric. In part, this was because of the conflict of values noted earlier, which has inhibited consensus on any sustained initiative. But in part, it was also because of woefully inadequate knowledge about what programs, in fact, "work." (Pragmatic concerns have been far less problematic to policies for the aged because, among other reasons, preparation for productive work is no longer an issue.) Neither the ideological nor the pragmatic barrier appears easily broachable.

In a more optimistic vein, we note that many of the public programs mounted in the service of equality of opportunity over the past several decades were essentially experimental, and in the interim much has been learned. Political leaders are now in a better position to separate the wheat from the chaff, if they so choose. (For example, Head Start, and nutrition programs for pregnant women and infants seem to work; relaxed educational standards do not.) And on the more philosophical side, Heclo has identified an emerging theme that appears to be catalyzing some promising public activity: "not that family responsibilities should be altered, but that certain collective provisions need to be improved to help functioning family units continue to function." Furthermore, there is another nascent theme that could strike a chord in the American public, if properly appealed to by political leaders. Growing international competition and a declining birth rate in this country could lead to an increasing awareness of the greater extent to which the national economic health in the future will depend upon how well *all* our children are prepared to assume productive economic roles. Appeals to collective self-interest may help serve to accomplish what appeals to social solidarity could not.

Beyond this critical problem of public education, the central dilemma for social policy will be to find more creative ways of balancing the interests of program targeting and program universality. The Reagan era has underscored the vulnerability of many of the means-tested social programs, especially those serving families with children; while at the same time budget constraints, rising poverty rates and a growing underclass among children, and persistent pockets of financial vulnerability among the elderly, have underscored the need for more concentration of public resources among subgroups of both of these dependent populations. Some reordering of public priorities and policies that places less emphasis on age per se is clearly in order. And because of the diversity of the problems to be addressed, a diversity of approaches will be required. There is no magic solution.

There are, however, numerous promising measures for improving the economic security of the aged in a highly targeted fashion.[8] The components of the principal means-tested programs that serve the aged—Supplemental Security Income (SSI) and Medicaid—have proven to be politically resilient; and modest liberalizations of these programs (for example, expanding Medicaid eligibility for long-term care—which is essentially not covered at all by Medicare, and raising SSI benefits to the poverty level) could go a long way toward improving the lot of the lowest income elderly at relatively modest public cost. In addition, there are several low-cost improvements that could be made in non-means–tested policies that would strengthen the income protection provided by both our private and public retirement systems to many of the most financially vulnerable elderly of modest means, particularly widows and divorcees. Possibilities here include facilitating the availability of reverse mortgages, which convert home equity into annuity payments, sharing of earnings records between spouses under certain circumstances for purposes of calculating Social Security benefits, and selective changes in the rules and tax incentives governing private pensions. Finally, the Medicare program could be modified to provide coverage for catastrophic acute and long-term care expenses that pose a serious threat to the economic security of all but the most affluent elderly.[9]

To help pay for such program expansions and otherwise relieve some of the budgetary pressures attending the rapid aging of the population, the affluent elderly could be required to finance more fully their own retirement and health care. This might eventually entail some across-the-board restraint in the current built-in growth of Social Security and Medicare benefits affecting today's and tomorrow's younger workers, who generally can expect to have a much higher standard of living in their retirement than the current aged and near-aged. But, if an across-the-board approach is adopted in the near future, it would undermine the achievements of the past several decades in greatly improving the economic security of the majority of the current aged and near-aged, who are highly dependent upon these two social insurance programs. What is most needed now is an approach that is targeted on the more affluent aged without unduly compromising the desirable universal features of current policies. This could best be accomplished through the tax system, by such measures as imposing income-related premiums to help finance part of Medicare, full taxation of social insurance benefits and other forms of wealth, and tighter restrictions on tax incentives for private pensions and retirement benefits for higher income retirees (especially those who retire early). Congress has taken some small steps in these directions in recent years, but considerably more could and should be done.

As with the targeting of policies for the elderly, the targeting of policies for children could be substantially improved by relatively modest adjustments to integrate better the tax and transfer systems. An expansion of the Earned Income Tax Credit (EITC), for example, could provide additional income assistance to working poor and near-poor families. Also, more intensive efforts to use the tax system to expand and enforce child support provisions—as has been pioneered in Wisconsin—appear to hold considerable promise for reducing single-parent families' dependency on AFDC (Garfinkel and McLanahan 1987). A more major change to the tax system would be to convert personal exemptions for children (and possibly adults) to credits, so that they would have the same value to families at all income levels (rather than increasing in value in line with the marginal tax rate applied to taxable income). Finally, such credits could be made refundable. In this case they would become a vehicle for providing financial assistance to families regardless of whether or not families had sufficient income to incur an offsetting tax liability and, therefore, supplant much, if not all, the need for the AFDC program.

These policies all have the advantage of increasing reliance on more universal approaches (in contrast to means-tested), while still providing greater assistance on balance to lower income families. However, the more extreme ones have the disadvantage of being highly redistributive—probably too much so for American tastes. In any event, they only address generalized income support needs. Consistent with our earlier observations, a complementary approach that emphasizes services supportive of families and enhanced human capital of children—particularly those "at risk"—is also required.

Here policymakers would have to be guided by both past experience and prospective experimentation regarding which policies are likely to be both politically popular and programatically effective and to determine the relative priority to place on parents as the means of helping children or direct services to children. The former would entail such things as greater financial assistance for day care, employment and training assistance for welfare recipients, and adolescent pregnancy and parenting programs; whereas the latter would entail greater emphasis upon such things as improving education standards, child health and nutrition, compensatory pre-school education (such as Head Start), programs for in-school youth at risk of failure, and more financial support for skill training and higher education for disadvantaged older youths.

If such policies are to result in a substantial improvement in the opportunities for and the abilities of today's and tomorrow's children to become more productive adults, they will require an investment of public resources far larger than has been provided in the recent past. Given the budget constraint we discussed earlier, some creative approaches to financing undoubtedly will be necessary. One possibility is use of the huge surpluses that will soon be accruing in the Social Security trust funds. If these surpluses are to be of any real benefit in easing the financial burden of the retirement of the baby boom, they must be used to enhance economic growth in the interim. One way in which this can occur is if they result in higher overall national savings (through forced public savings) and concomitant investment in physical capital than would otherwise occur. Alternatively, this could also result if some of the surplus went into human capital investment, which paid off in a more productive work force in the future. Furthermore, this approach to financing investment in America's children would reflect an explicit recognition of the mutual interdependence of well-being among all generations.[10]

Notes

1. Unless otherwise indicated through citations in the text and endnotes, the outcomes reported in the first section are either based on the data and analyses contained in earlier chapters of this volume or the income data routinely published by the U.S. Bureau of the Census gleaned from the dicennial censuses and the annual *Current Population Surveys.*

2. Interestingly, while the other factors have maintained their degree of importance over time, the influence of race, per se, has lessened considerably (Fuchs 1986).

3. We are here using the phrase "population heterogeneity" in the broadest possible sense, to encompass not just the racial and ethnic (black, Hispanic, white) divisions noted elsewhere in the volume, but also cultural and religious differences.

4. These three countries, as longstanding members of the British Commonwealth, share traditions that presumably serve to counterbalance somewhat the heterogeneity of their populations. Were it not for this identification with the British, we hypothesize that the Canadian poverty picture would look a lot more like that of the United States than it does.

5. Lampman's conclusions hold equally for all three major economic efficiency goals: stabilization, growth, and the production of a pattern of goods and services that are highly valued by consumers. We focus on the goal of economic growth here since that seems to be the one of most concern to policymakers.

6. These two scenarios also involve somewhat different assumptions about fertility, mortality and immigration rates, but these factors contribute in less major ways (than the differing assumptions about real earnings growth and health care cost inflation) to the differences in outlays as a percentage of GNP. See Palmer (1988) for further discussion of these projections and their implications for the financial status of Medicare and Social Security.

7. For example, other things being equal, a quarter of a percentage point higher annual growth rate in real GNP over twenty years will result at the end of the period in a real GNP that is about 5 percent higher ($250 billion in today's dollars) than it otherwise would be and a federal deficit more than $100 billion lower, mostly because of higher tax revenues.

8. See Palmer (1988) for background on the following discussion of possible changes in public policies toward the aged.

9. At the time of this writing, final enactment of a catastrophic acute care provision under Medicare appeared likely in 1988. Both houses of Congress passed bills in 1987 which would pay the full costs of all currently covered acute care services (plus prescription drugs) after Medicare enrollees incur out-of-pocket expenses in excess of prescribed limits. (These limits differ in the two bills and will have to be reconciled in conference; the final bill, if passed, will likely have a limit of just under $2,000, which will be raised over time in line with some appropriate index.) However, any such action will not address long-term care financing under Medicare and will still leave those of modest means not eligible for Medicaid exposed to acute care costs that could be a high percentage of their income.

10. Our focus throughout this chapter, and particularly in the last section, has been primarily on federal policies. However, we should note that some of the policy initiatives discussed in the last few pages (especially those for children) would fall under the purview of state and local governments, as well as the federal government. Also, state initiatives have been gaining increasing importance during the 1980s in various areas relevant to children and the aged, such as health care for the indigent, compensatory preschool education, child support enforcement, and work- welfare policy.

References

Fuchs, Victor. 1986. "Why are Children Poor." NBER Working Paper No. 1984. Cambridge, Mass.: National Bureau of Economic Research.

Garfinkel, Irwin, and Sara S. McLanahan. 1986. *Single Mothers and Their Children: A New American Dilemma.* Washington, D.C.: Urban Institute Press.

Ladd, E. C. Jr., and S. M. Lipset. 1980. "Public Opinion and Public Policy." In *The United States in the 1980's,* edited by Peter Daignum and Alvin Rabushka. Palo Alto, Calif.: Hoover Institute.

Lampman, Robert J. 1985. *Balancing the Books: Social Spending and the American Economy.* Washington, D.C.: National Conference on Social Welfare.

Palmer, John L. 1988. "Financing Health Care and Retirement for the Aged." In *Challenge to Leadership: Economic and Social Issues for the Next Decade,* edited by Isabel V. Sawhill. Washington: D.C.: Urban Institute Press.

———. 1987. "Income Security Policies in the United States: The Inevitability and Consequences of Retrenchment." *Journal of Public Policy* 7, no. 1 (January–March):1–32.

Smeeding, Timothy. 1985. "Full Income Estimate of the Relative Well-Being of the Elderly and the Nonelderly." In *Research in Economic Inequality: Volume I,* edited by Daniel Slottje. Greenwich, Conn.: JAI Press.

Wilensky, Harold L., and Lowell Turner. 1987. "Democratic Corporatism and Policy Linkages." Research Monograph 69. Berkeley, Calif.: Institute of International Studies, University of California.

About the Authors

Richard V. Burkhauser is professor of economics and senior research associate at the Institute of Public Policy Studies at Vanderbilt University. He has published widely on the behavioral and income distributional effects of government policy toward aged and disabled persons and is coauthor of *Public Policy Toward Disabled Workers: A Cross National Analysis of Economic Impacts.*

Sheldon Danziger is director of the Institute for Research on Poverty, Professor of Social Work, and Romnes Faculty Fellow at the University of Wisconsin–Madison. He is the author of numerous scholarly articles on poverty, income inequality, and social welfare programs and policies, and is the coeditor of *Fighting Poverty: What Works and What Doesn't.*

Greg J. Duncan is program director at the Survey Research Center and professor of economics at the University of Michigan. He codirects, with James Morgan, the Panel Study of Income Dynamics project and is principal author of *Years of Poverty, Years of Plenty.*

Robert Erikson is professor of sociology at the University of Stockholm and director of the Swedish Institute for Social Research. His research is concerned with social stratification and mobility and with social policy and living conditions. Recent publications include *Welfare in Transition, Living Conditions in Sweden 1968–1981,* coauthored.

Gosta Esping-Andersen is currently professor of Political and Social Science at the European University Institute in Florence. His research is on the influence of the public sector on labor market behavior. Recent publications include *Politics against Markets.*

Ross Finnie is a graduate student in economics at the University of Wisconsin–Madison, currently completing his dissertation on women's labor market earnings and job tenure patterns. He has published on black youth unemployment, the structure of inequality across major demographic groups, and the role of socioeconomic background factors in labor market earnings.

Johan Fritzell is a sociologist and research associate at the Swedish Institute for Social Research in Stockholm. He is presently working on income distributions and income determinants in welfare states.

Peter Gottschalk is professor of economics at Boston College and Research Associate at the Institute for Research on Poverty. He has published extensively in labor economics. Much of his work has focused on the impact of economic activity, demographic change, and public policy on poverty.

Stephanie G. Gould is a freelance writer and consultant currently working primarily with the Economic Development Institute of the World Bank. Previously she was director of the Case and Curriculum Development Program of the Kennedy School of Government at Harvard. She has authored and directed numerous publications and studies in public policy and management.

Daphne T. Greenwood is assistant professor of economics at the University of Colorado in Colorado Springs. Her research is in the areas of income and wealth distribution, the role of women in the economy, and tax policy analysis.

Robert Haveman is the John Bascom Professor of Economics at the University of Wisconsin–Madison, director of the Robert M. La Follette Institute of Public Affairs and Policy, and research associate at the Institute for Research on Poverty. His research is in the economics of poverty and income distribution, cost-benefit analysis, and the incentive effects of government taxes and transfers. Recent publications include *Poverty Policy and Policy Research.*

Hugh Heclo is Robinson Professor of Public Affairs at George Mason University in Virginia. He is currently working on problems of social welfare and American politics. His most recent book is *Policy and Politics in Sweden: Principled Pragmatism.*

Christopher Jencks is professor of sociology and urban affairs at Northwestern University, and a former professor at Harvard University and the University of California. His books include *The Academic Revolution, Inequality,* and *Who Gets Ahead?*

Alfred J. Kahn is professor of social policy and planning at Columbia University School of Social Work and codirector of the Cross-National Studies Research Program. His research is in income transfers and social services, with special attention to comparative social and family policies. Recent publications include *Child Care: Facing the Hard Choices, coauthored.*

Sheila B. Kamerman is professor of social policy and planning at Columbia University School of Social Work and codirector of the Cross-National Studies Research Program. Her research is in income transfers and social services, with special attention to comparative social and family policies. Recent publications include *The Responsive Workplace: Employers and a Changing Labor Force,* coauthored.

Shigemi Kono is director-general of the Japanese Institute of Population Problems, Ministry of Health and Welfare. In 1967–78 he was with the Affairs Office and later chief of the Estimates and Projections Section. His research is on demographic aspects of population aging and family demography. He has published widely on fertility and social implications of the population aging in Japan. Recent publications include *World Population* in Japanese.

Jack A. Meyer is the president of New Directions for Policy, a firm specializing in social science research and public policy evaluation. His current research is in the areas of demographics, long-term care, and the use of incentives to help youth at risk of dropping out of school. He has published extensively in the fields of social policy and health-care cost management. Recent publications include *Ladders Out of Poverty,* coeditor, and *Toward Ending Poverty Among the Elderly and Disabled,* coauthor.

Marilyn Moon has been director of the Public Policy Institute of the American Association of Retired Persons since April 1986. Prior to joining the Association, she worked as a senior research associate at The Urban Institute and a senior research analyst at the Congressional Budget Office. She has written extensively on Medicare, poverty, income distribution, and the measurement of social statistics. Recent publications include *Changing the Structure of Medicare Benefits: Issues and Options.*

Michael O'Higgins is a managing consultant with Price Waterhouse Management Consultants, London, and during 1987–88 a Principal Administrator in the Social Affairs Division of the Organization for Economic Cooperation and Development in Paris. He was previously a Reader in Social Policy at the University of Bath. He has published extensively on income distribution, public expenditure analysis, comparative social welfare and on the changing agenda of social policy. Recent publications include *Poverty, Inequality and the Distribution of Income*.

John L. Palmer is a senior fellow of The Urban Institute and codirector of the Changing Domestic Priorities project. His research interests are in economic and social policy. He has been an assistant professor at Stanford University, a senior fellow of The Brookings Institution, and an assistant secretary for the U.S. Department of Health and Human Services. His most recent book is *Perspectives on the Reagan Years* (1986).

Samuel H. Preston is chairman of the Sociology Department and director of the Population Studies Center, University of Pennsylvania. His principal areas of research are mortality, family, and formal demography. He is currently working on a monograph about American child mortality in the late nineteenth century. Recent publications include *Determinants of Mortality Change in Differentials in Developing Countries*.

Lee Rainwater is professor of sociology at Harvard University and Research Director of the Luxemburg Income Study at CEPS, in Luxemburg. His research work for the past several years has been concerned with comparative studies of social and economic well-being. He is coauthor of *Income Packaging in the Welfare State*.

Martin Rein is professor of social policy at the Massachusetts Institute of Technology in the Department of Urban Studies and Planning. He is coauthor of *Income Packaging in the Welfare State* and *Stagnation and Renewal in the Welfare State*.

Timothy Smeeding is professor of public policy and economics and director of the Center for the Study of Families, Children, and the

Elderly, Vanderbilt Institute for Public Policy Studies, Vanderbilt University. His research interests are in the economics of social welfare policy, cross-national comparisons of economic well-being and poverty, and the economics of aging. Recent publications include *Should Medical Care Be Rationed by Age?* and *International Perspectives on Income and Poverty Status* (editor).

Eugene Smolensky is professor of economics and a research affiliate of the Institute for Research on Poverty, at the University of Wisconsin–Madison since 1968. He has published widely on the determinants of the trend in income inequality and poverty in the United States during this century. He has also specialized in urban economics, and is known for his work on the construction of equivalence scales. Recent publications include *Public Expenditures, Taxes, and the Distribution of Income: The United States, 1950, 1961, 1970,* coauthored.

Barbara Boyle Torrey is the chief of the Center for International Research at the U.S. Bureau of the Census. Her research has been on the effect of population changes on public policy issues in the United States; she now is studying the same issues for other countries.

Barbara L. Wolfe is professor of economics and preventive medicine at the University of Wisconsin–Madison, and a Research Associate at the Institute for Research on Poverty. Her research is in the areas of health economics, economics of education and human resources. Recent publications include *The Relevance of Public Finance for Policy-Making,* coedited.

Edward N. Wolff is professor of economics at New York University and a former research associate at the National Bureau of Economic Research. He is also managing editor of the *Review of Income and Wealth.* His current research is in the areas of household wealth distribution, Marxian economics, and productivity growth. Recent publications include *Growth, Accumulation, and Unproductive Activity: An Analysis of the Postwar U.S. Economy.*

Index